FILE STRUCTURES
Theory and Practice

Panos E. Livadas

PRENTICE HALL, Englewood Cliffs, New Jersey 07632

Library of Congress Cataloging-in-Publication Data

LIVADAS, PANOS E.
  File Structures, theory and practice / Panos E. Livadas.
      p.   cm.
    ISBN 0-13-315094-1
    1. File organization (Computer science)   1. Title
QA76.9.F5L58   1990
005.74—dc20   89-71020

Editorial/production supervision: Edith Riker/Jeanne Jacobson
Cover design: Photo Plus Art
Manufacturing buyer: Margaret Rizzi/Lori Bulwin

To My Parents

The author and publisher of this book have used their best efforts in preparing this book. These efforts include the development, research, and testing of the theories and programs to determine their effectiveness. The author and publisher make no warranty of any kind, expressed or implied, with regard to these programs or the documentation contained in this book. The author and publisher shall not be liable in any event for incidental or consequential damages in connection with, or arising out of, the furnishing, performance, or use of these programs.

Printed in the United States of America

10 9 8 7 6 5 4 3 2 1

ISBN   0-13-315094-1

Prentice-Hall International (UK) Limited, *London*
Prentice-Hall of Australia Pty. Limited, *Sydney*
Prentice-Hall Canada Inc., *Toronto*
Prentice-Hall Hispanoamericana, S.A., *Mexico*
Prentice-Hall of India Private Limited, *New Delhi*
Prentice-Hall of Japan, Inc., *Tokyo*
Simon & Schuster Asia Pte. Ltd., *Singapore*
Editora Prentice-Hall do Brasil, Ltda., *Rio de Janeiro*

Contents

Preface   ix

1 Introduction   1

    1.1   Basic Concepts   1
             1.1.1   Files, 1
             1.1.2   Records, 2
             1.1.3   Insertion, Deletion, Update, 3
             1.1.4   Keys, 3
    1.2   Computer Systems   4
    1.3   Users   5
    1.4   File Processing Systems   7
             1.4.1   Logical and Physical Records, 8
             1.4.2   Logical and Physical File Structure, 14
             1.4.3   Access Methods, 14
    1.5   File Design 18
             1.5.1   Operations, 19
             1.5.2   Constraints, 20
             1.5.3   File Organizations, 21
             1.5.4   Performance, 22

2 Secondary Storage Devices   25

    2.1   Magnetic Tapes   25
        2.1.1   General Characteristics, 25
        2.1.2   Vertical and Longitudinal Parity Check, 26
        2.1.3   Density, Capacity, Utilization, 27
        2.1.4   Maximal and Effective Data Transfer Rate, 29
        2.1.5   Volume, Header, Trailer Labels, 32
        2.1.6   Fixed- and Variable-Length Records, 34
        2.1.7   Advantages and Disadvantages of Magnetic Tape, 36
    2.2   Magnetic Disks   36
        2.2.1   General Characteristics, 36
        2.2.2   Disk Capacity, 38
        2.2.3   Seek and Latency Time, 38
        2.2.4   Maximal and Effective Data Transfer Rate, 39
        2.2.5   Fixed versus Fixed-Head Disks, 40
        2.2.6   Average Seek Time, 40
        2.2.7   Disk Architecture, 42
        2.2.8   Clusters and Extents, 48
        2.2.9   Volume Table of Contents (**VTOC**) and File Labels, 48
        2.2.10 Loading Density and Storage Requirements, 49
    2.3   Exercises   50

3 Data Transfer   53

    3.1   Hardware   54
        3.1.1   Primary Storage, 54
        3.1.2   Secondary Storage, 54
        3.1.3   Central Processing Unit (CPU), 55
        3.1.4   Channel, 55
        3.1.5   Controller, 57
        3.1.6   I/O Buffers, 57
    3.2   Software   59
        3.2.1   Operating Systems, 59
    3.3   Case Studies: The MVT and MVS Operating Systems   79
        3.3.1   Multiprogramming With a Variable Number of Tasks (MVT), 79
        3.3.2   Multiple Virtual Storage (MVS), 90
    3.4   Exercises   94

4 Sequential Files   95

    4.1   Physical Sequential Files   96
        4.1.1   Tape Files, 96
        4.1.2   Disk Files, 99
    4.2   Physical Linked Sequential Files   103
        4.2.1   Unordered Files, 104
        4.2.2   Ordered Files, 105
    4.3   The Required I/O Time   107
    4.4   Exercises   110

Contents

4.5   Host Language: PL/1   112
    4.5.1   Data Definition Language, 112
    4.5.2   Data Manipulation Sublanguage, 113
    4.5.3   Examples, 123
4.6   Exercises   143

5   Direct Files   **145**

5.1   Basic Definitions   146
5.2   Deterministic Transformations   147
    5.2.1   Performance Analysis, 148
5.3   Hashing Transformations   150
    5.3.1   The Choice of the Hash Transformation, 151
    5.3.2   A Collection of Hashing Transformations, 157
    5.3.3   Loading a Hash File, 160
    5.3.4   Overflow Management Techniques, 161
    5.3.5   Load and Average Search Length Control, 190
5.4   Exercises   190
5.5   Host Language: PL/1   193
    5.5.1   Regional(1) Files, 194
    5.5.2   Regional(2) Files, 199
    5.5.3   Examples, 202

6   Indexed Files   **215**

6.1   Full Index Organization   216
    6.1.1   The Operations, 217
    6.1.2   Storage Requirements, 219
6.2   Indexed Sequential Files   219
    6.2.1   Multilevel Indexed Sequential File Organizations, 220
    6.2.2   Performance Analysis, 223
    6.2.3   A Simple Model, 226
    6.2.4   Reorganization Points of an Indexed Sequential File, 232
6.3   Exercises   234
6.4   ISAM File Organization   235
    6.4.1   The File Structure, 235
    6.4.2   The Operations, 238
    6.4.3   HOST LANGUAGE: PL/1, 241

7   Tree-Based Files   **253**

7.1   Binary Search Trees   253
    7.1.1   The Operations, 255
7.2   Threaded Binary Search Trees   268
7.3   Height-Balanced (AVL)-Trees   270
    7.3.1   The Rotations, 272
    7.3.2   The Rebalancing Operation, 274

7.3.3   *The Insert Algorithm, 277*
7.3.4   *The Performance, 278*
7.4   Paged Trees   282
7.5   B-Trees   284
7.5.1   *The Operations, 286*
7.6   B$^+$-Trees   297
7.6.1   *The Operations, 300*
7.6.2   *The Initial Loading Operation, 305*
7.7   Trie Structures   306
7.7.1   *The Operations, 310*
7.7.2   *Storage Requirements, 315*
7.8   *C-Trie* Structures   315
7.9   Exercises   317
7.10   VSAM File Organizations   318
7.10.1   *The File Structure, 318*
7.10.2   *Relative Record Files, 320*
7.10.3   *Entry-Sequence Files, 322*
7.10.4   *Key-Sequence Files, 322*

8 Multilist and Inverted Files   **326**

8.1   Queries   329
8.2   Multilist Files   330
8.2.1   *The Operations, 333*
8.2.2   *Cellular Multilists, 334*
8.3   Inverted Files   334
8.4   Exercises   336
8.5   *VSAM* File Organizations   338

9 External Sorting   **339**

9.1   Sorted Partition Files   340
9.1.1   *The Simple Sorted Partition Generator, 341*
9.1.2   *The Replacement Sorted Partition Generator, 342*
9.2   Balanced Merge Sorts   350
9.2.1   *The External Two-way Balanced Merge Sort, 351*
9.2.2   *The External m-way Balanced Merge, 358*
9.3   The *m*-Way Polyphase Merge   366
9.3.1   *The Initial Partition Distribution, 368*
9.3.2   *Estimating the Number of Passes Through the Data, 374*
9.3.3   *The Required I/O Time, 376*
9.4   The *m*-Way Cascade Merge   377
9.4.1   *The Initial Partition Distribution, 379*
9.5   Comparison of Sorting Methods   381
9.6   Exercises   382
9.7   Host Language: PL/1   385
9.7.1   *Data Manipulation Sublanguage, 385*

9.7.2   *Examples, 387*
9.8   Exercises   399

APPENDIX: The UNIX File System

401

A.1   The File System   401
          A.1.1   The Directory, 401
          A.1.2   I/O Buffers, 403
          A.1.3   Access Modes and Access Techniques, 404
A.2   Host Language: C   405
          A.2.1   Data Manipulation Sublanguage, 405
          A.2.2   The Logical READ Request, 407
          A.2.3   The Logical WRITE request, 409
          A.2.4   Positioning into the File, 410
          A.2.5   Closing a File, 411
A.3   An Example   411

Index

425

Preface

BASIC RATIONALE

In writing this book I have attempted to satisfy the need for an *introductory* textbook in files structures that would effectively address the following issues.

1. *Suitability for Classroom Use and Self-instruction.* An introductory text in any subject is primarily intended for novices; therefore, it must be their first, not last, book on the subject. As a first book, it must present the topics in a complete and "detailed" fashion; issues that may seem "trivial" to the experts are not so to novices. This obviously should *not* be accomplished at the expense of a an accurate and thorough treatment of the subject.

With such an approach the book becomes lengthy as is the case here; but, the responsibility of the instructor is to *navigate* the student through the book; and, he/she therefore may cover what he/she feels is appropriate. In addition, today Computer Science is not a bag of tricks anymore; it has evolved into a highly technological *science;* therefore, instruction should not terminate with the end of class. I feel that this text will help the student clarify and understand the answers to the "trivial" issues that they may not be presented during classroom time.

2. *Study of File Structures.* A number of textbooks using the general title "File Processing" confuse the issue of file structures with the issue of teaching

COBOL and PASCAL(!). In other instances "File Processing" is confused with Data Base Management. Despite the fact that Data Bases (and their associated courses) are becoming quite popular, the fact remains that a Data Base makes use of file structures. Hence, the study of File Organizations, in *both* their logical and physical level, provides a firm foundation for the study of Data Bases, a foundation in which most undergraduate students often lack experience and who have never truly had an adequate course in File Structures. A File Structures course *should* be a prerequisite to the first Data Base course.

This book discusses File Structures from many aspects thereby permitting different issues to be offered to different people. In particular, note the topics that are presented.

1. *Data Transfer Sequence.* The transfer rate of data between the data area of the application program and the external storage media is relatively slow. It is clear that this delay affects the performance of a file system. A textbook must provide the reader with an essential understanding of I/O facilities, file and operating systems. This understanding is necessary for the evaluation, design, and performance of file systems.

2. *Data Sublanguage.* Computer files require a language or sublanguage for their creation and manipulation. In addition, a novice must not only be exposed to the theoretical aspects of File Structures - all too important for design, evaluation and performance - but also to their implementation. Hence, a data definition and manipulation language must be presented and a number of programming illustrations are necessary.

3. *Comparative Performance Analysis.* The textbook must not only present the variety of available file organizations for both primary and secondary access methods; but, it must also present an analysis of their performance and in a number of instances, a comparative analysis between different file organizations. This way one can illustrate why in a particular case one file organization would be preferable over another.

This book is the outgrowth of four years of class notes and lectures and has been designed primarily for a course in Computer Science similar in content to the ACM curriculum '78 course CS5; but, it will satisfy the needs of Business students as well as computer professionals. The book does not break new ground in the field; rather, it attempts to make existing knowledge accessible and comprehensible to people unfamiliar with File Structures.

ORGANIZATION

Chapter 1 serves as an introduction to the topics that are covered in the book. Specifically the issues associated with design, access methods (primary and secondary), I/O, and performance of file organizations are presented.

Chapter 2 discusses secondary storage devices. Given that the processing of files is connected with the I/O facilities of the operating system, I chose the OS/MVS system not only because it is a widely used operating system but also because I could "tie it up" with PL/1. Additionally, in order to present real world examples relative to access times, effective data transfer rate, and storage requirements, I chose one specific secondary device. That device is the IBM 3350 disk. The concepts are easily extendable to other disk systems.

Chapter 3 discusses issues associated with file systems. The evaluation, design, and performance of file organizations requires an essential understanding of the file system.

The remaining chapters are divided into two parts. The first part, Chapters 4 through 8, discusses the issues as well as the performance of the file structures which chapters present *independent* of specific devices in addition to specific data manipulation languages. The second part of these chapters discusses the implementation of these file structures. Unfortunately, and it is important for the student to realize this, not every theoretical or proposed file structure can be implemented efficiently and/or directly in every system. The capabilities depend primarily on the host operating (file) system. For example, the UNIX operating system has no "built-in" file organizations. Every file structure under this system is a dynamic physically (linked) sequential file. Therefore, every other file organization can be implemented via user written application programs; the direct result is that different allocations of the physical blocks would not necessarily lead to the expected performance. On the other hand, very few file organizations supported by IBM's OS/MVS system directly support dynamic file structures; but, its file system directly supports a rich collection of such structures (organizations with strategic placement of the physical blocks) which can be manipulated via the powerful data sublanguage of PL/1.

For the above reasons and the fact that the subject matter of this book is *not* programming but file structures, and given that physical file structures are of crucial importance, I chose the OS/MVS system as the continuing thread for illustrating the concepts in this book. In addition, in order to provide the reader with *one* programming language (and with one version of that language) that facilitates the creation and manipulation of these file organizations, I had to choose a language which could easily interact with the OS/MVS system. PL/1 was that choice.

In conclusion, it is my belief that the choice of a high-level host language and of an operating system is not of so much importance given that when one must implement a file structure, the relevant manuals are available for consultation. Finally, even a non-PL/1 programmer will find the fully-commented PL/1 programming examples presented in this book as pseudo-code easy to understand and he/she will be able to convert these examples to any other high-level language[1] of his/her choice. Even so, every effort has been made to enable one

[1] Depending, of course, on the host operating system.

to *omit* all the programming examples and their discussion if he/she so wishes without materially detracting from an understanding of the balance of the text.

Sequential files are discussed in Chapter 4, Direct Files in Chapter 5, Indexed Files in Chapter 6, Tree Based Files in Chapter 7, and Multilist and Inverted Files in Chapter 8.

Chapter 9 presents, discusses, and compares the performance of some of the available external sorting algorithms.

USING THIS BOOK AS A TEXTBOOK

This book has been used as the main text in the three-semester-credit course File Structures at the Department of Computer and Information Sciences at the University of Florida for the last four years. The students enrolled in this course are both graduate and undergraduate students in Engineering, Liberal Arts and Sciences as well as Business students. The course is meant for those who have acquired respectable programming skills, knowledge of at least one modern high level language (preferably PL/I, PASCAL, or C), and exposure to advanced data structures (queues, stacks, trees). Courses, such as Operating Systems or Computer Architecture, would help to a certain degree, but, they are not prerequisites.

It is my experience that it is very difficult for an instructor to cover the entire book in class. Instead, my approach has been to present the most important topics in class and assign other parts of the book as background reading. Certain sections can be omitted altogether. I realize that what may be considered an important topic depends both on the background of the students and what the instructor feels is important. I always follow the sequence of topics as they are in the book. In particular, I rapidly cover Chapter 1 in its entirety; I rapidly cover approximately half of Chapter 2; also, I cover a subset of the topics presented in Chapter 3. All the topics in Chapters 4 through 8, the core of the book, are discussed in their entirety. Of course, the extent of the exposure of the students to Data Structures permits me to cover some areas (such as binary search trees and AVL trees) more quickly than others. Depending on the composition of the class, I always have time to present at least two of the external sorting methods that are discussed in Chapter 9.

Since I believe that the students learn by implementing file structures, I assign three to four programming assignments during the semester. Each of these assignments deals with the creation and maintainance of some of the file structures presented in this book. I provide my students with the freedom of selecting the host programming language and the host operating system. A number of students utilize the IBM environment and PL/I while others opt for the Unix environment and C[2].

---

[2] A brief discussion of this environment is presented in Appendix A.

ACKNOWLEDGMENTS

Many people have been helpful and supportive of my effort to write this book. First, I would like to thank Dr. Sam Navathe who encouraged me to proceed with the publication of this book after reading through my class notes. My friend Dr. George Logothetis supplied his technical assistance; Andy Wilcox kept things running smoothly(!); Dr. Chris Ward read the entire manuscript and made many useful suggestions and stimulated extensive discussions on a variety of topics throughout the text. Last but not least I wish to acknowledge and give my many thanks to Dr. John Staudhammer who provided me with continued encouragment and support throughout the years.

I would like to thank my many students (who used the first as well as subsequent drafts of this text) for their help in identifying areas of the book that needed more clarification and for their support. In particular, my many thanks to Mr. Patrick Leathem for helping to code, run, and debug the numerous programming examples presented. And it would be a great omission on my part not to mention my wife Debra who has given her support, understanding, and managerial assistance toward the production of this manuscript. My thanks also go to the editors at Prentice Hall, Jim Fegen and Tom McElwee; and to Edie Riker and Jeanne Jacobson for the production of the book.

1

Introduction

1.1 BASIC CONCEPTS

1.1.1 Files

The efficiency of an organization, be it a banking institution, an educational institution, or any firm that gathers extensive amounts of information[1] for future retrieval, depends on a system of filing that will allow one to access specific information in the most timely but least costly manner. This is necessary for both the functioning of the organization and its decision-making processes involved therein. Additionally, this information must be recorded and maintained in some fashion. As an example consider a banking institution. The information that must be recorded could be information on customers' checking or savings accounts, on loan applications, about employees of the banking institution, etc.

As one can see, the above discussion indicates that in a number of instances the entire "package" of information naturally tends to divide itself into a collection of subpackages of information, each of which has some homogeneity. In the

---

[1]Strictly speaking the term *information* refers to the meaning of the values of the data, whereas the latter term, *data* refers to the actual values that have been stored in a computer file. In this book we will use both terms interchangeably.

example above, we see at least four subpackages of information: checking accounts, savings accounts, loan applications, and the employee subpackage. Each such subpackage is referred to as a *file*. Hence, one can see that the organization—the banking institution—must record the information in four files, as illustrated in Figure 1.1.

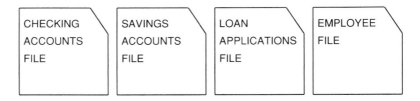

Figure 1.1   Four typical files maintained by a banking institution.

1.1.2 Records

The observant reader should have noticed that a file is nothing more than a collection of information relative to a number of related entities. The collection of information about an entity is what is referred to as a *record;* equivalently, a record is a collection of information about an *entity*.

Now, a record from the Checking Accounts file, which is understood to contain information about a customer's account, will be examined. The *minimal* amount of information that must be reflected in that record is the account number for that customer, the name of the customer, his or her address, and the current balance. Each of the above "pieces" of information is called a *field (item)* of the record. Therefore, we can state formally that a record is a collection of related fields. As an example, Figure 1.2 illustrates a typical record of the Checking Accounts file consisting of four fields. Notice that all records in the Checking Accounts file have the same *type;* i.e., each record consists of the same number and type of fields.

ACCOUNT	NAME	ADDRESS	BALANCE
9783-59-812	MARGIE WATERS	36 NORTH DRIVE, MIAMI	30562.26

Figure 1.2   A typical record of the Checking Accounts file. Notice the four fields of the record: *Account, Name, Address,* and *Balance*.

Therefore, the following formal definition of a file can be stated: A file is a collection of records of the same type.

1.1.3 Insertion, Deletion, Update

As stated earlier, this information, or equivalently, the files where the information is stored, must be maintained. Exactly what does the term "maintained" mean? Assume that a customer made a deposit into his or her savings account. Obviously the information on this account must be *updated* to reflect that fact, so the Savings Accounts file is said to be maintained. Similarly, if a customer closes a savings account, then the record for this customer must be *deleted* from the Savings Accounts file. Finally, as a last example, assume that a loan application was received from a new customer. Then the information (record) relative to this customer must be *inserted* into the Loan Applications file.

1.1.4 Keys

Consider the file of checking accounts. In order to satisfy a request such as "Find the *Balance* of *(Account = 9783-59-812),*" one must first *retrieve* the corresponding record from the file and then examine the contents of the *Balance* field. In particular, one is searching for that record whose contents of the *Account* field are identical to the account number of the customer in question. But, in order to retrieve that record it must first be *accessed*. There are a number of steps involved in accessing a record.

The first step consists of locating the *target* file, in our case the Checking Accounts file. The second step involves locating the *target* record among all the records of the target file by some access mechanism. For example, one access mechanism will locate the target record by starting with the very first record of the file and then examining each subsequent record one after another. Another access mechanism could follow a similar idea; that is, the records would be examined in order, but the search would begin with the last record of the file and proceed toward the beginning of the file.

No matter what the access mechanism used, the target record is that record whose *Account* field value is equal to 9783-59-812. What we really have seen here is that in most instances there is a field of a record whose contents identify that particular record *uniquely*. Such a field is referred to as the *primary key* of the record. Notice that the Account number of each customer is unique within our specific banking institution; therefore, that field can serve as the primary key. One can also see that the customer's *Name* field can not serve as a primary key, since there could be more than one customer with the same name, in which case that field is called a *secondary key*. In other words, a secondary key is a field that does identify the record, but this identification is not unique.

As an example, in Figure 1.3(a) one can see that the *Account* field can serve as a primary key, whereas the *Name* field can serve only as a secondary key, since there are at least two customers with the same name, Margie Waters; therefore, that field does not identify the record uniquely.

Account	Social Security	Name	Address	Balance
3654-24-321	182-55-0319	Margie Waters	18 Arlington, Alachua	2431.22
6314-87-675	157-91-0241	Mike Ekoff	1022 Duval, Melbourne	987.57
9783-59-812	210-94-3004	Margie Waters	36 North Drive, Miami	30562.26

(a)

Account	Social Security	Name	Address	Balance
6314-87-675	157-91-0241	Mike Ekoff	1022 Duval, Melbourne	987.57
3654-24-321	182-55-0319	Margie Waters	18 Arlington, Alachua	2431.22
9783-59-812	210-94-3004	Margie Waters	36 North Drive, Miami	30562.26

(b)

Figure 1.3 Two different sequential organizations of the same file. Records are organized in increasing order of their primary key value. The primary key in (a) is the *Account* field, while in (b) it is the *Social Security* field.

In addition, there could be more than one field that could serve as a primary key, as would be the case if the record had been furnished with an additional field, the *Social Security* field. That field, for example (as Figure 1.3 illustrates), could also serve as a primary key. Hence, one can see that in a number of instances there is more than one field that could serve as a primary key; for such cases, we refer to this type of field as a *candidate key*. In this instance the designer of the file must select *one* of the candidate keys to serve as a primary key, because, as will be seen later, in most instances a file is *organized* subject to the primary key. In Figure 1.3 one can see how the selection of the primary key affects the order of the records; also, observe that the records of that file have been organized in an *ordered sequential* fashion. In other words, the records are stored in sequence and their order is determined by their key values.

At any rate, in the case in which there is more than one candidate key, then the keys not selected are referred to as *alternate* keys. Before closing this section, it should be noted that there is not always a single field of a record that can serve as a primary key. But, in that case, one would look for a combination of two or more fields of that record that could serve as a primary key, in which case it would be referred to as a *composite key*.

1.2 COMPUTER SYSTEMS

In today's high-technology world, an organization such as our banking institution would utilize a computer system to aid in the creation and manipulation of its files. By a computer system we mean its two basic components, *hardware* and *software*.

The term *hardware* includes the CPU, primary memory, channels, controllers, and all the necessary electronic or electro-mechanical devices; the term "software" denotes all the programs necessary for the operation of the computer system and all the information stored therein. It should be noted here that the collection of all the information that is known as files is stored or resides in special hardware components collectively called *secondary storage devices*, or simply *secondary memory*, in which case these files are called *stored* or *computer* files. Primarily, secondary devices are *magnetic tapes, magnetic disks*, and *magnetic drums;* they are discussed in Chapter 2.

Figure 1.4 illustrates the hardware components of a typical computer system. Their purpose and function are discussed extensively in Chapters 2 and 3.

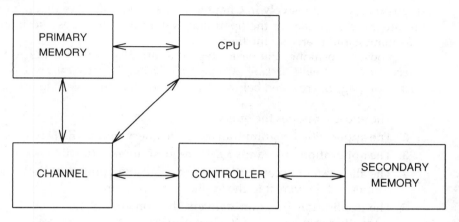

Figure 1.4   Hardware components of a computer system.

1.3 USERS

A number of people would like to access computer files in order to extract some kind of information; these people are known as *users*. Three major classes of users can be distinguished.

The first class of users consists of *end-users*. An end-user has at his or her disposal some special language usually referred to as a *query language*. For example, an end-user will enter into a terminal a query in the following fashion in order to access a record from the Checking Accounts file:

"Retrieve from Checking Accounts file Balance of Account 3654-24-321"

A second class of users consists of the so-called *application programmers*. This type of user employs one of the available high-level languages known as the *host language,* which permits him or her to *access, create,* and/or *manipulate* a computer file via a specific subset of that language usually referred to as a *Data*

Sublanguage. Each data sublanguage consists of two components; the first, known as the *data definition language,* permits the user to define the file organizations and their structures; the second permits the user to manipulate the file and is known as the *data manipulation sublanguage.*

Data sublanguages come in a variety of colors and flavors! This statement means that the data manipulation sublanguage provided with FORTRAN does not have the same capabilities as Pascal, for example, and vice versa. In addition, the data sublanguage provided with a high-level language depends primarily on the operating system's vendor.

The third and final class of users consists of *systems programmers.* A user in this class has available a low-level language, and his or her primary responsibility is the maintenance of the *file system.* Despite the fact that file systems are discussed more extensively in Chapter 3, one must note here that a file system is an integral component of the operating system that manages and maintains the information and therefore the files.

Loosely speaking, the basic steps that are required in order to satisfy the query *"Retreive from Checking Accounts file Balance of Account 3654-24-321,"* discussed on page 5, are listed below with notation that involves the users.

1. The end-user issues the query.
2. The application program translates the query into a *READ* request.
3. The application program's *READ* request invokes the file system.
4. The file system accesses the record from the computer file Checking Accounts and delivers it to the application program.
5. The application program delivers the contents of the *Balance* field of the currently received record to the end-user.

The following can be observed:

1. The application program is invoked as a response to an end-user's query. A moment's reflection on the example query given above is enough to convince one that the end-user is aware of the existence of the computer file Checking Accounts and also of the fields of each record. On the other hand, the end-user has no idea of the organization of the file, the number of bytes of each record, the size of the computer file, the access mechanism that is employed, or the device in which the file is stored. In other words, the end-user is not concerned with any technical details whatsoever. The only concerns of the end-user are:
   a. Receiving accurate information as a response to his or her queries.
   b. Fast response to those queries.
2. The file system is invoked whenever the application program needs to access and/or create a computer file via the user's Data Sublanguage, for example, as a response to an application program's *READ* request. The result is that the applications programmer *must* be aware of the

organization of the file, the record structure, and the available access mechanisms. On the other hand, he or she does not have to be concerned with the details of allocating or deallocating storage in the secondary device or even with invoking the proper access method.

Despite the obvious benefits of this approach, there is a tremendous disadvantage—namely, the use of the host language conceals from the applications programmer all the details pertaining to the actual manner in which the way the file is *stored* in secondary memory. The direct consequence is that the applications programmer is unable to make optimal use of the available tools and resources, since the available high-level language may not take advantage of all the features of the file system, which frequently leads to loss of efficiency and performance.

3. The file system, on the other hand, is the responsibility of the systems programmer, who obviously is aware of all the available tools and resources; moreover, he or she is capable of enhancing those provided by the operating system's vendor file system.

1.4 FILE PROCESSING SYSTEMS

The above discussion indicates that the end-user *indirectly* manipulates the corresponding file via a number of queries available to him or her. On the other hand, the applications programmer, being aware in advance of the different types of queries in which the end-user is interested, *designs* a file in such a way that all the queries can be satisfied and responses to each query are given in the minimum possible time. Moreover, recall that the applications programmer again must develop a layer of software referred to as the *Checking Accounts File Processing System* in between the end-user and the file system, which will provide access paths to the data in order to satisfy the end-user's request. In other words, a File Processing System is a collection of procedures that access the underlying stored file in order to satisfy those requests indicated by the end-user. Figure 1.5 illustrates the Checking Accounts file-processing system and the path that is followed in order to satisfy the end-user's request.

Observe that with the same rationale one can obtain three more file-processing systems, the Savings Accounts, Loan Applications, and Employee file-processing systems. In this way a set of four single-file-processing systems can be obtained that is called a *multifile-processing system*. Figure 1.6 illustrates that file -processing system, but the interface between the single-file-processing systems and the stored files is not illustrated in order to stretch the point that each processing system is capable of satisfying end-users' requests *relative* to the file that it accesses and relative to the initially defined requirements. The term *requirements* underscores the fact that at the time of creation of each file and of its corresponding file-processing system, the *designer*[2]

---

[2] The designer is usually the applications programmer.

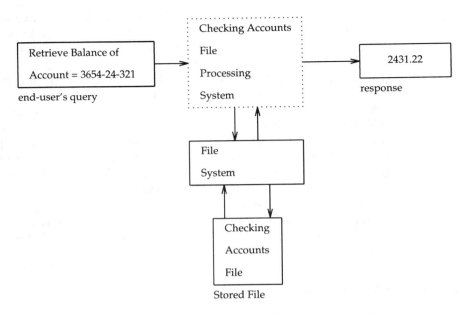

Figure 1.5   The checking accounts file-processing system.

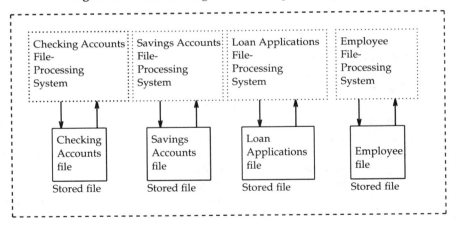

Figure 1.6   The four-file, multi-file processing system.

was aware of the type of processing that would be required for the respective stored file.

If at the time of development of the Checking Accounts file-processing system, the operation "Retrieve all *Accounts* whose *Balance* < 500.00" was not part of the requirements, then in order to satisfy that request, the corresponding File-Processing System must be enhanced by adding to it one more software component that aids in the satisfaction of the request.

At any rate, closer examination of a multifile-processing system reveals a number of critical inadequacies and problems. Some of these are listed and discussed below:

- **Data duplication.** As one can see it is not unusual that an employee of our banking institution would maintain a checking account in the same bank in which he or she works. The direct result is that at least two records of that employee will appear in at least two different computer files, the Employee file and Checking Accounts file. This phenomenon is referred to as *Data duplication*. One can see that beyond the obvious waste in required storage, the most important problem arising from data duplication is possibly the *lack of integrity* that the data can exhibit. For example, if an employee who maintains an account with this bank changes his or her address, there is a possibility that only one of the employee's records will be updated to reflect the new address; or, even if the change is made in both his records, there is a good possibility that one end-user will access the record in the file in which the change has not yet been made.

- **Program-data dependence.** Assume that a new requirement is added, that one would like to be able to obtain a list of all the employees who maintain a checking account with this bank. Notice that a new software component is needed that must cross-reference both Employee and Checking Account files. But there is a possibility that the two computer files are incompatible; i.e., one of the files could be a *stream* file, whereas the other could be a *record*[3] file; in such case, the software component required would be too difficult to implement. To add one more example, consider the case in which the designer has decided that the performance of the file system under the present file organization has been degraded. This is something that could very well happen and it could occur either because the banking institution has gained a significant number of new customers or because new requirements have been added. In such a case, the designer would implement a new file organization; but observe that the components of the corresponding file-processing system cannot perform their old function, since they are "tied up" to the initial file organization. In other words, the programs are dependent on the data.

In this book we will concentrate on developing and comparing a number of different single-file-processing systems.

---

[3] The difference between record and stream files lies in the way that data are transmitted between primary and secondary memory. Under stream I/O, data are *always* transmitted in character format. In other words, a stream file, unlike a record file, is *always* in character format. In this text we will assume that we are dealing with record files unless otherwise noted.

1.4.1 Logical and Physical Records

In this sequence we will be concerned primarily with the views of a record and a file from the perspectives of both applications and systems programmers. As the discussion in the previous section indicates, each of these two users has his or her own *view* of the records in a file. Usually the applications programmer's view is what is known as the *external view* of the record, whereas the systems programmer's view is known as the *internal view* of the record. The above-adopted terminology is justified from the simple observation that the applications programmer's view of a stored record is obstructed by the high-level language that he or she uses to access the records, whereas the systems programmer has a direct, from the inside, view of the stored record.

Let's examine and compare those two views more closely. To this end, assume that the applications programmer via his or her application program would like to perform the following very simple task: He or she desires to access the very first record of the ordered sequential Checkings Accounts file and print out only the name of the customer appearing in that record. Furthermore, assuming that the available host language is Pascal, a customer's record will be defined in the application program via the type of definition appearing in Figure 1.7. In addition, the applications programmer must declare a *program variable* CUSTOMER where he or she expects to receive the record.

```
TYPE
        CUSTOMER_RECORD = RECORD
                            Account : INTEGER;
                            Name    : ARRAY [1..20] OF CHAR;
                            Address : ARRAY [1..25] OF CHAR;
                            Balance : REAL;
                          END;

VAR
        CUSTOMER : CUSTOMER_RECORD;
```

Figure 1.7   The external view of the CUSTOMER_RECORD.

Then, the first record of the file can be retrieved from the stored file and delivered into the program variable CUSTOMER via a *READ* request that is issued by the application program. For example, this could be accomplished via a statement such as the one below:

```
READ (CHECKING_ACCOUNTS,CUSTOMER);
```

What has occurred is that data have been transferred into the application's *data area* or, equivalently, into the indicated program variable CUSTOMER in this case, in response to a *READ* request issued by the application program. What really has been transferred is the record in exactly the same way that the applications programmer perceived or viewed it. Hence, the *unit* of data transferred into the *data area* is a record and is referred to as a *logical record*. The READ request issued by the application program by extension is referred to as a *logical READ*.

The curious reader should have accumulated a number of important questions by now. First and foremost, a logical record has been delivered into the data area, but how? Whenever a logical *READ* request is issued, a number of events take place. All these events will be explained later, but for now it can be noted that an *input request* is formulated for a physical *READ* operation. The term *physical READ* refers to the fact that a certain amount of data must be transferred from secondary memory to primary memory. The transfer of data between primary and secondary storage is referred to simply as a *data transfer*. For reasons that will be explained shortly, a data transfer from secondary memory to primary memory, or conversely, does not transfer just one logical record but any number of logical records. In other words the *unit* of data transferred between primary memory and secondary memory as a response to a physical I/O request is a collection of logical records and is referred to as a *logical block*. The number of logical records per block is referred to as the *blocking factor*—a number that is user defined. If the blocking factor is equal to 1, then each logical block contains just one logical record; and in this case, one may say that the logical records are *unblocked*; otherwise, one would say that the logical records were *blocked*.

The logical block constitutes a portion of the area that was accessed into secondary memory as a response to a physical *READ* request. The area that is accessed and read into primary memory is what is referred to as a *physical block,* or *block;*[4] Figure 1.8 illustrates the general structure of a block. Closer examination of Figure 1.8 reveals that the other portion of the block is occupied by system data. The information stored by the file system in the "system data" area is of critical importance. The information recorded there reveals the *address* of that physical block, so that a verification can be made that the correct block was accessed; this information also aids the access method in *blocking* and *deblocking* the logical records.

System data	Logical record 1	Logical record 2	Logical record 3

Figure 1.8   A physical block with an assumed blocking factor of three.

As mentioned earlier, the first logical *READ* request causes the first logical record of the block to be delivered,[5] actually by the access method, to the

---

[4] An alternate definition for a physical record or block of a file stored in a magnetic disk device is that a block is the smallest addressable unit of the device.

[5] Unless *anticipatory buffering* is used. We discuss this topic further in Chapter 3.

program variable. In order for this to be possible, the access method must "strip" from the physical block the "system data" area and deliver just the block of logical records in a storage area in the primary memory referred to as the *input buffer;* then, the first logical record must be "separated," or *deblocked,*[6] from the logical block so that it may be delivered to the program variable that resides in the data area of the user's area.

During a logical *WRITE* operation the reverse process must take place; that is, the logical record must be transferred from the program variable to a storage area in memory referred to as the *output buffer,* where the logical records are blocked by the access method.

Figure 1.9 summarizes the above points. In particular, one can see that both buffers, as well as the program variable CUSTOMER, are initially empty. After the application program issues the first logical *READ* request, the access method accesses the first physical block of the file in question in secondary storage; the logical block is transferred to the input buffer and the access method deblocks the first logical record, R0, and delivers it to the variable CUSTOMER. Now, assuming that the second logical request is a *WRITE* request, the access method delivers the logical record, R0, from the variable CUSTOMER to the output buffer where the records are blocked. Notice that the next logical *READ* request will *not* cause a data transfer; the reason is that the "next" record is already in the buffer. Instead, the second logical record, R1, is delivered to the program variable CUSTOMER. Similarly, the next logical *READ*, the third one, will cause the next logical record, namely, R2, to be delivered to the program's data area.

It is very important to notice that the second physical I/O will occur only after the fourth logical *READ* request has been issued. This fact explains why logical records are blocked. To understand this, assume the following end-user's request: "Retrieve *all* records from the Checking Accounts file." It is obvious that in order to satisfy that request one must access *all* physical blocks of the stored file. Hence, the number of data transfers, a critical measure of the performance of a file-processing system required to perform this task, is equal to the number of physical blocks. Therefore, by blocking the records one considerably reduces the number of physical blocks required and consequently the number of data transfers required.

The above remark implies that the designer should select the maximum possible blocking factor, since the number of data transfers is strictly a decreasing function of the blocking factor. Theoretically, the value of the blocking factor could be arbitrarily large. As a matter of fact, if the blocking factor were

---

[6] The distinction between record and stream I/O should be more apparent now. In particular, under stream I/O the data transmitted to the Input Buffer and those transmitted to the Output Buffer are transmitted in character format. But, before the record is to be delivered from the Input Buffer to the program variable, the character data are *converted* to the indicated binary and/or binary coded decimal formats by the record definition. Similarly, when a record is to be delivered from the program variable to the Output Buffer area, then the reverse conversion takes place. On the other hand, under record I/O, no such conversions take place. In other words, the record is delivered *as is*. The reader undoubtedly has encountered a stream file in the form of the type *text* file supported by Pascal.

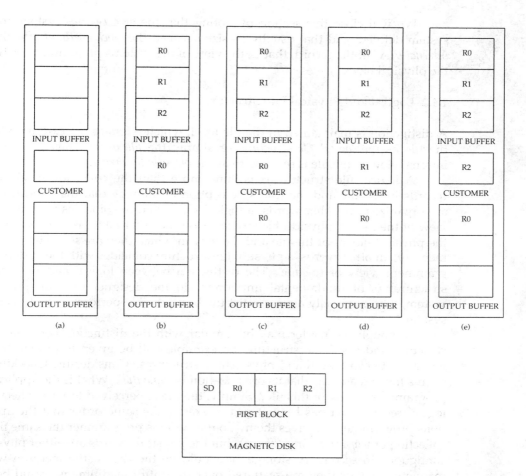

Figure 1.9 Physical block and logical record movement assuming single Input and Output Buffers: (a) Initially, (b) after the first logical *READ*, (c) after the first Logical *WRITE*, (d) after the second logical *READ*, and (e) after the third logical *READ*.

equal to the number of logical records then one could successfully argue that only one data transfer would be needed! But in practice, the value of the blocking factor is limited by the size of the buffers. Notice that the buffers reside in primary storage, a very precious commodity; therefore, an increase in the blocking factor will yield an increase in the size of the physical block and consequently an increase in the size of the required buffer. Hence, the designer is again faced with another task; namely, he or she must select an *optimal* blocking factor, optimal in the sense that it minimizes the number of data transfers subject to the available storage area allowed by the operating system for the required buffers. This issue will be addressed in subsequent chapters.

We will close this section by noting that the size of the "system area" is system defined and that usually its size is called the *block overhead;* finally, the *internal* view of the record, that is, the view of the systems programmer, is that of the physical block.

1.4.2 Logical and Physical File Structure

A distinction is maintained in the file level, which refers to the external view of the file as the *logical file structure,* or simply the *file organization,* whereas the internal view of the file is referred to as the *physical file structure.*

A logical file structure is nothing more than the collection of all logical records in the file and the user's perception of the way that the logical records are organized; in other words, a logical file structure coincides with the user's view of the file. A physical file structure, on the other hand, is a collection of all the physical blocks of the file and the way in which they are *stored* in secondary memory; in other words, a physical file structure coincides with the systems programmer's view of the file. The distinction between logical and physical file structures is of fundamental importance to the designer of a file-processing system, who obviously aims toward the best possible performance of his or her system.

Although the reader may be familiar with the distinction between a data structure and a storage structure, an example will be given to outline the difference between logical and physical file structures. Consider the Checking Accounts file and assume that its organization is *sequential.* What is the applications programmer's view of this file? Simply, the file is perceived to be a collection of logical records that has been stored in exactly the same order that the applications programmer perceives them. To the systems programmer the same file is a collection of *physical records (blocks),* but the physical records are either physically contiguous in secondary storage, as would be the case if the medium were a magnetic tape, or they are scattered over the entire medium, as would be possible in a magnetic disk. Their natural sequential order is preserved via *block pointers.* The former case refers to a *physical sequential file,* while the latter case, refers to a *physical linked sequential file.*

At the other extreme, the mere fact that the physical file structure is linked sequentially does not tell one anything whatsoever about the file organization. Just as a linked list in primary memory could represent either a stack data structure or a queue data structure, a physical linked sequential file could represent a sequential file organization, or an *indexed sequential* organization.

1.4.3 Access Methods

Consider a physical file structure. Recall that in order to retrieve a logical record, one must first access that particular physical block in secondary storage where the logical record resides. But a physical file structure consists of a number of physical blocks, so a path must be found through those blocks in such a way that the path leads to the physical block in question subject to the physical file structure. This path is referred to as the *access path* to the data. The *length* of an access path is defined to be the number of physical blocks that define that access path.

It must be clear that the access path to the data depends on a number of factors. First, the access path depends on the *search mechanism* employed; for the same physical file structure a sequential search mechanism will generate a different access path than one generated by a binary search mechanism. Secondly, the access path depends on the file organization; if the organization is sequential, then, unlike the case of *direct* file organization,[7] there is not a search mechanism that could generate an access path of length one for the retrieval of a unique logical record. Thirdly, the access path depends on the secondary storage medium where the physical file structure resides; if the storage medium is the magnetic tape, then the only physical file structure allowed is that of physical sequential; moreover, in this case, the only possible search mechanism is the sequential search.

A moment's reflection on the definition of the length of an access path will convince one that the number represented by this length is nothing more than the number of physical I/O accesses required in order to locate the target record, which turns out to be the most important element of the performance analysis.

An *access method* can now be defined as that method which provides one with an access path to the data. According to the previous discussion, it is not unusual for there to be a number of different access methods that could apply to a certain file organization.

The physical sequential file of Checking Accounts, consisting of 14 logical unblocked records as shown in Figure 1.10, illustrates two different access paths generated by the sequential and the binary access mechanisms as a response to "Retrieve record with *Account* = 937-94-3132." It is important to notice that the access path provided by the sequential access mechanism has a length of 10, whereas the one provided by the binary search mechanism has a length of only 2. More importantly, examination of Figure 1.10 indicates that the *mode* of accessing the physical records under a sequential search is *sequential* in the sense that in order to locate the "target" record, one must start at a particular block and continue the search by examining in order, one physical block after another. At the other extreme, the path generated by the binary search access mechanism indicates that the "target" record is located *not* by examining every preceding physical block; in other words, the *mode* of accessing the target record is *random*.

Hence, the access methods can be classified as either *sequential access methods* or *random access methods*, the classification depending on the access mode. The access paths generated by a sequential access method consist of only *sequential* accesses, whereas the paths generated by random access methods consist, in general, of a number of *sequential and* a number of *random* accesses. At any rate,

[7] This file organization is discussed in Chapter 5.

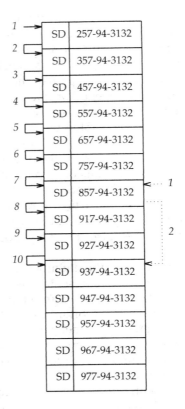

Figure 1.10 The two access paths generated for retrieval of a record with key 937-94-3132 by a sequential search (solid arrows) and a binary search (dotted arrows) access method from the Physical sequential file; the records are unblocked, and only the *Account* field of each logical record is shown.

the diagram in Figure 1.11 indicates the classification of the access methods according to their mode.

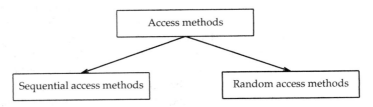

Figure 1.11 Classification of access methods.

In Chapter 3, one will find that an access method can also be defined and used in another context. Namely, the access method is that piece of software provided by the operating system's vendor, which is a part of the file system and serves as an interface between the application program and the physical file system. As one can see in this context, the access method will perform the function that we mentioned above, namely, it provides one with an access path to the data, but there are also a number of other functions associated with it. As a matter of fact, blocking and deblocking is one of these functions.

1.4.3.1 Primary and Secondary Access Methods.
Recall that it is the responsibility of the designer to be aware of the end-user's requirements. In other words, the designer must be aware of the types of queries that may be issued relative to the file that he or she is to design and, eventually, the file-processing system that will be implemented. These pieces of information are crucial and must be the first issues addressed. The reason is the following. If every operation associated with the records of a file, that is, retrieval, update, insertion and deletion, is based *only* on the primary key value, then the associated access method is called a *primary access method*. Otherwise, if some operations involve accessing records based also on secondary key values, then the associated access method is called a *secondary access method*. Subsequent chapters show that file organizations that perform efficiently for primary access methods become very inefficient in terms of performance for secondary access methods. Hence, if the retrieval of records is based on primary access methods, then a number of different file organizations, namely, those that perform well for secondary access methods, must be excluded from consideration at the very first stage of the design. Therefore, one more level may be added in the tree structure of Figure 1.11 and the tree structure of Figure 1.12 is thereby obtained in which access methods are classified according to what has been discussed so far.

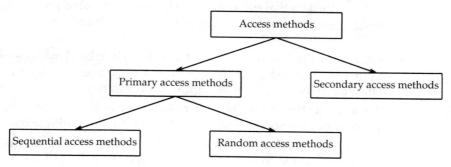

Figure 1.12   Classification of access methods.

An example is given that illustrates the previous point. In subsequent chapters one should observe that the logical records of a file are usually organized according to their primary key value, which of course leads to a different ordering of the logical records of the file even under the same organization. For example, in Figure 1.3 two sequential file organizations of the same file are shown. In particular, in Figure 1.3(a) the logical records of the file have been arranged in increasing order of their primary key value, which is assumed to be the

Account field, whereas in Figure 1.3(b) the logical records have been arranged in increasing order of their primary key value, which is assumed to be the *Social Security* field.

Assume the file organization in Figure 1.3(a) and also a physical sequential file structure for that file. Notice that the query

"Retrieve all records of customers where Balance > 500.00"

will cause *all* physical blocks of the physical file to be accessed in order to retrieve those logical records whose *Balance* field value exceeds 500.00 *independent* of the primary access method. One can see, then, that the length of the access path is equal to the number of physical blocks, an unacceptable figure.

1.5 FILE DESIGN

File design is the process of designing a file organization that satisfies the end-user's specified requirements and also minimizes the response time. The previous discussion and the above definition imply that the file-design process consists of two major steps. The first step, *logical file design*, consists of either selecting one of the available file organizations or designing a new file organization in such a way that the end-user's requirements are satisfied. The second step, *physical file structure design*, consists of a number of substeps concerning the design of the physical file. Despite the fact that some of the issues have already been encountered and the fact that these steps are discussed in subsequent chapters, *some* of the design issues that must be considered are listed below.

- **Selection of the *blocking factor*.** The value of the blocking factor affects the number of required physical blocks and consequently the total I/O time dedicated to the process of all logical records of the file.
- *Allocation* **of the I/O buffers.** Performance can be drastically improved in a number of instances as a result of the allocation of multiple buffers.
- *Size* **of the physical file.** Observe that in a number of instances the designer is limited to a selection from a specific subset of the available file organizations as a result of possible restrictions in the amount of secondary storage available to him or her.
- *Organization* **of the physical blocks of a file in secondary storage.** It must be clear that the I/O time required to traverse an access path depends to a great degree on the placement of the physical blocks in secondary storage.
- *Design* **or** *selection* **of the proper access method.** Recall that different access methods could be employed in the same file organization; moreover, these methods would yield different access paths.
- *Selection* **of the primary key among the list of candidate keys.** Since, as

was noted, normally logical records within files are organized according to their primary key; the selection of the primary key will affect the access paths to the data and consequently the length of these paths.

- **File *growth*. Some files increase and/or decrease in size as a result of insertions and deletions of logical records; these are called** *dynamic* files, as opposed to *static* files, in which those operations do not occur. In the former case, the size of the file grows at a rate proportional to the rate of insertions minus deletions. Hence, at the initial stage of the design, one must consider the anticipated positive growth of the file in order to estimate the length of the access paths.

- *Reorganization point.* In the case in which a file exhibits a high rate of insertions and deletions (*highly volatile* file) there will come a point at which the file must be *reorganized* either because the position of the logical records within the physical blocks causes very long access paths or because the file has grown to the point in which another file organization would perform considerably better than the initially selected file organization. That point is referred to as the reorganization point. The designer must estimate that point, since it is clear that it would be unreasonable to reorganize a file frequently; the cost would be much too high.

1.5.1 Operations

Observe that there is a natural mapping from the set of queries available to the end-user into the set of operations that are performed on the records of the corresponding file. Independent of the syntax of each particular query language, the set of possible operations on the logical records of a file can be classified as follows:

- *Retrieve_All.* This operation requires the retrieval of all logical records of the file.

- *Batch.* This operation requires the retrieval of a very large subset of the logical records of the file. An empirical rule that can be followed is that the number of logical records that are to be processed under this operation must be greater than 20% of the records of the file. Observe that the operation *Retrieve_All* is a special case of *Batch* operation. This latter term is synonymous with the term *sequential processing.*

- *Retrieve_One.* This operation requires the retrieval of just one specific logical record.

- *Retrieve_Next.* This operation requires the access of the logical record "next" to the currently accessed logical record.

- *Retrieve_Previous.* This operation is similar to the *Retrieve_Next* operation, but now the logical record "previous" to the currently accessed logical record must be retrieved.

- *Insert_One.* This operation requires the insertion of a new specific logical record in the file in a physical position depending upon the file organization.
- *Delete_One.* This is a request to delete a specific logical record from the file.
- *Update_One.* This is a request to retrieve a logical record, update a number of its fields, and rewrite the updated logical record in the same physical position from which it was retrieved.
- *Retrieve_Few.* This operation falls in between the corresponding *Retrieve_One* and *Batch* operations.

1.5.2 Constraints

There are two major constraints associated with the file-design process. The first constraint deals with the fact that applications programmers must limit their selection to the file organizations and access methods provided by the file system's vendor and the host language that they may have at their disposal. In this textbook a number of different file organizations that are *system-independent* will be developed and discussed. The rationale is that the reader must be exposed to a number of facts and issues associated with both file organizations and file systems so that he or she would be able to implement certain file organizations that are not provided by the operating system available to him or her on "top" of the file system. On the other hand, certain file organizations that are available under OS/MVS will be focused upon.

Second, there is usually a natural trade-off between storage allocated to a file and response time. In other words, an increase in allocated secondary storage space quite often results in a decrease in the response time. In general, the storage and response time are reciprocals of one another. Hence, the designer in a number of instances will be faced with the following dilemma. Is allocating more storage space, or, equivalently, selecting a more complex file organization, worth the gain in response time? The answer to this question depends on the specific circumstances, but much insight can be gained by comparing the percent gain in response time as a result of a certain percent increase in allocated storage. At any rate, there are cases in which the designer should not bother. After examining the two specific parameters listed below, one can see an indication of that fact:

- *Size* of the file. In the case in which the size of the file is small, the length of the access paths do not vary considerably between any two file organizations, whereas for a large file the opposite is true.
- *Amount of activity.* If a file is not to be processed frequently, then improving the response time is not as important as saving a considerable amount of storage. On the other hand, if a file is *active*, (processed often), then sacrificing storage space is probably worth the gain in response time.

1.5.3 File Organizations

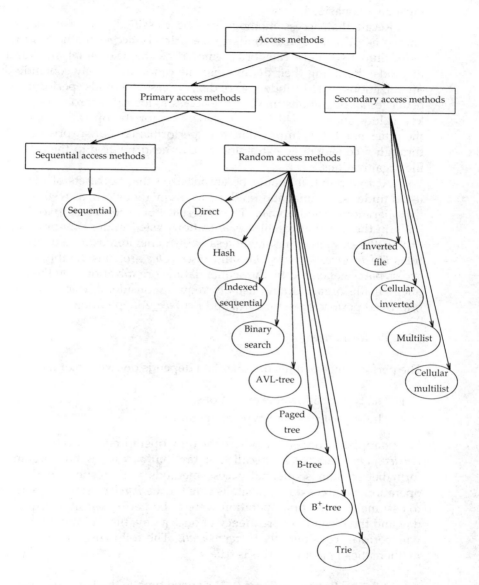

Figure 1.13   Classification of access methods and of file organizations.

File organization selection depends primarily on the *type* of operations that are to be allowed. Figure 1.13 illustrates three sets of file organizations that will be discussed in the text and the *category* to which each belongs. Despite the fact that all these organizations will be studied extensively, their fundamental differences must be emphasized.

Recall that access methods can be classified into two major categories, known as primary and secondary; the primary access method is further subdivided into two more categories, known as the sequential and random access methods. Recalling their definitions, one can immediately conclude that the file organizations listed under secondary access methods perform considerably better for *all* operations that require access to logical records based on secondary key values and—as will be indicated—also for the operation *Retrieve_Few*. On the other hand, this improvement in performance, not surprisingly, is achieved through a considerable extra storage overhead relative to the other two sets of file organizations.

At this point, it should be emphasized that both sets of file organizations listed under sequential and random access methods can, as well, support most of the operations listed above. The difference between those two sets lies principally in the fact that the file organizations listed under random access methods exhibit the property that the access paths generated as a response to the operations *Delete_One*, *Retrieve_One*, and *Insert_One* are considerably shorter than the access paths generated by the sequential file organization. On the other hand, sequential file organizations usually require considerably less storage and offer improved performance for *Batch* and *Retrieve_All* operations.

1.5.4 Performance

The performance of a file organization depends on two major factors:

1. The type of allowable operations.
2. The *frequency* of each type of operation.

For example, assume a file where the only operations allowed are the operations *Retrieve_One* and *Batch*. Recall that random access method organizations perform better than sequential access methods with respect to the *Retrieve_One* operation, whereas the opposite is true for the *Batch* operation. Now if one were to assume that the first operation were to be performed at a frequency of fifty a day and the second at a frequency of once a day, then a random file organization will perform considerably better *overall*. The following discussion will explain mathematically just why this is true.

1.5.4.1 Response Time.   Response time is the time that elapses from the moment an operation is initiated to the moment it is completed. Observe that in order for an operation to be completed a number of events must take place (explained further in Chapter 3). Each of these events requires a certain amount of time. For example, in a multiuser environment a certain amount of "wait time" is inevitable (from the moment that a physical I/O request is issued until the time that the data transfer takes place). This "wait time" is a result of the secondary

devices, which are very slow compared with primary memory; therefore, physical I/O requests are issued much faster than they can be serviced. The other required block of time is the actual time required for the data transfer plus some internal processing time, such as the time needed to update a logical record. Given the relative speeds of the primary storage on the one hand and of the secondary storage on the other, the amount of internal processing of the logical record is negligible compared to that required for a data transfer. Now, notice that the "wait time," which is system dependent, will occur for *any* file organization. Hence, a performance analysis between two file organizations is done solely on the required physical I/O time or, equivalently, on the I/O time required to complete all the required data transfers.

1.5.4.2 Search Length and Expected I/O Time. Consider two file organizations A and B and assume that only one operation $OPER$ is permitted in both files and that both files reside in the same type magnetic medium. Clearly, the better of the two file organizations will be the one that has the best *response time*, or equivalently, according to our preceding discussion, the one in which the *I/O time* required for the completion of the operation $OPER$ is minimal. Therefore, one must calculate the I/O time required in each case.

Recall that the length of the access path for each file organization subject to the access method can be derived. From now on the length of the access path will be referred to as the *search length* and will be denoted by SL. In particular, the notation $SL[OPER, A]$ will be employed to indicate the search length required for the operation $OPER$ under the file organization A. Recall also, that, in general, the access path consists of a number n_1 of sequential accesses (sa) and a number n_2 of random accesses (ra). Therefore, assume that

$$SL[OPER, A] = n_1 sa + n_2 ra \qquad [1.1]$$

Then, as will be seen in the next chapter, it is an easy matter to derive an expected value of the I/O time required for one sequential access, call it t_{sa}, and also the expected value of the I/O time required for one random access, call it t_{ra}. Then the above equation can be rewritten as

$$T_{I/O} = n_1 t_{sa} + n_2 t_{ra}$$

where $T_{I/O}$ denotes the expected I/O time. Hence, one can observe that there is a natural mapping from the search length into the I/O time; therefore, the *cost* of an operation will also be reflected by the search length.

It is important to notice that in a number of instances, no actual expected I/O time needs to be calculated. For example, if one assumes that

$$SL[OPER, B] = n_1 sa + m_2 ra \qquad [1.2]$$

then it is clear that by combining equations [1.1] and [1.2], the better performance will be obtained for file organization A if and only if $n_2 < m_2$. Similarly, if one assumes that

$$SL[OPER, A] = n_1 sba \qquad\qquad [1.3]$$

and also that

$$SL[OPER, B] = n_1 rba \qquad\qquad [1.4]$$

then clearly the file A organization is superior given that a sequential access *always* requires less or equal I/O time to a random access.

The last example indicates the case in which the estimation of $T_{I/O}$ is required. To this end, assume that

$$SL[OPER, A] = nsba$$

while

$$SL[OPER, B] = mrba$$

Then it must be clear that the actual I/O time needed to perform a sequential access and a random access must be found.

In certain instances, the derivation of the search length for a particular operation is impossible. Specifically, if one assumes the operation *Retrieve_One* is used, then it is easy to see that the search length is bounded below by one sequential access and above by a number of sequential accesses equal to the number of blocks in the file. In that particular case one derives an *average (expected)* search length denoted by *ASL*. For example, in the case at hand the average search length for the operation *Retrieve_One* is equal to the total number of accesses required to access all logical records of the file *independently* divided by the number of logical records in the file.

We will close this chapter by indicating the process by which the *SL* can be computed in the case in which there are two operations, $OPER_1$ and $OPER_2$, permitted in file A. In order for this to be possible, the frequencies of the two operations f_1 and f_2 (expressed in percent) must also be given. Then, the *SL* can be found via the equation

$$SL = f_1 \cdot SL[OPER_1, A] + f_2 \cdot SL[OPER_2, A] \qquad\qquad [1.5]$$

from which the I/O time can be calculated.

Finally, equation [1.5] can be generalized in the case of the presence of n operations, $OPER_1, OPER_2, \ldots, OPER_n$ of frequencies $f_1, f_2, \ldots, f_n$, respectively, via the following equation:

$$SL = \sum_{i=1}^{n} SL[OPER_i, A] \cdot f_i$$

2

Secondary Storage
Devices

As mentioned earlier, files are stored in secondary storage media. Secondary storage media could be cassettes, tape on reels, disks, drums, or punched cards. This chapter will focus primarily on magnetic tapes and magnetic disks. Each one will be examined in turn.

2.1 MAGNETIC TAPES

2.1.1 General Characteristics

A magnetic tape is a continuous plastic strip of mylar with a ferrous oxide coating. Tape lengths range from 200 to 6400 ft, but are typically 2400 ft, while their width is approximately 0.5 in.

The physical beginning and end of a tape are marked by two metallic strips called the *load point mark* and *end of reel mark*. These markers are electronically detected by photocells in the drive mechanism, enabling one to read and/or write on the tape only in between these two markers. The tape itself is divided into nine horizontal lines, called *tracks*, across its length.[1] Data are written onto

---

[1] There are also seven-track tapes.

the tape character by character. If data are recorded in EBCDIC[2] format, each character requires 8 bits to be represented. For example, the character 0 has the representation shown in Figure 2.1. This byte always is represented in parallel; i.e., the 8 bits will be recorded in 8 parallel tracks. This leaves one track free, which is used to record the *vertical parity bit*.

1	1	1	1	0	0	0	0

Figure 2.1 The EBCDIC representation of character 0. The most significant bit is the leftmost one.

Before the function of the vertical parity bit is explained, one should note that because of the anticipated frequent use of the tape, the edges of the tape physically deteriorate, so the most significant bit (bit 0) of the byte is stored towards the middle of the tape in order to protect it. Table 2.1 illustrates this.

TABLE 2.1. Nine-track tape (EBCDIC code)

Track Number	Bit Number	Tape
0	4	0
1	6	0
2	0	1
3	1	1
4	2	1
5	VPB	1
6	3	1
7	7	1
8	5	0

2.1.2 Vertical and Longitudinal Parity Check

The vertical parity bit is set to either 0 or 1 and is used for error checking. The mechanism for setting the parity bit is quite straightforward. When a byte (character) is to be written onto the tape, the number of 1s in the byte is counted, and the vertical parity is set to either 0 or 1 according to the parity convention. For even mode parity, the total number of 1s in the nine tracks must be even. In Table 2.1, the vertical parity bit has been set to 1, which assumes that the even parity mode was used.

In a number of cases, another parity check is performed to ensure that the block is written correctly. To do this, an extra byte is allocated at the end of each physical block. Each bit of that byte is called the *longitudinal parity bit*, and each such bit is set to zero or one to indicate the parity of the set of all bits of the block along the track to which this parity bit corresponds. Assuming that the parity

[2] Extended Binary Coded Decimal Interchange Code.

mode is even, if the total number of 1s along track 3 is an even number, then the longitudinal parity bit is set to zero. Notice that if both checks for parity, vertical and longitudinal, are utilized, the probability that an error escapes detection is very close to zero. In addition, the read head is positioned "after" the write head so that a parity check can be made immediately after each byte and block has been written, as Figure 2.2 illustrates. This method is known as *write verification*.

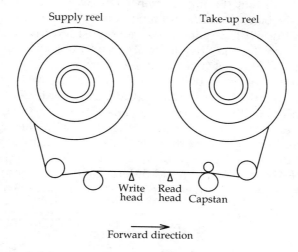

Figure 2.2.   A tape drive.

If now, during a read, the number of 1s in a byte turns out to be odd, then the controller (whose responsibility is the parity checking) calls an interrupt routine via the channel. This routine instructs the channel, and in turn the controller, to reread the physical record a number of times. If at a reread the byte in question is read with no error (which could very well happen either because of noise or accumulated dust on the tape), then the process continues; otherwise, an error is indicated.

2.1.3 Density, Capacity, Utilization

Tapes are also characterized by their *density*. Density is defined as the number of characters that can be recorded in an inch of tape and is measured in *bytes per inch (bytes/inch)*. Typical tapes are available with a density of 1600 bytes/inch. If the length and density of the tape is known, then the *capacity* of the tape can be found. The capacity of the tape is defined as the number of bytes (characters) that can be stored in the entire tape. In other words, if the density of the tape is D bytes/inch, and L indicates the length of the tape in inches, then the capacity of the tape is given by:

$$C = L \cdot D \text{ bytes}$$

For a typical tape of density 1600 bpi[3] and length equal to 2400 feet, the capacity of the tape can be found by:

$$C = 2400 \cdot 12 \cdot 1600 \text{ bytes} = 44 \text{ Megabytes}$$

Unfortunately, the entire tape can not be utilized in the sense that not all available storage can be used to store the user's data. The reason is the following. Recall that the unit of transfer between main memory and secondary storage is the block. In order for a block to be transmitted, as the result of a physical *READ* or *WRITE* request, the tape must already be mounted onto a tape drive. In order for the drive to be able to read or write from the tape correctly, the tape must move at a constant speed over the R/W head, typically on the order of 10 ft/s, a speed that is attained via the *capstan*, a small wheel that pulls the tape across the R/W heads (Figure 2.2). In order for the tape to reach this speed (since initially it was idle), a certain time must elapse. In that period of time, the portion of the tape that passes through the R/W head can not be written onto or read correctly.[4] Hence, each block must be preceded and followed by an unused portion of tape, which allows the tape to accelerate to a normal *READ/WRITE* speed and decelerate to a stop respectively. The unused portion of tape is called an *interblock gap (IBG)*. Figure 2.3 illustrates this concept.

IBG	BLOCK	IBG	BLOCK	IBG

Figure 2.3. Each physical block is surrounded by two interblock gaps *(IBG)*.

Hence, the *utilization U* of the tape is a function of both the block size *(BS)* and the interblock size *(GS)*. Namely, *U* is given by:

$$U = \frac{BS}{BS + GS}$$

For example, if $BS = GS$, then the utilization of the tape is 50%. Observe that the above equation can be rewritten as:

$$U = \frac{1}{1 + \dfrac{GS}{BS}}$$

Also note that when the quantity (GS/BS) approaches 0, *U* approaches 1; i.e., the utilization approaches 100%. Hence, increasing the *BS* for a fixed *GS* increases the utilization. Two obvious questions here are what are the optimal *GS* and *BS* sizes. The answer to the first question is that the *GS* must be the minimum

---

[3] Tapes of density 6250 bytes/inch are also popular.

[4] To prevent accidental writing on a magnetic-tape reel a small plastic ring, called the *file-protection ring*, is placed on the reel. Therefore, in order be able to write, the ring must be removed first. Some systems require the reverse process.

possible, and that minimum is a GS of length equal to 0.6 in.[5] The answer to the second question is a little more involved. If the BS is very large and the number and size of the records is fixed, then, as pointed out in Chapter 1, fewer transfers are needed to read/write the entire file, since a large BS indicates a larger *blocking factor (BF)*. This in turn means a fewer number of blocks. But, an increase in the BS necessitates an increase in the size of the input and output buffers. Hence a compromise must be implemented.

Consider a typical tape of density 1600 bytes/inch and of IBG size equal to 0.6 in. The utilization for different values of BS is calculated and listed in Table 2.2.

TABLE 2.2. Different values for the utilization of a 1600 byte/inch tape with a fixed interblock size (0.6 in.) and different block size values .

BS (in bytes)	U (%)
400	29.4
800	45.5
1200	55.6
1600	62.5
2000	67.6
2400	71.4
2800	74.5
3200	76.9

By using the data from Table 2.2, a graph of the utilization as a function of the block size can be obtained, as Figure 2.4 illustrates. Observe that the rate of increase in BS for steps equal to 400 bytes yields a significant increase in the rate of utilization for BS less than or equal to 2000. The increase in the rate of utilization for larger values of the BS is not as significant and would probably not justify the required increase in the size of the buffer. The above analysis indicates that a reasonable block size is in the neighborhood of 2000 bytes. There is another reason, which would indicate that the previous choice was an appropriate one, and this is the effective data transfer rate.

2.1.4 Maximal and Effective Data Transfer Rate

Recall that a tape drive can read/write at a speed of 10 ft/s. Hence, in theory one can read/write 192,000 bytes/second on a typical tape, as the following computation indicates.

$$10(\text{ft/s}) \cdot 12 \ (\text{in./ft}) \cdot 1600 \ (\text{bytes/inch}) = 192,000 \ (\text{bytes/second})$$

The number of bytes that potentially can be transferred in a period of time is

[5]System dependent.

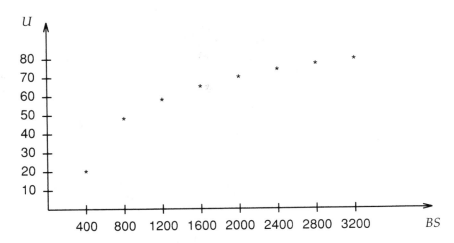

Figure 2.4   The utilization (*U*) as a function of the block size (*BS*).

called the *maximal data transfer rate (MDTR)*, or nominal transfer rate. However, this transfer rate is never attained. The reason is this: Assume that the time elapsed between the moment the process began to its completion is *T*. Clearly, the number of bytes transferred must be less than (*T·MDTR*), since a certain amount of time would have been wasted in starting and stopping the tape, and in the *IBG's*.

We therefore speak of the *effective data transfer rate (EDTR)*. EDTR is measured in bytes/second, giving the quantity, in bytes of user data, that can be transferred in a second. Let *T* again be the time spent to transfer the block, and let *r* be the time required to read just the user's data in the block. Then only a fraction *f* of the time *T* are data actually being transferred. This fraction is equal to the quotient of the time *r* spent to read just the user's data over the entire time spent for completion of the transfer.

The first quantity has been assumed to be *r*, and the second is the sum of three quantities; the time required to read the block *r*, the time required to start and stop the tape *ss* (in milliseconds), and the time spent in the interblock gaps *gt* (in milliseconds); i.e., $T = r + ss + gt$. Hence, the fraction of time *T* is:

$$f = \frac{r}{T} = \frac{r}{r + ss + gt} \qquad [3.1]$$

Notice that *gt* is equal to $[(GS/MDTR) \cdot 1000]$ ms, and since *r* is the time directly spent to read the block, *r* satisfies the equation

$$BS = \frac{r}{1000} \cdot MDTR$$

Substituting the values of *r* and *gt* from the above two equations into equation [3.1] and simplifying, we obtain:

$$f = \frac{BS \cdot 1000}{BS \cdot 1000 + ss \cdot MDTR + GS \cdot 1000}$$

Since the effective data transfer rate satisfies the equation $EDTR = f \cdot MTDR$, in view of the above equation we obtain

$$EDTR = \frac{BS \cdot 1000 \cdot MDTR}{BS \cdot 1000 + ss \cdot MDTR + GS \cdot 1000} \qquad [3.2]$$

Observe that the $EDTR$, as the above equation indicates, is a function of the BS for a given device since the GS is assumed to be fixed. Hence, the choice of the BS will affect the $EDTR$, a critical factor in performance.

Table 2.3 shows the $EDTRs$ for a typical tape for which GS is 0.6 in.; ss is 2 ms, and $MDTR$ is 192,000 bytes, for different values of BS.

TABLE 2.3 The effect of the block size (BS) on the $EDTR$ for the transmission of a single block.

BS (in bytes)	$EDTR$ (in bytes/second)
400	44,037
800	71,642
1200	90,566
1600	104,348
2000	114,833
2400	123,076
2800	129,730
3200	135,211

There are two important observations to be noted here. Firstly, we can see to what degree the presence of interblock gaps and the start/stop time affects the transfer rate. Secondly, our choice of BS equal to 2000 is a justifiable one.[6]

One might wonder how the transmission of k consecutive blocks ($k \geq 1$) could affect the $EDTR$. A simple analysis shows it is not significant. To see this, equation [3.2] can be modified to:

$$EDTR = \frac{k \cdot BS \cdot 1000 \cdot MDTR}{k \cdot BS \cdot 1000 + ss \cdot MDTR + k \cdot GS \cdot 1000}$$

Observe that it has been assumed that the tape drive reads in k consecutive blocks without intermediate starts/stops in the intervening $IBG's$.

Calculation of the $EDTR$ for different values of BS with the same parameters as in the previous example and $k = 5$ yields the data in Table 2.4. Combining the data from Tables 2.3 and 2.4, the graphical representation of the effective data transfer rate (Figure 2.5) can be obtained as a function of the block size. It is clear

[6]Notice that no system or controller overheads are assumed.

from the above figure that the number of blocks transmitted has little effect on the *EDTR*, for the assumed value of the start/stop time, considering the buffer overheads.

TABLE 2.4 The effect of the block size (*BS*) on the *EDTR* for the transmission of five consecutive blocks.

BS (in bytes)	*EDTR* (in bytes/second)
400	53,452
800	83,623
1200	103,004
1600	116,005
2000	126,449
2400	134,078
2800	140,117
3200	145,015

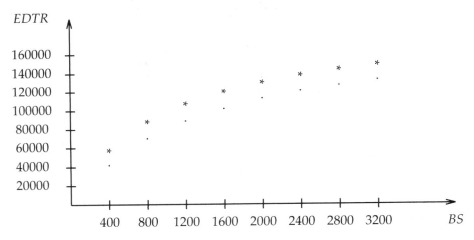

Figure 2.5   The *EDTR* as a function of the block size (*BS*). Two curves are shown. Points marked by an asterisk correspond to the curve for which $k = 5$, whereas points marked by a dot correspond to the curve for which $k = 1$.

2.1.5 Volume, Header, Trailer Labels

A tape reel in most systems—and, in particular, in IBM systems—is identified via its *volume label*. A volume label is an 80-byte block which resides immediately after the load mark point. (See Figure 2.6.) The *volume label number* must be a number between 1 and 8 that indicates the relative position within the current volume set; it occupies byte position 3. The *volume serial number* is a 6-byte numeric field which is a unique identification code that is assigned to the volume when it first enters the installation and is not changed until the tape is reinitialized; it occupies byte positions 4 through 9. Byte position 11 is a security byte. The owner's name and his or her identification are stored in byte positions 41 through 50. All other byte positions are unused.

VOL	VOLUME LABEL NUMBER	VOLUME SERIAL NUMBER	SECURITY	UNUSED	IDENTIFICATION	UNUSED

Figure 2.6   Tape volume label format.

The blocks of an individual file are delimited by two labels. The label preceding the first block of the file is called the *header* label, and the one that immediately follows the last block is called the *trailer* label.[7] (See Figure 2.7.) Each label is an 80-byte block; its format is given in Figure 2.8. Briefly, the *label identifier*, the first three bytes of the label, is used to indicate the type of label. For a header label, the content of the 3-byte field is the character string *HDR*. On the other hand, for a trailer field, the content of the field is the string *EOF* or *EOV*. If a trailer is used to mark the end of a file, then *EOF* is used. Otherwise, if the file is to be continued on the next reel of a multivolume set, then *EOV* is used to indicate that this is the physical end of the volume and the file continues on the next reel of tape. The one byte, *File Label Number* field, is set to 1, whereas the 17-byte *File Identifier* field uniquely identifies the entire file. The file/volume relationship is indicated by the 6-byte *File Serial Number* field. Order of the volume in a multifile set is indicated by the 4-byte *Volume Sequence Number* field, whereas the numeric sequence of a file within a multivolume set is reflected by the 4-byte *File Sequence Number* field. The 1-byte *File Security* field is set to 0 if no security protection is required; otherwise, it is set to 1. *Block Count,* a 6-byte field, is used only in trailer labels and records the number of blocks written onto the tape from the last header label to the current trailer label. The other fields are self-explanatory.

HEADER	IBG	BLOCK	IBG	.....	BLOCK	IBG	TRAILER

Figure 2.7   The file format layout.

---

[7] Usually, two special characters called the *tape marks* are written immediately after and immediately before the header and trailer labels, respectively.

Label identifier	File label number	File identifier	File serial number	Volume sequence number	File sequence number	Generation number	Version number of generation	Creation date	Expiration date	File security	Block count	System code

Figure 2.8   Header and Trailer Label format (IBM).

2.1.6 Fixed- and Variable-Length Records

To calculate the storage requirements for a file consisting of a number of records NR, a number of parameters must be considered. The first parameter deals with whether or not the records are of a fixed or variable size. Each case will be examined in turn.

Assume that all records have the same size RS. Then if the blocking factor is BF, the number of blocks, $NBLK$, can be found via[8]

$$NBLK = clg\left(\frac{NR}{BF}\right)$$

Here, it can be assumed that each block is filled entirely before the next block is written. Observe that it is unwise to leave empty slots in a block in anticipation that a new record is to be inserted at a later time. The reason is that in order to insert a record in a block, the block must first be read. After it is transferred into main memory and after the insertion has been completed, when that block is to be written out, the block has already passed through the R/W head. Hence, in order to be able to write the block "in place" one must read backwards. Despite the fact that there are tape drives that can read and/or write backwards, hardware imperfections may cause subsequent blocks to become unreadable.[9] The above discussion indicates that the operations of updating, inserting, and/or deleting a record cannot be done "in place" in tape files; the file, as well as all subsequent files that reside in this tape must be rewritten (see Chapter 4 for that process). Since the blocking factor is BF and the record size is RS, the size of each block BS must be:

$$BS = RS \cdot BF \text{ bytes}$$

assuming no system overhead. Observe that BS could be larger than the one calculated from the equation above, but this would lead to waste. Finally, then, the total storage (TS) requirement for that file is:

$$TS = NBLK \cdot (BS + GS) \text{ bytes}$$

---

[8] clg is used to denote the ceiling function; i.e., $clg(x) = \lceil x \rceil$. Recall that the ceiling of a real number x is the smallest integer that exceeds x. For example, $\lceil 3.2 \rceil = 4$, whereas $\lceil -3.2 \rceil = -3$.

[9] Some manufacturers claim that their tape drives are accurate enough to permit updating "in place."

Observe that GS, as before, is the size of the interblock gap, and the overhead associated with the header and trailer labels has been ignored in the above equation.

With respect to variable-length records, there are three principal implementations. First, one could indicate to the system that the logical records are of variable length and that they are unblocked. In the case in which a record of size RS is to be written, the system allocates a block of size $(RS+8)$ bytes. The extra 8 bytes are two 4-byte fields. The first field, the *block descriptor word (BDW)*, contains the size of the block BS. The second field, the *record descriptor word (RDW)*, contains the size of the record RS (Figure 2.9).

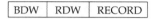

Figure 2.9   Variable-length (unspanned) unblocked record format.

Second, one could indicate to the system that the logical records are of variable length and that they are to be blocked within a block of size BS and a blocking factor of BF. In this case the system allocates a block of size $(BS+4)$. The first four bytes, the overhead, form the block descriptor word. The first record is then written by attaching the RDW to it. Now, if the next record, together with its RDW, can fit into the current block, the record is written here; otherwise, the record is written into the "next" block and the process is repeated (Figure 2.10).

BDW	RDW	RECORD 1	RDW	RECORD 2	FREE

Figure 2.10   Variable-length (unspanned) blocked records.

Third, one could indicate that the logical records are of variable length and that they are to be blocked within a block size of BS. But, the records must be spanned. *Spanning* means that if a record does not fit into the current block, then the record is "chopped off" into two segments. The first segment is put into the incomplete block to bring it up to size, and the second segment is placed into the "next" block. With this type format even records of a size larger than the size of the block can be accommodated. In order for the access method to be able to deblock records, the system replaces the RDW with the *segment descriptor word (SDW)*. Consider the case of a record that could be split into more than two segments. A segment could either be the last segment of a record, the first segment of a record, an entire record, or an intermediate segment. The SDW contains two subfields. The first subfield indicates the length of the following segment and the second subfield contains a code that indicates the nature of the segment (first segment, last segment, intermediate segment). Figure 2.11 illustrates this format.

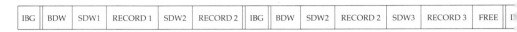

Figure 2.11   Variable-length spanned blocked records (IBM) format. A file of three records requiring two blocks.

Observe that implementation of variable-length logical records requires an extra overhead per block compared to records of a fixed size. The extra overhead for unspanned and unblocked records is the sum of the *BDW* field, the required *RDW* field, and the unused portion at the end of each block whose expected length will be (*RS*/2), where *RS* is the size of the largest (in terms of length) record in the file. Hence, spanned records could potentially save a significant amount of storage compared with unspanned records. However, blocking and deblocking of spanned records is done by the access[10] method at a considerable additional computational cost.

2.1.7 Advantages and Disadvantages of Magnetic Tape

It is clear that if a file resides on a tape, then the records of that file must be processed sequentially. That is, in order to access a record, all preceding blocks must be accessed. Hence, by their nature, tape drives are sequential devices, and the only file structure that is allowed in a tape is a physical sequential structure. Moreover, a record can not be updated in place. The direct result is that the entire file must be rewritten. Nevertheless, the low cost of magnetic tape makes it an attractive way to store data rather than on a more expensive direct-access device. Magnetic tape is also the most efficient way of transferring data from one computer system to another, the only requirement being that the systems must be compatible, regardless of manufacturers. In addition, magnetic tapes are compact and portable, facilitating off-line storage.

2.2 MAGNETIC DISKS

2.2.1 General Characteristics

As shown in the previous section, tape drives are sequential devices. Disks, on the other hand, support both sequential accesses and random accesses. Recall that random access means that a record can be accessed directly (via an address) without having to access all preceding records. It is for this reason that magnetic disks are called *direct access storage devices (DASD)*. Basically, a disk, or a disk pack, is a collection of platters. The platters, all of equal size, are permanently mounted in their centers on a spindle. Each surface of a platter consists of a

---

[10] Under *queued access methods* only. (See the next chapter.)

collection of concentric rings called *tracks*. Tracks are numbered in sequence, usually with the track closest to the outside edge numbered as track 0 (Figure 2.12). Data are encoded on each track in a serial representation (Figure 2.13).

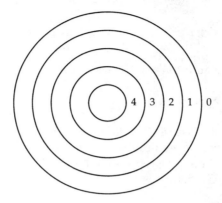

Figure 2.12   A platter with five tracks.

The *capacity of a track (TC)* is defined as the number of bytes that can nominally be stored on a track. Despite the fact that the circumference of the tracks toward the center of the platter is less than those further from the center, all tracks normally[11] have the same capacity, since the *density* of the tracks toward the center is greater than those nearer the periphery.

Figure 2.13   The encoded (EBCDIC) representation of character 1.

A *cylinder* is the set of all tracks with the same number in a pack, i.e., the tracks from each platter. The cylinder number is the common number of all tracks that define it. For example, cylinder 8 is the set of all tracks bearing the track number 8. In order to address a specific track of the disk, two parameters are needed. First, the number of the cylinder must be specified; and second, the relative number of the track within the cylinder must be indicated. The track at the top-most surface is usually referred to as track 0, the one in the "next" recording surface is referred to as track 1, and so on. (See Figure 2.14.)

---

[11] Systems do exist in which all tracks do not have the same capacity.

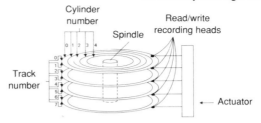

Figure 2.14   A disk with 5 cylinders and 8 tracks per cylinder.

2.2.2 Disk Capacity

The *capacity of a disk (DC)* is defined as the number of bytes that can be stored on it. In particular, if the number of cylinders is represented by NC, the number of tracks per cylinder is represented by TPC, and the capacity of each track is denoted by TC, then:

$$DC = NC \cdot TPC \cdot TC \text{ bytes}$$

The IBM 3350[12] disk has 555[13] cylinders, 39 tracks per cylinder, and a capacity of 19,254 bytes per track. Hence, the capacity of the disk is:

$$DC = 555 \cdot 39 \cdot 19{,}256 \text{ bytes} = 397 \text{ megabytes}$$

2.2.3 Seek and Latency Time

In order to either read or write from a disk, the disk must be mounted on a disk drive. The disk drive causes the disk to rotate continuously at a constant speed about its *spindle*. The IBM 3350 disk performs one revolution every 16.7 ms. In addition, the disk drive has an *actuator*[14] mounted to it. A set of arms of equal length are mounted to the actuator, and at the end of each arm is a set of R/W *heads*. There are as many R/W heads as there are tracks per cylinder or, equivalently, as the number of recording surfaces. The R/W heads float on a cushion of air over the spinning platters. The distance between the R/W heads and the platters is referred to as the *head flying distance* and it is usually on the order of 100 millionths of an inch.

To service a request in a certain block residing on a certain track of a specified cylinder, the actuator has to move (under the disk controller's control) from the current cylinder to the requested one. The time elapsed is referred to as *seek time*. The R/W head corresponding to the requested track must be activated

---

[12]In the *native* mode. The IBM 3350 is capable of emulating either a set of two IBM 3330 disk packs or just one 3330 disk pack in the other two modes.

[13]And five alternate tracks.

[14]Some disks are supplied with two *independent* actuators, independent in the sense that their movements are independent. For example, the IBM 3370 disk has two actuators, the first of which can service only tracks 0 through 5, whereas the second can service only tracks 6 through 11 of the 12 tracks in each cylinder.

since only one R/W head can be active at a time. The time required to activate a R/W head is called *head-switching time*. Moreover, an additional delay may occur. Namely, one must wait until the beginning of the requested physical block is positioned immediately below the R/W head before the block can be accessed. This rotational delay is called the *latency time*.

2.2.4 Maximal and Effective Data Transfer Rate

There is a simple relationship between track capacity TC, maximal data transfer rate $MDTR$, and the time that is required for one complete revolution RT of the disk, namely,

$$MDTR = \frac{TC}{RT} \text{ bytes/second}$$

The rationale for the above equation is that during a revolution the contents of an entire track can be either read or written. To obtain a perspective of the magnitude of the $MDTR$, the $MDTR$ for an IBM 3350 disk will be calculated. Recall that for this disk the TC is 19,254 bytes, whereas the RT is equal to 16.7 ms. Hence, the above equation yields:

$$MDTR = 19254 \cdot \frac{1000}{16.7} = 1.1 \text{ megabytes/second}$$

One can see how much greater is the $MDTR$ of a disk compared to that of a tape; moreover, data transfers of this magnitude are impossible to be attained. If it is assumed that the time that elapsed between the instant in which the request began service until the transfer was completed is r, only during a relatively small fraction of that time was the user's data actually being transferred, since seek time, latency time, and other not as significant factors absorb the larger portion of time, r.

Assume that the "target" record resides in a known block. In order for this block to be accessed by the controller, a certain overhead time exists. This time is the sum of three delays, seek time ST, head-switching time, and latency time LT. The second term, head-switching time, can be assumed to be 0 and will be ignored. Hence, the delay is the sum of ST and LT. Now, consider that the block is about to be read. No matter what format is used, conceptually the block consists of two portions. The first portion consists of system data such as information identifying the block, its length, etc. The second portion is the one that contains user's data; the first portion will be called the *block overhead* and its size will be denoted by BOS; the second portion of the block, in which user's data are contained, will be referred to as the *data subblock* and its size denoted by DBS. Observe that the total time, TT, spent to service the request is:

$$TT = ST + LT + \frac{BOS + DBS}{MDTR}$$

Hence, the portion of time in which user's data were transferred is given by (t/TT). The time spent directly reading the data subblock is t, but t is equal to

$(DBS/MDTR)$. Taking into account that the $EDTR$ is related to $MDTR$ via the equation $EDTR = t/TT) \cdot MDTR$ the following equation can be obtained:

$$EDTR = \frac{DBS}{ST + LT + \dfrac{BOS + DBS}{MDTR}} \text{ bytes/second}$$

For purposes of illustration, it will be assumed that the disk is an IBM 3350 again. The exact value of ST depends on the number of cylinders that the actuator has to travel. In this case, assume that ST is equal to 25 ms, and that the latency time is 8.3 ms, since this time is equal, on the average, to half the time required to perform one disk revolution. For BOS equal to 185 bytes and DBS equal to 2000 bytes, the above formula yields:

$$EDTR = \frac{2000}{25 + 8.3 + \dfrac{2000 + 185}{\dfrac{19{,}254}{16.7}}} = \frac{2000}{25 + 8.3 + 1.9} = 56{,}818 \text{ bytes/second}$$

The above calculations indicate that despite the fact that time is "wasted" due to overheads, the dominant quantity in the delay is the seek time, in the absence of which the dominant quantity becomes the latency time.

2.2.5 Fixed versus Fixed-Head Disks

Observe that if the seek time was not present, then the effective data transfer rate soars to approximately 196,078 bytes/second. The seek time can be eliminated if the disk drive is equipped with an actuator, which provides an R/W head per track, per cylinder[15]. In that case, no seek is required. Such disks are called *fixed-head* disks, as opposed to the ones that were introduced at the beginning of this section, which are called *movable-head* disks. It should be clear that fixed head disks are much more expensive than movable disks given the additional complexity of the controller's circuitry and multiple heads; thus, we will assume that the disk is a movable head disk unless otherwise noted.

Fixed disks, on the other hand, are magnetic disks in which the recording media are not removable. Conversely, disks in which the recording media are removable are called *removable* disks.

2.2.6 Average Seek Time

In the previous section, it was shown that the seek time had a significant effect on the $EDTR$. Therefore, the calculation of the exact value of the seek time is most

---

[15]Certain disk packs come with fixed R/W heads over only a subset of the set of available cylinders. As an example, the IBM 3344 disk pack has 560 cylinders, and there is a feature in which the actuator assembly provides fixed R/W heads only for the first two cylinders.

important for the determination of the *EDTR*. One might suppose that if he or she knew the distance (in terms of the number of cylinders) that must be traveled and the time required to move between two adjacent cylinders, then the product of these two quantities would return the seek time. Unfortunately, that is not the case. This is because the time required to travel a distance d, i.e., $t=f(d)$, is not linear. This suggests that in order to evaluate the seek time for each single random access, one must know the distance that must be traveled. To avoid such complicated calculations, the *average seek time* is derived and its value is used as the seek time. The process under which the average seek time is calculated is explained subsequently.

Initially the distribution of the accesses must be known. In our case we make the assumption that the accesses are distributed randomly. In other words, assume that the probability of moving from any one cylinder to any other cylinder is equally likely. Also assume that the disk has n cylinders, numbered from 0 to $(n-1)$, with the cylinder numbered $(n-1)$ being closest to the spindle. Denote by $p[l]$ the probability that the length of the seek, in terms of cylinders, is equal to l and by $s[l]$ the actual seek time required for a seek of length l. Then the average or expected value of the seek time, s, is given by

$$s = \sum_{j=0}^{n-1} (s[j] \cdot p[j])$$

since the length of the seek could be between 0 and $(n-1)$. The values of $s[j]$ for different j are provided by the manufacturer, whereas the values for the probabilities $p[j]$, according to our assumption, are derived below.

First, assume that the R/W head is positioned over cylinder k, as Figure 2.15 illustrates. Then, a seek of length l is possible toward the center of the disk if and only if $(k \le (n-1)-l)$, whereas a seek is possible towards the outer surface of the disk if and only if $(k \ge l)$. Hence, the probability of a seek of length l is given by

$$p[l] = \sum_{t=0}^{(n-1)\,|\,-l} r[t] + \sum_{q=l}^{n-1} r[q]$$

where $r[t]$ is the probability of a seek of length l from the current cylinder t to the inside of the disk and $r[q]$ is the probability of a seek of length l from the current cylinder q to the outside of the disk. But we assumed that $r[t]=r[q]$ for all t and q between 1 and $n-1$. So it remains for $r[t]$ to be calculated.

To accomplish this, assume again that the current position is over a cylinder k. Now, one can travel to any one of the $n-1$ remaining cylinders. Given that cylinder k could be any of the n cylinders, it can be seen that the total number of combinations of cylinders that one may travel between is given by $n(n-1)$. Hence for all t between 1 and $n-1$, $r[t]=[1/n(n-1)]$. Hence

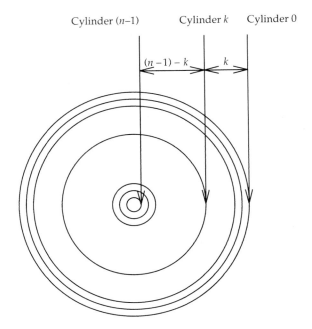

Figure 2.15 The current position of the R/W head.

$$p[l] = \frac{1}{n(n-1)} \cdot [\sum_{t=0}^{(n-1)-l} 1 + \sum_{q=l}^{n-1} 1]$$

$$= \frac{1}{n(n-1)} \cdot [((n-1)-l+1) + ((n-1)-l+1)]$$

$$= \frac{2(n-l)}{n(n-1)}$$

Clearly, $p[0]$ is equal to $(1/n)$, but this is immaterial in calculating the average value of the seek s, since $s[0] = 0$. Finally,

$$s = \sum_{j=1}^{n-1} [s[j] \cdot \frac{2(n-j)}{n(n-1)}]$$

$$= \frac{2}{n(n-1)} \sum_{j=1}^{n-1} [s[j] \cdot (n-j)]$$

2.2.7 Disk Architecture

Recall that in a direct access device a block can be accessed directly (randomly) via its address. These devices are classified into two categories: *sector addressable devices* and *block addressable devices*. Their difference lies in the addressing scheme employed. Each of these categories will be examined below.

2.2.7.1   Sector Addressable Devices.   In sector addressable devices, each track is divided into a fixed number of *sectors,* each one of which has the same fixed capacity. The process of dividing each track into sectors can be carried out either by the manufacturer, in which case one speaks about *hard sectoring,* or by the disk controller, subject to user's defined requirements, in which case one speaks about *soft sectoring.*

In either case, a sector is the smallest addressable unit. Its physical boundaries are detectable by its physical beginning. Its capacity is known to the disk drive, in the case of hard sectoring, or via special markers that are written on the disk surface by software during the formatting process, in the case of soft sectoring.

Observe that since sector size is predefined, a record of small length will generate unused storage at the end of a sector, whereas a record of length longer than the sector size will require more than one sector to be stored. Both these phenomena will be present in the case of variable-length records. In any case, methods similar to those discussed with tapes are employed to store records. Some file systems, like VAX/VMS, employ yet another scheme to handle variable length records and eliminate any unused space. In this case the length of a record is not stored; instead, the first record is stored at the beginning of the first sector of the physical file. Each record is terminated by using a special character, such as a carriage return or a line feed, that is supplied by the user. The access method uses that special character, known as a *record terminator,* to block and deblock records. Note that this scheme resembles the spanned variable record format used earlier. The only difference is that a block here could be either a sector or a number of sectors which is usually user defined. As an example, a sector addressable device manufactured by IBM is presented below.

The IBM 3310 Disk.   The IBM 3310 disk is a sector addressable device, and its architecture is referred to as *fixed-block architecture (FBA)* according to IBM terminology. Each track contains 33 sectors, of which only 32 are available to the user. Each sector ("block" in IBM terminology) has a capacity of 600 bytes, but only 512 bytes of these can hold user data. These 512 bytes of user data constitute a *FBA-block* in IBM terminology.

The address of each block is given in terms of its displacement from the very first block of the disk. That displacement is referred to as the *physical block number.* Notice that a physical block number of 6 indicates the address of the seventh block, assuming of course that the block with physical block number 0 is the first block. Finally, during I/O operations the controller resolves the physical block number into three components — a cylinder number, a track number within the cylinder, and a block number within the current track. This address is used to activate the correct R/W head and then those three components are compared via the controller with the three 1-byte fields (a part of the 88-byte system overhead per block) of each sector on the track until the correct one is located.

The unit of transfer for the IBM 3310 is referred to as the *control interval (CI).* A *CI* is the amount of user data that can be transferred between primary and secondary storage in response to a physical I/O request. The range of a control interval is between 1 and 64 *FBAs*, — in other words, between 512 and 32,768 bytes. IBM provides the user with tables that will assist one in determining the number of *FBAs* per control interval, which depends on the logical record size and the blocking factor. This section closes with the observation that all the parameters, such as control interval size, blocking factor, and the number of logical blocks per control interval can be defined by the user subject to the IBM-provided table mentioned above.

2.2.7.2 Block Addressable Devices. In these devices, the size of the block, as well as the blocking factor, is user defined. This means that the number of blocks can vary from track to track. Most IBM-manufactured devices are block addressable devices. Two different block formats are supported: *count data* format and *count-key data* format. In either case, the diagram of a track is shown in Figure 2.16 and the significance of each field follows.

IM	HA	IBG	BASE BLOCK	IBG	DATA BLOCK	IBG	DATA BLOCK	IBG

Figure 2.16 Track format (IBM). Only the first portion of the track is shown.

1. *IM: Index marker* is a hardware marker indicating the physical beginning of a particular track that is electromagnetically detected.

2. *HA: Home address* contains information about that track. Specifically, this field contains five subfields, three of which contain the cylinder number, the head number, and the physical address corresponding to this track. The fourth field, a flag, is used to indicate a defective or an operative and a primary or an alternate track. The last field is a 2-byte field used for a cyclic check.

COUNT AREA	ISBG	DATA AREA

Figure 2.17 The format of the base block. The format of the data blocks is the same.

3. The *base* or *track descriptor block* is the first block in the track and contains only system information, not user data; its structure, the same for both formats, is shown in Figure 2.17.

   a. *Count area* indicates the address of an alternate track if that track is defective, etc. There is also a key length subfield, which is set to zero, independent of the format used. The number of its fields is the same as in the count area of a data block (see below).

b. *Data area* is an area 10 bytes long that contains information about how much unused space is in this track and a 2-byte subfield used for the cyclic check.

4. *IBG:* Interblock gaps are system gaps whose size varies according to the block size and the number of blocks allocated per track.

The difference between count data and count-key data formats lies in the structure of the data blocks, and each one is examined in turn.

Count Data Format

The diagram of a data block is shown in Figure 2.18.

Figure 2.18   The format of a count-data data block. Notice the format of the data area.

1. The first field, the *address marker, A,* a 2-byte field, indicates the physical beginning of the data block.
2. The *intersubblock gaps, ISBGs,* are required in order to permit the switching of the operation of the R/W head from read to write and vice versa.
3. The *Count Area* field contains eight subfields. Three of these fields constitute the *identifier* for the particular block and contain the cylinder number, the head number, and the block number. The integer value stored in the fourth field, the *key-length* field, is the one that determines the format used. If that value is equal to zero, then it implies that count-data format was used; otherwise, the count-key data format was used and the value of this field indicates the length of the key in bytes. The fifth field, the *data length* field, indicates the length of the data area (user data only); the sixth field contains a *flag* field whose contents are the same as that of the flag field in the count area; the seventh field is a *cyclic check*[16] 2-byte field; and, the last field contains the physical address of the block.
4. The *Data Area* is the area in which user data is stored. In Figure 2.18 a blocking factor of $n + 1$ was assumed.

Note that the block overhead here is fixed by the system, and its length (fields *A, Count Area,* and *ISBGs*) is equal to 185 bytes.

---

[16] This topic is covered in the next section.

Count-Key Data Format

The basic difference between the count data and count-key data formats lies in the structure of the blocks, specifically in the presence or absence of the *Key Area* field and the data area. In the case of the count-key data format, the data block format is given in Figure 2.19, and the significance of each of its fields follows.

| A | ISBG | COUNT AREA | ISBG | KEY AREA | ISBG | DATA AREA |

Figure 2.19 The count-key block format.

1. **A.** This field has the same significance as in count data format.

2. **Count area.** The only difference here is that the key length is set to the length of the key in bytes.

3. **Key area.** This field contains the key of the last (rightmost) record of the following data area.

4. **Data area.** This area can be formatted in one of two ways, formatting with *nonembedded* or with *embedded keys*. No matter which format is used, the key appearing in the key area is attached to the beginning of the data area. In the case of embedded keys, the remainder of the data area is the same as in the count data format; in nonembedded format, the key of each record is attached to the beginning of that record. Figures 2.20 and 2.21 illustrate these two formats assuming a blocking factor of $n + 1$, records R0, R1,..., Rn, and of keys 0, 1, 2, ..., n respectively.

| n | 0 | R0 | 1 | R1 | .... | n | Rn |

Figure 2.20 The data area: count-key nonembedded key data format.

| n | R0 | R1 | R2 | .... | Rn |

Figure 2.21 The data area: count-key embedded key format.

The block overhead for count-key data format is larger than that in count data format. First, the presence of the key area forces the allocation of a new *ISBG*, which causes the block overhead to increase to 267 bytes. Second, there is an additional overhead due to the presence of the key area and the formatting of the data area. The block overhead is the sum of the above two quantities. In particular, if the length of the key is k bytes and the blocking factor is BF, then the overhead in the case of embedded key formatting is $(267 + 2 \cdot k)$ bytes, whereas the overhead for nonembedded key formatting is equal to the above overhead plus $(BF - 1) \cdot k$ bytes.

The above-defined quantities are of real importance to both the applications and the systems programmer. The reason for this is that only an integral number of blocks can be allocated by the system per track; therefore, a portion of the track will be unused, which will cause the utilization to fall.[17] To see this, consider the case when the unused portion of the tracks is ignored for a blocking factor, BF, of 10, key of length 10 bytes, and a record size equal to 200 bytes. For embedded key formatting, the utilization is $[2000/(267 + 2000 + 2 \cdot 10)]$, or approximately 87.4%; for nonembedded key formatting, the utilization falls to 83.7%. However, the utilization calculated above is misleading. To recognize this, evaluate the track utilization for the data in the above example. The track size is 19,254 bytes. Given the overhead of the base block, the available storage area for the data falls to 19,069 bytes. Assuming nonembedded key formatting, the number of blocks that can be stored in this track is the floor of the quotient of storage area size over block size. Hence, the number of blocks is $flr\,(19{,}069/(387 + 2000))$, or 7 blocks.[18] The number of bytes of user data is equal to $7 \cdot (2000)$, or 14,000 bytes. Hence, the track utilization is $(14{,}000/19{,}254)$, or 72.7%.

Before closing this section it should be emphasized that the above-derived formulas relative to the utilization are only approximate. As a matter of fact the actual values of the utilization are less than those derived above. The reason is that, as in the case of tapes, physical blocks are "separated" by interblock gaps. Unlike the case of tapes, the *IBGs* here have no *fixed* size. As a matter of fact their size is a function of both the blocksize and the specific device. Their exact values can not be derived even from special tables that are provided by the manufacturer. From now on the interblock gap sizes will be ignored.

Parity Checking.   Parity checking for data stored in disk devices differs considerably from that performed for data stored in tape devices. First, we note that it is the disk controller's responsibility to perform parity checking. For example, during a physical *WRITE* operation the controller removes the transmitted parity bit from each byte of each logical record of the physical block that is to be written, whereas during a physical *READ* operation the controller reconstructs that bit in each byte of each logical record as it is transmitted.

Instead of parity, two bytes that are called the *cyclic check redundancy* bytes are coded. In addition, during the *WRITE* operation four more bytes are calculated and collectively are called the *error correction code;* those bytes are appended to the data area of each data block. If during a subsequent *READ* operation the cyclic check fails, then the error correction code is used to aid in the correction of the error.

---

[17] Certain disks permit a physical block to be continued from one track to the next. Disks as such are said to support *track overflow*.

[18] flr is used to denote the floor function; i.e., $flr(x) = \lfloor x \rfloor$. Recall that the floor of a real number x is the greatest integer that does not exceed x. For example, $\lfloor 3.2 \rfloor = 3$ while $\lfloor -3.2 \rfloor = -4$.

2.2.8 Clusters and Extents

When a physical file is to be created a component of the file system must allocate the requested amount of external storage, i.e., a collection of physical blocks; these blocks could be dispersed over the entire disk. A collection of *contiguous* (physically adjacent) blocks is referred to as a *cluster;* the number of blocks in the cluster is referred to as the *cluster size.* Furthermore, an *extent* is a collection of contiguous tracks and/or cylinders. In general the file system will allocate multiple extents for a physical file (up to 16 in an IBM environment) unless an explicit request for contiguous allocation is made to it by the user.

2.2.9 Volume Table of Contents (*VTOC*) and File Labels

As in the case of tapes, a disk is identified via its *volume label,* which usually resides in the first track of the first cylinder. Its format and length are given in Figure 2.22.

VOL	VOLUME LABEL NUMBER	VOLUME SERIAL NUMBER	SECURITY	VTOC ADDRESS	UNUSED	IDENTIFICATION	UNUSED

Figure 2.22   Disk volume label format (IBM).

The observant reader will notice that the only difference between disk volume labels and tape volume labels is that the first five bytes of the first field labeled unused in Figure 2.7 are used here to indicate the address of the *volume table of contents (VTOC).*

The *VTOC* serves as the *disk directory.* In other words, the *VTOC* contains all the necessary information relative to the physical location and organization of all physical files residing on this disk. The information relative to each physical file is contained in a set of up to six different *types* of *file labels* linked via block pointers. The types of file labels[19] employed and their number depends on the file organization employed and the physical size of the file; their format will be discussed in detail in Chapter 3.

The format of the first file label in the linked list will be discussed briefly here in order to illustrate to the reader that the file headers reflect the file structure of the file. This label is a 140-byte area consisting of a number of fields. The first field, the *File Name* field, is a 44-byte area where the name of the physical file is stored. A number of fields were encountered also in the header labels for tape files such as *File Serial Number, Volume Sequence Number, Creation and Expiration Date.* A 1-byte field, the *Format Identifier,* indicates the type of label in question. The *Physical Record Format, Block Length, Logical Record Length,* and *Key Length* fields are self-explanatory. If the *Key Length* field is not zero, then the location of

---

[19] Data set control block (*DSCB*) in IBM terminology.

the key field within a logical record is recorded in the *Key Location* field. Note here that the location is expressed as a number of bytes that reflects the distance between the beginning of the key field and the physical beginning of the stored record; this distance is usually referred to as the *offset* of the key. The organization of the file, sequential, indexed sequential, and so on, is reflected by a 2-byte field known as the *File Type* field.

Finally, recall that in IBM systems, a file can be allocated up to 16 extents. In the file label those extents are reflected by a collection of fields. In particular, the number of extents allocated to the file is indicated by the *Extent Count* field; each extent is assigned an *Extent Sequence Number* such as first, second, and so on. Furthermore, the type of each extent is indicated by the *Extent Type Indicator;* the address of the beginning and end of each extent is stored in the *Upper* and *Lower Limit* fields. Observe that the last logical record in the file may not be stored in the last block. In other words the *logical* and *physical end* of the file may be different. The physical end of the file is indicated by the last extent, whereas the address of the last logical record in the file is stored in the *Last Record* field. The last field of the file label is a *Pointer* field that is utilized to *link* this file label to another.

2.2.10 Loading Density and Storage Requirements

Observe that with disk files a record can be updated "in place" after the block in which the target record resides has been accessed at an additional cost of one sequential access. Loosely speaking this is possible, since a physical *READ* operation transfers the block into the input buffer in main memory after the block has been located where the record in question is modified; given that the internal processing time is negligible, a physical *WRITE* operation causes the block to be written in its initial position upon the next revolution.[20] Similarly, records can be inserted "in place." In order for this to be possible the block must not be full; otherwise, more than one sequential access is needed. The number and mode of the access, sequential and/or random, depends on the file organization, as will be seen in later chapters. In any case, if insertions of records in the lifespan of the file are anticipated, then it is prudent to intentionally leave empty *slots* in each block to permit relatively inexpensive insertion operations. The ratio of the storage area utilized by user data and the storage area allocated to user data is called *loading density*. For example, if the fixed-length records are of size *RS*, the blocking factor *BF* is 10, and loading density *LD* is 80%, then the number of records that must be stored in each block, with the possible exception of the very last one of the file, is called the *effective blocking factor (EBF)* and is given by:

$$EBF = flr(BF \cdot LD)$$

In this case, the *EBF* turns out to be 8; i.e, at initial loading eight records must be stored in each block. It is a simple matter now to calculate the number of

[20] The exact mechanism of the *READ* operation transfer is discussed in Chapter 3.

cylinders (*NC*) required to store a file consisting of number of records (*NR*). One first calculates the number of blocks (*NBLK*) required via

$$NBLK = clg\left(\frac{NR}{EBF}\right)$$

Then, the number of tracks required is calculated, taking into consideration the track capacity (*TC*) and the fact that the size of the physical block *BS* is the sum of the block overhead and the data area, the latter quantity being equal to the product of *BF* and *RS*. The number of tracks (*NT*) is given by the equation:

$$NT = clg\left(\frac{NBLK}{flr\left(\dfrac{TC}{BS}\right)}\right)$$

Finally, the number of cylinders required depends on *NT* and the number of tracks per cylinder (*TPC*) and is given below:

$$NC = clg\left(\frac{NT}{TPC}\right)$$

Notice that the above equation is valid only under the assumption that each file is stored in a new cylinder.

2.3 EXERCISES

1. The IBM 3420/8 tape drive has the following characteristics: Density = 1600 bytes/inch, IBG length = 0.6 in., v = 200 in./s, and rewind v = 800 in./s. A file of 20,000 fixed-length records must be stored on a new tape of length 2400 ft. The size of each logical record is 170 bytes. Physical records are to be of size 1024 bytes.
   a. Find the capacity of the tape.
   b. Find the utilization.
   c. Find the MDTR.
   d. Find the EDTR for the transmission of two consecutive blocks.
   e. Assuming that the tape drive is ready to write the first block (at the physical beginning of the tape), find the minimum time to write the file onto the tape and to rewind the tape.
2. A file with 20,700 fixed-length logical records is loaded on a new 3350 disk. The file structure is physical sequential and the first block is written at the physical beginning of cylinder number 0. The *JCL* statement indicates a logical record length of 200 bytes and a blocking factor of 16. Assuming that

no interblock gaps are present and that the format used is count data find the following.

  a. The number of cylinders required to store the entire file.

  b. The utilization of the allocated file space.

  c. The track utilization.

  d. The time required to write the entire file onto the disk, assuming that initially the R/W head is positioned over cylinder 0.

3. The GTD and IBM 3420/8 tape drives have the following characteristics:

Tape Drive	Density	IBG	Start/Stop time	R/W speed	Rewind speed
GTD	D bpi	I"	S ms	RW"/sec	RS"/sec
IBM 3420/8	6250 bpi	0.6"	1 ms	200"/sec	640"/sec

A file of 2 million fixed-length records must be stored on tape. The length of each record is 90 bytes. Blocks are to be 2048 bytes. Assuming no block overhead and unspanned records for the GTD tape drive, develop equations which define the following.

  a. The blocking factor.

  b. The minimum expected time to write the file onto tape and rewind the tape assuming the R/W head is ready to write the first block.

  c. The effective data transfer rate.

  d. Evaluate all equations that were derived in parts (a) through (c) using the device characteristics of the IBM 3420/8 tape drive.

4. The DEC RM03 disk drive has the following characteristics: 832 cylinders/disk, 5 tracks/cylinder, 32 sectors/track, 512 bytes/sector, IBG 114 bytes/sector, 8 ms/(one cylinder seek), average seek time 30 ms, and latency of 8.3 ms. Answer the following questions by stating all your assumptions.

  a. What is the storage capacity of the disk?

  b. What is the maximum data transfer rate?

  c. Suppose that enough sectors are to be written to fill 20 consecutive cylinders. What is the minimum expected time needed to perform this operation?

  d. Suppose all data blocks that were written in part (c) are to be read in reverse order. Estimate the time to perform this operation.

5. A new disk drive has the following characteristics: C cylinders/disk, 1 track/cylinder, S sectors/track, D bytes/sector, IBG G bytes/sector, M ms/(one cylinder seek), average seek time A ms, and average latency of L ms. Suppose that the operating system allows block sizes to be defined in terms of an integral number of sectors. For example, a block of $2 \cdot D$ bytes would be stored in two consecutive sectors, each sector containing D bytes.

K blocks are to be written in order of ascending block numbers (i.e., 1, 2, 3,..., K). Each block is stored in B consecutive sectors. Assuming that all K blocks can be written on a single track, derive an equation for the expected time to read these K blocks in the order K, $K-1$, $K-2$,..., 2, 1. Clearly define your approach to solving this problem and state all your assumptions.

3

Data Transfer

Computer files require a language for their creation and manipulation. Most of the high-level languages such as PL/I, COBOL, FORTRAN, and PASCAL contain a data sublanguage dedicated to this task. Despite the obvious advantage that a user is not to be concerned with the the system-level implementation details, there are a number of critical disadvantages associated with the use of only high-level languages. First, each high-level language provides the applications programmer with a *different* data language and set of capabilities; therefore, the programmer must tailor the application work subject to the constraints imposed by the high-level language, instead of the *performance* of the application. Second, the high-level data manipulation sublanguages conceal from the user the inner workings of the system; therefore, the user cannot improve the overall performance of the application. Finally, if the user's application program is coded in a high-level language, then it is often difficult to use the entire access subsystem directly, and therefore in many instances the user must rely only on the limited set of processing features provided by the high-level language in question.

One moment's reflection on the previous paragraph indicates that the evaluation, design, and performance of file systems requires an essential understanding of how the system *works*. In particular, one must be aware of the underlying system software responsible for the transfer of data between primary and secondary storage. But the software *drives* the hardware; and in order for the software to achieve its best performance, one must take into account the different devices connected to the system and the way that the software communicates with them in order to take full advantage of the functions of both the principal hardware and software components of a computer system. The important aspects for a student of file systems will be summarized in this chapter.

3.1 HARDWARE

The *hardware* of a computer system, consisting of processors, storage devices, and I/O devices, can be represented in a general way as in the diagram in Figure 3.1.

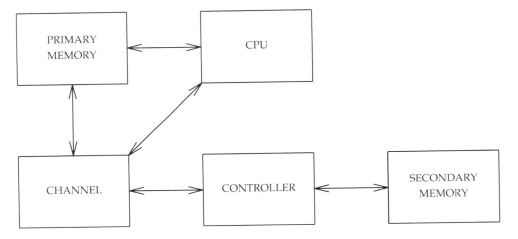

Figure 3.1   Hardware components of a computer system.

The fundamental characteristics of each of these components are discussed below.

3.1.1 Primary Storage

All programs that are being executed by the hardware are stored in *primary* or *main storage (memory)*. These programs could be either user programs or programs required to assist in the execution of user programs such as assemblers, compilers, loaders, etc. Chief among the latter programs is the *operating system*, a large and complex software product whose function is to manage all the resources of the computer.

3.1.2 Secondary Storage

Primary storage is a very expensive commodity; therefore, one must get the most out of its use. Hence, programs that are not being executed as well as large data files are not stored in main memory.[1] Instead, they are stored in *secondary (auxiliary, external) storage* that permits the storage of massive amounts of information. Secondary storage usually consists of magnetic tapes, magnetic disks, and drums.

3.1.3 Central Processing Unit (CPU)

The CPU contains the electronics necessary to execute the machine language instructions and control the transfer of data between main and secondary memory. Typically, CPU's are capable of executing anywhere from 1 million to 50 million instructions per second (MIPS) at the present level of technology.

3.1.4 Channel

As noted above the CPU is operating at electronic speeds on the order of microseconds.[2] At the other extreme, secondary memory devices are operating at electro-mechanical speeds on the order of milliseconds. The reason for the slow speeds of electro-mechanical devices (disks) is that when a request for transmission of data is issued, the first step is to locate the "target" data in the secondary storage device. Thus the read/write head of the drive must be *moved* in such a way that it is positioned over the physical beginning of the "target" data. That "movement" requires not only the aid of electronic signals but also the aid of mechanical parts. It is these parts that cause the delays. To see the magnitude of these delays, note that a moderate estimate of the time required to complete a data transfer from the time that the request was issued is 25 ms. Assuming a CPU capable of executing 2 MIPS, then with the data transfer of 25 ms, the CPU is capable of executing $2{,}000{,}000 \cdot 0.025$, or $50{,}000$, instructions, which obviously could be equivalent to $0.025 \cdot 50{,}000{,}000$, or $1{,}250{,}000$, instructions for a computer capable of executing 50 MIPS. Thus if the task of managing and supervising the transfer of data were assigned to the CPU, it would be idle most of the time waiting for the completion of the transfer.

To relieve the CPU of this duty one uses the *channel*. The channel is another type of processor with its own instruction set, instruction counter, and control logic. When a request for a physical data transfer is issued, the CPU loads the channel's instruction counter with the beginning address of a program that has been loaded in the main memory known as the *channel program*. It then signals the channel to start executing this program. The CPU is now relieved of the data transfer task and is therefore free to perform other tasks.

3.1.4.1 Cache Memory.
Since only one processor can access main memory at a time, the channel interrupts the CPU, in mid-execution if necessary,

---

[1] There is one more important reason that forces the information to be stored in secondary storage devices. Primary memory is a volatile medium, whereas secondary storage is nonvolatile.

[2] Recall $1\,\mu s = 10^{-6}$ s and $1\,ms = 10^{-3}$ s.

whenever it needs a new instruction or whenever it is ready to transmit data between main and secondary storage. In a number of instances the CPU executes instructions not from main memory but instead from a very fast memory, *cache memory*, where the instructions that the CPU must execute have been loaded from main memory ahead of time. With this enhancement the channel interrupts the CPU only occasionally. It should be noted here that only relatively small cache memories are used because of their high costs.

3.1.4.2 Selector, Byte Multiplexor, Block Multiplexor Channels. Assume that a physical I/O request is issued to write a physical block onto the disk. Here is the pseudocode of the required channel program.

```
Perform a ''seek'';
Find the correct block;
Write the block from address;
```

In the above pseudoalgorithm the term "seek" requires two steps; the first step is to perform a seek to find the required cylinder and the second is to activate the write head of the appropriate track. The first step is a mechanical movement and this requires, as we have seen, an average of 25 ms. Therefore, the channel cannot execute the second channel command until the seek operation has been completed, and the channel remains idle between the two channel commands. Given that the seek can be completed only by the controller[3] means that the channel will remain idle for a period of time before it resumes execution with the next channel command. Hence, utilization of the channel may be increased by attaching to it more than one device; so while one device is busy and not using the channel, a new physical I/O operation may be initiated on another device attached to the channel. In order to be able to implement such channel multiprogramming one needs special types of channels. The following paragraphs are discussions of three popular channel types.

A *selector channel* can be connected to up to 256 different devices; but only one device can be selected at a time. In other words a device is selected, the physical I/O operation is completed, and then another device is selected and the process is repeated. These channels are, therefore, usually used with high-speed devices.

A *byte multiplexor channel* may also be connected to as many as 256 different devices. The byte multiplexor interleaves the transmission of bytes from the different devices to which it is connected. Notice that unlike the selector channel, this channel does not need to wait for the physical I/O to be completed in a device. Since it interleaves bytes, the byte multiplexor channel must be connected to slow-speed devices such as card readers and printers.

---

[3]Controllers are discussed in the following section.

Finally, a *block multiplexor channel* resembles a byte multiplexor in that the channel does not need to wait for a channel program to be completed; therefore, it can execute multiple-channel programs. Unlike the byte multiplexor, this channel interleaves the transmission of blocks from the different devices to which is connected; therefore, these devices must operate at high speeds.

3.1.5 Controller

A channel program issues commands to read or write data, to locate data physically in the external storage, and so on. However, since each secondary device has its own characteristics, there is a need for another component that interprets and executes those channel commands subject to the device that it "controls." In other words, a component is directly connected to a channel at one end and to a secondary device at the other end. This provides the interface between the standard I/O software interface of the channel and the device dependent characteristics. This component is referred to as the *device controller*. Since the channel provides a standard I/O interface, each channel can be connected to more than one controller, while each controller can be connected to several secondary storage devices provided that they are all of the same type. Figure 3.2 illustrates the above-discussed points.

3.1.6 I/O Buffers

As mentioned earlier, a physical *READ* request could cause a *unit* of data to be transferred from secondary storage to primary storage, whereas a physical *WRITE* request could cause a unit of data to be transferred from primary to secondary storage. The unit of transferred data is defined to be the *block,* where the block is defined to be a set of records. Hence, each application's program area contains at least one storage area large enough to receive a logical block[4] (in response to a physical *READ* request) and another storage area the size of a block whose contents are transmitted to secondary storage as a result of a physical *WRITE* request. The former area is referred to as the *input buffer;* the latter is known as the *output buffer.*

Assume the situation in Figure 3.3, where single input and output buffers have been allocated and a blocking factor of three is used. Also assume that the user's application program has just issued the first logical *READ* request. Since the Input Buffer is empty,[5] the access method will find the first block in the

---

[4] If variable length records are employed, then the buffer area must be larger than the logical block in order to accommodate the *BDW* and *RDW* fields.

[5] Unless *anticipatory buffering* is used. In other words, certain access methods anticipate the subsequent issue of a logical *READ* request, the moment in which an *input* file is *opened* via an *OPEN* statement (which must precede any logical I/O request), formulate a request for a physical *READ,* and cause the first block of data to be transferred into the Input Buffer.

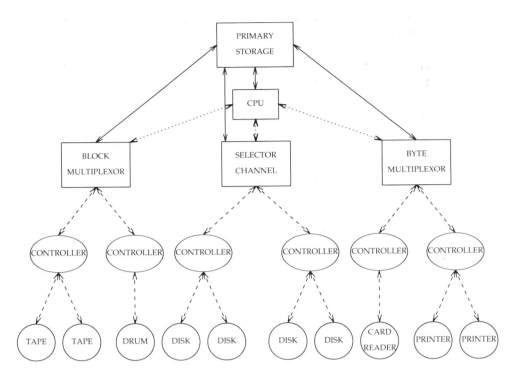

Figure 3.2   A typical hardware configuration.

secondary device, in our case, the magnetic disk; that logical block will be transferred into the input buffer, while *at the same time*, the first logical record, R0, will be delivered to the structured variable, which resides in the data area of the user's area, indicated by the application program.

Recall that a new physical *READ*, (the transmission of the second block), will take place upon issue of the fourth logical *READ* request. The reason for this is that the access method will not find the "next" record, R3, in the input buffer, since the input buffer is empty,[6] so a block transfer request will be issued.

Similarly, the first logical *WRITE* request does not trigger a data transfer; instead, the access method delivers the record from the data area to the "next" available slot in the output buffer. In Figure 3.3 the first logical *WRITE* request, assuming that it was preceded by the first logical *READ* request, will cause the logical record R0 to be delivered from the data area to the first slot in the output buffer. When the third logical *WRITE* request is issued, the access method will deliver the third record R2 to the "next" slot in the output buffer; at this instant it will detect a *full* buffer. The access method, anticipating a new logical *WRITE* request, will formulate a data transfer request.

---

[6] The exact mechanism is explained later.

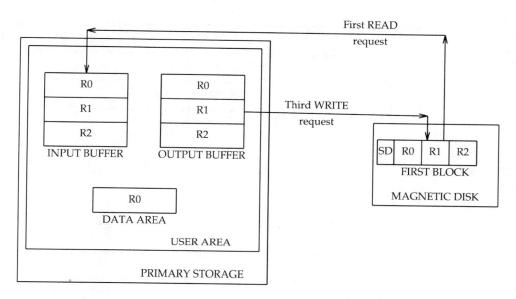

Figure 3.3 Block and record movement assuming single input and output buffers.

3.2 SOFTWARE

3.2.1 Operating Systems

As mentioned earlier, the use of channels permits the CPU to perform other tasks while a data transfer is in progress. In particular, it is clear that the "other" tasks could be that the processor serves another user's job. In other words, today's systems are *multiprogramming systems* in which the processor switches from one program to another if the former requests a data transfer. The CPU starts the channel; while the channel is servicing the request of the first program, the processor starts or resumes execution of another program. It is clear that all these transitions must take place in an orderly fashion; and as a matter of fact, this is done under the supervision of the *operating system.* An operating system is a computer program designed to manage the system's resources; a *multiprogramming system* is a system in which there are several processes in a "state of execution" at the same time.

Recall from Figure 3.1 that there are three major classes of resources. First, there is primary storage or simply *memory;* second, there are the *processors;* and third, there are secondary storage devices, or simply *I/O devices.* We define another resource here, the *file system.* This resource has the task of controlling the creation, assignment, updating, and general manipulation of computer files. The operating system that is responsible for managing these resources consists basically of four primary components, which are illustrated in Figure 3.4. We now consider these resources and their responsibilities below.

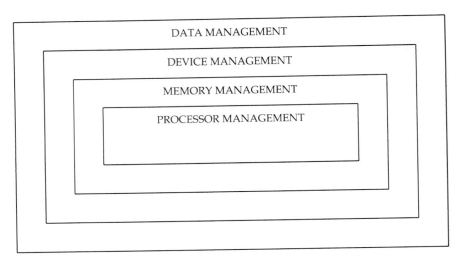

Figure 3.4 The four primary components of a multiprogramming operating system.

3.2.1.1 Memory Management Component. The primary functions of the memory management component are to allocate storage areas to processes that request them, to release the storage area allocated to a process that is no longer active and to decide which of the processes requesting storage is to receive it.

3.2.1.2 Processor Management Component. This component actually consists of a number of entities, which are illustrated in Figure 3.5. The *job scheduler* decides which of the jobs that are submitted to the system will be allowed next into the system. The *processor scheduler* is assigned the task of deciding to which job the processor will be dedicated next and for what period of time. Finally, the *traffic controller* keeps track of the processors and the status of the processes.

One of the principal functions of a processor scheduler is to provide the users with *fair* and *efficient* scheduling. One aspect of efficient scheduling is the *minimization* of the average waiting time for the jobs on the system.

Job scheduler	Processor scheduler	Traffic controller

Figure 3.5 The three primary components of the processor management component.

Briefly, some of the available scheduling algorithms will be mentioned and compared.

CPU Scheduling Algorithms.   One should note that only one application program *(job)* can be executed by the CPU at any instant in time. It therefore can be said that the job has *control* of the CPU, or simply, *control*. The *CPU scheduler* is the component of the processor scheduler that decides for how long and in which order the jobs in the system will gain control. In the following paragraphs, some of the possible mechanisms through which a job gains control of the system will be presented.

First, there is the *first come, first serve (FCFS)* policy. Under this policy the first job (or, equivalently, its region) gains control of the processor and does not relinquish it until the job is finished. As an example, if the order of arrival of only three jobs together with their corresponding required processor service times are as given in Table 3.1(a), then it is easy to see that the average waiting time is given by the sum of the waiting times divided by the number of jobs. If it is assumed that the difference in the time of their arrivals is negligible, then it can be seen that the first job does not have to wait any time, the second must wait 100 µs which is the time required for the first one to be processed; and the third job must wait 110 µs, the time required for the first two jobs to finish. Hence, the average waiting time is given by $(100 + 110) / 3 = 70$ µs, which is an unacceptable figure. This policy *favors* lengthy jobs, speaking in terms of service times.

TABLE 3.1 The order of arrival of three jobs and their required corresponding processor service times.

Job Number	Service Time		Job Number	Service Time
1	100 µs		3	5 µs
2	10 µs		2	10 µs
3	5 µs		1	100 µs
(a)			(b)	

Another policy that could be implemented is the *shortest job next (SJN)*. This policy allows the job that requires the least processor service time to be serviced next. Assume that the processor scheduler must select the next job to be serviced from the ones that appear in Table 3.1(a). According to the established policy, the jobs will be serviced in the order of job 3 first, job 2 second, and finally job 1 third, as in Table 3.1(b). Following the same reasoning as in the previous case, it can be seen that the average waiting time falls to $(5 + 10) / 3 = 5$ µs, a considerable improvement. But, if new jobs arrive while the first job is executing, then theoretically the third job could wait forever because, as can be seen from Table 3.1(b), continuously arriving jobs that require less than 100 µs would be processed

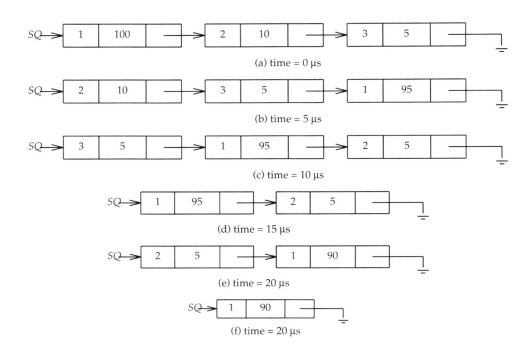

Figure 3.6 The service queue and the job in service at five intervals in time. The quantum is assumed to be equal to 5 μs.

before it. Hence, one can see that this policy represents the other extreme in that it *favors* the shortest jobs.

A fair compromise is the *processor sharing* policy of scheduling. Under this method jobs are serviced *in* the order that they arrive; *but* the processor is dedicated to a job only for a short period of time, called a *slice (quantum)*. If during that slice of time a job has not been completed, then the job is suspended, the intermediate results are saved, the job is placed at the end of the queue, and the processor dedicates itself to the "next" job, namely, the one that is in the front of the queue. Finally, if the job is completed before it consumes the allocated slice of time, then the next job is serviced. This discussion closes by noting that the *size* of the slice depends on the computer center's environment, on the required overhead for saving and restoring the intermediate results, and on the status of processes. Control of time slicing is done by the *dispatcher*.

Figure 3.6 illustrates the *service queue (SQ)* that is maintained by the processor scheduler and the number of steps required in order for all three jobs to be serviced under the assumptions that the order in which the processor scheduler initially finds them is as in Table 3.1(a), and that no other jobs arrive in the mean time. Each node in the service queue has three fields; the first indicates the job identification number; the second, the remaining service time required, and the third, a pointer to the next job. Finally, the slice time has been assumed to be equal to 5 μs, an unreasonably small quantity in actual practice.

3.2.1.3   Device Management Component.

Keeping track of the devices, channels, and controllers is a task assigned to the *I/O traffic controller*. Deciding to which request the device will be dedicated next is a task that is assigned to the *I/O scheduler;* again some of the available scheduling algorithms are discussed below. Finally, once the next job to be serviced has been selected by the I/O scheduler, the channel is signaled to start executing the channel program tasks that are assigned to the *I/O device handler*. Figure 3.7 illustrates these basic components of the device management component. Notice that each secondary storage device has its own peculiarities; therefore, different devices have different device handlers.

I/O job scheduler	I/O device handler	I/O traffic controller

Figure 3.7   The three primary components of the device management component.

Device Scheduling Algorithms.   Recall that in certain instances the access method will issue a physical I/O request in response to a logical I/O request issued by the application program. Recall also that execution of a physical I/O consumes a significant amount of time; therefore, normally physical I/O requests arrive much faster than they can be serviced. The direct result is that a long *list* for such requests is formed, one list per device. It is the responsibility of the I/O scheduler to ensure that the average wait for the service of a request for each particular device is minimal. Before any of the available disk scheduling algorithms are discussed, a simple observation will be made—namely, the primary reason for the delay encountered during the execution of a physical I/O request is the seek time. Therefore, the primary goal of a "good" scheduling algorithm is to minimize the seek time. This, in turn, requires minimizing the *number* of cylinders traveled in order to service all arriving requests.

Assume that the channel is dedicated to just one movable-head magnetic disk device. Notice that only one physical I/O request *(job)* can be serviced by the channel at a time.

The *I/O scheduler* is a component of the processor scheduler that orders the requests arriving at each list associated to a device. In the following paragraphs some of the possible ordering algorithms are presented.

First, there is the *FCFS* policy. Under this policy jobs are serviced according to their order of arrival. In other words, the list of requests is nothing but a queue. Notice that this policy does not consider the required seek time needed to service the jobs; therefore, no attempt is made to minimize that time.

There are two additional scheduling policies that are designed to minimize the total distance, in terms of cylinders, traveled by the R/W heads, in order to service all the physical I/O requests pertaining to this device. Under these policies the list of requests is implemented not as a queue but instead as a double-linked list, so that when a new I/O request arrives it is inserted in the list *in order* relative to the cylinder number to which the request was issued. In other words, the list of requests is ordered in increasing order of the cylinder number to which the requests apply.

Under the first policy, *shortest cylinder next (SCN)*, the request that is serviced next is the one whose cylinder is closest in terms of physical cylinder distance from the one that just finished. In other words, the request that uses a cylinder that is either to the *left* or to the *right* of the current cylinder is the request that will be serviced next.

Under the second policy, *SCAN*, the R/W head is moving in one specific direction and the R/W head services any request on a cylinder over which it passes. When there are no more requests to be serviced in that direction, then the actuator switches its direction and the process is repeated.

Figure 3.8 illustrates the *service request (SR) list* that is maintained by the I/O scheduler for each of the three scheduling policies discussed above, under the assumption that jobs 2 through 4 arrive before the completion of job 1. It is clear that after completion of the first request, the next request to be serviced depends on the policy being used at the time. For example, under *FCFS* the next job to be serviced would be job 2; under *SCN* the next job would be job 3; and, under *SCAN*, assuming that the present direction of movement of the actuator is toward the interior of the disk, the next job would be job 4.

The *FCFS* policy is clearly inferior to the other two policies, whereas the determination of the "best" policy among *SCN* and *SCAN* [7] depends on the environment and, specifically, on the distribution of arrival times of the requests and distribution of the cylinder number of the requests.

3.2.1.4 Data Management Component.
The primary responsibility of the data management component is the management of computer files. Specifically, it keeps track of the location of the physical file, its use, its status, opening and closing the file, allocating external storage according to the needs of the application program, and keeping track of the I/O buffers, secondary devices, and their characteristics. This complex but highly important component of the operating system is usually referred to as the *file system*.

---

[7] It is not difficult to see that the *SCAN* policy favors the latest-arriving jobs and the jobs whose requests are for cylinders nearest to both innermost and outermost cylinders. The first problem can be avoided via the *N-SCAN* policy, under which requests arriving during a sweep are grouped together and ordered for service during the return sweep. The second problem can be addressed via the *C-SCAN* policy, under which the R/W head is moved directly to the outermost cylinder after the innermost sweep has been completed.

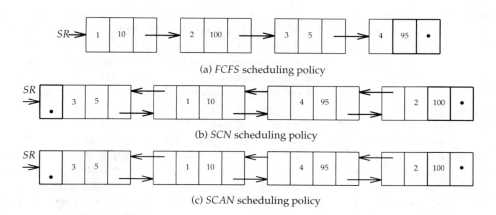

(a) *FCFS* scheduling policy

(b) *SCN* scheduling policy

(c) *SCAN* scheduling policy

Figure 3.8   The request list that depicts each of the three discussed policies. Each node on the list reflects a request; the first field of each node contains the job number, and it also reflects the order of its arrival. The second field reflects the number of the cylinder where the physical I/O request is to be performed. Notice that the job in service is job number 1 in all cases.

In the following sections some of the tasks of this system will be discussed.

Access Modes and Access Techniques.   Recall that the access method serves as the interface between an application program and the file system. In other words, any logical I/O request issued by an application program must be handled by the access method.

The *access mode* is the mode by which an application program must access logical records from a physical file. The number of access modes depends on three factors: the operating system's vendor, the secondary storage medium, and the file organization. For example, IBM file systems support a file organization called VSAM, whereas VAX file systems do not. In addition, if the physical file resides on a tape, then by default its structure is physical sequential and by default again, the only possible access mode is the *sequential access mode.* On the other hand, if the Physical Sequential file is residing on a disk, then the access mode could be either a sequential access mode or a *random access mode.* As a matter of fact, in some instances the access mode employed to access the records of a file can be changed each time the file is used. Again the combination of different access modes allowed in a file depends on the file system and the file organization employed.

Under the sequential access mode, a "target" record is located by starting at a particular point in the physical file and continuing in order one record after the other until the record is located. At the other extreme under random access mode, the target record is located not by examining every preceding record but instead via an address. These modes will be studied in detail in subsequent chapters.

Recall that as a result of a logical *READ* request the access method will either deliver the next record into the program variable in the data area when the input buffer is not empty, or it will formulate a physical I/O request in which case the application program loses control while the physical record transfer takes place. Strictly speaking, this remark is not always true. There are two techniques, *synchronous I/O* and *asynchronous I/O,* through which an application program can handle record operations. The first mechanism places the program in a *wait* state until the transfer is complete. On the other hand, if the reading of the record is done asynchronously, the application program may continue to run (i.e., is not placed in a wait state) unless some other application gains control; it may regain control before the transfer of the record into the data area is completed. If the applications programmer is not aware that asynchronous I/O has been employed, he or she may proceed with the update of an erroneous record, namely, the one currently in the data area instead of the new one. Access methods that employ synchronous I/O are said to use *queued access technique,* whereas access methods that employ asynchronous I/O are said to use *basic access technique.* Most systems include a *WAIT* routine so a user who is operating in asynchronous I/O may issue a *WAIT* request so the application will be placed into a wait state until the record transfer to the data area is completed.

It is important to be aware of one other significant difference between these two techniques. With queued access technique, the corresponding access method automatically blocks, deblocks, and buffers, whereas basic access techniques perform only physical block transfers; and blocking/deblocking is the responsibility of the application program.

This discussion closes by stating that most of the high-level languages support synchronous I/O operations and that the access method that must be employed for a file structure depends on the file organization[8] and the available file system.

The Directory.   Recall from Chapter 2 that the physical files that reside in a volume can be located via the *VTOC* of each volume. In a computer system one usually finds multiple volumes; therefore, the question arises how can a specific physical file be located in response to a user request. Observe that the location of the target file depends on two major components, the *user name* and the *physical name* of the file. Notice that in a multiuser environment, one cannot access a file by just its physical filename, such as *myfile,* since there could be several users who have named their files with the same name. In other words, the *owner* of the file that is to be accessed must be known. The file system, realizing this fact, permits each user to create her own *directory;* that is, a *file* is created where the physical filenames of the files that the user owns are stored. Furthermore, the file system designer realizes that several files may pertain to a

---

[8] As an example, the only access method that may be employed for sequential files is that whose mode is *sequential* and whose technique is *queued.* On the other hand, at least two access methods may be employed in the case of an *Indexed Sequential* file.

similar function and should be grouped together. Hence, the users are provided with an extra flexibility; i.e., users can create different directories within their directory so that files of a "similar" nature can be grouped together. These latter directories are called *subdirectories*.

For example, consider a user with user name *user1* who owns a set of files in which a subgroup of those files contain letters that the user has received. Another subgroup of files contains letters that the user is to send; and another subgroup consists of just one file containing a telephone directory that the user maintains. A possible organization of his or her directory is presented in Figure 3.9.

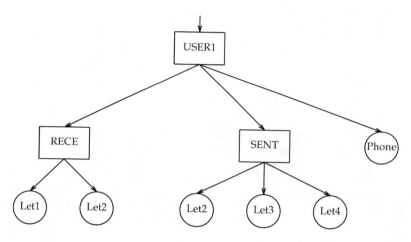

Figure 3.9   User's USER1 directory.

Notice that this directory contains two subdirectories, *RECE* and *SENT*, the former stands for the set of received letters (let1 and let2) and the latter, for the set of letters (let2, let3, and let4) to be sent. Another file under the filename "phone" contains the user's phone directory. Notice that the structure of Figure 3.9 permits the user to have two or more files to bear the same filename provided they do not belong in the same subdirectory.

The above observation is a direct result of the fact that the structure, a tree structure, is a directed acyclic graph. Therefore, the absence of cycles indicates that each file can be identified uniquely by its path from the root of the directory to the file (which always occupies a leaf position).

The above discussion suggests that the system maintains its own directory, in which each user's directory is treated as a subdirectory. Figure 3.10 illustrates a system's directory, usually referred to as the *master directory*, which assumes that there are a total of three users and a total of eight files. Notice that in a tree structure each file can be accessed via its path from the root, which is appropriately called the *pathname* of the file. For example, the pathname of *file1* of *user1* is *root/user1/file1*, whereas the pathname of *file3* of *user2* is *root/user2/sub2/file3*.

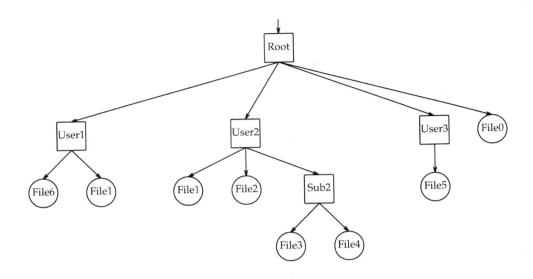

Figure 3.10   A master directory. Note that "square" nodes represent subdirectories, whereas "round" nodes represent files.

The important thing to notice is that a directory *is* a file. Hence, one must select a file structure to physically store the directory in external storage. Despite the fact that this is the goal of subsequent chapters, a possible file structure for the master directory of Figure 3.10 is given in Figure 3.11, which is presented as a preview of things to come.

Notice the structure in the top level. This structure contains 13 contiguous physical blocks with physical block numbers from 1 to 13, respectively. In addition, each block contains an area where a pointer can be stored. Observe that the block pointer of the first block points always to a file which contains the master directory. Each logical record of this file contains three fields, the first of which contains the physical name of a file or subdirectory. The second field contains a physical block pointer that points to a block at the topmost level. The third and last field is a bit field in which the bit is set to 1 whenever the physical name appearing in the first field of that logical record represents a subdirectory; otherwise the bit is set to 0. Observe that every block pointer at the topmost level of the structure, except the first one, could point to either a file, as is the case with the block pointers in blocks 2, 3, 4, and 10, or to the location where the "target" physical file is stored, as is the case with the block pointers in blocks 5 through 9 and 11 through 13. In other words, a pointer in Figure 3.11 that points to a circle would in reality point to the header label of the file in the case of a single volume environment; or it would point to the *VTOC* of the corresponding volume in the case of a multivolume environment. In the latter case the *VTOC* must be searched in order to locate the target file.

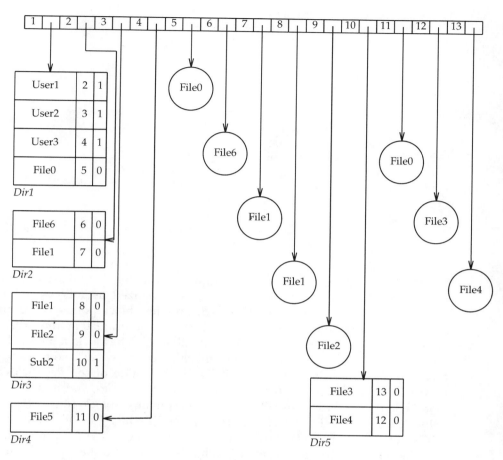

Figure 3.11   A file structure that is a possible implementation of the directory in Figure 3.10.

Table 3.2 illustrates the pseudoalgorithm employed for searching the above structure. First, assume that the pathname has been stored one name per location in the array *p*. In addition, the function *Block_Pointer* accepts a block number as an argument and returns the pointer that was stored in the pointer field of that block. The procedure *Access* expects a block pointer as an argument and it accesses this file. The function *Search* searches the currently accessed file for the logical record whose filename field contents matches the Physical filename, and it returns the pointer that is stored in the block pointer field of that record. In addition, the Boolean field *Directory_Flag* is set according to the value of the Boolean field in the logical record. Finally, the procedure *Search_VTOC* searches the *VTOC* of the volume pointed by the *Look_Ahead* pointer for the file header of the file with the name field contents equal to *Physical_name*.

TABLE 3.2 The search pseudoalgorithm.

```
Algorithm Search;

[1]      i ← 1;
[2]      Physical_Name ← p[i];
[3]      Physical_Block_Number ← i;
[4]      Look_Ahead ← Block_Pointer(Physical_Block_Number);
[5]      Found ← False;
[6]      While not(Found) do
              {Access(Look_Ahead);
               Look_Ahead ← Search(Physical_Name);
               If not(Directory_Flag) then Found ← True
                                      else
                                           {i ← i+1;
                                            Physical_Name ← p[i];}}
[7]      Search_VTOC(Look_Ahead,Physical_Name);
```

Let's trace the above pseudoalgorithm to locate file *file3* whose pathname is *root/user2/sub2/file3*. Then, the array *p[i]* is initialized as follows: *p*[1]=*root*, *p*[2]=*user*2, *p*[3]=*sub*2, and *p*[4]=*file*3. Now, the first block points to *dir1* and examination of the contents of its logical records indicate that the *Look_Ahead* pointer is set to 3 and the value of *Found* is still false. The block pointer of block 3 points to *dir3;* the logical record with filename equal to *sub2* indicates that the *Look_Ahead* pointer must be set to 10 while the value of the flag field *Found* remains the same. Finally, block number 10 points to *dir5*, and it is easy to see that the logical record whose filename is *file3* contains a block pointer that points to block number 13. But, more importantly, the *Directory_Flag* field indicates that this is not a directory. Hence, the value of the variable *Found* is set to true; the main loop of step 6 of the pseudoalgorithm is exited, and the block pointer field of the 13th physical block points to the target volume, where its *VTOC* is searched for that header whose filename contents is *file3*.

Secondary Storage Space, File Storage Space. In this section two important issues will be addressed. First, what is the mechanism by which the file system allocates storage in response to a user's request? Second, what is the mechanism by which the access method can access the particular block within a given file that contains the target record? At the outset, it should be noted that there are a number of different of mechanisms employed, and here we will concentrate on only a few of them.

Device Storage Allocation. First and foremost the file system must be aware of what blocks are in use and which are free. One popular way is by use of a *bit map*. A bit map is a sequence of bits where the number of bits is equal to the number of blocks that can be allocated in the device. In other words, there is a *one-to-one* correspondence between bit positions and block positions. The *i*th bit of the bit map will correspond to the block with physical block number equal to i. In this way, if the ith block is already allocated to a file, then the ith bit of the bit map is set to 1; otherwise, it is set to 0. Hence, when a block is requested, it is a simple matter to search the bit map for the occurrence of an entry equal to 0. Notice that the principal advantage of this technique is that the amount of storage required for the bit map is minimal; therefore, this file can be permanently placed in primary storage. On the other hand, this technique becomes inapplicable if the blocks have variable sizes because the conversion from a physical block number to an actual disk address is impossible to calculate.

Another approach would be to ignore the already allocated blocks and to keep track of only the free blocks. One of the ways this can be accomplished is by keeping all the free blocks in a linked list and which is referred to as a *free chain*. In this case only the address of the first block of the chain needs to be known, since every other free block can be located via pointers. Allocating a block under this scheme is very simple; just allocate the first block in the chain. Similarly, when a block is deallocated, that block is placed at the beginning of the chain and the chain is repaired. This method works equally well for both fixed or variable length blocks. The only drawback is that in the case of variable-length blocks, the allocation of a block must be handled via some algorithm. To see this, suppose that a request is issued for the allocation of a block of size 1000 bytes. If the first block in the free chain has a length less than 1000 bytes, an algorithm will be needed to consolidate several blocks that are adjacent members of the same cluster from this chain in order to satisfy the request. In addition, the algorithm must be carefully designed in order to effectively handle the *fragmentation* of secondary storage.

File Storage Allocation.   Most of the observations made in the previous section apply here as well. In particular, if all blocks have a fixed length, then each file has a *file allocation table* associated with it, where a bit map, similar to the one used above, is stored and where the bit positions' values are set to 1 to reflect the fact that the corresponding block has been allocated to *this* file, while bit positions that have been set to zero indicate that the corresponding blocks have not been allocated to this file. Notice again that this technique does not work in the case of variable length blocks; in addition, if the blocks allocated to this file are not contiguous, a logical byte address to physical byte address mapping will assume some overhead.

As mentioned before, another method that will work in both fixed- and variable-length blocks is the *chained block* method. In this case only the address of the first block of the file needs to be known.

Another method that works well for both fixed and variable length blocks is the method that employs *file maps*. In this case a file of logical records is created for each file. Each logical record corresponds in a *one-to-one* fashion to a block in the file; that is, the ith logical record corresponds to the ith block and contains just two fields. The first field reflects the *length*, and the second reflects the *address* of the block to which it corresponds. Notice that this file can be extremely large; in some instances it may require a considerable amount of both storage and processing time in order to locate a specific entry for a block. Again, as before, the designer must find the most efficient file structure to represent the *file map,* which is the topic of subsequent chapters. In passing, we mention that a possible solution could be the creation of a file map file for the file map file, analogous to the directory of directories.

I/O Buffers .   Consider a sequential file *MASTER* in order to see how one could update the logical records of this file. Since all processing of the logical records can be done only in primary storage, the logical records must first be transferred via physical *READ* requests to an input buffer and then transferred to the data area where they are updated; finally they are written out in secondary storage from the output buffer via physical *WRITE* requests. Referring to Figure 3.3, it can be seen that the first logical *READ* request, assuming a queued access method, will cause the transfer of the first logical block into the input buffer and the transfer of the first logical record from the buffer into the indicated program variable in the data area of the applications program.

One may wonder how the access method keeps track of the current record in the input buffer and also of the current record in the output buffer. The file system that has the responsibility of allocating the buffers maintains a set of two pairs of pointers. Each pair of pointers is associated with a buffer. The first pointer of the pair points to the address in main storage of the first byte of the respective buffer. That pointer is called the *input buffer pointer (IBP)* for the case of the input buffer and *output buffer pointer (OBP)* for the case of the output buffer. The second element of each pair points to the current "slot" in the associated buffer; the pointer to the current slot of the input buffer is known as the *current input buffer pointer (CIBP),* and the pointer to the current slot in the output buffer is known as the *current output buffer pointer (COBP).* Figure 3.12(a) illustrates the initial situation, which is the situation before the first logical *READ* request.

The pseudoalgorithm in Table 3.3 indicates the events that take place in response to a logical *READ* request.

TABLE 3.3 The sequence of events that are taking place as a result of each logical *READ* request.

```
Algorithm logical_READ;

If IBP = CIPB then
                    {perform a Physical Read;
                     while transfer_not(complete) do
                            wait;}
    deliver logical record pointed to by CIPB to indicated program variable;
    CIPB ← CIPB + length(delivered logical record);
    If CIPB = IPB + Size(Buffer) then CIPB ← IBP;
```

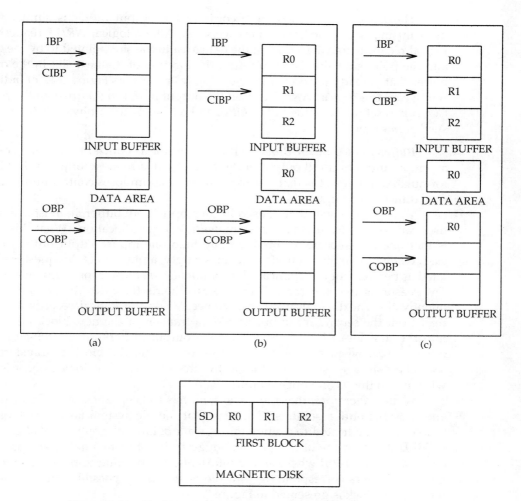

Figure 3.12 Block and record movement assuming single input and output buffers. (a) Initially, (b) after the first logical *READ*, and (c) after step (b) and the first logical *WRITE*.

Observe that the first step is the examination of the input buffer. If it is empty, indicated by the fact that the values of the two pointers *IBP* and *CIBP* are equal, as in Figure 3.12(a), then a request for a physical I/O is issued; otherwise, the record pointed to by the current input buffer pointer is delivered to the program area. At any rate, after the delivery of the logical record to the data area is completed, the *CIPB* is adjusted to point to the next "slot" in the buffer by adding to its value the length of the logical record that was just delivered. Figure 3.12(b) illustrates the result of this step. Finally, a test is performed to see whether the *CIPB* pointer points to a location outside the buffer; in that case, its value is set to the value of the *IBP*, which reflects an empty buffer.

The mechanism of writing records to the output buffer is similar to the mechanism just outlined, with one exception. After a logical *WRITE* request, the logical record is transferred from the data area to the slot pointed to by the *COBP* and the pointer's value is set to reflect the location of the next slot in the output buffer that is ready to receive the next logical record, as Figure 3.12(c) indicates. But in case this logical *WRITE* caused the output buffer to fill up, then the pointer *COPB* is reset to the value of the *OPB,* and a request for a physical *WRITE* is issued at *this* time.

Buffer Pool Control Block.   It is important to notice that whenever either an empty input or a full output buffer is detected, a request for a physical I/O is formulated; the result is that the application program loses control until the physical transfer is completed.

To avoid the wait time caused by an empty input buffer, in most instances a user can request from the file system *multiple buffer* allocation. What this means is that one can allocate to this file more than one input/output buffer. In this case, when the first input buffer becomes empty, a physical I/O request is formulated as before, but the application program *does not* lose control for lack of data. The reason is that the second input buffer holds the next "block" and consequently the "next" logical record. Hence, while the logical records are being read from the second input buffer, a data transfer of the next block takes place into the first input buffer. Similarly, the output buffers can be *flip-flopped.* In other words, when an output buffer becomes full, the block is transferred to secondary storage; subsequent logical writes will cause the logical records to be written into the second output buffer.

Notice, therefore, that the file system has to keep track of multiple buffers and multiple buffer pointers. The way that the file system keeps track of multiple buffers dedicated to a single file is via a pointer, the *buffer pool block pointer (BPBP).* As the name of this pointer suggests, it points to a data structure called *buffer pool block (BPB)* where all the information pertaining to the set of allocated multiple buffers corresponding to a file is stored. A possible structure for the buffer pool block is presented in Figure 3.13.

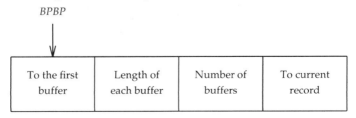

Figure 3.13   The buffer pool block.

Notice that the first field of the *BPB* contains the address of the first buffer, *IPB* or *OPB,* of the pool of allocated buffers; the second field indicates the physical length of each of the buffers in this pool; the number of buffers in this pool is reflected in the third field; and finally, the *CIBP*, or *COPB*, depending on whether or not the pool is an input or output buffer pool, is stored in the last field.

Data Event Control Block List.   The above discussion centered around the fact that the file system must keep track of all buffer pools allocated to a single application program, various status information pertaining to each buffer pool, and the physical files to which these buffer pools are allocated. A possible solution to the above problem is presented next.

Information pertaining to *each* buffer pool is stored in a data structure usually referred to as the *data event control block (DECB)*. Despite the fact that the number of fields in this structure depends primarily on the access method employed, a general description of such a block is presented in Figure 3.14.

A brief explanation of the purpose and function of each of the fields of the *DECB* follows:

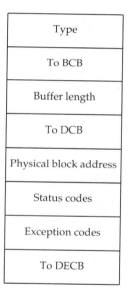

Figure 3.14   The data event control block.

- The *Type* field indicates the type of processing as well the type, input or output, of the associated buffer pool.
- The next field is a pointer field that points to the buffer control block associated with it.
- The *Buffer Length* field indicates the number of bytes that must be read or written.
- The next field is a pointer to the *data control block (DCB)* where all

information relative to the associated physical file structure, such as *data block size*, *logical record length*, and *organization*, is stored.[9]

- The *physical block address (PBA)* is a disk pointer that points to the "next" block that will be transferred from or to the buffer, a direction that is indicated by the *type* of buffer. Notice that the access method employs the *DCB* structure in order to calculate the address of the "next" block.

- The *Status Codes* field, as its name suggests, contains codes that indicate the status of the latest logical I/O operation requested. For example, one code indicates that the I/O operation is in *progress*; another code indicates that the operation was completed *successfully*; a third code indicates that the operation was completed *unsuccessfully*.

- The *Exception Codes* field contains codes that signify how an unsuccessful completion must be handled and it depends on the returned status code.

- Finally, each buffer pool is associated with a *DECB*; since there could be more than one buffer pool allocated, one could have more than one *DECB*. Therefore, the collection of *DECBs* that correspond to a single file are linked together via the last field of each *DECB*, the *DECB pointer*.

Hence, the *data event control block list (DECBL)* is the linked list of the above defined *DECBs*.

The Data Control Block List.   Observe that a set of buffers is dedicated to a specific file. In other words the file is the *owner* of each of these allocated buffers. But an application program can operate on more than one file at the same time; hence, there are multiple sets of buffers in existence for the same application program—in particular, a set of buffers corresponding to each *open*, or *active*, file. The file system keeps track of owners of each set of buffers via a data structure that allocates the *DCB*, where all the information is stored relative to the active file that this control block represents. In Figure 3.15 a general description of such a block is presented.

To DECB	Physical file structure	Logical record structure	To UCB	To DCB

Figure 3.15   The *Data Control Block*.

The first field of the *DCB* is a pointer to the beginning of the *DECBL* associated with this file; the second and third fields, Physical File Structure and Logical Record Structure, respectively, describe, as their names suggest, the physical file structure of the file in question, whereas the fourth field contains a pointer to the *Unit Control Block (UCB)*. The *UCB* is a data structure that contains all the

---

[9] The *data control block* is discussed in the next section.

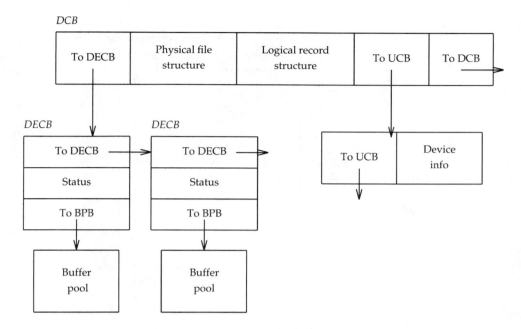

Figure 3.16   The data structure consists of the *file control block*, the *I/O buffer control block* list, the *I/O buffers*, and the *device unit block* list corresponding to a single file.

information relative to the device (unit) where the physical file resides. Notice that the latter three fields of the *DCB* were stored at the moment the file was *opened*, and the information was derived from the file header.

In this way the *DCBs* corresponding to the active files used by the application program are maintained in a linked list usually referred to as the *DCB list*. The size of this list is equal to the number of active files utilized by the application program, since there is one *DCB* node per active file.

Finally, Figure 3.16 illustrates the multilist structure, consisting of the *DCB* list, *DECB* list, and the corresponding buffers for one of the active files. Notice that there is a pointer from the *UCB* to another *UCB*, which must be present in the case of a multivolume file.

Locate Mode Processing.   In an earlier section we noted that in order to update a logical record, we must transfer the record from the input buffer area to the data area where the record is to be updated and then transfer that updated record into the output buffer. This procedure requires *two* main memory transfers of the logical record, and its processing is generically known as *move mode* processing.

Instead, one could have updated a record while it was in the buffer and in that case one speaks about *locate mode* processing. Notice that under this type of processing, a logical record must be "moved" only once from the input buffer to

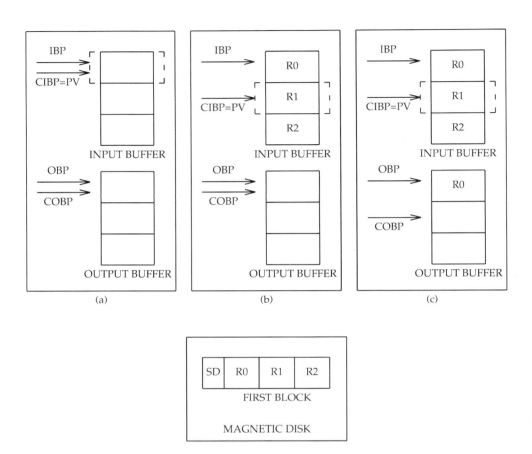

Figure 3.17 Block and record movement assuming single input and output buffers under locate mode input buffer processing. (a) Initially, (b) After the first logical *READ*, and (c) After step (b) and the first logical *WRITE*.

the output buffer. In addition, under this mode the record can be updated while in the input buffer or in the output buffer. In the former case we say that *input buffer* processing is employed, whereas in the latter we say that *output buffer* processing is employed.

In terms of implementation, the technique that is employed is to allocate a program variable, say *PV*, not in the data area but instead in the area overlaying the slot in the input (output) buffer where the record to be updated resides. Figure 3.17 illustrates the technique. Notice that this is a very easy task, since the slot where the record resides is pointed to by the buffer pointer. We will see actual implementations of this technique in subsequent chapters.

3.3 CASE STUDIES: THE *MVT* AND *MVS* OPERATING SYSTEMS

Recall that the primary responsibility of the memory management component is the allocation of primary storage to a process that requests it. The policy used by this component in allocating storage space is what basically differentiates between operating systems. In this section we will briefly discuss two major types of operating systems: partitioned memory systems and demand-paged memory systems. In particular, the two major representatives of those two systems are *multiprogramming with a variable number of tasks (MVT)*[10] and the *multiple virtual storage (MVS)*,[11] both of which are supported by IBM. The *MVS* operating system, a very popular operating system, is based on the older and outdated *MVT* system that is still in use today.

Despite the fact that the memory partition systems are considered archaic, we will study them first for two reasons. First, understanding this type of operating system makes the understanding of virtual systems much easier; second, the sequence of data movement is basically the same in the two systems.

Before we present this system we would like to warn the reader that our goal is to present the major features of those systems, which are going to serve as the starting point for a detailed study of operating systems via the available manuals in their respective computer system installations.

3.3.1 Multiprogramming With a Variable Number of Tasks (*MVT*)

We begin this section with the assumption that we just submitted an application program to the system. We will try to explain the sequence of events that take place under an *MVT* system from this moment until the first physical I/O is completed in response to our application program's first logical I/O request.

3.3.1.1 Primary Storage Allocation.   Under *MVT*, primary memory is divided into *regions (partitions)*, where each region contains a user's *entire* job. In other words each user's job selected for execution, by the job scheduler, is allocated a region where the job is loaded by the *loader*. The region allocation and deallocation is done *dynamically* under the *MVT* system. In other words, each job is allocated as much real storage as needed and, therefore, the size of these regions vary. Notice that under the partitioning scheme the number of regions and, consequently, the number of jobs in real memory are severely limited, given the amount of available space and the size of each job. Figure 3.18 illustrates the *MVT* allocation scheme, in which there are only four user jobs in the system that occupy the four regions, respectively. Notice also that the operating system occupies a significant portion of low memory and that there is free space available for allocation.

---

[10] Released in 1967.
[11] Released in 1974 and also referred to as OS/VS2.

Primary memory

Figure 3.18   Memory partition into four regions.

3.3.1.2 Region Partitions.   Let's assume now that the *job scheduler* decided which of the waiting jobs must be loaded into memory. A region is allocated within the *free area* where the user's job is loaded. The natural question is, What are the contents of the region? The answer is that each region is further subdivided into a number of partitions. In particular, there are the following partition areas:

1. The *application program* area, where the user's compiled code resides.
2. The *data area,* where the requested program variables of the application's program are allocated.
3. The *channel program* area, where the channel program will be stored as soon as it is constructed.
4. The *buffer* area[12] where the I/O buffers will be allocated.
5. The *data control block* area, where the data control blocks will be allocated.[13]
6. The *access method* area, where the properly invoked access method will be allocated.

Figure 3.19 illustrates these partitions within a region.

3.3.1.3 Gaining Control.   Let's suppose that the job just selected by the *job scheduler* was ours. Observe that at some point the *multiprogramming supervisor* will give *control* to our region. Since only one program[14] can be executed at a time, our region initially has no control; that is, our program is in a wait state until the multiprogramming supervisor decides to *switch* control from some other region to ours. There are a number of circumstances under which a region can lose control. We will state two of them that are important for our development.

1. The application program in that region is out of data. In that case, since a considerable amount of time will elapse until the formulated request for a physical I/O read is completed, the multiprogramming supervisor, instead of keeping the CPU idle, will switch control to some other region.

[12] Strictly speaking, the buffers could be outside the region.
[13] Data control block is the IBM terminology for the file control block.
[14] *MVT* allows only 15 jobs to run concurrently.

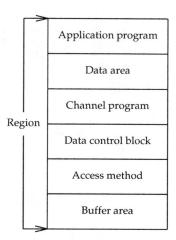

Figure 3.19   The partitions within a region.

2. The application program has "used up" all its allocated time *slice.*

3.3.1.4 *VTOC*, File Space, Device Allocation Space.   Recall that the file system is responsible for maintaining a file directory, allocating space to a physical file, and also keeping track of the free space on each device. Under *MVT,* all these pieces of information are recorded, as we emphasized in Chapter 2, in a set of labels each referred to as *data set control block (DSCB)* that reside in the *VTOC* of each volume. There are six different format *DSCBs, DSCB1* (a format 1 *DSCB)* through *DSCB6;* all have the same length (140 bytes) and their formats are distinguishable by the 44th byte, which carries the *label format.*

Before we discuss these labels in detail, we first illustrate the layout of *VTOC* in Figure 3.20. Notice that the first label of each *VTOC* is a format 4 *DSCB* referred to as *VTOC descriptor.* As its name suggests, this describes the *VTOC* file. The second label of each *VTOC* is a format 5 *DSCB* referred to as *device allocation table.* As its name suggests, it keeps all information relative to the available space in the volume. The file space relative to a file is described via a chain of labels of formats 1, 2, and 3, where the first label of the chain is a format 1 *DSCB.* One can see that there are as many chains as physical files that reside in this volume.

VTOC Descriptor.   The *VTOC* descriptor layout is presented in Figure 3.21, and the significance of each of its fields follows.

- **Key identifier.** A 44-byte area that contains 22X'04'.
- **FI.** The *format identifier,* a 1-byte field, indicates the type of label and in this case 4 is set to 4.
- **Last DSCB1.** This field, a 5-byte area, indicates the address of the last *DSCB1* label in the *VTOC.* The first two bytes indicate the cylinder, the

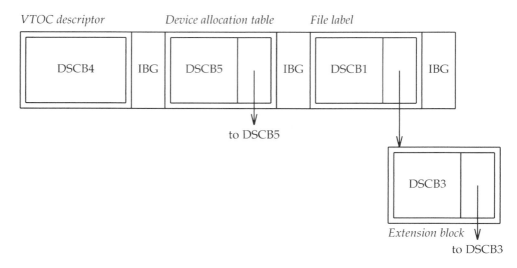

Figure 3.20   *VTOC* layout.

Key identifier	FI	Last DSCB1	DCSBs number	VTOC description	Device description	VSAM file	To DSCB6	Extent description

Figure 3.21   The *VTOC* descriptor (*DSCB4*) label.

next two bytes indicate the track within the cylinder, and the last byte indicates the block number within the track where the DSCB1 label has been stored.

- **DSCB's number.** This 2-byte area indicates the number of labels in the *VTOC*.

- **VTOC description.** A 9-byte area that indicates the number of alternate tracks and, more importantly, the number of extents allocated to *VTOC*.

- **Device description.** A 14-byte area that describes the device. In particular, the device size, the track length, the number of labels per track, and device constants such as tolerance are recorded there.

- **VSAM file.** The 19-byte area contains information if there are *VSAM* files stored in this volume.

- **Extent description.** This 10-byte area records the *first* extent allocated to the VTOC. The first five bytes indicate the address of the first block in this extent, whereas the last 5-byte address indicates the address of the last block in this extent.

- **To DSCB6.** This 5-byte area contains a block pointer to a *DSCB6* label that is used to record the information of up to 26 extents. Notice that if the *VTOC* occupies more than 27 extents, then the additional extents can be recorded in a number of *DSCB6* labels that are linked together.

Device Allocation Table.   Recall that the available storage in this volume is recorded in the second label in the *VTOC*, a *DSCB5* label. Its format is illustrated in Figure 3.22.

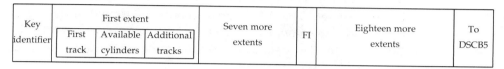

Key identifier	First extent			Seven more extents	FI	Eighteen more extents	To DSCB5
	First track	Available cylinders	Additional tracks				

Figure 3.22   The device allocation table (*DSCB5*) label.

- **Key identifier.** This 4-byte area contains 4X'05'.
- **First extent.** This 5-byte area indicates the *first* available extent. In particular, the first 2-byte subfield indicates the relative track address of the extent, the second 2-byte subfield indicates the number of unused cylinders in this extent, and the last field indicates the number of any additional unused tracks in this extent.
- **FI.** This 1-byte field indicates, as before, the format of this label and has been set to 5 in this case.
- Up to 25 more extents can be specified in this label by utilizing the 35-byte *Seven* and the 120-byte *Eighteen More Extents* fields.
- **To DSCB5.** In the case in which more than 26 extents are available, the *DSCB5* label can be linked to another label of the same type via this block pointer field.

File Space.   The space allocated to each file in a volume is reflected by its *file space* label. The fields of *DSCB1* are illustrated in Figure 3.23, and their significance is outlined below.

Filename	FI	Dates	Number of extents	FO	Record format	Block length	Record length	Key length	Key position	Ind	Free bytes	Three extents	To DSCB3 or DSCB2

Figure 3.23   File space (*DSCB1*) label.

- **Filename.** The file name is recorded in this 44-byte area.
- **FI.** As before, this is the format identifier that has been set to one in this case.

- **Dates.** This area contains a number of subfields. The first reflects the *creation date*, the second, the *expiration date*, and the third, the *date of last reference* to this file.

- **Number of extents.** This 1-byte field indicates the number of extents allocated to this file.

- **FO.** This 2-byte field indicates the file organization and, therefore, the format of the blocks (count data or count-key) is determined.

- **Record format.** This 1-byte area records the format of the logical records employed. For example, whether the format is of fixed or variable size.

- **Block length.** The data block size indicated by the user is recorded in this 2-byte field.

- **Record length.** This field records the size of the logical records in the file. In the case of fixed length records, this field is equal to that length, whereas in the case of variable-length records, this field reflects the size of the longest record in the file.

- **Key length.** In this 1-byte field the system records the user-defined length of the key of the logical records.

- **Key position.** This field indicates the distance of the key field from the beginning of the logical record. Certain access methods retrieve logical records from their key value, so their *offset*, or key position, must be known.

- **Ind.** This area contains a number of subfields, such as the protection of the file, that are collectively referred to as *file indicators*. The interested reader could consult the respective IBM VMS manuals for the description of these subfields.

- **Free bytes.** This field records the number of free bytes on the *last* track associated with this file.

- **Three extents.** As the title of this 30-byte area suggests, this is where the information related to the first three extents allocated to this file is recorded. Each extent description consists of 10 bytes and four subfields. The first 1-byte area reflects the *type* of extent. For example, if the type setting is X'15', this indicates the extent that was allocated on cylinder boundaries; however, a setting of the type field to X'00' indicates that no extent has been allocated. The second field, the *Extent Sequence Number* field, indicates the relative sequence of this extent in the set of allocated extents. Finally, the third and fourth fields, each 4 bytes long, indicate the *lower* and *upper limit* of the associated extent. Each limit is described via the cylinder (2 bytes) and track within the cylinder (2 bytes) numbers.

- **To DSCB3 or DSCB2.** The last field is a block pointer field that could point to either of the two labels. *DSCB2* labels are present if and only if the organization is *ISAM*. Notice that a *DSCB2* label could also point to a *DSCB3* label. The purpose of a *DSCB3* label is to permit the recording of up to 13 more extents allocated to a file that the *DSCB1* label associated with this file cannot accommodate. The layout of the *DSCB3* label, which is referred to as *extension data set control block,* is illustrated in Figure 3.24. The fields of that label are self-explanatory; we only note that the key identifier is set to 4′X0′.

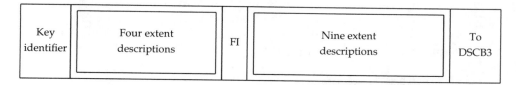

Key identifier	Four extent descriptions	FI	Nine extent descriptions	To DSCB3

Figure 3.24   The extension data set control (*DSCB3*) label.

3.3.1.5   The First Logical I/O.   At any rate, our region has gained control. Let's assume that our application program is ready to issue the first logical I/O request from a file under the physical filename *MASTER.*

Recall that in order for a physical I/O to take place the access method, among other things, must construct the channel program. But in order for the access method to perform its task a number of important parameters must be known, such as the physical filename of the file and its structure. These parameters are known to the access method via the *DCB,* which is constructed from the information available in two sources: first, the *job control language (JCL)* statements that accompany the high-level source of the application program and, second, the *required DECLARE* and *OPEN* statements.

JCL is a language that permits the user to communicate directly with the operating system, whereas the *OPEN* and *DECLARE* statements are provided by the employed host language. It is important to notice that a file must first be *DE-CLARED* and *OPEN,*[15] in that order, before any logical I/O requests are issued pertaining to this file.

The DECLARE Statement.   The purpose of the *DECLARE* statement is twofold; first, it provides a way which the user may use any valid symbolic filename—that is any syntactically correct name and not the *actual* physical filename of the file, for the file that he or she intends to use; and second, it is the way which the user indicates to the file system the file's organization. For example Table 3.4 depicts the syntax of the *DECLARE* statement available in PL/1.

TABLE 3.4 The PL/I DECLARE statement.

DECLARE FILE **SYMBOL** RECORD ENV(**CONSECUTIVE**)

Notice the presence of a number of keywords such as *DECLARE, FILE,* and *RECORD.* The first two keywords are self-explanatory, whereas the function of

---

[15]Certain high-level languages combine both steps into one.

the keyword *RECORD* indicates a record format file as was explained in Chapter 1. The keyword *ENV*, short for environment, indicates that the file organization follows. In our case the file organization is *CONSECUTIVE*, which is the PL/I terminology for a sequential file. Up to this point the file structure of the file and its physical filename are undefined. The way that the file system becomes aware of these two is known to the system via the *JCL*, which is supplied with our source. As an example, the *JCL* statement for this file could have either one of two different formats (a) or (b) appearing in Table 3.5.

TABLE 3.5 The two possible sets of *JCL*.

//GO.**SYMBOL** DD DSNAME=**MASTER**,DISP=(**OLD**,**KEEP**),UNIT=**DISK**

(a)

//GO.**SYMBOL** DD DSNAME=**MASTER**,DISP=(**NEW**,**CATLG**),UNIT=**DISK**,

// DCB=(RECFM=**FB**,LRECL=**30**,BLKSIZE=**3000**), SPACE=(**TRK**,**(5,2)**),

// VOL=SER=**123**

(b)

In both sets of *JCL*, the values of the keyword parameters appear in bold letters. Before we explain the information contained in those *JCL* statements, we note that the *JCL* statement appearing in Table 3.5(a) is all that is needed in the case in which our file *MASTER* had been *created* previously, whereas the *JCL* statements appearing in Table 3.5(b) are needed at the time of *creation* of the file.

1. The first part of the *JCL* statement is what accomplishes the *mapping* from the symbolic filename *SYMBOL* to the physical filename *MASTER*. In particular the *DD* keyword stands for *data definition*, and the *DSNAME* stands for *dataset name*, where Dataset means file in IBM terminology.

2. The *DISP* keyword stands for *DISPOSITION* and informs the file system whether or not the file is to be created at this time *(NEW* or *OLD)*, and also what the file system is supposed to do with the file after the file is *CLOSED*. After an *OLD* file is used, then either we will *KEEP* it or we will *DELETE* it. Now in the case of *NEW* file, we will either *DELETE* it or keep it; therefore, its existence must be recorded in the master directory, *CATALOGUE* in IBM terminology, in which case we *CATLG* that file.

Observe that in Table 3.5(a), the file *MASTER* is assumed to be an *OLD* file; therefore, the file is already catalogued and all the information relative to its structure is already stored in its *file label*. On the other hand, the file *MASTER* is assumed to be a *NEW* file in Table 3.5(b); its physical structure is indicated via the second *JCL* statement, and the storage device where the file will be stored is indicated by the third *JCL* statement.

At this point we mention that the *CATALOGUE,* which resides on a special volume called *SYSRES,* has stored the physical filenames in it together with a pointer to the volume in which each file resides. Hence, in order for the file system to locate the *OLD* file *MASTER,* it first examines the *VTOC* of the *SYSRES* volume in order to locate the *CATALOGUE;* then the logical records of that file are searched to locate the filename *MASTER.* If successful, the volume pointer to the disk where the file *MASTER* resides is extracted. Finally, the *VTOC* of that disk is searched for the location of the file label for our file. Figure 3.25 illustrates these steps.

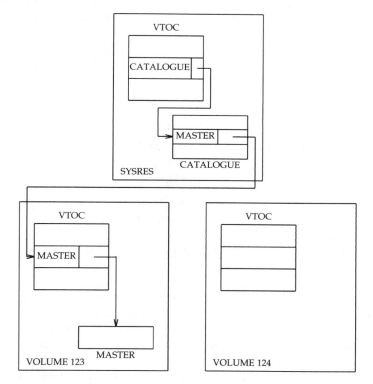

Figure 3.25   The SYSRES volume.

Finally, observe that the physical data block[16] has a size of 3000 bytes, as *BLKSIZE (Blocksize)* indicates; the size of the logical records is 30 bytes, as indicated by *LRECL (logical record length);* a *fixed block (FB) size* is used as *RECFM (record format)* indicates; and a request for a seven-track allocation is made to the file system via the *SPACE* parameter.

---

[16] Count-data format is used with consecutive files.

At any rate, the following events take place in response to a *DECLARE* statement. First, the information from the *file label*, in the case of an *OLD* file, is copied into the *job file control block (JFCB)*, so that the entire information about the physical file is copied into main memory. Therefore, subsequent accesses to the blocks of the physical file are dictated from main memory. Second, the information contained in the *DD* statement supplements and overrides the information contained in the *JFCB*. Third, the *DCB* statement is used to supplement and override the contents of the *JFCB* which is copied into the *DCB*.

The OPEN Statement. The OPEN statement serves two primary purposes. First, it indicates to the system the subsequent use of this file. In particular, each file is *OPENed only* for one purpose; the purpose is for *input* (read logical records only), or for *output* (write logical records only), or possibly for *update* (update logical records of the file). The second purpose that the OPEN statement serves is to indicate the file organization; consequently, the proper access method will be invoked. In the system/370 there are seven access methods; they are as follows:

1. *Queued Sequential Access Method (QSAM).*
2. *Basic Sequential Access Method (BSAM).*
3. *Queued Indexed Sequential Access Method (QISAM).*
4. *Basic Indexed Sequential Access Method (BISAM).*
5. *Basic Direct Access Method (BDAM).*
6. *Basic Partitioned Access Method (BPAM).*
7. *Virtual Storage Access Method (VSAM).*

Notice that basic or queued indicates the access technique employed. Sequential, indexed sequential, direct, partitioned, and *VSAM* are the five file organizations[17] supported by most IBM File Systems.

At any rate, the *OPEN* statement causes the proper access method to be invoked and the linked lists are built as shown in Figure 3.16.

When the first logical I/O request is issued, a number of events take place. In order to facilitate the listing of these events we assume that this was a logical *READ* request. First, the access method gains control and examines the contents of the input buffer. If the logical record is there, it is deblocked and delivered by the access method to the indicated program variable. Otherwise, a physical data transfer must take place. The access method in that case builds the channel program, which is discussed below.[18]

---

[17] We note that the subset of access methods available to the applications programmer depends on both the file system and the host language at his or her disposal. In addition the access methods *QISAM, BISAM,* and *VSAM* are not available under MVT.

[18] If necessary, the access method may repeatedly build channel programs to reach the required physical block.

The Channel Program.   Recall that the channel relieves the CPU of managing the requested data transfer. On the other hand, the channel cannot start an operation unless it is instructed to do so by the CPU. In other words, the relationship between the CPU and the channel is a master-slave relationship, where the CPU is the master and the channel is the slave. The CPU and channel communicate via either *instructions,* when the CPU is communicating with the channel, or *interrupts,* when the channel is ready to communicate with the CPU. There are primarily three instructions available to the CPU in order to communicate with the channel—namely, *START, TEST,* and *STOP.*

A *START* instruction is a signal to the appropriate channel to perform some kind of I/O. The channel receives from the CPU three major pieces of information:

1. Its channel number, identifying the channel.
2. The device number connected to the channel where the physical I/O is to be performed; as we will see shortly, more than one device can be connected to the same channel.
3. The channel program that must be executed by the channel. Notice that each different user I/O request potentially requires a different channel program. Hence, when the request is issued, the beginning address of the channel program associated to that I/O request is placed in a fixed memory address called *channel address word (CAW),* where the channel can retrieve it, and therefore can start its execution.

Notice that a *START* instruction may be rejected by the channel and no physical I/O is performed in this case. There are a number of reasons for which the channel can reject the CPU I/O request, the two major ones being that either the channel/device is not operational or that the channel/device is busy. At any rate, the CPU can detect the reason by examining the *condition code (CC)* or by examining the contents of the *channel status word (CSW),* which contains the information relative to the status of the channel.

The status of a specific channel and device can be determined via the *TEST* instruction, which sets the *CC.* Finally, the CPU can terminate a physical I/O operation at any time by issuing a *STOP* instruction.

At the other end, the channel is communicating with the CPU via *interrupts.* There are a number of various reasons the channel could interrupt the CPU. For instance, the channel may have attempted to execute an invalid *channel command* (that is, an instruction of the channel program), or the channel may have executed the last channel command while the device was still busy executing the interpreted channel command, as would be the case when the channel program must transfer the contents of the output buffer to a printer device for printing. Given the relatively slow operation of the printer, as opposed to the transfer of data by the channel from the output buffer to the printer device, the channel transfers the data into the printer device's buffer. Therefore, the channel has finished execution of the channel program while the printer device is still busy printing the remaining data from its buffer. Notice also, that when the printer device has finished its work, it will notify the channel, which in turn will notify the CPU via an interrupt of this event.

The natural question is how does the CPU become aware of the reason that caused the interrupt. The answer again is given by the contents of the *CSW*. As an example, if the reason for the interrupt is that the channel has finished its work, then bit 36 of the *CSW* is set; otherwise, if the reason is that the printer device has finished its work, then bit 37 of the *CSW* is set. In addition, the address of the channel/device that caused the interrupt can be found by examining the contents of the *program status word.*

The Request Element. When the access method is ready to request a data transfer, the access method places the address of the channel program together with the address of the input buffer into a data structure called the *request element,* which is placed into the *request queue* (IBM's terminology for request list), and informs the I/O supervisor. The access method loses control, assuming a queued access method, and some other partition gains control. Eventually, there comes a point at which our request must be serviced. The I/O supervisor places the address of the channel program into the *CAW,* which resides at a fixed memory address and starts the channel, which accesses and executes the channel program. When the block has been transferred into the input buffer, the multiprogramming supervisor will eventually give control to our job, and the access method will deliver the logical record into the program variable. Figure 3.26 illustrates the sequence of events that have been discussed up to this point.

3.3.2 Multiple Virtual Storage (*MVS*)

Recall that the number of user jobs in main memory under *MVT* at any time is severely limited by the *size* of the jobs. In particular, it would be impossible to execute a job whose size is larger than the free area in main memory, or, by extension, larger than main memory. Designers of operating systems realized that these limitations could be overcome by loading in primary memory only a certain *portion* of the user's job instead of its entirety. Using this approach, not only will more user jobs be allowed into the system, but also, a single job's size could exceed that of primary memory.

To accomplish this task, a partition similar to the one allocated under *MVT* is allocated to each user's job *but* not in primary memory. Instead, it is allocated in a very fast secondary device referred to as *virtual memory* and the user's entire job is loaded into the allocated partition. In order to execute the user's program, as we mentioned earlier, a portion of the user's job must be loaded into primary memory, which is appropriately referred to as *real memory* (in order to distinguish from virtual memory). Only a portion of the program is loaded into real memory by the job scheduler. At the time of loading of the user's job into its allocated partition, it is subdivided into a number of "pieces." In particular the

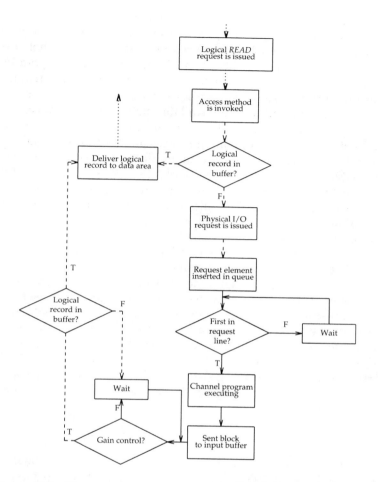

Figure 3.26   The sequence of events that take place as a response to a logical *READ* request. Dotted arrows indicate that the *application program (AP)* has control; dashed arrows indicate that the *access method* has control; and solid arrows indicate that some other *AP* has control.

program is subdivided[19] into an ordered set of *segments,* where each segment is usually on the order of 64K bytes starting with segment number 0, then number 1, and so on. Each segment is further subdivided into an ordered set of *pages,* usually 32 pages; hence, we have page 0 of segment 0, page 1 of segment 0, and so on.

For each user's job, a *page* (or a number of pages) is loaded in real memory from virtual memory. Therefore, from each job at each instance in time there

---

[19]There are a number of different virtual memory management systems. The MVS memory management system is presented here.

exists, in real memory, an *application program page,* an *access method page,* a *buffer page,* and a *channel program page.* At the time our partition gains control for the first time, pages must be transferred into real memory, where execution will take place. It is the responsibility of a new component of the operating system, the *paging supervisor,* to load a number of pages from virtual to real memory. To make this possible, the paging supervisor must be aware of the location of the pages in virtual memory and also the available slots in real memory, called *blocks,* where the pages will be loaded. The mechanism under which this is accomplished is straightforward. The operating system maintains a set of *tables* that are resident in real memory; these tables contain all the necessary information. Specifically two tables are associated to each job; first, there is a *virtual (file) page table* that records the locations of the pages in virtual memory; second, there is a *page map table* that indicates the block allocated to each page of the pages that are executed in real memory. In addition, there is a global *memory block table* that indicates the status, free or otherwise, of each block in real memory.

The observant reader would have noticed that there are two important issues that arise under such a system.

Initially, when the job scheduler loads the user's job into virtual memory, addresses that are associated with the instructions of a user's job are relative to virtual memory and are therefore referred to as *virtual addresses.* When a page is *paged in,* the address of each instruction as well as the addresses of the operands of each instruction are virtual addresses. For example, let's assume that page 10 of segment 0 has been paged in the block at real address FF0000 (hex) and the first instruction in this page—that is, the instruction at location 0 (hex) of that page—is to be executed (Figure 3.27). Notice that the virtual address of this instruction is

$$(10 \cdot 2k) \text{ decimal} = 2800 \text{ hex}$$

Furthermore, assume that the instruction is an unconditional branch instruction to virtual location 280C hex. We see that the CPU will try to execute a branch to location 280C hex in real memory. Hence, the CPU needs to know the real address to jump to. In particular the correct instruction that must be executed next must be the one at real address

$$FF0000 + 00000C \text{ hex} = FF000C \text{ hex}$$

since the instruction is an offset of C hex bytes from the beginning of page 10 of segment 0, and the latter has been loaded at real address FF0000 hex. Hence, every virtual address must be translated to a real address. In theory, this conversion could be done via software. However, the routine required would drastically slow down the CPU. In order to speed up the process, the conversion from virtual to real addresses is done via hardware, specifically by *dynamic address translation (DAT).*

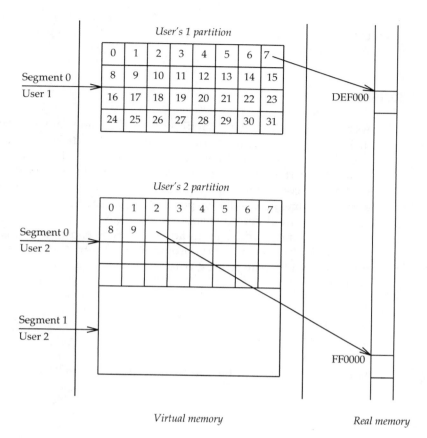

Figure 3.27 Real and virtual memories. The subdivision of the two jobs into segments and further into pages is shown. Notice that page 7 of segment 0 (user 1) has been paged in at real location DEF000, whereas page 10 of segment 0 (user 2) has been paged in at real location FF0000.

Secondly, if we assume that only one page is loaded and if we assume that in our previous example the branch was to take place at a location that is more than 2K bytes away, then the instruction that must be executed *will not* yet be in real memory, a phenomenon referred to as a *page fault*. In that case the paging supervisor is informed, and it *swaps* the page currently in real memory with another from virtual memory. The particular page selected from virtual memory by the paging supervisor to replace the one in real memory depends on the paging algorithm employed. There are a number of different algorithms[20] available, but they are beyond the scope of this book.

[20] We note here for the benefit of the readers who are familiar with operating systems issues that the algorithm employed under *MVS* is the *least recently used (LRU)* algorithm.

We close this chapter by noting that the sequence of data transfers under MVS is the same as under MVT except for the continuous paging of buffers and channel programs.

3.4 EXERCISES

1. Assume that a channel is dedicated to only one movable-head magnetic disk device. The number of cylinders in this disk is equal to 100; the cylinders are numbered consecutively, with the address of the outermost being 0 and the innermost 99. We assume that the arrival of requests, as well as the corresponding required service times, are exponentially distributed with means λ and μ, respectively, whereas the corresponding cylinder requests are randomly distributed. Assume that the seek time required to move from one cylinder to an adjacent one is constant and equal to s milliseconds. Write a simulation program to measure the average waiting time for 10,000 read/write requests that the following policies will yield.

   a. *FCFS*

   b. *SCN*

   c. *SCAN*

   d. *N-SCAN*

   e. *G-SCAN*

Compare your results with the observations made in the "Device Scheduling Algorithms" section.

4

Sequential Files

In Chapter 1 the statement was made that sequential file organizations offer improved performance for the operations *Batch* and *Retrieve_All*. The term *sequential file* implies that *logically* the records are stored consecutively—that is adjacently, in the order that the end-user perceives them. In particular, one can then distinguish between *ordered* and *unordered* sequential files. An ordered sequential file organization stores the logical records sequentially but in increasing (decreasing) order according to their primary key values, whereas an unordered sequential file organization stores the logical records consecutively but not in any specific order.

At the physical level, blocks that are stored "consecutively" are either

1. Stored in such a way that they are physically adjacent and therefore reside in the same and only extent; or
2. Stored in such a way that they belong to different clusters and, therefore, belong to more than one extent, with their logical adjacency maintained via *disk pointers*.

In the former case one speaks about a *Physical Sequential file,* whereas in the latter case one speaks of a *Physical Linked Sequential file.*

The latter physical structure is preferable over the former in the case in which the file is a highly volatile one in the sense that the magnitude of the number of required operations *Insert_One* and *Delete_One* is quite large. This will become apparent in the following paragraphs.

Before we proceed, the notation that will be used throughout this chapter is presented. *NR* denotes the number of logical records in the file *S*; *BF* and *EBF* denote the blocking factor and effective blocking factor, respectively. Finally, *NBLK* denotes the number of blocks in the file *S*.

4.1 PHYSICAL SEQUENTIAL FILES

At the outset it should be apparent that the physical sequential structure is the only allowable file structure for files that reside in the tape medium. Despite the fact that such implementation is possible for files that reside on a disk, these files are studied separately. The reason for this, as was emphasized in Chapter 2, is that one cannot update, insert, and/or delete a logical record "in place" with tape files, which is always possible with disk files. The result is that the search length for the same operation will depend on the magnetic medium employed.

4.1.1 Tape Files

The performance of Physical Sequential files that reside on tapes will be examined. Assume that the file resides on just one tape; moreover, assume no interference from other jobs in the system. Two cases will be considered—unordered and ordered files.

4.1.1.1 Unordered Files.   Notice that the only available mode of processing is the sequential mode. Hence, in order to *retrieve* every record of the file all blocks must be accessed; therefore, it is easy to see that

$$SL[Retrieve\_All, S] = NBLK \quad sba$$

where *sba* stands for sequential block access. On the other hand, the search length for the operation *Retrieve_One* varies between one *sba* and *NBLK sba*, depending on the relative location of the logical record in the physical file. Therefore, the *average* search length must be derived. Recall that the average search length is defined as the ratio of the total number of accesses required to access all logical records in the file *independently* over the number of records in the file. Notice that in this particular case the *BF* is equal to *EBF*; therefore, in order to access all logical records in the first block, *BF sba* accesses are needed, since each logical record in the first block can be retrieved in exactly one *sba*. Similarly, a logical record residing in the second block can be retrieved in two *sba*; therefore, all logical records of this block can be retrieved in exactly $(2 \cdot BF) sba$. In general, then, all records of the *i*th block in the file can be retrieved *independently* with exactly $(i \cdot BF)\ sba$. Therefore, the average search length is given by

$$ASL\,[Retrieve\_One\,,\,S] = \frac{\displaystyle\sum_{i=1}^{NBLK} i \cdot BF}{NR}\ sba$$

or

$$ASL\,[Retrieve\_One\,,\,S] = BF \cdot \frac{\displaystyle\sum_{i=1}^{NBLK} i}{NR}\ sba$$

$$= \frac{1}{\dfrac{NR}{BF}} \cdot \frac{NBLK \cdot (NBLK + 1)}{2}\ sba$$

$$= \frac{1}{NBLK} \cdot \frac{NBLK \cdot (NBLK + 1)}{2}\ sba$$

and finally we obtain

$$ASL\,[\boldsymbol{Retrieve\_One}\,,\,S] = \frac{NBLK + 1}{2}\ \boldsymbol{sba}$$

It is worth noting that the above formula is not valid in the case in which the target record does *not* exist in the file; in that case, the search length is equal to *NBLK* sequential block accesses.

A moment's reflection should be enough to convince the reader that the search length of the operations *Insert_One, Delete_One,* and *Update_One* is very large, which would make these operations prohibitive. Hence, almost *never* would one use such files if the intent is to permit these three types of operations.

4.1.1.2 Ordered Files. One should note at the outset that ordered files have a disadvantage relative to unordered files; that disadvantage is the considerable cost associated with the required initial sorting operation of the given file.[1] Do the benefits of this particular file organization offset the associated disadvantages? The answer will depend on whether the operations that were not supported by the unordered files are required. If the answer is yes, and in particular if the number and frequency of these operations is high, then as one will see this is the preferred file structure.

First, notice that in the case in which the target record exists, the search length for the operation *Retrieve_All* as well as the average search length for the operation *Retrieve_One* is the same as before. In the opposite case the search length is smaller than that of unordered files given that one can decide if that record exists on the *average* after $(1 + NBLK)/2\ sba$.

Second, the operations *Insert_One, Delete_One,* and *Update_One* can be performed but not in a random fashion; instead, they are performed under a mode

---

[1] External sorting is discussed extensively in Chapter 9.

known as *Batch Mode Update Processing*. Similarly, the operations *Batch* and *Retrieve_Few* can be performed under a mode known as *Batch Mode Retrieval Processing*. Both of these modes are based on the same idea that is outlined below.

Assume that *Batch Mode Update* is to be performed. First, let *MASTER_FILE (MF)* be an ordered physical sequential file containing all logical records. In addition, let *TRANSACTION_FILE (TF)* be a file containing all logical records that are to be either updated, deleted, and/or inserted into the *MF*. It is worth noting that the logical records of the *TF* contain an operational field, *oper_type*, which indicates the type of operation that is to be performed relative to that logical record; for instance, *i* could mean insert, whereas *d* could mean delete.

The first step of the *Batch Mode* consists of sorting the logical records of the *TF* according to their primary key values, and in particular, sorting them in the same order as the logical records of the *MF* file. Let *NEW_TRANSACTION (NTF)* be the filename of the generated sorted file (Figure 4.1(a)). Now three tape drives are needed. The tape mounted on the first drive will contain the file *MF*; the tape on the second drive, the file *NTF*; and the tape on the third drive, the physical sequential file *NEW_MASTER (NM)*, which is the file that will contain the "updated" logical records of the *MF* (subject to the operations) and the logical records of *NTF* (Figure 4.1). Then both files *NTF* and *MF* are input files to the software package *Batch Update*, which is explained below.

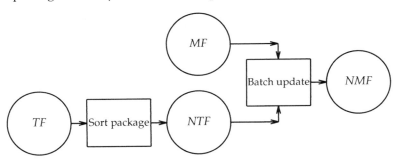

Figure 4.1 Batch mode processing.

Initially, the first block from each of the files *NTF* and *MF* is transferred via appropriate *READ* requests to their respective input buffers *NTF_BUF* and *MF_BUF*. The key of the first logical record from the *NTF_BUF* is compared with the keys of all records in the *MF_BUF*; if no match is found, then the block from *MF_BUF* is written out via the *NMF_BUF* output buffer into the *NMF* file. Otherwise, the logical record of the matched logical record from the *MF_BUF* is updated according the *oper_type* code; it is then written out to the *NMF_BUF*. In this case, the next record[2] from the *NTF_BUF* is selected and the process is repeated. At any rate, the process is repeated until the logical end of one of the files *NTF* or *MF* is reached. In the former case the remaining logical records from

---

[2] If the input buffer *NTF_BUF* is empty, a new physical transfer takes place.

the *MF*, if there are any, are written via the *MF_BUF* and *NMF_BUF* into the *NMF* file; otherwise, all remaining logical records from the *NTF*, if there any, are written[3] via the *NTF_BUF* and *NMF_BUF* into the *NMF*. In either case the *NMF* eventually becomes the new *MASTER(MF)* file.

It should be clear that the search length for this operation is the sum of three terms. First, *all* logical records, and therefore *all* blocks, $NBLK_{MF}$, and $NBLK_{NTF}$ must be read from both files *MF* and *NTF*, respectively. Secondly, a number of sequential accesses is required to *create* the *NMF*. The number of these accesses is clearly equal to the number of blocks, $NBLK_{NMF}$, that must be written. Therefore, assuming no interference from other jobs in the system we obtain

$$SL\,[BatchUpdate\,,MF] = \left[NBLK_{MF} + NBLK_{NTF} + NBLK_{NMF}\right]\,sba$$

The number of blocks of the *NMF* is easily derived. In particular, the number of logical records in this file is equal to the number of logical records in the *MF* plus the number of logical records, NR_I, that must be inserted minus the number of logical records, NR_D, that must be deleted. In symbols we obtain

$$NBLK_{NMF} = clg\left\lceil \frac{NR_{MF} + NR_I - NR_D}{BF_{NMF}} \right\rceil$$

In general the blocking factor of the *NMF* is not equal to the blocking factor of *MF*.

4.1.2 Disk Files

Again, as in the case of tape files, one should distinguish between unordered and ordered files. Each one is examined in turn.

4.1.2.1   Unordered Files.   In this case again, the search length consists of exactly *NBLK sba*.[4]

Similarly, the *average* search length for the operation *Retrieve_One* is equal to $(1 + NBLK)/2\ sba$ in the case in which the target record exists, whereas it is equal to *NBLK sba* if the target record does not exist.

Notice that with disk files the operation *Update_One* can be done in place. The mechanism is straightforward. First, after an *average* number of $(1 + NBLK)/2sba$'s, the logical record is located; the block that contains the logical

---

[3] Insertion is the only possible operation in this case.

[4] Recall that under our model a sequential access indicates that a logical record is retrieved after all its preceding records have been retrieved; a random access indicates that a record is retrieved via an address. Notice that in order to calculate the I/O time required, the device specifics as well as the file attributes must be known. In other words, if the file is stored consecutively on a track-by-track basis so that it occupies just one cylinder extent, then the time required for one sequential access will be equal to t_{sa}; if the file occupies an extent comprised of two cylinders, then one of the sequential accesses will require I/O time equal to t_{ra}.

target record is already in the input buffer. This record is updated in main memory, the block is updated, and it is then written out on the disk. Given that the internal processing time is negligible, it is clear that the output buffer can be written out to the same block location on the disk in the "next" revolution. Hence, the average search length is given by

$$ASL[Update\_One, S] = \left\lceil \frac{1 + NBLK}{2} + 1 \right\rceil \quad sba$$

Similarly, we can see that both operations *Delete_One* and *Insert_One* can be done in place. It is clear that the average search length for the first operation is equal to that of the operation *Update_One*. One should also note that it is wise to delete a record by flagging it. In other words, initially an extra field, a flag field, is allocated as part of each logical record; when a record is deleted then its flag is set to indicate a deleted record.

The search length of the operation *Insert_One* depends on the employed mechanism, and there are a number that could be employed. Two of them are presented here.

The first mechanism depends on the fact that the file system keeps track of the block in the file that contains the *last* logical record. Assuming that the activity of the file has been predetermined to be such that the number of future insertions is considerably larger than the number of future deletions, one may initially allocate a number of extra blocks that were originally empty at the end of the file where the records will eventually be inserted. In this case the operation *Insert_One* can be performed very quickly, since the search length will vary between *1 rba* (random block access) + *1 sba* and *1 rba* + *2 sba*. The random access is required to access the block that contains the last logical record; one sequential access is required to rewrite the updated block; and one extra sequential access have been will be needed in the case in which the initially accessed block is full and the next block must be accessed.

The reader may jump to the conclusion that this is the most efficient way to perform insertions in this case. This is *not* true because if the frequency of the requested operation *Retrieve_One* is very high, then the average search length for this operation could considerably exceed the one calculated above. Given that logical records tend to cluster at the end of the file and that a number of deletions will have been performed, many unnecessary accesses will have been made. Another approach would be to employ a initial loading density of less than one. In this case, a number of logical record slots will be empty in each block; then if a record is to be inserted, a block at a time is retrieved until one is found in which the flag of some logical record is set. The logical record is then inserted in this block. Under this scheme the cost of the operation is equal to the cost of the operation *Delete_One*.

4.1.2.2 Ordered Files. To retrieve all logical records from a physical sequential file, one must access all blocks of the file; therefore

$$SL[Retrieve\_All, S] = NBLK \quad sba \qquad\qquad [4.1]$$

With regard to the operations *Retrieve_One*, *Insert_One*, *Delete_One*, and *Update_One*, there are a number of different algorithms that may be employed. To see this, note that since this is a disk file each physical block has a unique address associated with it. In this case the file system is able to calculate the address of each block requested.

For example, a possible access mechanism is the use of a *binary search* performed on the blocks. At each step of the search the address of the "middle" block must be calculated; the block that is accessed is transferred to main memory where a comparison of the keys of the logical records in this block versus the key of the target record takes place. If a match is found the search is completed. Otherwise, taking advantage of the fact that the logical records are ordered, one can decide whether the logical record will be in the preceding or the succeeding blocks of the file. After this determination has been made, the middle block is accessed and the process is repeated. Recall that an *upper bound* for a binary search (and, thus, for the search length) is given by

$$SL[Retrieve\_One, S] = clg(\log_2(NBLK)) \quad rba \qquad\qquad [4.2]$$

Notice that the accesses are random since each block is accessed via its address. We are stating without a proof that the *average search length* is given by

$$ASL[Retrieve\_One, S] = clg\left(\log_2\left\lceil\frac{NBLK}{2}\right\rceil\right) \quad rba \qquad\qquad [4.3]$$

Another search scheme that could be employed is the *step search*. Under this mechanism the sth block is accessed and examined; if the target record is there, the search is completed. If the key of the target record is smaller than the key of the first logical record of the accessed block, then a sequential search *backward* is initiated from the current block; thus, if the record exists it must reside in the $s - 1$ preceding blocks. On the other hand, if the key of the target record is greater than the key of the last record in the accessed block, then the sth successor block from the accessed block is accessed and the process is repeated. The determination of the upper bound for this search is found as follows. First, a number of $clg(NBLK/s)$ random block accesses[5] are required, followed by at most $(s - 1)$ sequential block accesses for the backward single steps; therefore

$$SL[Retrieve\_One, S] = clg(\frac{NBLK}{s}) \quad rba + (s - 1) \quad sba$$

We are now ready to derive the *average* search length for the same operation under this mechanism. To this end the total number of accesses to access all NR records of the file *independently* must be derived. Notice that a total number of

[5] The worst case.

$$BF \cdot \left[s \; rba + \sum_{i=1}^{s-1} i \; sba \right] \tag{4.4}$$

accesses will *independently* retrieve all logical records residing in the first s blocks of the file. To see this, observe that 1 *rba* is required in order to retrieve a logical record from the sth block; in addition, 1 *rba* + 1 *sba* is required to access a logical record from the preceding block of the sth block, while 1 *rba* + 2 *sba* are required to access a logical record of the $(s-2)$nd block. Continuing in this fashion it can be seen that 1 *rba* + j *sba* are required to retrieve a logical record from the $(s-j)$th block for every j such that $0<j<s$. Hence, the total number of accesses required to retrieve all logical records of the first s blocks *independently* is given by the second term of equation [4.4]. Moreover, each block is assumed to contain BF logical records so that the total number of accesses to access all logical records of the first s blocks is given by equation [4.4].

To access the set of all records belonging to blocks $s+1$ and $2s$, we need

$$BF \cdot \left[(2 \cdot s) \; rba + \sum_{i=1}^{s-1} i \; sba \right] \tag{4.5}$$

where the additional s random accesses are required because two random block accesses are needed for the $(2s)$th block to be accessed. In general, then, in order to access all logical records belonging to the group of blocks from $js+1$ to $(j+1)s$

$$BF \cdot \left[(j \cdot s) \; rba + \sum_{i=1}^{s-1} i \; sba \right]$$

or

$$BF \cdot \left[(j \cdot s) \; rba + \left(\frac{(s-1) \cdot s}{2} \right) sba \right] \tag{4.6}$$

accesses are needed. But $j = 1, 2, ..., clg\,(NBLK/s)$; therefore, the total number of accesses will be the sum of all accesses given by [4.6] for the given range of index j. Hence,

$$ASL\,[Retrieve\_One\,,\,S] = \frac{\displaystyle\sum_{j=1}^{clg\,(NBLK/s)} \left[BF \cdot \left((j \cdot s) \; rba + \frac{(s-1) \cdot s}{2} \; sba's \right) \right]}{NR}$$

$$= \frac{\left[\displaystyle\sum_{j=1}^{clg\,(NBLK/s)} (j \cdot s) \right] rba + \left[\displaystyle\sum_{j=1}^{clg\,(NBLK/s)} \left(\frac{(s-1) \cdot s}{2} \right) \right] sba}{\dfrac{NR}{BF}}$$

The right side of the above equation can be rewritten as

$$\dfrac{\left[\dfrac{s \cdot clg(\dfrac{NBLK}{s}) \cdot (clg(\dfrac{NBLK}{s}) + 1)}{2}\right] rba + \left[\dfrac{clg(\dfrac{NBLK}{s}) \cdot (s-1) \cdot s}{2}\right] sba}{NBLK}$$

and, by assuming a continuous environment and simplifying, we obtain

$$\dfrac{\left[\dfrac{s \cdot (\dfrac{NBLK}{s}) \cdot \left[(\dfrac{NBLK}{s}) + 1\right]}{2}\right] rba + \left[\dfrac{(\dfrac{NBLK}{s}) \cdot (s-1) \cdot s}{2}\right] sba}{NBLK}$$

Finally

$$ASL[Retrieve\_One, S] = \frac{1}{2} \cdot \left[\left[\frac{NBLK}{s} + 1\right] rba + (s-1) sba\right] \qquad [4.7]$$

Similarly, one can show that a sequential search will require, on the average,

$$ASL[Retrieve\_One, S] = \frac{NBLK + 1}{2} \ sba$$

This section closes with the remark that the *average* cost of the other three operations, *Insert_One*, *Delete_One*, and *Update_One*, is equal to

$$\left[ASL[Retrieve\_One, S]\right] + \left[1 \ sba\right] \qquad [4.8]$$

where the first term depends, as was mentioned above, on the type of search mechanism employed, and the second term is the cost of rewriting the updated block.

4.2 PHYSICAL LINKED SEQUENTIAL FILES

Despite the fact that earlier it was demonstrated that one could, with clever programming, perform the *Insert_One* operation relatively inexpensively on a physical sequential file, the sequential file structure proves to be inefficient in a number of instances. In particular, for a highly active file in which the frequency of the operations *Delete_One* and *Insert_One* is very large in relation to the operation *Retrieve_All*, one should choose to employ a *Physical Linked Sequential File*. Such a file preserves the ordering of logical records, *but* the blocks are not contiguous. However, their "adjacency" is preserved via block pointers. As will become apparent shortly, the blocks could be dispersed on the entire disk; therefore, one could assume that each block access is a random access.

Again, a Physical Linked File could be an *ordered* as well as an *unordered* file. In either case, the mode of accessing is necessarily *sequential;* the reason for this is that a binary search mechanism, even for an ordered physical linked sequential file, is impossible to be implemented. This is a direct result of the fact that the address of the "middle" block of the file cannot be calculated.

It is easy to show that the operation *Retrieve_One*, for the case in which the target logical record exists, will require, on the average,

$$ASL\,[Retrieve\_One, S\,] = \left\lceil \frac{1 + NBLK}{2} \right\rceil \; rba$$

If the target record does not exist, it will require

$$SL\,[Retrieve\_One, S\,] = \left\lceil NBLK \right\rceil \; rba$$

Both equations are valid for both ordered and unordered files. In addition, it is clear that, independent of the ordering of the file, the search length for the operation *Retrieve_All* is given by

$$SL\,[Retrieve\_All, S\,] = \left\lceil NBLK \right\rceil \; rba$$

On the other hand, the number of accesses for the operation *Insert_One* differs considerably between ordered and unordered files. Although there are a number of possible ways to perform the insertion operation, an example algorithm for unordered and ordered files will be presented below. Before the algorithms are described, one should note that a considerable savings will occur if double input buffers are allocated. The analysis below assumes this fact.

4.2.1 Unordered Files

In the beginning, the first block of the file is accessed at a cost of one random block access. If the block is not full (that is, it is not an *overflow* block), the record is inserted in that block; it is then rewritten at an additional cost of one sequential block access. On the other hand, if the first block is an overflow block, the allocation of a *new* block is requested from the file system. Before the new block is accessed at a cost of one random block access, the address of the first block of the file is saved. When the new block is accessed the logical record is inserted there; the saved block pointer is written on the link field of that new block. This block is rewritten at an additional cost of one sequential block access (Figure 4.2).

Therefore, one can conclude that

$$1 \; rba + 1 \; sba \leq SL\,[Insert\_One, S\,] \leq 2 \; rba + 1 \; sba$$

On the other hand, the *average* search length for the operation *Delete_One* is given by

$$ASL\,[Delete\_One, S\,] = \left\lceil \frac{1 + NBLK}{2} \right\rceil \; rba + 1 \; sba$$

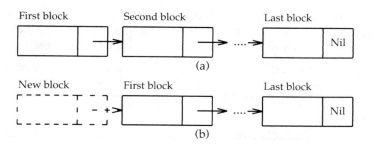

Figure 4.2 Inserting a logical record for the case in which the first block is full: (a) before and (b) after the insertion.

where the first term indicates the number of random accesses to retrieve the target block, and the second term is the cost of rewriting the block after the flag of the record has been set. At this point it has been assumed that even if the deletion of the record causes an empty *underflow* block, the block is not deleted, since a future insertion into it is anticipated.

4.2.2 Ordered Files

It is clear that using the algorithm recently described, the cost of the *Delete_One* operation for ordered files remains the same as in the case of unordered files above.

With respect to the *Insert_One* operation, the cost is higher. Before the algorithm is described, the notation $max(i)$ will be used to denote the largest of the keys of all logical records in the ith block of the file; it should be clear that the logical record *should* be inserted in the particular block j such that the $max(j)$ value is greater than the key of the logical record.[6] According to our previous discussion the location of this block requires, on the average, $(1 + NBLK)/2$ random accesses.

After the target block j has been located, if the block is not an overflow block the logical record is inserted there at an additional cost of 1 *sba* (Figure 4.3(a)); otherwise, if the preceding block that is currently in the first input buffer is not an overflow block and if the key of the record to be inserted is less than $min(j)$, then the logical record is inserted there and the block is rewritten at an extra cost of 1 *rba* + 1 *sba* (Figure 4.3(b)). In the case in which the target block is full and its predecessor block is either full or the key of the record to be inserted is greater than $min(j)$, a request for a new block to be allocated will be issued at an extra cost of one random block access. The new block is transferred to the second buffer; the address of the link field of the preceding block, still in the input buffer, is copied into the link field of the newly allocated block. The record is

---

[6] If the key of the logical record is greater than $max(j)$ for every j, then the record should be inserted in the last block.

inserted there, and the new block is written out[7] at an additional cost of one sequential block access. Its address is inserted into the link field of the preceding block, which is rewritten at an additional cost of 1 *rba* + 1 *sba* (Figure 4.3(c)).

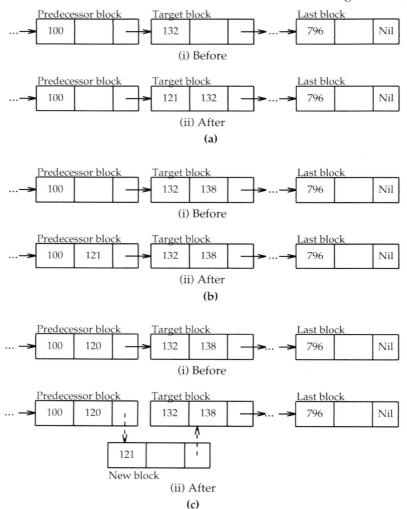

Figure 4.3   The Physical Linked Sequential file before (i) and after (ii) the insertion of the logical record with key 121. Three cases are shown: (a) the target block is not an overflow block, (b) the target block is an overflow block while the predecessor block is not, and (c) both the target and predecessor blocks are full.

---

[7] It is wise to redistribute the logical records so that a potential insertion into the preceding block at a later time will not encounter an overflow block.

Notice that the operation *Retrieve_Previous* is expensive for such a file structure. One could argue that no additional accesses are needed, since the *previous* record belongs in the same block and, therefore, is currently in the buffer. But the probability that the previous record is in the same block as the one currently accessed is equal to $((BF - 1)/(NR - 1))$, since, excluding the currently accessed record, there are $(BF - 1)$ logical records in this block; the previous record could be any one of $(NR - 1)$ remaining logical records in the file. It is clear that this probability is very close to zero; therefore the expected number of accesses in order to access the predecessor block is equal to that of the *Retrieve_One* operation, since a new search from the physical beginning of the file must be initiated.

In the case in which the frequency of that operation is very large, one could allocate more storage and maintain a *doubly linked* sequential file, as opposed to the *singly linked* sequential files that we have discussed in this section. One should immediately notice that only one random access is needed for the operation *Retrieve_Previous* but at a considerable, additional overhead. In particular, one extra pointer must be allocated in each block that will be employed to point to the preceding block; but, in addition, the cost of the operation *Insert_One* increases, since more pointers must be maintained in the case in which a new block must be allocated. Figure 4.4 illustrates such a file structure.

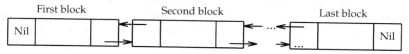

Figure 4.4   A Doubly Linked Physical Sequential file.

The performance of this file structure parallels that of singly linked sequential files and their analysis remains as an exercise for the reader.

4.3 THE REQUIRED I/O TIME

In Chapter 1 it was noted that there is a natural mapping from the set of length paths into the I/O time. In this section an example is given. Assume the following:

1. An ordered physical sequential file, S, consisting of NR number of records of fixed-length RS bytes, blocking factor BF, and loading density equal to 1.
2. The only allowable operations are: *Retrieve_All* with a frequency of ϕ_1 operations/day, *Retrieve_One* with a frequency of ϕ_2 operations/day, and *Delete _One* with a frequency of ϕ_3 operations/day.
3. The access mode for the operation *Retrieve_All* is sequential, whereas the search mechanism for the other two operations is a step search with a step of m.
4. The disk device is an IBM 3350.

Under the above assumptions and equation [1.5] it can be seen that the average search length is given by

$$ASL = \alpha_1 \cdot SL\,[Retrieve\_All\,,S\,] + \alpha_2 \cdot SL\,[Retrieve\_One\,,S\,] + \alpha_3 \cdot SL\,[Delete\_One\,,S\,]$$

where

$$\alpha_1 = \frac{\phi_1}{\phi_1 + \phi_2 + \phi_3}\,,\quad \alpha_2 = \frac{\phi_2}{\phi_1 + \phi_2 + \phi_3}\,,\quad \alpha_3 = \frac{\phi_3}{\phi_1 + \phi_2 + \phi_3}$$

and the values of α_i indicate the percent of time the respective operations are performed. Taking into account equations [4.1], [4.7], and [4.8], the above equation yields:

$$ASL = \alpha_1 \cdot NBLK\ sba + \frac{\alpha_2 + \alpha_3}{2} \cdot \left[\left[\frac{NBLK}{m} + 1 \right] rba + (m-1)\ sba \right] + \alpha_3\ sba$$

or, by mapping into the I/O time,

$$T_{I/O} = \alpha_1 \cdot NBLK \cdot t_{sa} + \frac{\alpha_2 + \alpha_3}{2} \cdot \left[\left[\frac{NBLK}{m} + 1 \right] \cdot t_{ra} + (m-1) \cdot t_{sa} \right] + \alpha_3 \cdot t_{sa}$$

Notice that if we operate in a multiuser environment, then the $T_{I/O}$ attains its largest value because, in this case, all t_{sa} must be replaced by t_{ra}. At the other extreme the best value for $T_{I/O}$ is obtained under the assumptions of a single-user environment and a file that is stored in a single extent comprised of just one cylinder. In the latter case no seek is required for any access; therefore all t_{ra} times must be replaced by t_{sa}.

At any rate, the I/O time is calculated below subject to the above-derived equation. If s denotes the average seek time, l the average latency time, and v the $MDTR$, we obtain

$$t_{sa} = l + (BS/v),\ \text{and}\ \ t_{ra} = s + l + (BS/v) \tag{4.9}$$

Hence, $t_{ra} = s + t_{sa}$; in addition, $\alpha_3 + \alpha_2 = 1 - \alpha_1$ and $T_{I/O}$ become

$$T_{I/O} = \alpha_1 \cdot NBLK \cdot t_{sa} + \alpha_3 \cdot t_{sa}$$

$$+ \frac{1 - \alpha_1}{2} \cdot \left[\left[\frac{NBLK + m}{m} \right] \cdot (t_{sa} + s) + (m-1) \cdot t_{sa} \right]$$

Or, by rearranging,

$$T_{I/O} = s \cdot (NBLK+m) \cdot \left[\frac{1 - \alpha_1}{2m} \right]$$

$$+ \left\{ \alpha_1 \cdot NBLK + \left[\frac{1 - \alpha_1}{2m} \right] \cdot \left[(NBLK + m) + m \cdot (m-1) + \alpha_3 \right] \right\} \cdot t_{sa}$$

Hence

$$T_{I/O} = (s \cdot NBLK + s \cdot m) \cdot \left[\frac{1 - \alpha_1}{2m} \right]$$

$$+ \frac{\left\{ \left[2m \cdot \alpha_1 + 1 - \alpha_1 \right] \cdot NBLK + \left[(1 - \alpha_1) \cdot (m^2 + \alpha_{3)} \right] \right\}}{2m} \cdot t_{sa}$$

By letting

$$\gamma = \frac{2m \cdot \alpha_1 + 1 - \alpha_1}{2m}, \quad \delta = \frac{\left[(1 - \alpha_1) \cdot (m^2 + \alpha_3) \right]}{2m}$$

the above equation becomes

$$T_{I/O} = \left[\gamma \cdot NBLK + \delta \right] \cdot t_{sa} + (s \cdot NBLK + s \cdot m) \cdot \left[\frac{1 - \alpha_1}{2m} \right] \qquad [4.10]$$

But, $NBLK = clg((RS \cdot NR)/BS)$. Assuming again a continuous environment, we obtain $BS = NBLK/(RS \cdot NR)$. Replacing this value of BS in [4.9], we obtain

$$t_{sa} = l + \left[\frac{RS \cdot NR}{NBLK \cdot v} \right]$$

Letting $\beta = (RS \cdot NR)/v$, the above equation yields

$$t_{sa} = l + \left[\frac{\beta}{NBLK} \right]$$

By replacing the value of t_{sa} found above and after simplification, equation [4.10] becomes

$$T_{I/O} = \left[\gamma \cdot l + \frac{s \cdot (1 - \alpha_1)}{2m} \right] \cdot \mathbf{NBLK} + \left[\frac{\beta \cdot \delta}{\mathbf{NBLK}} \right] + \left[\beta \cdot \gamma + \delta \cdot l + \frac{s \cdot (1 - \alpha_1)}{2} \right]$$

The reader should have noticed that the above equation indicates that the I/O time is a function of the number of blocks $NBLK$; therefore, not only can the performance of our file be measured, but the I/O time can be minimized by choosing an appropriate BS, which will yield the desired number of blocks.

To this end, notice that

$$\frac{dT_{I/O}}{dNBLK} = \left[\gamma \cdot l + \frac{s \cdot (1 - \alpha_1)}{2} \right] - \left[\frac{\beta \cdot \delta}{NBLK^2} \right]$$

and that

$$\frac{d^2 T_{I/O}}{dNBLK^2} = \left[\frac{2 \cdot \beta \cdot \delta}{NBLK^3} \right]$$

But the second derivative remains positive for all values of $NBLK$; therefore, the function $T_{I/O}$ attains its absolute minimum at its critical value.

Therefore, the absolute minimum of that function is obtained for

$$NBLK = \sqrt{\frac{\beta \cdot \delta}{\gamma \cdot l + \frac{s \cdot (1 - \alpha_{1})}{2m}}}.$$

4.4 EXERCISES

1. Assume that **FILE1** is an ordered physical sequential disk file. Derive the *average* search length for the operation *Retrieve_One*. Assume the file consists of $NBLK$ number of blocks, the effective blocking factor is EBF, the loading density is equal to one, and the access mode is sequential.

2. Consider equation [4.7]. Show that the $ASL[Retrieve\_One, S]$ becomes minimal for the value of s equal to $\sqrt{NBLK}$.

3. Assume that **FILE2** is an ordered doubly linked sequential file. Find the average search length of the operation *Delete_One* under the assumptions that double input buffers are employed and that, in the case of an underflow block, the latter block is deallocated.

4. Compare the storage requirements of physical sequential structures, physical linked sequential structures, and physical doubly linked sequential structures.

5. The IBM 3420/8 tape drive has the following characteristics: Density = 1600 bytes/inch, IBG length = 0.6 in., v = 200 in./s, rewind v = 800 in./s. A physical sequential file of 20,000 fixed-length records is to be stored on a brand new tape of length 4800 ft. The size of each logical record is 170 bytes. Physical records are to be of size 1170 bytes.

   (a) Assuming that the tape drive is ready to write the first block (at the physical beginning of the tape), find the minimum required time to write the file onto the tape.

   (b) Find the average time required for the operation *Retrieve_One*.

   (c) Assume now that a record must be deleted. Find the time required to perform the operation.

6. The DRT 3420 tape drive has the following characteristics:

```
Tape Drive   Density          IBG       Start/Stop time   R/W speed    Rewind speed
----------   -------          ---       ---------------   ---------    ------------
DRT 3420/8   6250 bytes/inch 0.6 in.          1 ms        200 in./sec  640 in./sec
```

An ordered file of 2 million fixed-length records has been stored on this tape. The length of each record is 90 bytes. Blocks are 2048 bytes (assuming no block overhead and unspanned records). An ordered transaction file has been stored on another tape and each of its records is furnished with an extra field, 2 bytes long, indicating the type of transaction that is to be performed. If there are 200,000 insertions, 50,000 deletions, and 400,000 updates to be performed, estimate the time required for the batch update of this file. State all your assumptions.

7. A physical sequential file with 20,700 fixed-length logical records of size 200 bytes is to be loaded on a brand new IBM 3350. Assume that
   • No interblock gaps are present;
   • The format used is count data; and
   • In a period of 6 mo. it is estimated that 300 *Retrieve_All* operations and 40 *Delete_One* operations will be performed.
   Find the blocking factor that minimizes the required I/O time given that the access mode is sequential.

8. A new IBM disk is a sector addressable device. There are 8 sectors per track, 512 bytes per sector, 10 tracks per cylinder, and 500 cylinders. The latency time is 24 ms and the average seek time is s ms. A *static* file of 100 logical records each having a length equal to 512 bytes is to be stored. The only operation that must be performed is the operation *Retrieve_All*. It is calculated that the internal memory processing time is equal to 3 ms. Assuming a single input buffer allocation of size 512 bytes, unblocked records, and no block overhead, suggest a physical file structure for this logical file so that the retrieval operation is performed in the minimal possible time and then find that time. A diagram may be needed to illustrate the physical file structure.

9. A static physical sequential file is stored on a single disk that has the following characteristics: average seek time A milliseconds, seek for one cylinder M milliseconds, average latency of L milliseconds, C cylinders/disk, T tracks/cylinder, and B blocks/track. The file consists of Z blocks and occupies an integral number (greater than one) of consecutive cylinders.
   a. Derive an equation that estimates the expected time to read the file.
   b. Reanswer part a, assuming that the time to process the records (in main memory) of a block and to issue the next read request is P milliseconds, where P satisfies

   $$\frac{2 \cdot S}{B} < P < L$$

   c. Taking into account the inequality above, describe a storage strategy for this sequential file so it will reduce the required time to process the entire file.
   d. What is the improvement in performance by adopting your storage strategy?

4.5 HOST LANGUAGE: PL/1

4.5.1 Data Definition Language

The PL/1 data definition language supports sequential files that are referred to as **CONSECUTIVE** files. In the case of a **CONSECUTIVE** disk file, the block format is count data[8] and the blocks comprise just one extent; therefore, the structure is physical sequential. Note that for all practical purposes a set of punched cards containing records constitutes a sequential file.

One should also be aware that the only access mode supported is sequential and that the only access technique employed is queued.

4.5.1.1 Declaring a CONSECUTIVE File. Every file must be declared before its used; the required PL/1 statement and its format is given below:

```
DCL (logical_filename) FILE RECORD ENV(CONSECUTIVE);
```

Recall from Chapter 3 that the *logical_filename*[9] is tied-up with the appropriate physical filename referred to in IBM terminology as the *Data Set Name* **(DSNAME)** via the appropriate *JCL* statement referred to as the *Data Definition* **(DD)** statement. Hence, the file organization becomes known to the file system via the declaration statement above, whereas the file structure becomes known via the other required parameters (attributes) such as blocksize, logical record length, etc. These parameters are defined via a *JCL* statement known as the *Data Control Block* **(DCB)** statement.

For example, assume that the only file declarations appearing in the source code were

```
DCL (FILE1) FILE RECORD ENV(CONSECUTIVE);
DCL (FILE2) FILE RECORD ENV(CONSECUTIVE);
```

and that the *JCL* statements accompanying the source were as in Table 4.1. Notice that **FILE1** refers to the **OMASTER** file and that **FILE2** refers to the **NMASTER** file. Moreover, both files are physical sequential; **NMASTER** is a file of logical records of fixed size (30 bytes); and the implied blocking factor is 100. In addition, an allocation of six primary and two secondary tracks is requested via the **SPACE** parameter.[10]

---

[8] See the relevant discussion in Chapter 2.

[9] Often referred to as the Data Definition Name (DDNAME).

[10] The interested reader should consult a manual for further discussion of the SPACE parameter.

TABLE 4.1. The JCL statements.

```
//GO.FILE1 DD DSNAME=OMASTER,DISP=(OLD,KEEP),UNIT=DISK,

//GO.FILE2 DD DSNAME=NMASTER,DISP=(NEW,CATLG),UNIT=DISK,

// DCB=(RECFM=FB,LRECL=30,BLKSIZE=3000), SPACE=(TRK,(6,2))

// VOL=SER=123
```

The PL/1 language, running under OS/MVS, permits[11] the definition of the **DCB** parameters (or file attributes) in the declaration statement instead of in the *JCL* statement. All such parameters must be placed after the keyword **CON-SECUTIVE** and inside the parentheses. The allowable parameters, their syntax, and meaning are given in Table 4.2.

TABLE 4.2 The allowable **DCB** parameters in PL/1 under OS/MVS.

PARAMETER	MEANING
F	Fixed size, unblocked records
FB	Fixed size, blocked records
V	Variable size, unblocked records
VB	Variable size, blocked records
BLKSIZE(S)	Data sublock of size s bytes
RECSIZE(L)	Logical records of length L bytes
BUFFERS(N)	Allocate N buffers to the file

As an example, the declaration of **FILE2** above could have been

```
DCL (FILE2) FILE RECORD ENV(CONSECUTIVE FB RECSIZE(30) BLKSIZE(3000));
```

4.5.2 Data Manipulation Sublanguage

4.5.2.1   Opening a CONSECUTIVE File.   Recall that in order to perform an operation on a file that file must first be opened. The format of the PL/1 statement that accomplishes this task follows

```
OPEN FILE (logical_filename) OPTIONS
```

where the word **OPTIONS** indicates the *type* of operation that is to be performed on the file. Note that the selected **OPTIONS** depend also on the medium

---

[11] Not a standard PL/1 feature.

employed. Table 4.3 indicates the available options and the media to which they apply.

TABLE 4.3 The allowable **OPTIONS** and operations.

OPTION	DISK FILES	TAPE FILES	READ	WRITE
INPUT	Yes	Yes	Yes	No
INPUT BACKWARDS	No	Yes	Yes	No
OUTPUT	Yes	Yes	No	Yes
UPDATE	Yes	No	Yes	Yes

Examination of Table 4.3 indicates that in the case at hand, the case of CONSECU-TIVE files, a file is opened for a *specific* operation:

- A file opened for INPUT or INPUT BACKWARDS can only be read. No writes are permitted. Moreover, the **OPTION INPUT BACKWARDS** can be used only if the tape drive (to which the tape containing the file is mounted) permits such operation.
- A file opened for OUTPUT can only be written to. No reads are permitted. Therefore, this Option is selected *only* in the case in which a *new* file is to be created; for example, in the case of batch processing, the *NMF* file would have been used as an OUTPUT file. The reason is that since only writes are permitted, records that are to be inserted can be inserted only at the end of the file.
- A file opened for UPDATE can be read and written to. Notice that this option is available only for disk files because, as was mentioned earlier, in these devices one can *update* a logical record in place. Moreover, by using a loading density less than one, the user can *insert* records at any place in the file assuming, of course, that there is room available. This can be accomplished, as was mentioned in Section 4.1, via the insertion of *dummy* records at the time of initial creation of the file. Then if one wishes to insert a logical record, the file is opened for UPDATE, the blocks are read consecutively until a dummy record is found, and the desired record to be inserted is written over the dummy[12].
- Notice that no DELETE operation is supported in this case. Deletion can be done via clever programming. Specifically, either batch mode processing is employed or the file is opened for UPDATE. In the latter case the blocks are read sequentially until the target record is located; then a dummy record is written in its place.

---

[12]Notice that this assumes an unordered sequential file. The algorithm is considerably more complex in the case of an ordered sequential file.

The *Data Definition Language* (DDL) facilitates the processing of CONSECUTIVE files, which contain either fixed-length or variable-length records. Processing of these files differs depending on the DDL; therefore, we examine each facility separately.

4.5.2.2 Fixed-Length Records.

As was noted in Chapter 3, in a number of instances *locate mode processing* is faster than *move mode processing*. In the former case the structured variable to which the record is to be delivered must overlay the logical record in the buffer area[13] so that the logical record does not actually "move" to the data area. Therefore, it can be processed while still in the buffer. In the latter case, the structured variable must be allocated in the data area of the application program. Each case is examined in turn.

Move Mode Processing.   For simplicity assume throughout that FILE1 consists of a collection of logical records, each of which consists of exactly two fields: the first, the NAME field, is a character string of length 16; the second, the AGE field, is an integer variable. Furthermore, assume that fixed length logical records are blocked with a blocking factor of 100. Under the previous assumptions the declaration for a physical sequential file will be as follows:

```
DCL (FILE1) FILE RECORD ENV(CONSECUTIVE FB RECSIZE(20) BLKSIZE(2000));
```

Then storage must be allocated in the data area of the application program where the logical record is to be moved. A possible declaration for the structured variable MOVEAREA follows:

```
DCL 1  MOVEAREA
       2  NAME   CHAR(16),
       2  AGE    | FIXED BINARY(31);
```

The Logical READ Request.   Whenever "reads" are permitted, a logical record can be read via the following PL/1 statement:

```
READ FILE (logical_name) INTO (program_variable);
```

Each time the above statement is executed, the access method will deliver the next logical record from the input buffer into the storage allocated to the structured variable that has been defined earlier in the source and in such a way that its *type* agrees with that of the logical record.

For example, if file FILE1 is opened for INPUT, then the first time that the statement

```
READ FILE (FILE1) INTO (MOVEAREA);
```

---

[13] Input or output, depending on the kind of processing.

is executed, the first logical record of the file, i.e., the first logical record from the first block, is delivered[14] to the location indicated by the MOVEAREA variable.

The Logical WRITE Request.   There are two statements related to "write" requests in which their use depends entirely on the chosen OPTION. In the case in which the file has been opened with the option OUTPUT, the statement that *must* be used is the following.

```
WRITE FILE (logical_filename) FROM (program_variable);
```

In particular, if file FILE1 has been opened for OUTPUT, then the first time that the statement

```
WRITE FILE (FILE1) FROM (MOVEAREA);
```

is executed, the contents of the 20 bytes starting at location MOVEAREA will be moved to the very first slot of the first[15] output buffer. When the buffer gets full, its contents will be written out in the first block of the physical file.

On the other hand, if the file has been opened with the UPDATE option, the write statement that *must* be used is

```
REWRITE FILE (logical_filename) FROM (program_variable);
```

In particular, if the file FILE1 has been opened with the option UPDATE, then the first time that the statement

```
REWRITE FILE (FILE1) FROM (MOVEAREA);
```

is executed, the logical record that is stored at location MOVEAREA is written over the same "slot" in the buffer where the last READ statement "read" from. As an example, consider the sequence of the following four statements.

```
READ FILE (FILE1) INTO (MOVEAREA);
READ FILE (FILE1) INTO (MOVEAREA);
MOVEAREA.AGE=35;
REWRITE FILE (FILE1) FROM (MOVEAREA);
```

Assuming that the first statement above is the first logical READ issued by the application program, then one can see that execution of the second logical READ causes the second logical record to be delivered to the location MOVEAREA. The third statement causes the contents of the AGE field to be overwritten by the entry 35, and the fourth statement causes the updated record at location MOVEAREA to be written over the second logical record in the buffer.

[14] Via the MVC (machine code) instruction.
[15] By default, two buffers are assigned by the PL/1.

Locate Mode Processing.   Recall that a memory data transfer may be eliminated and memory conserved by processing a logical record while it is in the buffer. The way in which the logical record can be accessed while in the buffer is via a *pointer* that points to it. Therefore, a pointer variable must be allocated that eventually will contain the *address* of the logical record that is to be accessed. Given that a logical record is nothing else to the access method but a collection of bytes, the pointer variable should be declared in such way that

1. It points to the logical record; and
2. It permits us to access the fields of the record.

Recall that the **MOVEAREA** declaration, in the case of move mode processing, was as follows:

```
DCL 1  MOVEAREA
       2  NAME   CHAR(15),
       2  AGE    | FIXED BINARY(31);
```

The declaration needed for locate mode processing is as follows:

```
DCL 1  MOVEAREA    BASED(BUF_PTR),
       2  NAME   CHAR(15),
       2  AGE    | FIXED BINARY(31);
```

Notice the difference in syntax between the above two declarations; the semantic difference is explained below.

A pointer variable, **BUF_PTR**, to point to a structure of the type **MOVEAREA** has been allocated. It is important to observe that no memory is allocated for the **MOVEAREA** structure in contrast with move mode processing. The above construct indicates, via the keyword **BASED**, that the pointer variable will point to 20 bytes of memory starting at the location indicated by **BUF_PTR**. In other words, the **MOVEAREA** will "overlay" the 20-byte area pointed to by **BUF_PTR**.

At run time the access method will store the address of the current logical record into the **BUF_PTR** variable; this mechanism is distinctively different for *input* and *output* mode processings. In other words a file opened with the option **INPUT** admits only *input buffer* processing, whereas a file opened with the option **OUTPUT** supports only *output buffer* processing. Each of these two techniques will be examined below.

Input Buffer Processing.   Only reads are permitted to this file; the corresponding PL/1 statement for move mode processing is

```
READ FILE (logical_filename) INTO (program_variable);
```

In this case, we do not want to move the record; therefore, the **INTO** clause does not apply and is not used here. Instead, the following PL/1 statement is issued that performs a logical *READ*.

```
READ FILE (logical_filename) SET (pointer_variable);
```

The SET clause requests that the access method supply at run time the address of the logical record into the pointer_variable; therefore, the logical record can be accessed and manipulated via the variable program_variable. Figure 4.5 illustrates these concepts. The first logical READ issued via

```
READ FILE (FILE1) SET (BUF_PTR);
```

causes the access method to access the very first record in the buffer and to set the contents of BUF_PTR (1000 hex in this case) to the address of this logical record. The second logical read will cause the access method to access the next logical record (the second in this case) and to set the contents of the BUF_PTR to the address of that record, and so on.

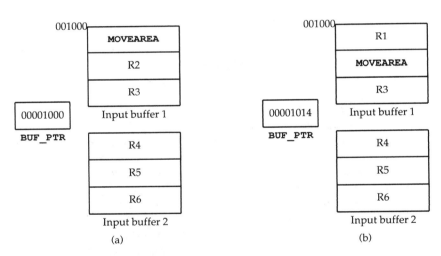

Figure 4.5 The BUF_PTR points to the first logical record in the first buffer (at address 1000 hex) as a result of the first logical READ FILE (FILE1) SET(BUF_PTR) (a), while BUF_PTR points to the second logical record in the first buffer after the second such logical READ. In either case, the MOVEAREA overlays the logical record in the Input Buffer.

In either case, the current record, the one pointed to by the BUF_PTR, can be updated via the the MOVEAREA variable and can be written out to an output file FILE2 via the WRITE statement presented earlier, i.e., via

```
WRITE FILE (FILE2) FROM (MOVEAREA);
```

Output Buffer Processing. The processing of a logical record in the output buffer consists of two basic steps:

1. The contents of the `pointer_variable` must be updated to reflect the *address* of the next slot in the output buffer that is to receive the logical record.
2. The logical record must be moved to that location where it can be processed.

The first step is accomplished via the following statement:

```
LOCATE (program_variable) FILE (logical_filename);
```

The second step is accomplished via the READ statement:

```
READ FILE (logical_filename) INTO (program_variable);
```

As an example, let FILE1 and FILE2 be two CONSECUTIVE files where the first file has been opened for INPUT and the second file has been opened for OUTPUT. Consider the sequence of the following two statements:

```
LOCATE (MOVEAREA) FILE (FILE2);
READ FILE (FILE1) INTO (MOVERAREA);
```

Also, assume that the LOCATE and the logical READ are the first such statements encountered in the application program. The first statement will cause the contents of the pointer BUF_PTR to be set to the address of the first slot of the output buffer allocated to FILE2; the direct result is that the MOVEAREA variable overlays the 20 bytes starting at the location indicated by the BUF_PTR. It is worth mentioning that the first logical record in the input buffer allocated to FILE1 has not yet been moved into the output buffer. The next logical read moves the record to the first slot of the output buffer. At this point the application program can process the record via the MOVEAREA variable. Figure 4.6 illustrates these concepts.

We close this section by noting that the contents of the output buffer are transferred to secondary memory when the buffer reaches capacity.

4.5.2.3 Variable-Length Records.

Assume that both files, FILE1 and FILE2, have been declared as CONSECUTIVE files and have been opened for INPUT and OUTPUT, respectively. In addition, assume that they both contain two classes of logical records, 1 and 2, each of different lengths. More precisely, assume that class 1 consists of records of two fields, a 16-byte character field (NAME) and a 4-byte integer field (AGE). Logical records of class 2 contain an extra field, a 12-byte character field (PHONE). In order to be able to distinguish between the two types of records, a 1-byte character field, CLASS, is

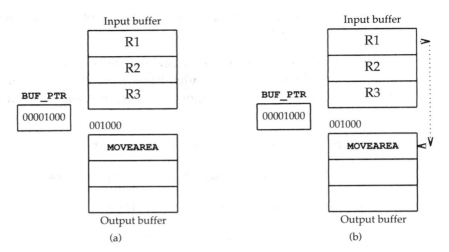

Figure 4.6   (a) The **BUF_PTR** points to the first logical record in the output buffer (at address 1000 hex) as a result of the first **LOCATE (MO-VEAREA) FILE (FILE2);** and, consequently, the **MOVEAREA** structure overlays the 20 bytes at this address, and (b) the logical record **R1** is moved there as a response to **READ FILE (FILE2) INTO (MOVEAREA).**

allocated in which the character representing the class to which the logical record belongs is recorded. Therefore, two areas must be allocated, **CLAS1AREA** and **CLAS2AREA**, where the logical records of class 1 and class 2, respectively, must be moved in order to be processed.

Hence, the declaration of the two files follows:

```
DCL (FILE1) FILE RECORD ENV(CONSECUTIVE VB RECSIZE(33) BLKSIZE(3000));
DCL (FILE2) FILE RECORD ENV(CONSECUTIVE VB RECSIZE(33) BLKSIZE(3000));
```

It is true that the access method can block and deblock; but the question is, how does the application program know to which class the "next" logical record to be read belongs so that it can be properly processed? Or, for that matter, how does it know to which class it belongs so that the appropriate **READ FILE (FILE1) INTO .. request** is issued? The answer is that the application program cannot do this.[16] The only possible way is that an area in main storage **MOVEAREA** of size equal to the largest of the two type logical records must be allocated and the access method must be instructed via the appropriate logical **READ** requests to transfer the logical record there. In addition, the two areas **CLAS1AREA** and **CLAS2AREA** must be allocated storage at the *same location* as the **MOVEAREA** so those

---

[16] One could argue successfully that the application program will know the class to which the "next" logical record belongs if, and only if, the *CLASS* field of each logical record contains the class of its logical successor record. In order for this to be possible, the type of the very first logical record must be known in advance, an unrealistic requirement.

areas overlap. We READ INTO the MOVEAREA; then, by examining the first byte at this location one can decide to which class the record belongs. From that point on the record can be processed by the application program by using either the CLAS1AREA or the CLAS2AREA declaration depending on the class.

Therefore, the following declarations are employed

```
DCL 1  CLAS1AREA    BASED(CLAS1_PTR),
       2  CLASS  CHAR(1),
       2  NAME   CHAR(16),
       2  AGE    FIXED BINARY(31);
DCL 1  CLAS2AREA    BASED(CLAS2_PTR),
       2  CLASS  CHAR(1),
       2  NAME   CHAR(16),
       2  AGE    FIXED BINARY(31),
       2  PHONE  CHAR(12);
```

As in the case of fixed-length records, either move or locate mode processing may be employed.

Move Mode Processing.   In move mode processing, the MOVEAREA structure variable is declared as follows:

```
MOVEAREA CHAR(33);
```

Now storage for all three variables can be allocated in such a way so that they overlap. PL/1 returns the address of a variable via ADDR(variable). Hence, all that is required is to set both pointer variables to the address of MOVEAREA. In particular,

```
CLAS1_PTR = ADDR(MOVEAREA);
CLAS2_PTR = ADDR(MOVEAREA);
```

is needed; the logical READ takes the form

```
READ FILE (FILE1) INTO (MOVEAREA);
```

Now if a test such as IF CLAS1.CLASS='1' returns true, then the logical record at hand belongs to class 1; otherwise, it belongs to class 2. Figure 4.7 illustrates these concepts.

Locate Mode Processing.   In either case—input or output buffer processing—the same strategy is followed as in the case of fixed-length record processing. In particular, the same *pointer* variable is assigned to either class of records, i.e., the following declarations are used:

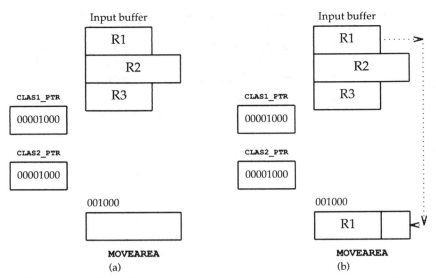

Figure 4.7   (a) Both pointers, `CLAS1_PTR` and `CLAS2_PTR`, point to the location (001000 hex) where `MOVEAREA` has been allocated storage as a direct result of the two statements, `CLAS1_PTR=ADDR(MOVEAREA)` and `CLAS2_PTR= ADDR(MOVE AREA)`. (b) The first logical record `R1` is moved into the `MOVERAREA` as a result of the first logical `READ FILE (FILE1) INTO MOVEAREA;`

```
DCL 1  CLAS1AREA    BASED(CLAS_PTR),
       2  CLASS   CHAR(1),
       2  NAME    CHAR(16),
       2  AGE     FIXED BINARY(31);
DCL 1  CLAS2AREA    BASED(CLAS_PTR),
       2  CLASS   CHAR(1),
       2  NAME    CHAR(16),
       2  AGE     FIXED BINARY(31),
       2  PHONE    CHAR(12);
```

   Input Buffer Processing. ◄ The two areas, `CLAS1AREA` and `CLAS2AREA`, and the logical record are forced into an overlap situation in the input buffer. In other words

```
            READ FILE (FILE1) SET (CLAS_PTR);
```

is issued. Then the logical record's class can be found via a simple test of the form `IF CLAS1AREA.CLASS='1' THEN ...;` and the record can be processed according to the requirements. Figure 4.8 illustrates this sequence of events.

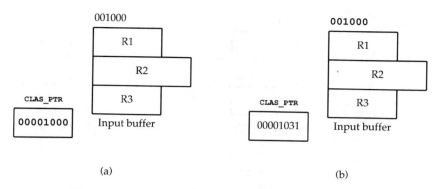

Figure 4.8 (a) Pointer `CLAS_PTR` points to the location (001000 hex) as a result of the first `READ FILE (FILE1) SET(CLAS_PTR);;` and, therefore, both areas, `CLAS1AREA` and `CLAS2AREA`, overlap the first logical record. (b) The `CLAS_PTR` has been updated as a result of the second `READ FILE (FILE1) SET(CLAS_PTR);` and, therefore, it points to the second logical record.

Output Buffer Processing. Similarly one could force the two areas to overlap the slot in the output buffer where the next record is to be moved and processed. Recall that this is accomplished via the following two statements:

```
LOCATE (CLAS2AREA) FILE (FILE2);
READ FILE (FILE1) INTO (CLAS2AREA);
```

Figure 4.9 illustrates these concepts.

4.5.2.4 Closing a File. Assume the desired operations have been performed on a file. In the case of an OUTPUT file, the possibly partially filled contents of the buffer must be written out, and all storage areas associated with that file in the application program's area[17] must be deallocated. All these operations can be accomplished via the following statement:

```
CLOSE FILE (logical_filename);
```

4.5.3 Examples

A number of applications programs are presented below that perform several operations on CONSECUTIVE files. The purpose of these programs is to expose the reader to the capabilities of PL/1 data sublanguage; therefore, the programs are written in such a way as to emphasize these capabilities. In other words, we intentionally avoid error checkings.

---

[17] Refer to Chapter 3.

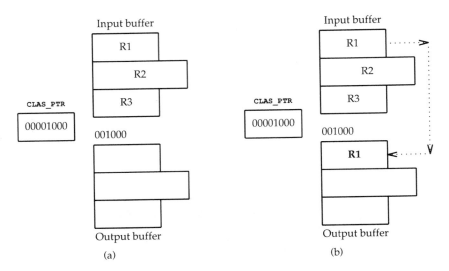

Figure 4.9 (a) The `CLAS_PTR` points to the first logical record in the output buffer (at address 1000 hex) as a result of the first `LO-CATE (CLAS2AREA) FILE (FILE2)`; consequently, both the `CLAS1AREA` and `CLAS2AREA` structures overlay at this address. (b) The logical record `R1` is moved to that area as a response to `READ FILE (FILE1) INTO (CLAS2AREA)`.

4.5.3.1 Fixed-Length Records.   Assume that the first task is to `CREATE` the Checking_Accounts file that was encountered in Chapter 1 as a `CONSECUTIVE` file. For the sake of simplicity, this file will be referred to as the `CHECKS` file hereafter.

The PL/1 declaration of the logical records of this file in view of Figure 1.7 follows.

```
DCL 1 CHECKSAREA
      2   ACCOUNT CHAR(11),
      2   NAME     CHAR(20),
      2   ADDRESS CHAR(15),
      2   BALANCE FLOAT DECIMAL(16);
```

The Creation of the CHECKS File.   Assume now that each customer's record has been punched on an 80-column card and the format of each is given below.

```
DCL 1 CARDSAREA,
      2 ACCOUNT  CHAR(11),
      2 NAME      CHAR(20),
      2 ADDRESS  CHAR(15),
      2 BALANCE  PIC'999999V.99',
      2 FILLER    CHAR(34);
```

The PL/1 code that reads the set of data cards and creates the CHECKS file is given below.

```
CREATE:PROC OPTIONS(MAIN);
/*
** Declare the CARDS file as a CONSECUTIVE  file, and the type of the structured
** variable, CARDSAREA, where each logical record of the file will move.
*/
      DCL CARDS FILE RECORD ENV(CONSECUTIVE F RECSIZE(80)),
           1 CARDSAREA,
                2 ACCOUNT  CHAR(11),
                2 NAME     CHAR(20),
                2 ADDRESS  CHAR(15),
                2 BALANCE  PIC'999999V.99'
                2 FILLER   CHAR(34);
/*
** Declare the CONSECUTIVE CHECKS file, and the type of the structured
** variable, CHECKSAREA, where each logical record of the file will move.
*/
      DCL CHECKS FILE RECORD ENV(CONSECUTIVE FB RECSIZE(54) BLKSIZE(540)),
           1 CHECKSAREA,
                2 ACCOUNT  CHAR(11),
                2 NAME     CHAR(20),
                2 ADDRESS  CHAR(15),
                2 BALANCE  FLOAT DECIMAL(16);
/*
** Declare a Boolean variable and initialize it to true.  When
** the logical end of file CARDS is reached set this variable to false.
*/
      DCL BEOF BIT(1) INIT('1'B);
      ON ENDFILE(CARDS) BEOF='0'B;
/*
** Open the CARDS file for INPUT and the file CHECKS for OUTPUT. Notice that
** that at this time the DCB is built; and,two buffers are allocated to CHECKS file.
*/
      OPEN FILE(CARDS) INPUT, FILE(CHECKS) OUTPUT;
/*
** Transfer the first logical record of the CARDS file into the CARDSAREA.
*/
      READ FILE (CARDS) INTO (CARDSAREA);
/*
** As long as the end of file of the CARDS file is not reached, build
** a logical record of the CHECKS file into the CHECKSAREA
```

```
*/
      DO WHILE (BEOF);
             CHECKSAREA.ACCOUNT = CARDSAREA.ACCOUNT;
             CHECKSAREA.NAME    = CARDSAREA.NAME;
             CHECKSAREA.ADDRESS = CARDSAREA.ADDRESS;
             CHECKSAREA.BALANCE = CARDSAREA.BALANCE;
/*
** Write the constructed logical record from the CHECKSAREA into the next
** available slot in the output buffer.  Notice that whenever an output
** buffer reaches capacity its contents are transmitted to the secondary device
** and the output buffers are flip-flopped.
*/
             WRITE FILE (CHECKS) FROM (CHECKSAREA);
/*
** Get the next logical record from the CARDS file.
*/
             READ FILE (CARDS) INTO (CARDSAREA);
      END;
/*
** All done.  Close the CHECKS file.
*/
      CLOSE FILE(CHECKS);
 END;
/*
** The JCL follows
*/
/*
//SYSPRINT DD SYSOUT=A
//GO.CHECKS DD DSNAME=UF.CHECKS,DISP=(NEW,CATLG),UNIT=SYSDA,
//                          SPACE=(TRK,(6,2))
//GO.CARDS DD *
Data cards go here.
/*
```

Now it may be assumed that the file CHECKS is sorted in increasing order of the primary keys.

The Update of the CHECKS File.   Assume that the file CHECKS has been created and that we are faced with the task of changing the ADDRESS of a certain customer.

In particular, assume that a single card contains two fields, the ADDRESS and the ACCOUNT number of a customer whose address must be changed. The format of the card is given below.

```
        DCL 1 CARDSAREA,
              2 ACCOUNT  CHAR(11),
              2 ADDRESS  CHAR(15),
              2 FILLER   CHAR(54);
```

The code that accomplishes this task is given below.

```
UPDATE: PROC OPTIONS(MAIN);


    DCL CARDS FILE RECORD ENV(CONSECUTIVE F RECSIZE(80)),
        1 CARDSAREA,
            2 ACCOUNT  CHAR(11),
            2 ADDRESS  CHAR(15),
            2 FILLER   CHAR(54);
    DCL CHECKS FILE RECORD ENV(CONSECUTIVE FB RECSIZE(54) BLKSIZE(540)),
        1 CHECKSAREA,
            2 ACCOUNT  CHAR(11),
            2 NAME     CHAR(20),
            2 ADDRESS  CHAR(15),
            2 BALANCE  FLOAT DECIMAL(16);
/*
** Open the CARDS file for INPUT  and the file CHECKS for UPDATE.
*/
    OPEN FILE(CARDS) INPUT, FILE(CHECKS) UPDATE;
/*
** Transfer the only logical record of the CARDS file into the CARDSAREA.
*/
    READ FILE (CARDS) INTO (CARDSAREA);
/*
** Create for purposes of comparison a dummy CHECKS logical record.
    CHECKSAREA.ACCOUNT  =  ' ';
/*
** If the value of the current logical record's ACCOUNT field from the CHECKS
** file is less than that of the current logical record's ACCOUNT field from
** the CARDS file, read the next logical record from the CHECKS
** file and repeat this test.
*/
    DO WHILE(CHECKSAREA.ACCOUNT< CARDSAREA.ACCOUNT);
        READ FILE(CHECKS) INTO (CHECKSAREA);
    END;
/*
** If the values of the ACCOUNT fields are equal then perform the update.
** In particular, change the ADDRESS and WRITE the updated record in place.
```

```
*/
      IF (CHECKSAREA.ACCOUNT = CARDSAREA.ACCOUNT)
          THEN DO;
                  CHECKSAREA.ADDRESS = CARDSAREA.ADDRESS;
                  REWRITE FILE(CHECKS) FROM (CHECKSAREA);
                  END;
/*
** All done.  Close the CHECKS file.
*/
      CLOSE FILE(CHECKS);
 END;
/*
** The JCL follows
/*
//SYSPRINT DD SYSOUT=A
//GO.CHECKS DD DSN=UF.CHECKS,DISP=(OLD,KEEP),UNIT=SYSDA
//GO.CARDS DD *
Data cards go here.
/*
```

Batch Mode Update of the CHECKS File.   Assume that a batch update of this file must be performed. Also assume that each operation is represented by a single card of input that contains the two fields ACCOUNT and UP_TYPE, a 1-byte character field that may take the values I and D. The first code value indicates that the target record must be inserted; the second indicates that the target record must be deleted. Moreover, the set of cards is sorted in increasing order of the ACCOUNT field.[18] Two algorithms are presented below that perform the same task but with a different scheme of internal processing of the records.

Move Mode Processing.   The following PL/1 code performs the Batch update of the logical records of the CHECKS file.

```
MVMDUP: PROC OPTIONS(MAIN);

      DCL CARDS FILE RECORD ENV(CONSECUTIVE F RECSIZE(80)),
          1 CARDSAREA,
              2 UPTYPE   CHAR(1),
              2 ACCOUNT  CHAR(11),
              2 NAME     CHAR(20),
              2 ADDRESS  CHAR(15),
              2 BALANCE  PIC'999999V.99',
              2 FILLER   CHAR(24);
```

[18] Normally, the unordered set of cards are read into a CONSECUTIVE file, *TF*, that is sorted; then the update operation takes place.

```
DCL CHECKS FILE RECORD ENV(CONSECUTIVE),
    1 CHECKSAREA,
        2 ACCOUNT  CHAR(11),
        2 NAME     CHAR(20),
        2 ADDRESS  CHAR(15),
        2 BALANCE  FLOAT DECIMAL(16);
```

```
/*
** The NCHECKS file will be the new CHECKS file.  Notice that the type of its
** records have been defined to be the same as those of the CHECKS file
** via the LIKE keyword.
*/
    DCL NCHECKS FILE RECORD ENV(CONSECUTIVE FB RECSIZE(54) BLKSIZE(540)),
        1 NCHECKSAREA LIKE CHECKSAREA;

    DCL BEOF1 BIT(1) INIT('1'B),
    BEOF2 BIT(1) INIT('1'B);
    ON ENDFILE(CARDS)   BEOF1='0'B;
    ON ENDFILE(CHECKS) BEOF2='0'B;
/*
** Open the two files CARDS and CHECKS for INPUT and the file NCHECKS for OUTPUT
*/
    OPEN FILE(CARDS) INPUT, FILE(CHECKS) INPUT, FILE(NCHECKS) OUTPUT;
    READ FILE(CHECKS) INTO (CHECKSAREA);
    READ FILE(CARDS) INTO (CARDSAREA);
/*
** As long as the logical end of the file CARDS is not reached, repeat the
** sequence.
/*
    DO WHILE(BEOF1);
/*
** As long as the ACCOUNT field of a logical record from the CHECKS file
** remains less than that of the current logical record from the CARDS file, write
** the former record into the NCHECKS file, read the next logical record from the
** CHECKS file, and repeat the same test.
/*
        DO WHILE
            ((CHECKSAREA.ACCOUNT< CARDSAREA.ACCOUNT) & (BEOF2));
            WRITE FILE(NCHECKS) FROM (CHECKSAREA);
            READ FILE(CHECKS) INTO (CHECKSAREA);
        END;
/*
** An operation must be performed.  If the ACCOUNT value is the same and
```

```
** if the UP_TYPE is equal to I, ignore the current CARDS record;
**  otherwise, delete the current CHECKS logical record.
*/

            IF (CHECKSAREA.ACCOUNT = CARDSAREA.ACCOUNT)
                THEN DO;
                    IF (CARDSAREA.UPTYPE = 'I')
                        THEN DO;
                            WRITE FILE(NCHECKS) FROM (CHECKSAREA);
                            READ FILE(CHECKS) INTO (CHECKSAREA);
                            END;
                        ELSE DO;
                        READ FILE(CHECKS) INTO (CHECKSAREA);
                            END;
                    END;
/*
** Insert the current CARDS logical record into the NCHECKS file.
*/
            ELSE DO;
                    IF (CARDSAREA.UPTYPE = 'I')
                        THEN DO;
                            NCHECKSAREA.ACCOUNT = CARDSAREA.ACCOUNT;
                            NCHECKSAREA.NAME    = CARDSAREA.NAME;
                            NCHECKSAREA.ADDRESS = CARDSAREA.ADDRESS;
                            NCHECKSAREA.BALANCE = CARDSAREA.BALANCE;
                            WRITE FILE(NCHECKS) FROM (NCHECKSAREA);
                                END;
                    END;
/*
** Get the next logical record from the CARDS file and repeat.
*/
            READ FILE(CARDS) INTO (CARDSAREA);
        END;
/*
** Write all remaining logical records in the CHECKS file into the
** NCHECKS file.
*/
        DO WHILE(BEOF2);
                WRITE FILE(NCHECKS) FROM (CHECKSAREA);
            READ FILE(CHECKS) INTO (CHECKSAREA);
        END;

        CLOSE FILE(NCHECKS);
END;
```

```
/*
//SYSPRINT DD SYSOUT=A
//GO.CHECKS DD DSN=UF.CHECKS,DISP=(OLD,KEEP),UNIT=SYSDA
//GO.NCHECKS DD DSN=UF.NCHECKS,DISP=(NEW,CATLG),
//      UNIT=SYSDA,SPACE=(TRK,(6,2))
//GO.CARDS DD *
Data cards go here.
/*
```

Locate Mode Processing. We distinguish between input and output buffer processing.

Input Buffer Processing. The PL/1 code below performs the same task as the algorithm of the previous section but employs locate input buffer mode processing.

```
INBFUP:PROC OPTIONS(MAIN);
/*
** The pointers LOC1, LOC2, and LOC3 will point to the current logical records
** in the buffers allocated to CARDS, CHECKS, and NCHECKS files respectively.
*/
    DCL LOC1 POINTER, LOC2 POINTER, LOC3 POINTER,
    ADDR BUILTIN;

    DCL 1 CARDSAREA   BASED(LOC1),
            2 UPTYPE   CHAR(1),
            2 ACCOUNT  CHAR(11),
            2 NAME     CHAR(20),
            2 ADDRESS  CHAR(15),
            2 BALANCE  PIC'999999V.99',
            2 FILLER   CHAR(24);

    DCL 1 CHECKSAREA BASED(LOC2),
            2 ACCOUNT  CHAR(11),
            2 NAME     CHAR(20),
            2 ADDRESS  CHAR(15),
            2 BALANCE  FLOAT DECIMAL(16);

    DCL 1 NCHECKSAREA BASED(LOC3),
            2 ACCOUNT  CHAR(11),
            2 NAME     CHAR(20),
            2 ADDRESS  CHAR(15),
            2 BALANCE  FLOAT DECIMAL(16);
```

```
      DCL (CARDS,CHECKS) FILE RECORD ENV(CONSECUTIVE);
      DCL NCHECKS FILE RECORD ENV(CONSECUTIVE FB RECSIZE(54) BLKSIZE(540));


      DCL BEOF1 BIT(1) INIT('1'B),
      BEOF2 BIT(1) INIT('1'B);
      ON ENDFILE(CARDS) BEOF1='0'B;
      ON ENDFILE(CHECKS) BEOF2='0'B;


      OPEN FILE(CARDS) INPUT, FILE(CHECKS) INPUT, FILE(NCHECKS) OUTPUT;
/*
** LOC2 points to the first logical record in the input buffer
** associated with the file CHECKS while
** LOC1 points to the first logical record in the input buffer
** associated with the file CARDS.
*/
      READ FILE(CHECKS) SET(LOC2);
      READ FILE(CARDS) SET(LOC1);


      DO WHILE(BEOF1);
          DO WHILE
              ((BEOF2)&(CHECKSAREA.ACCOUNT < CARDSAREA.ACCOUNT));
/*
** Notice that the CHECKSAREA overlays the logical record in the
** input buffer allocated to CHECKS.
*/
                  WRITE FILE(NCHECKS) FROM (CHECKSAREA);
                  READ FILE(CHECKS) SET(LOC2);
          END;
          IF (CHECKSAREA.ACCOUNT = CARDSAREA.ACCOUNT)
              THEN DO;
                  IF (CARDSAREA.UPTYPE = 'I')
                      THEN DO;
                          WRITE FILE(NCHECKS) FROM (CHECKSAREA);
                          END;
                      ELSE DO;
                          READ FILE(CHECKS) SET(LOC2);
                          END;
                  END;
              ELSE DO;
                  IF (CARDSAREA.UPTYPE = 'I')
                      THEN DO;
/*
** A logical record is to be inserted.  The pointer LOC3 is set to point to the
** beginning byte of the CARDSAREA.ACCOUNT;  the direct result is that the
```

```
** NCHECKSAREA overlays in this address; therefore, the UPTYPE field will
** not be written out.
*/
                                      LOC3 = ADDR(CARDSAREA.ACCOUNT);
                                      WRITE FILE(NCHECKS) FROM (NCHECKSAREA);
                                      END;
                         END;
              READ FILE(CARDS) SET(LOC1);
        END;


        DO WHILE(BEOF2);
              WRITE FILE(NCHECKS) FROM (CHECKSAREA);
              READ FILE(CHECKS) SET(LOC2);
        END;


        CLOSE FILE(NCHECKS);
END;

/*
//SYSPRINT DD SYSOUT=A
//GO.CHECKS DD DSNAME=UF.CHECKS,DISP=(OLD,KEEP),
//    UNIT=SYSDA
//GO.NCHECKS DD DSNAME=UF.NCHECKS,DISP=(NEW,CATLG),
//    UNIT=SYSDA,SPACE=(TRK,(6,2))
//GO.CARDS DD *
Data cards go here.
/*
```

Output Buffer Processing.   We present the code below that performs the following task. The **BALANCE** field of certain customers is updated. Each customer's transaction is recorded in a single input card. Specifically, only two fields are present in this card: the **ACCOUNT** number of the customer and the amount of the transaction **AMOUNT**. Notice again that the cards as well as the **CHECKS** file are sorted in increasing order of the **ACCOUNT** field.

```
OTBFUP: PROC OPTIONS(MAIN);
    DCL BUF_PTR POINTER;

    DCL CARDS FILE RECORD ENV(CONSECUTIVE F RECSIZE(80)),
        1 CARDSAREA,
             2 ACCOUNT  CHAR(11),
             2 AMOUNT   PIC'999999V.99',
             2 FILLER   CHAR(60);
```

```
     DCL CHECKS FILE RECORD ENV(CONSECUTIVE),
          1 CHECKSAREA BASED(BUF_PTR),
               2 ACCOUNT  CHAR(11),
               2 NAME     CHAR(20),
               2 ADDRESS  CHAR(15),
               2 BALANCE  FLOAT DECIMAL(16);

     DCL NCHECKS FILE RECORD ENV(CONSECUTIVE FB RECSIZE(54)
                              BLKSIZE(540));

     DCL BEOF1 BIT(1) INIT('1'B), BEOF2 BIT(1) INIT('1'B);
     ON ENDFILE(CARDS) BEOF1='0'B;
     ON ENDFILE(CHECKS) BEOF2='0'B;


     OPEN FILE(CARDS) INPUT, FILE(CHECKS) INPUT, FILE(NCHECKS) OUTPUT;


     READ FILE(CARDS) INTO (CARDSAREA);
/*
** The first statement sets the pointer BUF_PTR to point to the first logical
** record slot in the output buffer.  The second statement delivers the
** first logical record from the CHECKS file to that location where
** the record can be processed.  The buffer is written out
** whenever it gets full.
*/
     LOCATE CHECKSAREA FILE(NCHECKS);
     READ FILE(CHECKS) INTO(CHECKSAREA);


     DO WHILE(BEOF1);
          DO WHILE
             ((CHECKSAREA.ACCOUNT < CARDSAREA.ACCOUNT)&(BEOF2));
               LOCATE CHECKSAREA FILE(NCHECKS);
               READ FILE(CHECKS) INTO (CHECKSAREA);
          END;

          IF (CHECKSAREA.ACCOUNT = CARDSAREA.ACCOUNT)
               THEN DO;
                    CHECKSAREA.BALANCE = CHECKSAREA.BALANCE +
                              CARDSAREA.AMOUNT;
                    LOCATE CHECKSAREA FILE(NCHECKS);
                    READ FILE(CHECKS) INTO (CHECKSAREA);
                         END;
          READ FILE(CARDS) INTO(CARDSAREA);
```

```
        END;
        CLOSE FILE(NCHECKS);
END;


/*
//SYSPRINT DD SYSOUT=A
//GO.CHECKS DD DSN=UF.CHECKS,DISP=(OLD,KEEP),
//   UNIT=SYSDA
//GO.NCHECKS DD DSN=UF.NCHECKS,DISP=(NEW,CATLG),
//   UNIT=SYSDA,SPACE=(TRK,(6,2))
//GO.CARDS DD *
Data cards go here.
/*
```

4.5.3.2   Variable-Length Records.   Assume that the first task is to CREATE the *Loan Applications* file, which was encountered in Chapter 1, as a CONSECUTIVE file; for the sake of simplicity, hereafter this file will be referred to as the LOANS file.

Assume that the logical records of this file belong to two distinct classes, CAR and MORTGAGE loans.[19] The PL/1 declarations of the logical records of this file according to the class to which they belong follows:

```
DCL 1 CAR_TYPE BASED(BUF_PTR),
        2 CLASS    CHAR(1),
        2 ACCOUNT CHAR(11),
        2 NAME     CHAR(20),
        2 ADDRESS CHAR(15),
        2 MAKE     CHAR(10),
        2 YEAR     CHAR(4),
        2 AMOUNT   PIC'999999V.99';
DCL 1 MORTGAGE BASED(BUF_PTR),
        2 CLASS    CHAR(1),
        2 ACCOUNT CHAR(11),
        2 NAME     CHAR(20),
        2 ADDRESS CHAR(15),
        2 HADRES   CHAR(15),
        2 YEAR     CHAR(4),
        2 AMOUNT   PIC'999999V.99';
```

Assume now that each customer's record has been punched in an 80-column card.

---

[19] Assume that no customer applies for both types of loans.

The Creation of the LOANS File. The PL/1 code below is employed in
order to **CREATE** the **LOANS** file.

```
CREATE:PROC OPTIONS(MAIN);
/*
** Notice that the logical record length is defined to be equal to the size
** of the largest record plus an additional 8 control bytes.  Moreover,
** the blocksize definition includes 4 extra required bytes.
*/
    DCL (LOANS) FILE RECORD ENV(CONSECUTIVE VB RECSIZE(82) BLKSIZE(1644));
    DCL (CARDS) FILE RECORD ENV(CONSECUTIVE);
/*
** The declaration of the pointer variable that will be employed to
** force the three  areas to overlap follows.  Notice the declaration of
** the built in function ADDR
*/
    DCL BUF_PTR POINTER;
    DCL ADDR BUILTIN;
/*
** The declaration of the two types of records follows.
*/
    DCL 1 CAR_TYPE BASED(BUF_PTR),
          2 CLASS   CHAR(1),
          2 ACCOUNT CHAR(11),
          2 NAME    CHAR(20),
          2 ADDRESS CHAR(15),
          2 MAKE    CHAR(10),
          2 YEAR    CHAR(4),
          2 AMOUNT  PIC'999999V.99';
    DCL 1 MORTGAGE BASED(BUF_PTR),
          2 CLASS   CHAR(1),
          2 ACCOUNT CHAR(11),
          2 NAME    CHAR(20),
          2 ADDRESS CHAR(15),
          2 HADRES  CHAR(15),
          2 YEAR    CHAR(4),
          2 AMOUNT  PIC'999999V.99';
/*
** The area to which each logical record from the CARDS file will be read.
*/
    DCL CARDAREA CHAR(80);

    DCL BEOF BIT(1)INIT('1'B);
    ON ENDFILE(CARDS)BEOF ='0'B;
```

```
      OPEN FILE(CARDS) INPUT,FILE(LOANS) OUTPUT;
/*
** Force all three areas CAR_TYPE, MORTGAGE, and CARDAREA to overlap.
*/
      BUF_PTR = ADDR(CARDAREA);

      READ FILE(CARDS) INTO (CARDTEST);
/*
** As long as the logical end of CARDS file is not reached, repeat.
*/
      DO WHILE(BEOF);
          IF CAR_TYPE.CLASS = 'C'
               THEN WRITE FILE(LOANS) FROM (CAR_TYPE);
               ELSE WRITE FILE(LOANS) FROM (MORTGAGE);
            READ FILE(CARDS) INTO (CARDTEST);
      END;
      CLOSE(LOANS);
END;


/*
//SYSPRINT DD SYSOUT=A
//GO.LOANS DD DSNAME=UF.LOANS,DISP=(NEW,CATLG),
//   UNIT=SYSDA,SPACE=(TRK,(6,2))
//GO.CARDS DD *
Data cards go here.
/*
```

Hereafter, it may be assumed that the file LOANS is sorted in increasing order of the primary keys.

The Update of the LOANS File.   Assume that the file LOANS has been created and that we are faced with the task of changing the ADDRESS of a certain customer.

In particular, assume that a single card contains two fields, the ADDRESS and the ACCOUNT number of that customer whose address must be changed. The format of the card is given below.

```
      DCL 1 CARDSAREA,
            2 ACCOUNT  CHAR(11),
            2 ADDRESS  CHAR(15),
            2 FILLER   CHAR(54);
```

The code that accomplishes this task is given below.

```
UPDATE:PROC OPTIONS(MAIN);

    DCL (CARDS) FILE RECORD ENV(CONSECUTIVE);
    DCL (LOANS) FILE RECORD ENV(CONSECUTIVE VB RECSIZE(82) BLKSIZE(1644));
    DCL BUF_PTR POINTER;

    DCL 1 CARDSAREA,
            2 ACCOUNT  CHAR(11),
            2 ADDRESS  CHAR(15),
            2 FILLER   CHAR(54);
    DCL 1 CAR_TYPE BASED(BUF_PTR),
            2 CLASS    CHAR(1),
            2 ACCOUNT  CHAR(11),
            2 NAME     CHAR(20),
            2 ADDRESS  CHAR(15),
            2 MAKE     CHAR(10),
            2 YEAR     CHAR(4),
            2 AMOUNT   FLOAT DECIMAL(16);
    DCL 1 MORTGAGE BASED(BUF_PTR),
            2 CLASS    CHAR(1),
            2 ACCOUNT  CHAR(11),
            2 NAME     CHAR(20),
            2 ADDRESS  CHAR(15),
            2 HADRES   CHAR(15),
            2 YEAR     CHAR(4),
            2 AMOUNT   FLOAT DECIMAL(16);

/*
** Declaration of the MOVEAREA to which each logical record from the LOANS
** file will be read.  Notice that the first assignment statement below causes
** all three areas to overlap.
*/

    DCL MOVEAREA CHAR(74);
    DCL ADDR BUILTIN;
    BUF_PTR = ADDR(MOVEAREA);

    DCL BEOF BIT(1)INIT('1'B);
    ON ENDFILE(LOANS)BEOF ='0'B;

    OPEN FILE(CARDS) INPUT,FILE(LOANS) UPDATE;

    CAR_TYPE.ACCOUNT = ' ';
    READ FILE(CARDS) INTO (CARDSAREA);
```

```
        DO WHILE((BEOF) & (CAR_TYPE.ACCOUNT < CARDSAREA.ACCOUNT));
             READ FILE(LOANS) INTO (MOVEAREA);
        END;


        IF (CAR_TYPE.ACCOUNT = CARDSAREA.ACCOUNT)
            THEN DO;
                 CAR_TYPE.ADDRESS = CARDSAREA.ADDRESS;
                 IF CAR_TYPE.CLASS = 'C'
                     THEN DO;
                          REWRITE FILE(LOANS) FROM (CAR_TYPE);
                          END;
                     ELSE DO;
                          REWRITE FILE(LOANS) FROM (MORTGAGE);
                          END;
                 END;

END;
/*
//SYSPRINT DD SYSOUT=A
//GO.LOANS DD DSNAME=UF.LOANS,DISP=(OLD,KEEP),
//   UNIT=SYSDA
//GO.CARDS DD *
Data cards go here.
/*
```

Batch Mode Update of the LOANS File.   Assume that a batch update of this file must be performed. Also assume that a single card of input contains the two fields ACCOUNT and UP_TYPE, a 1-byte character field that may take the values I and D. The first code value indicates that the target record must be inserted; the second indicates that the target record must be deleted. Moreover, the set of cards is sorted in increasing order of the ACCOUNT field.[20] Again, there are three different algorithms that can be employed relative to the internal processing of records to accomplish this task. We present below the code that performs the update by employing move mode processing. The reader is encouraged to provide the missing comments to the code below.

```
BATCH: PROC OPTIONS(MAIN);

    DCL BEOF1 BIT(1) INIT('1'B), BEOF2 BIT(1) INIT('1'B);

    DCL LOC1 POINTER, LOC2 POINTER, LOC3 POINTER,
    ADDR BUILTIN;
```

---

[20] Normally, the unordered set of cards will be read into a CONSECUTIVE file, *TF,* which will be sorted; then the update operation will take place.

```
     DCL CARDS FILE RECORD ENV(CONSECUTIVE F RECSIZE(80)),
         1 CARDSCAREA BASED(LOC1),
               2 UPTYPE   CHAR(1),
               2 CLASS    CHAR(1),
               2 ACCOUNT  CHAR(11),
               2 NAME     CHAR(20),
               2 ADDRESS  CHAR(15),
               2 MAKE     CHAR(10),
               2 YEAR     CHAR(4),
               2 AMOUNT   PIC '999999V.99';

     DCL 1 CARDSMAREA BASED(LOC1),
               2 UPTYPE   CHAR(1),
               2 CLASS    CHAR(1),
               2 ACCOUNT  CHAR(11),
               2 NAME     CHAR(20),
               2 ADDRESS  CHAR(15),
               2 HADRES   CHAR(15),
               2 YEAR     CHAR(4),
               2 AMOUNT   PIC '999999V.99';

     DCL CARDIN CHAR(80);
     DCL LOANS FILE RECORD ENV(CONSECUTIVE),
         1 LOANSCAREA BASED(LOC2),
               2 CLASS    CHAR(1),
               2 ACCOUNT  CHAR(11),
               2 NAME     CHAR(20),
               2 ADDRESS  CHAR(15),
               2 MAKE     CHAR(10),
               2 YEAR     CHAR(4),
               2 AMOUNT   FLOAT DECIMAL(16);

     DCL 1 LOANSMAREA BASED(LOC2),
               2 CLASS    CHAR(1),
               2 ACCOUNT  CHAR(11),
               2 NAME     CHAR(20),
               2 ADDRESS  CHAR(15),
               2 HADRES   CHAR(15),
               2 YEAR     CHAR(4),
               2 AMOUNT   FLOAT DECIMAL(16);

     DCL LOANSIN CHAR(82);

     DCL NLOANS FILE RECORD ENV(CONSECUTIVE VB RECSIZE(82) BLKSIZE(540)),
```

```
        1 NLOANSCAREA BASED(LOC3),
                2 CLASS     CHAR(1),
                2 ACCOUNT CHAR(11),
                2 NAME      CHAR(20),
                2 ADDRESS CHAR(15),
                2 MAKE      CHAR(10),
                2 YEAR      CHAR(4),
                2 AMOUNT    FLOAT DECIMAL(16);

    DCL 1 NLOANSMAREA BASED(LOC3),
                2 CLASS     CHAR(1),
                2 ACCOUNT CHAR(11),
                2 NAME      CHAR(20),
                2 ADDRESS CHAR(15),
                2 HADRES    CHAR(15),
                2 YEAR      CHAR(4),
                2 AMOUNT    FLOAT DECIMAL(16);

    DCL NLOANHOLD CHAR(74);
    LOC1 = ADDR(CARDIN);
    LOC2 = ADDR(LOANSIN);
    ON ENDFILE(CARDS)  BEOF1='0'B;
    ON ENDFILE(LOANS) BEOF2='0'B;

    OPEN FILE(CARDS) INPUT, FILE(LOANS) INPUT, FILE(NLOANS) OUTPUT;
    READ FILE(LOANS) INTO (LOANSIN);
    READ FILE(CARDS) INTO (CARDIN);

    DO WHILE(BEOF1);
        DO WHILE
          ((LOANSCAREA.ACCOUNT< CARDSCAREA.ACCOUNT) & (BEOF2));
          IF (LOANSCAREA.CLASS = 'C')
                THEN WRITE FILE(NLOANS) FROM (LOANSCAREA);
                ELSE WRITE FILE(NLOANS) FROM (LOANSMAREA);
            READ FILE(LOANS) INTO (LOANSIN);
        END;
        IF (LOANSCAREA.ACCOUNT = CARDSCAREA.ACCOUNT)
            THEN DO;
                IF (CARDSCAREA.UPTYPE = 'I')
                    THEN DO;
                        IF (CARDSCAREA.CLASS = 'C')
                            THEN WRITE FILE(NLOANS) FROM (LOANSCAREA);
                            ELSE WRITE FILE(NLOANS) FROM (LOANSMAREA);
                        END;
```

```
                                        ELSE DO;
                                            READ FILE(LOANS) INTO (LOANSIN);
                                            END;
                                    END;

                            ELSE DO;
                                IF (CARDSCAREA.UPTYPE = 'I')
                                    THEN DO;
                                        IF (CARDSCAREA.CLASS = 'C')
                                            THEN DO;
                                                LOC3 = ADDR(CARDSCAREA.CLASS);
                                                WRITE FILE(NLOANS) FROM (NLOANSCAREA);
                                                    END;
                                        ELSE DO;
                                            LOC3 = ADDR(CARDSMAREA.CLASS);
                                            WRITE FILE(NLOANS) FROM (NLOANSMAREA);
                                            END;
                                        END;
                    END;
                    READ FILE(CARDS) INTO (CARDIN);
                END;


            DO WHILE(BEOF2);
                IF (LOANSCAREA.CLASS = 'C')
                    THEN WRITE FILE(NLOANS) FROM (LOANSCAREA);
                    ELSE WRITE FILE(NLOANS) FROM (LOANSMAREA);
                READ FILE(LOANS) INTO (LOANSIN);
            END;


            CLOSE FILE(NLOANS);

        END;


        /*
        //SYSPRINT DD SYSOUT=A
        //GO.LOANS DD DSN=UF.LOANS,DISP=(OLD,KEEP),UNIT=SYSDA
        //GO.NLOANS DD DSN=UF.NLOANS,DISP=(NEW,CATLG),
        //     UNIT=SYSDA,SPACE=(TRK,(6,2))
        //GO.CARDS DD *
        Data cards go here.
        /*
```

4.6 EXERCISES

1. Convert the program CREATE to a robust program.
2. Convert the program BATCH to a robust program.
3. The first task is to CREATE the Loan Applications file, which was encountered in Chapter 4, as a CONSECUTIVE file; for the sake of simplicity, this file will hereafter be referred to as the LOANS file.

Recall that the logical records of this file belong to two distinct classes, CAR and MORTGAGE loans. The PL/1 declarations of the logical records of this file according to the class to which they belong follows:

```
DCL 1 CAR_TYPE
      2 CLASS      CHAR(1),
      2 ACCOUNT    CHAR(11),
      2 NAME       CHAR(20),
      2 ADDRESS    CHAR(15),
      2 MAKE       CHAR(10),
      2 YEAR       CHAR(4),
      2 AMOUNT     PIC'999999.99';

DCL 1 MORTGAGE
      2 CLASS      CHAR(1),
      2 ACCOUNT    CHAR(11),
      2 NAME       CHAR(20),
      2 ADDRESS    CHAR(15),
      2 HADRES     CHAR(15),
      2 YEAR       CHAR(4),
      2 AMOUNT     PIC'999999.99';
```

Assume now that each customer's record has been punched in an 80-column card, and the cards have been sorted in increasing order. Notice that a certain customer could file for both types of loans but could not apply for two or more loans of the same type.

a. You are to write a PL/I robust program to create the LOANS file. You will probably have to decide on a new type of logical record for the LOANS file so it could reflect the number and the type of the loan applications filed by each customer.

b. The second task is to write a robust program to perform a batch update of the file that you created in the first step. Also assume that a single input card is reflecting a single transaction. The format of each card depends on the type of the transaction. Specifically, the first column contains a character. The value of the character could be D, 1, 2, 3, or 4.

In the case in which the character's value is D, then the second field reflects the ACCOUNT of the customer that must be deleted.

In the case in which the character's value is a 1 or a 2, then a record must be inserted, its type depending on the value of the character. A 1 indicates a CAR_TYPE loan application, whereas a 2 shows a MORTGAGE application.

In the case in which the character's value is a 3 or a 4, then a record must be updated to reflect a second application for the other type of loan from a customer. The loan's type depends on the value of the character. A 3 indicates a CAR_TYPE loan application, whereas 4 shows a MORTGAGE application. You may assume that the set of input cards corresponding to the transactions is sorted in increasing order of the ACCOUNT field.

Use a blocking factor of 5 and assume no more than 1000 records in the LOANS file.

When the file LOANS is created, reopen it for output and print out a report containing all logical records in the file. Similarly, when you update the file, reopen the new file (you may assume no more than 1200 records) and print a report containing all logical records. You are expected to comment your code fully. You may use any mode of processing.

5

Direct Files

In the previous chapter we demonstrated that in order to retrieve a record from a Physical Sequential file an average number of accesses bounded by $clg(\log_2(NBLK))$ random accesses and $clg((NBLK + 1)/2)$ sequential accesses is required, depending on the search method employed. Under the general title *random processing* the aim is to obtain file organizations in which retrieval of a record requires just one or very near to one random access. There are basically two methods by which this can be accomplished; both methods are based on the same idea. Namely, that given the primary key of the target record, this key will be resolved to a disk *address* and this address will be used to access the record. The mechanism by which the key is transformed into an address distinguishes these two methods. The first method uses the idea of the *index*, whereas the second uses the *key-to-address (KTA)* transformation. An index is basically a record in which the key is stored alongside the address of the record, whereas a key-to-address transformation is a mapping, user defined, that maps the key to an address. Despite the fact that we will discuss both of these techniques extensively, it should be noted that their basic difference lies in the fact that if an index is used, then the indexes must be stored, whereas if the *KTA* is used, then the address is internally computed. Files that use the latter method are called *Direct files* and we will elaborate on them in the following paragraphs of this chapter.

5.1 BASIC DEFINITIONS

When a file is to be created, the user must specify the number of blocks that are required. Since a block[1] is the smallest addressable unit, this is equivalent to saying that the number of addresses must be specified. This number is referred to as the *address space (R)*. In addition, the number of records that can be stored in each block must be defined. This number is referred to as the *address size (B)*. It should be clear that if the number of records in the file is equal to *NR*, then only a fraction of the available file space is utilized. This fraction is known as the *load factor (LF)* and can be obtained by

$$LF = \frac{NR}{R \cdot B} \qquad [5.1]$$

Observe that the load factor must be kept as high as possible; otherwise, much of the allocated storage is wasted.

The *KTA* transformation, as was mentioned above, is a mapping f with the domain being the set of primary keys[2] and the range being the address space. If, for some key k, it is assumed that

$$f(k) = s$$

then the address s is referred to as the *home address* of the logical record whose key is equal to k. That address corresponds to the physical block number relative to this file. In other words, the first block is identified by the address 0, the second by the address 1, and the last block by the address $R - 1$; when a block of address s is to be accessed, then the address s is converted to a three part disk address.[3]

It is known that the cardinality of the set of mappings from the record space into the address space is given by

$$R^{NR}$$

Setting R equal to 10 and NR equal to 5, it can be seen that the number of available mappings is equal to 100,000. One can therefore see the monumental task that the designer faces. In addition, only a relatively small subset of these mappings is *one-to-one*, which means that the probability of selecting a *KTA* that is not one-to-one is quite high. Notice that an $n : 1$ transformation could cause two distinct keys k_1 and k_2 to be mapped into the same address. In this case, the

---

[1] The term *bucket* is often used instead of *block*.

[2] We may suppose that all primary keys are nonnegative integers. If they are not, then before the *KTA* is applied the primary key is mapped to a nonnegative integer and the transformation is applied to that latter integer. Notice that such conversion is required if and only if the primary keys contain alphabetic characters. There are a number of such mappings, the most common of which is the one that converts each alphabetic character of the key to the corresponding EBCDIC code followed by the addition of all codes that were obtained.

[3] In the case of a multivolume file, the block address is converted to a four-part disk address, the first part being the volume address.

two records with keys k_1 and k_2 respectively are said to be *synonyms;* this phenomenon is known as *collision.* Observe that if the address size is equal to one, then a single collision will cause one of the two synonym records not to be placed in its home address, since that address is occupied by the other record. The former record, that is the record that could not be stored in its home address, is referred to as an *overflow* record. Where the overflow record is stored depends on the overflow technique used; a number of these techniques will be examined shortly. But the fact remains that no matter what is the employed technique, overflow records require more[4] than one random access to be accessed, since already one random access was performed to access the home address.

Observe that the presence of overflow records is detrimental to the performance of a Direct file, whereas absence of overflow records will lead us to our goal—namely, *just one* access is required to retrieve any record.

Hence, the key-to-address transformations can be grouped into two classes. First, the class of all 1:1 transformations is called the class of *deterministic transformations,* and the class of all $n : 1$ transformations is referred to as the class of *hashing transformations.* Notice that in a number of textbooks authors refer to *Hash files,* and already one can see that a Hash file *is* a Direct file. The only distinction between Hash and Direct files is the nature of the *KTA* as was mentioned earlier; that distinction will be maintained here.

No matter to which class the *KTA* belongs, it must be clear that records in Direct files can be processed in a sequential fashion, but seldom can they be processed in increasing order of the keys; in such a case the transformation is called a *sequence-preserving* transformation.

5.2 DETERMINISTIC TRANSFORMATIONS

Consider a file of 1000 records. Assume that the primary keys are integers, namely, 0 to 999. It is a simple matter to devise a deterministic transformation. Actually, the mapping f defined by

$$f(k) = k$$

will map each key *key* to a unique address; in addition, it provides us with a bonus; namely, this transformation is a sequence-preserving transformation. As a matter of fact, an address space of 1000 and a declared address size equal to 1 is all that is needed. Moreover, one can use an address size of 100 as an example to facilitate faster overall sequential processing of the entire file. In this case, the above transformation f must be composed with the mapping g defined[5] by

$$g(k) = k \ div \ 100$$

Here, an address space of just 10 is needed, but in both cases the loading factor

---

[4] According to our model.

[5] The operator *div* represents integer division.

remains at 100%. One should have noticed that the composition of the two mappings f and g is not a 1:1 mapping, *but* the mapping f *is 1:1*. The only reason that the mapping g is used is to facilitate record blocking. We will be able to see that the access methods for Direct file organizations do not block/deblock records; but in some instances it will be shown that records can be blocked, and for that matter deblocked, by the application program.

Why then is the design of a deterministic transformation such a monumental task? To understand this, let's restate the above problem. Again the file is to contain 1000 logical records. Again the primary keys are integers; *but* each key is a six-digit, nonnegative integer. Observe that the number of six-digit, nonnegative integers is 10^6, or 1,000,000. Hence, the set of the 1000 keys of the logical records could be any subset of these 1,000,000. It is needless to say that even if one knew the keys, and, therefore, their distribution beforehand, then still the values of the keys must be "controllable" as they were in the previous example. Hence, a possible solution would be to allocate 1,000,000 addresses. But then the loading factor is only 0.001%, an unacceptable figure. Moreover, it is difficult to see that deterministic procedures assume *static* files. To see this, note that in the first example, the insertion of a new record with key 1235 would have necessitated both a new transformation and a reloading of the file.

5.2.1 Performance Analysis

Assume a Direct file consisting of NR number of records of address space R and address size B. The physical structure of this file is physical sequential consisting of R blocks. The operation *Retrieve_One* will require exactly one random access, since the access of the target record is done via the address calculated internally by the *KTA*. On the other hand, the operations *Insert_One*, *Delete_One*, and *Update_One* require an additional sequential access needed to rewrite the "updated" block.

As was mentioned earlier, the file structure facilitates sequential processing, specifically at the cost of R sequential block accesses. But the probability that the *KTA* is sequence-preserving is very small. If the operation *Retrieve_All* required the retrieval of records in increasing order of their keys, then the cost of the operation would vary according to the technique used. Two possible techniques are discussed in the following paragraphs.

The first technique requires that the file be sorted before the records are retrieved. One can see that the extra encountered overhead[6] is considerable.

The second technique avoids the sorting of the file by maintaining the underlying physical sequential structure as an ordered sequential file. But the latter structure being ordered sequential implies that the physical location of each stored record is *dependent* on its primary key value but *independent* of the address calculated via the *KTA*. As an example, consider a set of five logical records with

---

[6] For a discussion of external sorting, refer to Chapter 9.

integer keys 10, 12, 14, 3, and 4. Assume an address space of $R = 5$ and address size $B = 1$. In addition, assume that the *KTA* transformation f is defined via

$$f(k) = k \bmod 6$$

It should be easy to see that the transformation f is deterministic and not sequence preserving. For the particular example above, the file structure is presented in Figure 5.1.

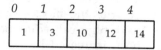

Figure 5.1   The Direct file.

Observe that in order to facilitate sequential processing of the logical records of this file, in increasing order of their keys, the file structure must be of the form illustrated in Figure 5.2.

```
   0    1    2    3    4
 +----+----+----+----+----+
 | 1  | 3  | 10 | 12 | 14 |
 +----+----+----+----+----+
```

Address space

Figure 5.2   The sequential file structure.

If the operation to be performed is *"Retrieve record with key 12,"* then the key will be mapped under our *KTA* to address 0; but as Figure 5.2 illustrates, the logical record has been stored at location 4. Therefore, our claim that the physical storage location of the record is *independent* of the address yielded by the *KTA* has been established. To be able then to retrieve each record randomly and to be able to sequentially process the logical records in increasing order of the keys, the following modifications must be made in the file structure of Figure 5.1.

- First, the logical records are stored in an ordered physical sequential structure as in Figure 5.2.
- Since the records have been relocated, another physical sequential file is created that serves as a look-up table for the file structure developed above. In other words, when a key is mapped into an address, it is the address of a record in the look-up table. Each record in the look-up table consists of just one field which is a pointer to the block that contains the target logical record.

After these modifications Figure 5.3 illustrates the new structure.

The price that has been paid in order to avoid sorting the file consists of two parts; first, extra storage equal to $R \cdot PS$ bytes must be allocated in order to

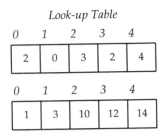

Figure 5.3   The modified Direct file.

facilitate the look-up table; second, extra accesses are needed in order to perform the other operations. Specifically, two random accesses are needed now for the operation *Retrieve_One*, whereas the cost of the operation *Insert_One* has been increased by one extra random access required to access the look-up table plus one sequential access to rewrite the block pointer plus the cost of the operation *Insert_One* in the ordered, physical sequential file. Finally, the cost of the operation *Delete_One* has been increased by just one random access, the access required to access the look-up table.

5.3 HASHING TRANSFORMATIONS

We have seen that the *KTA* transformation maps keys into addresses. In particular, if a set of keys *K* is given, then one obtains a new set of addresses *A* via *KTA(K) = A*. If the distribution of the elements of the generated set *A* is *uniform*, then the transformation *KTA* is the "best" hashing transformation. Assuming an address size of *B*, one can see that under the assumption that the distribution of the generated addresses is uniform, *each* address will receive approximately the *same number* of logical records *m*; in this case, choosing an address size equal to the value of the integer *m* will cause all logical records to be stored in their home addresses, no overflow records will exist,[7] and, more importantly, the loading factor will remain very high.

In the general case, on the other hand, the distribution generated is not necessarily uniform; therefore, overflow records are unavoidable with a direct result of an increase in the average search length of the *Retrieve_One* operation. Hence, in this case there are a number of crucial factors that must be considered in the design phase; these will be discussed below.

Assume that a Hash file of *NR* logical records is to be created, and let *h* be the hashing transformation employed. Then a few critical questions must be answered.

---

[7]Unless, of course, the number of collisions is too great.

1. How many overflow records are anticipated? How are they distributed? How can they be minimized?
2. What is the load factor? How can it be increased?
3. What is the average search[8] length? How can it be minimized?

These three important questions are intertwined; in other words, the choice of a certain parameter will affect the value of another. Some obvious examples are detailed so the reader can achieve a better insight into the interaction between the parameters.

1. Changing the hashing function will necessitate a change in the generated distribution and, therefore, in the number of overflow records.
2. For the same hashing function, h, the number of overflow records can be decreased by choosing a larger address size.
3. By choosing a larger address size for the same address space and hashing function, the load factor decreases and, therefore, the utilization.

5.3.1 The Choice of the Hash Transformation

Recall that in the case of Direct files the mapping KTA generated a uniform distribution. Hence, the answer to the general question, Which of the hashing transformations h_1 or h_2, is best? is determined by which is *closest* to the uniform distribution. Notice that this will lead to an exhaustive search among all possible transformations. Therefore, we adopt the following convention; a hashing transformation is *acceptable* if, and only if, the generated distribution is *better* than the random distribution. In other words, a hashing transformation may be adopted if it yields a better distribution than that of the random distribution. We now consider the random distribution.

5.3.1.1 The Random Distribution.   Under the random distribution one assumes that the addresses returned by the hashing transformation are *random*. In other words, no matter where the current key hashed to, each address has an equal probability of receiving the next record. As an example, consider the case of an address space equal to 100. Then the probability that the next record will hash to address 0 is equal to the probability that the key will hash to address 10, and so on. In other words each location has a probability equal to 0.01 that it will receive the next record. Notice that this probability depends only on the address space and is independent of the address size.

We will show below the following theorem:

Let the address space consist of *NBLK* addresses, let *NR* be the number of the logical records in the file, and let D_h denote the function that for each nonnegative integer

---

[8] Relative to the operation *Retrieve_One* unless otherwise noted.

n returns the *expected number* of addresses that receive *exactly* n logical records under the transformation h. Then if the distribution generated by the hashing transformation h is the random distribution, then $D_h \equiv P$, where

$$P(n) = \binom{NR}{n} \cdot R \cdot \left[\frac{1}{R}\right]^n \cdot \left[1 - \frac{1}{R}\right]^{NR-n} \qquad [5.2]$$

for every nonnegative integer n.

Despite the fact that the above result is well known, we proceed with its proof.

Proof.   Let $S = \{ k_{i_1}, k_{i_2}, k_{i_3}, ..., k_{i_n}\}$ be the keys of an *arbitrary* but fixed subset of n logical records from the set of NR records. We claim that the probability $p(n)$ that only this subset of logical records maps to the same address j is given by

$$p(n) = R \cdot \left[\frac{1}{R}\right]^n \cdot \left[1 - \frac{1}{R}\right]^{NR-n} \qquad [5.3]$$

To prove the claim, let j_0 be an *arbitrary* but fixed address. Clearly the probability that a record is assigned the address j_0 is equal to $1/R$, whereas the probability that a record is assigned some address other than j_0 is equal to $1 - 1/R$). Hence, the probability that all n keys of the set S are mapped to address j_0 is given by $(1/R)^n$, whereas the probability that all other $(NR - n)$ logical records whose keys do not belong to S are assigned addresses other than j_0 is given by $[1 - (1/R)]^{(NR-n)}$. Hence, the probability that only the records with keys in S are assigned the address j_0, whereas all other records are mapped to other addresses is equal to the product of the above two probabilities. In symbols

$$\left[\frac{1}{R}\right]^n \cdot \left[1 - \frac{1}{R}\right]^{(NR-n)}$$

But the address j_0 can take exactly R values; hence, the product of R and the above probability yields the desired probability $p(n)$ and the claim has been established.

Notice now that S is an arbitrary subset of n elements. Since the number of subsets of n elements of the set of NR records is given by

$$\binom{NR}{n}$$

then the desired probability $P(n)$ is given by the product of $p(n)$ and the number of those subsets of length n. In symbols

$$P(n) = \binom{NR}{n} \cdot R \cdot \left[\frac{1}{R}\right]^n \qquad [5.4]$$

The Poisson Distribution.   Below, an approximating equation for $P(n)$ will be derived that will permit an easier computation of the values of $P(n)$. In particular we will show the following:

The random distribution can be approximated by the Poisson distribution. In symbols

$$P(n) \approx \frac{R}{n!} \cdot \left[\frac{NR}{R} \right]^n \cdot e^{-\frac{NR}{R}} \qquad [5.5]$$

for every nonnegative integer n.

Observe that since $NR \gg n$, we obtain that $(NR - n) \approx NR$. Replacing $(NR - n)$ with its approximating value in equation [5.4] yields

$$P(n) = \left[\begin{array}{c} NR \\ n \end{array} \right] \cdot R \cdot \left[\frac{1}{R} \right]^n \cdot \left[1 - \frac{1}{R} \right]^{NR} \qquad [5.6]$$

In addition

$$\left[\begin{array}{c} NR \\ n \end{array} \right] = \frac{NR!}{n! \, (NR - n)!} \qquad [5.7]$$

But

$$\frac{NR!}{(NR - n)!} = NR \cdot (NR - 1) \cdot (NR - 2) \cdots (NR - n + 1) \qquad [5.8]$$

Again, since $(NR - n) \approx NR$, it may be inferred that each term of the product of the right-hand side of the above equation can be approximated by NR; since there are exactly n terms in the product, equation [5.8] yields

$$\frac{NR!}{(NR - n)!} = NR^n \qquad [5.9]$$

Equation [5.7] in view of [5.9] yields

$$\left[\begin{array}{c} NR \\ n \end{array} \right] = \frac{NR^n}{n!} \qquad [5.10]$$

Combining equations [5.6] and [5.10]

$$P(n) = \frac{NR^n}{n!} \cdot R \cdot \left[\frac{1}{R} \right]^n \cdot \left[1 - \frac{1}{R} \right]^{NR} \qquad [5.11]$$

is obtained. Rearranging yields

$$P(n) = \left[\frac{R}{n!} \right] \cdot \left[\frac{NR}{R} \right]^n \cdot \left[1 - \frac{1}{R} \right]^{NR} \qquad [5.12]$$

Comparing equations [5.2] and [5.12], one can see that in order to complete the proof it must be shown that

$$e^{-NR/R} \approx \left(1 - \frac{1}{R}\right)^{NR} \qquad [5.13]$$

To this end one can see that the binomial theorem yields

$$\left(1 - \frac{1}{R}\right)^{NR} = \sum_{v=0}^{NR} \binom{NR}{v} \cdot 1^v \cdot \left(-\frac{1}{R}\right)^{NR-v} \qquad [5.14]$$

Again, as before, it can be shown that

$$\frac{NR!}{v!} \approx \frac{NR^{NR-v}}{v!} \qquad [5.15]$$

and, therefore, equation [5.14] in view of [5.15] yields

$$\left(1 - \frac{1}{R}\right)^{NR} = \sum_{v=0}^{NR} \frac{NR^{NR-v}}{v!} \cdot \left(-\frac{1}{R}\right)^{NR-v} \qquad [5.16]$$

But

$$\sum_{v=0}^{NR} \frac{NR^{NR-v}}{v!} \cdot \left(-\frac{1}{R}\right)^{NR-v} = \sum_{v=0}^{NR} \frac{\left(-\dfrac{NR}{R}\right)^{NR-v}}{v!} \approx \sum_{k=0}^{\infty} \frac{\left(-\dfrac{NR}{R}\right)^{k}}{k!} = e^{-NR/R}$$

and, therefore, the claim has been proved.

It is worth noting that the derived equation indicates that the number of records mapped to a specific address is *independent* of the address size but *dependent* on the address space and the ratio NR/R.

As an example, consider a file of address space equal to $R = 2000$. Let the number of records to be stored in the file be $NR = 1500$. Assuming that the hashing function gives rise to the random distribution, and the equation derived above applies; one obtains

$$P(n) = \frac{2000}{n!} \cdot \left(\frac{1500}{2000}\right)^{n} \cdot e^{-1500/2000} = \left(\frac{2000}{e^{0.75}}\right) \cdot \left(\frac{0.75}{n!}\right)^{n}$$

The above equation for different values of n gives:

$$P(n) \approx \begin{cases} 945 & \text{if } n = 0 \\ 708 & \text{if } n = 1 \\ 266 & \text{if } n = 2 \\ 66 & \text{if } n = 3 \\ 12 & \text{if } n = 4 \\ 02 & \text{if } n = 5 \\ 01 & \text{if } n = 6 \\ 00 & \text{if } n > 6 \end{cases}$$

The above calculations indicate that if the hashing function generates the random distribution, then assuming that $R = 2000$ and $(NR/R) = 0.75$, the keys of the records are mapped in such way so that 945 addresses will receive no records; 708 addresses will receive 1 record; 266 addresses will receive 2 records; 66 addresses will receive 3 records; 12 addresses will receive 4 records; 2 addresses will receive 5 records; and, finally, only 1 address will receive 6 records.

5.3.1.2 The Number of Overflow Records.

It is a simple matter to calculate the number of overflow records, NOR, if the generated distribution function D_h is known. Assume an address size B, and consider the number of addresses that receive an arbitrary but fixed number, j, of logical records. But in order for each such address to receive exactly j overflow records, it must receive a *total* of $B + j$ logical records. We know that the number of addresses that could receive exactly $B + j$ records is equal to $D_h(B + j)$. But each such address will contribute exactly j overflow records; therefore, the total number of overflow records that are contributed from *all* of these addresses is equal to $j \cdot D_h(B + j)$ logical records. But j can take any integer value greater than 0; therefore, the total number of overflow records generated by this hashing function is given by

$$NOR = \sum_{j=1}^{\infty} \left[j \cdot D_h(B+j) \right] \qquad [5.17]$$

The above sum is a finite sum, since the function $D_h(n)$ is a decreasing function of n. Specifically, one can show that there exists a fixed nonnegative integer j_0 that depends on h such that $D_h(i) = 0$ for all integers $i \geq j_0$.

As a numerical example consider the hash file of the previous section. It is assumed that the address size B is equal to 2. Since $D_h=P$, equation [5.17] yields that

$$NOR = \sum_{j=1}^{\infty} \left[j \cdot P(2+j) \right] \qquad [5.18]$$

From the calculated values of $P(n)$, it can be seen that $P(2 + j) > 0$ if and only if $j \leq 4$. Equation [5.18] becomes

$$NOR = \sum_{j=1}^{4} \left[j \cdot P(2+j) \right] = \sum_{j=3}^{6} \left[j \cdot P(j) \right] \qquad [5.19]$$

or, by expanding and substituting,

$$NOR = 3 \cdot P(3) + 4 \cdot P(4) + 5 \cdot P(5) + 6 \cdot P(6) = 3 \cdot 66 + 4 \cdot 12 + 5 \cdot 2 + 6 \cdot 1 = 262$$

5.3.1.3 Address Size and Space, Load Factor.

It should be clear that an increase in either the address size or the address space will yield a decrease in the number of overflow records. But given that the loading factor is denoted by

$$LF = \frac{NR}{R \cdot B} \qquad [5.20]$$

one can see that an increase in either quantity, R or B, will have the unfortunate side effect of a decrease in the magnitude of the load factor and consequently of the utilization. As a matter of fact the magnitude of the utilization is considerably less than that of the load factor. This is due to the fact that calculation of the utilization involves a consideration of the size of the block overhead which is ignored in calculation of the load factor. In practice, a loading factor of less than 0.6 is unacceptable.

The discussion in the previous paragraph indicates that in a number of instances, one would be interested in reducing the number of overflow records but, at the same instant, in maintaining the load factor above an acceptable level. In order for this to be possible the denominator of equation [5.20] must remain less than a fixed quantity α. Each increment in the value of B will require a suitable decrease in the value of R in order for the product $R \cdot B$ to remain less than the desired value α. The question that arises is whether or not such a scheme will affect the number of overflow records. The answer is yes. Recall that equation [5.5] is independent of the address size B, but it is dependent on the ratio NR/R. Observe that a decrease in the value of R causes an increase in the ratio NR/R; therefore, in turn the value of $P(n)$ will be larger for small n than its previous value for each value of $n > 0$. The direct result is that *more* addresses will receive 1, 2, ... records, as opposed to the previous case, in which there is a smaller value of the ratio NR/R. Given that the address size is now larger, each address can accommodate more records than it did previously; that indicates a smaller number of overflow records.

A numerical example will be given to justify empirically the theoretical conclusions drawn in the previous paragraph. The value $NR = 6000$ and eight different values for the address space R ranging from 1000 to 6000 will be used. In addition, for each case an initial address size of one will be used that will be incremented nine times with an increment of one; the hashing function will generate the random distribution. By repeated applications of equations [5.5], [5.17], and [5.20], the quantities (expressed in percentage) of the overflow records and load factor that appear in Table 5.1 are obtained. Notice that an asterisk indicates a nonexistent file structure with corresponding parameters R and B.

Observe any row j of the overflow records portion of Table 5.1. It can be seen that when $R \rightarrow \infty$ or, equivalently, when $(NR/R) \rightarrow 0$, then the number of overflow records decreases. Similarly, each column k of the same table indicates that when $B \rightarrow \infty$, the number of overflow records decreases again. But the corresponding row (j) and column (k) of the Load Factor portion of Table 5.1 indicate that the load factor decreases simultaneously. If the present situation is $NR/R = 1.20$ and $B = 1$, then with the use of the tables in Table 5.1 one can see that $LF = 60.0$ and that approximately 33% of the logical records of the file overflow. If the address size B is *increased* to 5 and the address space is *decreased* in such a way that $NR/R = 3.0$, then the same tables again indicate that the percent of overflow records has been *reduced* to 4.46, whereas the loading factor *remains* at 60 percent.

TABLE 5.1 The effect of the address size B and the address space R on the load factor and on the number of overflow records, assuming random distribution of the addresses over a file of NR = 3000 logical records.

	Overflow Records (%)							
	Ratio (NR/R)							
B	0.50	0.75	0.86	1.00	1.20	1.50	2.00	3.00
1	21.32	29.63	29.63	32.81	36.74	*	*	*
2	28.00	6.53	8.08	10.29	13.65	18.65	27.00	*
3	0.39	1.13	1.57	2.27	3.60	5.91	10.82	22.39
4	0.03	0.17	0.25	0.40	0.79	1.56	3.69	10.62
5	0.00	0.03	0.03	0.05	0.15	0.34	1.07	4.46
6	0.00	0.00	0.00	0.00	0.03	0.05	0.26	1.66
7	0.00	0.00	0.00	0.00	0.00	0.00	0.04	0.55
8	0.00	0.00	0.00	0.00	0.00	0.00	0.00	0.15
9	0.00	0.00	0.00	0.00	0.00	0.00	0.00	0.03
10	0.00	0.00	0.00	0.00	0.00	0.00	0.00	0.00

	Loading Factor (%)							
	Ratio (NR/R)							
B	0.50	0.75	0.86	1.00	1.20	1.50	2.00	3.00
1	50.00	75.00	85.71	100.00	*	*	*	*
2	25.00	37.50	42.86	50.00	60.00	75.00	100.00	*
3	16.67	25.00	28.57	33.33	40.00	50.00	66.67	100.00
4	12.50	18.75	21.43	25.00	30.00	37.50	50.00	75.00
5	10.00	15.00	17.14	20.00	24.00	30.00	40.00	60.00
6	8.33	12.50	14.29	16.67	20.00	25.00	33.33	50.00
7	7.14	10.71	12.24	14.29	17.14	21.43	28.57	42.86
8	6.25	9.38	10.71	12.50	15.00	18.75	25.00	37.50
9	5.56	8.33	9.52	11.11	13.33	16.67	22.22	33.33
10	5.00	7.50	8.57	10.00	12.00	15.00	20.00	30.00

5.3.2 A Collection of Hashing Transformations

Recall that our goal is to select a hashing function so the generated distribution is better than random. The three most widely used hashing functions, *digit analysis*, *division method*, and *radix transformation*, are presented and discussed in the following paragraphs.

5.3.2.1 Digit Analysis.

The digit analysis method is applied whenever the distribution of the primary keys is known. This method will be explained by an example. Assume a set of $NR = 10000$ records and that the largest key consists of exactly six digits. The first step is the determination of the frequency of

TABLE 5.2 Digit analysis of 10,000 six-digit primary keys.

	Frequency Table					
	Digit Position within Key					
Digit	1	2	3	4	5	6
0	50	1008	54	970	3005	1000
1	950	1012	876	999	10	900
2	2000	999	1345	1056	98	1050
3	1000	997	134	892	199	950
4	0	996	765	1098	1103	1020
5	10	993	1002	1087	1714	980
6	0	1003	18	988	264	995
7	990	987	2875	993	951	1005
8	3000	996	1402	1049	453	930
9	2000	1009	1529	868	2203	1070

each possible digit 0 through 9 in each fixed digit position j of the primary key for $j = 1, 2, 3, ..., 6$. The result is presented in Table 5.2. Assuming now an address space of 999, it can be seen that three digits must be selected to form an address. Closer examination indicates that the digit positions 2, 4, and 6 exhibit the most uniform distribution from the six digit positions. Hence, given any key the hashing transformation will map it into the address formed from the three digits from positions 2, 4, and 6; as an example, the key 784572 will be mapped to the address 852.

5.3.2.2 Division Method.

The division method employs the transformation that maps a key x to an address that is equal to the remainder of the division of the key by a *fixed* positive integer m. In symbols, $x \to x \bmod m$. Notice that the remainder of the division of x by the integer m is always less than m; therefore, m must be carefully selected in such a way that it minimizes the collisions and, in turn, the number of overflow records. For example, for an address space R of 1000 addresses a choice of m such as 11 will yield an unreasonably large number of collisions because all records will have home addresses from 0 to 10. It should be clear that if the integer m is prime then the collisions are minimized. In particular, if the prime m is chosen to be the smallest prime number that is equal to or exceeds the address space, then one can see that the range of the transformation can be greater than the address space. In that case one of the methods that will be presented in the following paragraphs may be employed to map the located address to an address in the range of the address space.

Notice that this method preserves whatever uniformity exists among the keys of the logical records. Consider again an address space R of 100 and m equal to 53; then one can see that all logical records with primary keys from 5300 to 5352 are mapped into the addresses from 0 to 52, respectively. On the other hand, if the keys are distributed in a nonuniform fashion, then the address distribution is worse than random.

This section closes by noting that it has been observed that another satisfactory choice for the integer m is an odd integer whose prime factors are greater than 20.

5.3.2.3 Radix Transformation. It was noted earlier that the prime division method in the case of non-uniform keys usually generates an address distribution that is worse than random. In such cases the *radix transformation*, which usually yields distributions very close to random, is employed. This method utilizes a mapping that maps the decimal key to an address by considering the decimal number to be a number represented in another base, usually 11.

> Example. Consider the decimal key 326. Then that key is mapped to address 391, as the following computation indicates.
>
> $$3 \cdot 11^2 + 2 \cdot 11^1 + 6 \cdot 11^0 = 391$$

The use of the discussed hashing transformations could generate addresses that are outside the address space. In these cases another transformation can be applied that aims to "shorten" those addresses. These transformations are discussed briefly below; we also note that in a number of instances they can serve as stand-alone hashing transformations.

5.3.2.4 Truncation Method. The truncation method is a variation of the division method and consists of dividing each key x with an integer m where m is equal to some integral power of 10. In symbols

$$x \to x \bmod m, \text{ where } m = 10^n$$

This method provides one with $(n-1)$-digit addresses; it also preserves the uniformity of the keys. It is worth noting that the generated distribution is not as uniform as the one provided by the division method; this is due to the fact that the high-order digits of the primary key do not contribute in the calculation of the resulting address.

> Example. Using this method and with hashing function $f(x) = x \bmod 10^3$, the key 12365 will hash to address 365, whereas the key 1001322 will hash to 322.

5.3.2.5 Midsquare Method. Under the midsquare method, the calculated address is influenced by all digits of the primary key. Specifically, the mapping is the composition of two mappings; the first maps the key to its square; then the second mapping extracts a fixed number of digits (usually equal to the number of digits that form the address) from the middle of the key.

> Example. Consider the key 1845 and an address space of 100000. The first mapping maps the key to $1845^2 = 3404025$. The second mapping should extract five digits from the middle of the key; therefore, the key is mapped to the address 40402.

In certain instances, in order to scramble the result further, the number formed by the nonextracted digits is added to the extracted number in order to form the address. For instance, this method would cause the key 1845 of the previous example to be mapped to the address 35 + 40402 = 40437.

5.3.2.6 Shift Folding.   The advantage of the shift folding method is that all digits of the key participate in the formation of the address. Particularly, the given key is partitioned from left to right in a number of subnumbers, each of which, except possibly the last one, contains as many digits as the number of digits of the required address. Then all these sub-numbers are added together to form the required address. In the case in which the sum produces a carry out of the high-order digit, then either the carry is discarded or it is added to the result.

> Example: Consider the key 93876542319 and an address space of 1000. The four subnumbers 938, 765, 423, and 19 are formed. The required address is found by adding these four numbers; in particular, if it is assumed that the carry is discarded, then the key is mapped to 145; otherwise, it is mapped to 147.

5.3.2.7 Boundary Folding.   Notice that in the above method the key is formed by adding the extracted subnumbers. Since addition usually preserves patterns, the following variation method, called boundary folding, is sometimes used to scramble the result further; the first and last subnumbers, the boundary subnumbers, are reversed just prior to the addition. As an example, the key of the previous example will be mapped to the address 839 + 765 + 423 + 910, which yields either 937 or 939, depending on the method employed in handling the carry out of the high-order digit position.

5.3.3 Loading a Hash File

Assume that it has been decided that the address space is R, the address size is B, and the appropriate hashing transformation h has been selected. In this section the two possible ways by which the hash file $HASH$ can be loaded or equivalently created are detailed. It can be assumed that all logical records of the file have been punched on cards, which will constitute the physical sequential file $CARDS$.

5.3.3.1 Direct Loading.   If *direct* loading is employed, each logical record of the file $CARDS$ is read, its primary key k is hashed via the hashing transformation to an address $h(k)$, the corresponding block of the file $HASH$ is accessed, and its contents are examined. If the block is not full, the record is inserted there; otherwise, the current logical record is written out to a physical sequential file $OVLOW$. This process is repeated until all logical records (cards) have been read. At this point the file $HASH$ contains no overflow records, and all such records are contained in the $OVLOW$ file. The next step is the loading of those latter records; the method that is followed depends on the overflow management technique employed. The above steps are illustrated in Figure 5.4.

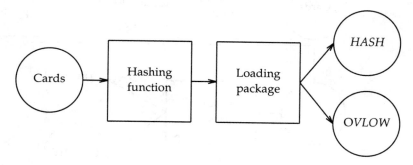

Figure 5.4   Direct loading of a hash file.

    5.3.3.2 Sequential Loading.   If *sequential* loading is utilized, each logical record of the file *CARDS* is read, its primary key k is hashed via the hashing transformation to an address $h(k)$, the latter address is inserted into a newly introduced field of the logical record, and the new logical record is written to a physical sequential file *REGN*. When all logical records of the file *CARDS* have been read, then the logical records of the file *REGN* are sorted in increasing order of the "address" field, and the records are written out to the physical sequential file *SORTED*. Then the logical records of the *SORTED* file are read in a sequential fashion; the nonoverflow records are written in their home addresses in the *HASH* file; and the overflow records are written out to the *OVLOW* file. Finally, the records of the latter file are loaded according to the overflow management technique employed. The above-defined steps are illustrated in the form of a diagram in Figure 5.5.

5.3.4 Overflow Management Techniques

In this section certain available techniques are described that are designed to handle the overflow problem.

    5.3.4.1 Open Addressing.   When a collision occurs in open addressing, the blocks in the address space are searched from the home address to which the logical record was hashed until a free address space is found, where the record is inserted. There are two ways that this search can be performed; each will be examined in turn.

    Linear Search.   Consider the following situation. A hash file with address space R equal to 13 and address size B equal to 1 has just been loaded with three logical records of keys 13, 6, 25, and 9, respectively. Assume that the hashing

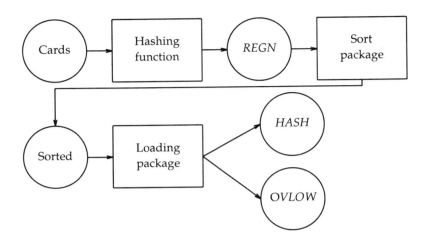

Figure 5.5 Sequential loading of a hash file.

transformation, h, is given by $h(k) = k$ mod 13. At this stage no overflow records are present; the situation is illustrated in Figure 5.6.

0	1	2	3	4	5	6	7	8	9	10	11	12
13						6			9			25

Figure 5.6 The *HASH* file.

Now assume that a request for inserting a logical record with key 26 has been issued. The key is hashed via the hashing mapping to address 0, but block number 0 is full, since it is occupied by the synonym logical record with key number 13. The new record, therefore, is an overflow record. Under the linear search[9] each and every subsequent location starting from the ,home address of the logical record is examined until an empty slot is found. In this case the first empty slot is at location 1; therefore, the record is inserted there. If the next request is "*insert logical record with key 64*", then the new record collides with the record with key 25. In that case a new linear search is initiated starting at location 12. Since block 12 is the last block of the file, a wrap-around to the beginning of the file is performed, and the linear search is resumed from that location. Clearly, then the new logical record must be inserted at location 2. Figure 5.7 illustrates the *HASH* file after the insertion of two new records; the algorithm, in pseudocode form, is given in Table 5.3.

The reader should be wondering what would happen if the next request is for an insertion of the logical record with key number 27. This key will be

---

[9] Often referred to as linear probing.

0	1	2	3	4	5	6	7	8	9	10	11	12
13	26	64				6			9			25

Figure 5.7   The *HASH* file after the insertion of two logical records with keys (in this order) 26 and 64, respectively.

TABLE 5.3   The insert algorithm (linear search).

```
Algorithm Insert;

Home_Address ← h(k);
i ← Home_Address;
Found ← False;
while ( (location i is full) and (not Found) ) do
     {i ← (i+1) mod (address space);
        if (i = Home_Address) then Found ← True;}
if (Found) then write('file full')
            else insert record in location i;
```

mapped to address 1; but that address is occupied by the logical record with key 26. *But* the latter record is an overflow record, or, equivalently, the home address of the record with key 27 is occupied by a logical record that is *not* a synonym. The direct result is that the new record should be treated as an overflow record, whereas it is not. Therefore, one could jump to the conclusion that the average search length would increase unnecessarily in this case, since more than one access is required for the insertion of the new record. Hence, a possible remedy would be that in the case in which the home address of a record is occupied by a record that belongs to a different home address, then the latter record is "pumped" to the nearest empty location (found by a linear search), and the new record is inserted in its home address. Figure 5.8 indicates the two file structures as a result of the two different insert algorithms.

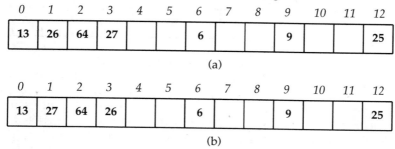

0	1	2	3	4	5	6	7	8	9	10	11	12
13	26	64	27			6			9			25

(a)

0	1	2	3	4	5	6	7	8	9	10	11	12
13	27	64	26			6			9			25

(b)

Figure 5.8   The *HASH* file after insertion of the logical record with key 27 (a) without "pump" and (b) with pump.

With the new insert routine, the number of overflow records is reduced but at extra computational cost required by the new insert routine. The question of whether or not that extra overhead cost is beneficial depends on whether or not the average search length for the *Retrieve_One* operation has been improved.

Let's calculate the average search length for each case. Table 5.4 indicates that the average search length in both cases is equal to [(8 *rba* + 5 *sba*)/7], which indicates no improvement whatsoever.

TABLE 5.4 The required accesses for retrieval of each logical record under the two different "insert" algorithms.

Record Key	No Pump Accesses	Pump Accesses
6	1 *rba*	1 *rba*
9	1 *rba*	1 *rba*
13	1 *rba*	1 *rba*
25	1 *rba*	1 *rba*
26	1 *rba* + 1 *sba*	1 *rba* + 3 *sba*
27	1 *rba* + 2 *sba*	1 *rba*
64	2 *rba* + 2 *sba*	2 *rba* + 2 *sba*

It should be clear that a new insertion affects the average search length. In particular, the search length could either increase or decrease. If the new record is not an overflow record, then the search length decreases; but if the record to be inserted is an overflow record, then the search length will increase provided that its *displacement* (the distance between the block where the record is to be inserted and its home address block) is sufficiently large. As an example, consider the file *HASH* where the logical records have been inserted in the following order: 13, 9, 25, 26, 64, 27, 17, 31, 42, 40, 23, and 24. Assuming the simple insertion algorithm, the file is illustrated in Figure 5.9.

0	1	2	3	4	5	6	7	8	9	10	11	12
13	26	64	27	17	31	42	40		9	23	24	25

Figure 5.9 The *HASH* file after the insertion of nine logical records with keys (in this order) 13, 9, 25, 26, 64, 27, 17, 31, 42, 40, 23, and 24.

It should be easy to see that the average search length is equal to [(14 *rba* + 5 *sba*)/12]. If the key of the new record to be inserted hashes to location 8, then the average search length is given by [(15 *rba* + 5 *sba*)/13], which is less than the previous search length. On the other hand, if the key of the new record to be inserted hashes to location 9, then the average search length increases to [(16 *rba* + 15 *sba*)/13].[10]

[10]Given the relatively small size of this file we can see that the file can be stored in just one cylinder; therefore, in terms of I/O time, 1 *rba* = 1 *sba*.

At any rate one can conclude that if deletion operations are considered, then the average search length increases as the loading factor approaches 1.0, since at initial loading most of the records have been loaded at their home addresses, but the deletions would have removed a considerable number of records from their home addresses.

The Delete_One Operation   Up to this point calculations of the average search length for the *Retrieve_One* operation did not consider the situation in which a number of records have been deleted from the file.

It should be clear that deletion of a record consists (as before) of flagging the record. This suggests that an extra flag field, *empty_flag*, must be allocated per logical record, and it is set whenever the corresponding logical record is deleted. *But* as the reader should have noticed, with this method subsequent *Retrieve_One* requests for certain logical records could yield erroneous *"record not found"* diagnostics. Consider the hash file of Figure 5.10(a) and the same file, Figure 5.10(b), after deletion of the logical record with key 26.

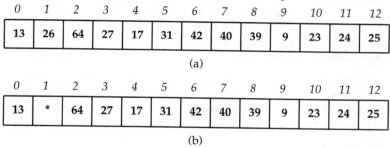

(a)

(b)

Figure 5.10   The *HASH* file (a) before and (b) after deletion of the logical record with key 26. The asterisk indicates a flagged record.

If the next operation to be performed is *retrieve record with key 26*, then the first location to be examined is location 0. Since this location is occupied, the next location, location 1, must be examined. But location 1 is empty; therefore, the search for the record should be suspended, since under the linear search method the overflow record with key 26 would have been expected to be in that location. Hence, one approach would be to let the search examine every location, which would lead to an unacceptable number of accesses; in the case in which the record did not in fact exist, the entire file would have to be searched. Instead, the following scheme is employed. An extra field, *Block_Flag*, is allocated per block that is set in addition to the *Empty_Flag* flag whenever a record is deleted. In this way an unsuccessful search for the retrieval of a record is recognized and subsequently terminated whenever a location is encountered in which the *Block_Flag* is not raised. Notice that the insert algorithms must be modified in order to take advantage of this modification in record and block structures.

We close this section by discussing the phenomenon of *primary clustering* exhibited by the linear search, which as we will see shortly , leads to a relatively large average search length for retrieval of the records. This phenomenon is based on the fact that when two keys are hashed to addresses that are "close" to each other, then the two corresponding logical records will *compete* for the same storage locations. For example, assume an address space of 10, an address size of 1, and an initially empty file. Notice that the probability, p_j, that the first insertion will be inserted into location j for $j = 0, 1, ..., 9$ is equal to 0.1. Assume now that the first record was inserted at location 0; the probability p_1 that the second record will be inserted at location 1 is then twice as great as the probability p_j that the record will be inserted in any of the positions $j = 2, 3, ..., 9$, because the record will be inserted there in either of the cases hashed at location 0 or 1. Continuing in this fashion one can see that a long sequence of successive full locations tends to become longer. In particular, when the load factor approaches 1.0, the sequences become so long that overflow records are stored further and further away from their home addresses, with the direct result that unacceptably large average search lengths are required for all operations such as *Insert_One*, *Delete_One*, and *Retrieve_One*.

The problem of primary clustering is addressed by *random probing*, or equivalently, *non-linear search*, which will be discussed in the next section.

Nonlinear Search.   Under this method, the linear search method is replaced by a non-linear search. There are a number of different methods that fall into this category, and here only two of them will be discussed: *rehashing* and *double hashing* methods.

Rehashing.   Reheashing employs a second hashing function, *r*, referred to as the *rehashing function*, which is chosen in such a way that it generates a random (and not a successor) address where a record that overflows from its home address would attempt to be stored. In the event that the newly generated location is full, the rehashing function is employed to generate a new random address. This process is repeated as many times as is necessary until an available location or a full file is detected. The latter condition would be detected in the event that the function *r* generated the home address of the record at hand.

If *h* and *r* denote the hashing and the rehashing function, respectively, and if *k* denotes the key of a logical record that is to be inserted into the Hash file, then the algorithm appearing in Table 5.5, in pseudocode form, illustrates the mechanism discussed in the previous paragraph.

It should be clear that a "good" rehashing routine must satisfy the following requirements:

1. It must generate addresses in a random fashion.
2. It must examine each and every location of the address space.

TABLE 5.5. The insert algorithm (rehashing method.)

```
Algorithm Insert;

Home_Address ← h(k);
i ← Home_Address;
Found ← False;
while ( (location i is full) and (not Found) ) do
      {i ← r(i);
         if (i = Home_Address) then Found ← True;}
if (Found) then write('file full')
            else insert record in location i;
```

Consider the following example. Assume that the address space R is equal to 100 and that the address size B is equal to 1. Moreover, assume that immediately after the initial loading, all addresses of the form $2 \cdot j$ for $j = 0, 1, ..., 49$ are occupied by logical records, whereas all remaining addresses are empty. Assume that the rehashing function r is defined by

$$r(i) = (i + 4) \bmod 100$$

If a request is made for a logical record to be inserted and if its key is hashed to an even address, $i = 2n$, then the record is an overflow record. The rehashing function r is applied to location i and yields $(2n + 4) \bmod 100$. Independent of the value of the nonnegative integer n, the expression $(2n + 4)$ is equal to some even number; therefore, the remainder of its division by 100 will yield an even address. In short, any subsequently generated address using the rehashing function r will yield an even address; eventually, in view of the algorithm in Table 5.5, a full file will erroneously be detected. Hence, this rehashing function is an unacceptable one. A moment's reflection is enough to convince one that the reason the irregularity arose is that the numbers $p = 4$ and $q = 100$ have a common factor. Therefore, all such problems could be resolved if one were to pick the integers p and q such that $(p, q) = 1$; in other words, p and q are relatively prime. Hence, an acceptable choice would have been a function such as

$$r(i) = (i+3) \bmod 100$$

Double Hashing.   If the rehashing function is chosen carefully, then the primary clustering problem can be resolved, but another drawback appears, namely, the phenomenon of *secondary clustering*. Specifically, when two keys are hashed to the *same* location, they compete for the same random addresses generated by the primary rehashing function. This problem is addressed via a number of different ingenious schemes; one of these will be detailed here, the *double rehashing* method. Using this method in addition to the *primary hashing* function, h_1, a second hashing function, h_2, referred to as the *secondary hashing* function, is employed. In the case of an overflow record with key k, the rehashing function r is used to generate random locations. Recall that the rehashing function is given by

$$r(i) = (i + q) \bmod p$$

But in this case the term q is not constant; instead, it is selected in such a way so that $q = h_2(k)$. As an example consider an address space of 12, an address size of 1, and the following functions.

$$h_1(k) = k \bmod 13, h_2(k) = k \ (\bmod \ 7)+1, \qquad r(i) = (i + h_2(k)) \bmod 13 \quad [5.21]$$

Also assume that location number 3 is occupied. Then both logical records with keys 16 and 3 will collide at address 3. The sequence of locations that will be generated by the rehashing function for the record with key 16 will be generated according to the rehashing function $r(i) = (i + h_2(16)) \bmod 13$, or equivalently by $r(i) = (i + 3) \bmod 13$, which yields

$$6, 9, 12, 2, 5, 8, 11, 1, 4, 7, 10, 0, 3$$

whereas the sequence of locations that will be generated by the rehashing function for the record with key 3 will be generated according to $r(i) = (i + h_2(3)) \bmod 13$, or $r(i) = (i + 4) \bmod 13$, which yields

$$7, 11, 2, 6, 10, 1, 5, 9, 0, 4, 8, 12, 3$$

So one can see that the secondary clustering problem has been solved. In addition, the following example indicates the improvement in performance of the *Retrieve_One* operation attained by using this method. In Figure 5.11 the *HASH* file of the previous section is illustrated under the transformations of equation [5.20].

0	1	2	3	4	5	6	7	8	9	10	11	12
13	64	26		17	31	42	40	27	9	23	24	25

Figure 5.11 The *HASH* file after the insertion of nine logical records with keys (in this order) 13, 9, 25, 26, 64, 27, 17, 31, 42, 40, 23, and 24.

Notice that only (15/12) *sba* are needed on the average for the *Retrieve_One* operation compared to (19/12) *sba* that were required by using the linear search method.

This section closes by noting that the use of the nonlinear search method solves the clustering problem. However, there is a considerable increase in the cost of the operation *Delete_One* to the point that for all practical purposes, this method is unacceptable in an environment where the frequency of delete operations is high.

5.3.4.2 Chaining. The major disadvantage of the open addressing technique is that the required search length for the operation *Delete_One* is so high that it is practically unacceptable. A remedy to this problem would be a method in which the overflow records from a specific, fixed address could easily be identified. One popular technique that accomplishes this is one involving chaining the overflow records from an address with their home address via pointers.

By using this method the storage area can conceptually be thought of as comprising two "areas". The first area consists of all blocks that accommodate *home records* (i.e., records in their home addresses), and the second area consists of all of the blocks that contain overflow records. The former area is referred to as the *primary area* whereas the latter is referred to as the *overflow area*. There are two different techniques; each is based on whether or not the overflow area is a "part" of the primary area, and each will be examined in turn below.

Coalesced Chaining.   The coalesced chaining method uses the blocks of an address space R in such a way that they accommodate both home records and overflow records. We will examine this method by discussing separately the two distinct cases that may arise.

Address Size Equal to 1.   As remarked above, since the physical file is used both as a primary and as an overflow area, then this implies that all blocks will have address size equal to 1. When an overflow record is to be inserted, an empty block is allocated and the record is inserted there. Notice that in order to facilitate the allocation of a new block, all nonfull blocks are maintained in an ordered (according to their home address) circular linked list, and the pointer to the beginning of this list *Free_Chain* pointer is saved. When an overflow record is to be inserted the record is placed in the block pointed to by the *Free_Chain* pointer; the home address is linked to that block via an internal to the home records pointer; and, if the latter block reaches its capacity, that block is removed from the free chain and the *Free_Chain* pointer is reset to the next nonfull block.

Notice that in our case there is the possibility that when a record is hashed to an address i, the address is occupied by an overflow record from another home address. In order then for the application program to know the situation that exists, an extra *Block_Pointer* is allocated per block that serves as the *header* pointer to the list of records that collide at this address. Figure 5.12 illustrates the structure of each block.

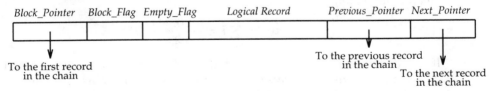

Figure 5.12   The structure of each block of a hash file with address size equal to 1 and coalesced chaining overflow technique. The fields *Previous_Pointer, Next_Pointer*, and *Empty_Flag* are attached to the logical record.

Returning to the case in which the home address of a logical record is occupied by an overflow record from a different home address, the insert routine can be modified in order to maintain ordered chains. In particular the overflow record should be deleted and inserted in the next available block; the pointer field of its "predecessor" logical record in the chain emanating from its home address should be updated in such way that it points to this block; and the new record should be placed in its vacated home block. Furthermore, when a record is deleted its chain must repaired in such a way that no empty slots are present in this list that would affect the search length of subsequent retrievals. Specifically, if the record was deleted from its home address, then the "next" record from its list must be inserted into its home address, the pointers must be reset accordingly, and the now-vacated block must be inserted into the *free_chain* list. The previously suggested operations require a considerable amount of overhead in the case of the two basic operations *Insert_One* and *Delete_One*. But the lists are maintained so that the average length of future *Retrieve_One* operations in this file is performed with the minimum possible search length.

The points stated in the previous paragraph are illustrated in Figure 5.13. Specifically, a Hash file employing the hashing function $h(x) = x$ mod 13, coalesced chaining overflow technique, an address size of 1, and an address space of 12 is created in each case (whether chains are maintained or not). It is assumed that the keys of the logical records are arriving in the following order: 13, 26, 0, 1, 14, 17, 15, 16, 19, and 31. An exercise for the reader will be to verify the file structures of Figure 5.13 and also to verify that the average search length improves from 2.1 to 1.4 by maintaining ordered chains. The insert algorithm is given in Table 5.6.

It is a rather simple matter now to calculate the average search length for the operation *Retrieve_One* under the assumption that the chains are maintained as indicated above. To this end consider a chain of n records. It should be clear that the number of random accesses required to retrieve the first record of the chain is equal to 1 and that the number required to retrieve the second record independently is equal to 2. Continuing in this fashion we obtain that the number of random accesses required to access the ith record of this chain is equal to i *rba*. Then the total number of accesses $\tau(n)$ required to retrieve all records of this chain independently is given by

$$\tau(n) = \sum_{i=1}^{n} i = \frac{n \cdot (n+1)}{2} \quad rba \qquad [5.22]$$

If the distribution function generated by the employed hashing function h is denoted by D_h, then we have seen that the number of chains containing exactly n records is given by $D_h(n)$; therefore, the total number of accesses required to access all logical records from all overflow chains that contain exactly n records is

$$D_h(n) \cdot \tau(n) \quad rba$$

Hence, the number of accesses to access all records in the file is

$$\sum_{n=1}^{\infty} \left[D_h(n) \cdot \tau(n) \right] \quad rba$$

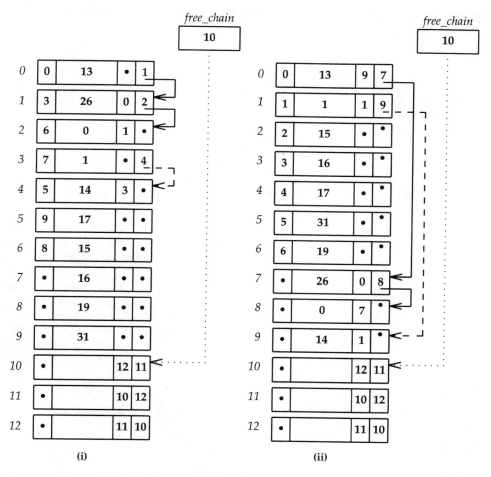

Figure 5.13   Coalesced chaining (i) without and (ii) with chain repair.

By taking into account equation [5.22], we obtain the *average search length*

$$ASL\,[Retrieve\_One\,,H] = \sum_{n=1}^{\infty} \frac{n \cdot (n+1) \cdot D_h(n)}{2 \cdot NR} \;\; rba$$

We close this section by noting that the cost of the operations *Delete_One* and *Insert_One* can be found by adding to the above cost the overhead required for the maintenance of ordered linked lists. The second case follows.

Address Size Greater than 1.   Observe that the fundamental difference between this case and the one just discussed is that there exists the possibility that a home address i could contain logical records whose home address is i and also logical records that overflow from another home address j with $i \neq j$.

TABLE 5.6 Coalesced Chaining (*B* = *1*) : the Insert algorithm. The algorithm *Repair_Free_Chain* is given in Table 5.7.

```
Algorithm Insert;

if Free_Chain = Nil then write('file full') and exit;
Home_Address ← h(k);
Save ← Home_Address;
if (Save.Block_Flag = False)
  then
      {Save.Block_Pointer ← Save;
       Repair_Free_Chain(Free_Chain,Save);
       Save.Previous ← Nil}
  else
      {if (Save.Block_Pointer = nil) then
                                      {Save.Block_Pointer ← Free_Chain;
                                       Save ← Free_Chain;
                                       Repair_Free_Chain(Free_Chain,Save);
                                       Save.Previous ← Nil}
                                else
                                    {Last ← Save.Block_Pointer;
                                     while (Last ≠ nil) do
                                            {Save ← Last;
                                             Last ← Save.Next_Pointer;}
                                     Last ← Save;
                                     Save ← Free_Chain;
                                     Last.Previous.Next ← Save
                                     Repair_Free_Chain(Free_Chain,Save);}}
Save.Next ← Nil;
Save.Block_Flag ← True;
insert the logical record in location save;
exit;
```

TABLE 5.7 The Repair_Free_Chain Algorithm.

```
Algorithm Repair_Free_Chain(Free_Chain, Save);
Length(Free_Chain) = Length(Free_Chain) - 1;
if (Length(Free_Chain) = 0) then Free_Chain ← Nil
                       else
                           {if ( Free_Chain = Save ) then Free_Chain ← Save.next
                            Save.Previous.Next ← Free_Chain;
                            Save.Next.Previous ← Save.Previous;}
exit;
```

Moreover, there is the possibility that subsequent records that are mapped by the hashing function to address *i* will be treated as overflow records from address *i*. This is because certain slots of the block number *i* will contain logical records whose home addresses are different than *i*. Again the remedy is the dedication of some extra computational overhead required to maintain ordered chains as often as possible. Figure 5.14 illustrates a Hash file with address space 7 and address size 3, with a hashing function defined by *h(k)* = *k* mod 7, and with an

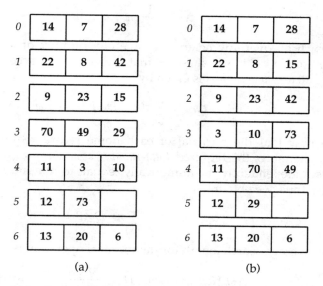

Figure 5.14 Coalesced Chaining   (a) without and (b) with chain
repair.

overflow management technique of coalesced chaining. The keys of the logical
records according to the order of their arrival are 14, 7, 9, 22, 8, 28, 42, 23, 15, 70,
13, 20, 6, 49, 11, 29, 12, 3, 10, and 73. It is worth noting that the total number of
accesses required in order to retrieve all records of this file is 32 and 26 accesses
for cases (a) and (b) of Figure 5.14, respectively, which indicates that the savings
in access time is considerable.

The derivation of the average search length for the retrieval operation is
quite involved mathematically. Hence, the *maximum* possible search length, i.e.,
the average search length for the worst case, will be derived below. Then for a
practical analysis, we will know that the *ASL* is never greater than the worst case.

It should be clear that the worst case will be obtained when the n overflow
records associated with an address are not clustered together or in the extreme
case when each of those overflow records is stored in a different block.

To access the first record from this chain of overflow records, two random
accesses are needed; one will be needed to access the home block and one to
access the "overflow" block. With the same reasoning it should be easy to see
that the access of the jth record of this overflow chain will require $j + 1$ random
accesses. Hence, the total number of accesses $\tau(n)$ required to access all logical
records of such a chain independently is given by

$$\tau(n) = \sum_{j=1}^{n}(j+1) = \left[\sum_{j=2}^{(n+1)} j\right] = \left[\sum_{j=1}^{(n+1)} j\right] - 1 = \left[\frac{(n+1)\cdot(n+2)}{2}\right] - 1 \quad rba$$

or, by simplifying,

$$\tau(n) = \frac{1}{2} \cdot n \cdot (n + 3) \quad rba \qquad [5.23]$$

Since such an overflow chain can have any number of logical records greater than or equal to 1, it is easy to see that the number of accesses, α_{OR}, required to retrieve all *overflow records* is given by

$$\alpha_{OR} = \sum_{n=1}^{\infty} \tau(n) \cdot D_h(B + n) \quad rba \qquad [5.24]$$

Notice now that the retrieval of each home record requires just one random access; therefore, the required *total number of accesses, α_{NOF}*, to access all home records independently is numerically equal to the number of those home records; thus, we obtain

$$\alpha_{NOF} = NR - \sum_{n=1}^{\infty} n \cdot D_h(B + n) \quad rba$$

and the average search length for the retrieval operation is given by

$$ASL\,[Retrieve\_One,\,H] = \frac{[\alpha_{NOF} + \alpha_{OR}]}{NR} \quad rba$$

It is a relatively easy matter to find a lower bound for the average search length; specifically, the lower bound is obtained for the value of the average search length that applies in the *best case*. The derivation of this quantity is left as an exercise for the reader.

Separate Overflow Area. This technique does not employ the overflow area as a part of the primary area. In other words, the home addresses are reserved exclusively for home records; similarly, the overflow area consists of blocks whose addresses are reserved exclusively for records that overflow from the home addresses. Such a scheme can be implemented in one of two ways: The overflow area is allocated to the same file as that of the primary area, or the overflow area can be allocated to a different file other than the one in the primary area. The latter technique is referred to as separate file overflow area technique in order to distinguish it from the former. The distinct advantage of the separate file overflow technique is that a different address size can be used for the overflow area than that of the primary area.

Independent of the technique used, management of the overflow records must be decided. One possible scheme is that the overflow records be maintained in a chained fashion and, moreover, that overflow blocks be reserved exclusively for records that overflow from the *same* home address. The latter remark ensures that there would never be a case in which an overflow block would contain two records that are not synonyms. Whether or not the chains are repaired depends on the type and the frequency of the operations. In Figure 5.15 the separate file overflow area technique is illustrated over the same file as in Figure 5.14. Notice that the policy implemented is that overflow blocks are reserved for synonyms.

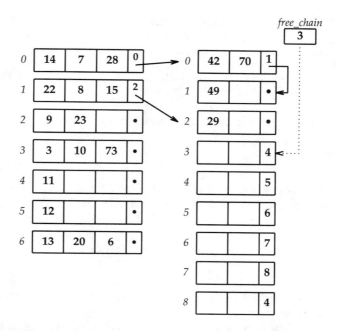

Figure 5.15 Separate file overflow method. Observe that the address size of the primary file is 3, whereas that of the overflow file is 2; also, not all links are shown.

The Average Search Length.   Assume a Hash file with address space R, which employs the separate file overflow area technique and which has an address size for both the primary and overflow file equal to B; the hashing function h will generate a distribution given by D_h.

The worst case occurs when, as a result of a large number of insertions and deletions, the records are stored in such a way that the home address is full, while all other synonyms can be found in the overflow area; in particular, there will be *just* one overflow record per address. The computation of the average search length for this case parallels that of the worst case of coalesced chaining with an address size equal to one and is left as an exercise for the reader.

We will concentrate now on deriving the *lower bound* for the average search length—i.e., the average search length for the best case. The best case occurs when *no empty* record slots exist in each and every block chain corresponding to a home address—in other words, when the synonyms are clustered together. Figure 5.16 illustrates such a typical chain. Consider such a typical chain with n overflow records. Closer examination of Figure 5.16 indicates that the total number of overflow blocks, T, is given by

$$T = clg \left\lceil \frac{n}{B} \right\rceil$$

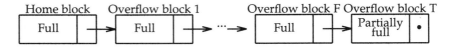

Figure 5.16 A typical chain of T overflow blocks (best case). All overflow blocks 1, 2, ..., F are full.

whereas the number of *full* overflow blocks, F, is given by

$$T = flr \left[\frac{n}{B} \right]$$

Now the total number of required accesses will be calculated in order to retrieve *all overflow* records of this chain independently. To accomplish this, the total number of accesses, $\tau_F(n)$, required to access all logical records from the full overflow blocks must be calculated first; then the total number of accesses, $\tau_T(n)$, to retrieve all records of the last overflow block, T, of this chain will be calculated.

Observe that $(i + 1)$ accesses are required to access the ith overflow block of this chain since all i overflow blocks must be accessed in addition to the home block. Since the number of records in this block is equal to B, it can be seen that $[(i+1) \cdot B]$ *rba* accesses are needed to access all records in this block. Hence, we obtain that

$$\tau_F(n) = \sum_{i=1}^{F} [(i + 1) \cdot B] \quad rba \qquad [5.25]$$

On the other hand, to access the last block of the chain, one needs $(T + 1)$ *rba*. Since the number of records in this block is equal to $(n - F \cdot B)$, then the number of accesses required to access all records of this block is given by

$$\tau_T(n) = (T + 1) \cdot (n - F \cdot B) \quad rba \qquad [5.26]$$

Combining equations [5.25] and [5.26] yields the total number of accesses τ_{NOR} required to access all records of all overflow chains independently:

$$\tau_{NOR} = \sum_{n=1}^{\infty} \left[[\tau_F(n) + \tau_T(n)] \cdot D_h(B + n) \right] \quad rba$$

But the number of accesses, τ_{HR}, required to retrieve all records from their home addresses is equal to τ_{HR} *rba*, since only one random access is needed in order to access any one of these records. Therefore, the equation $\tau_{HR} = NR{-}NOR$ is used to obtain the *average search length* in this case,

$$ASL[Retrieve\_One, H] = \left[\frac{NR - NOR + \tau_{NOR}}{NR} \right] \quad rba$$

5.3.4.3   Extendible Hashing.   So far we have seen a number of different methods that can be employed to manage overflow records generated as a result of collisions produced by hashing functions. In this section we will describe a relatively new technique that splits the corresponding physical block whenever an overflow record is generated during an insertion operation and which is followed by a rearrangement of the logical records (of the split block) in such a way that there are no overflow records per se. The direct result is that this method leads to an average search length of one random access for the retrieval of any record from that file.

The associated physical file structure employed in this case is a two-level structure. The data set, the collection of physical blocks, resides in the lower level, whereas the *index set*, which indexes the blocks of the data set, resides in the upper level. The physical file structure over a file of 10 logical records is presented in Figure 5.17. Notice that a number preceeded by the percent symbol, such as %010, represents the binary representation of an unsigned decimal integer; in this case the decimal number is 2.

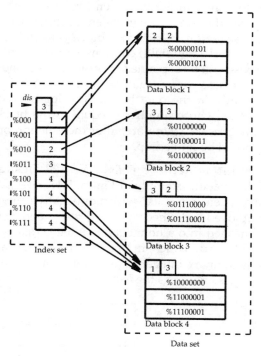

Figure 5.17   A physical hash file structure of 10 logical records with extendible hashing.

Let's examine this physical structure closer. Note that the first component of the index set, labeled in Figure 5.17 by *dis*, is referred to as the *depth of the index set.* The value of *dis* is always a positive integer and identifies the number of remaining components in the index set; this number is equal to 2^{dis}. In this case *dis* = 3; therefore, there are 8 more components in this set with the address of the first being 0, of the second, 1, and of the last, 7. Each of these addresses requires exactly *dis* bits to be specified as an unsigned binary integer; in our case the binary representations of these addresses are listed alongside their respective locations. Each of these 2^{dis} components contains a pointer to a data block of the data set, *but* not all pointers are necessarily distinct. In other words, the number of data blocks in general is less than or equal to 2^{dis}. Notice that the size, in bytes, of each component of the index set is system and implementation dependent, but undoubtedly this size is relatively small. Therefore, the size of the index table is relatively small. The previous observation suggests that for files that are not so large their index set could be resident in main memory at all times by allocating multiple buffers if necessary. On the other hand, for very large files the index set could be implemented as another file whose structure could be one of the plethora of file structures presented throughout this book that would yield the best performance under the given circumstances. To simplify the discussion, we will assume throughout that the entire index set is resident in main memory. The physical structure of each data block is as in Figure 5.18. The first field, the *Depth of Data Block (ddb)* field, contains a positive integer that satisfies $ddb \leq dis$, and its purpose will be explained shortly. The second field, the *Number of Records (NR)* field, contains a nonnegative integer that indicates the number of logical records currently in the data block. The logical records, R_i, are stored in the remaining fields whose number is equal to the blocking factor. Notice that no flag fields are present; therefore, after the deletion of a logical record the remaining ones should be moved up.

The Operation Retrieve_One. We will illustrate *Retrieve_One* by concentrating on the specific example of Figure 5.17. We have assumed that the logical records have been furnished with nonnegative integer keys, and the hashing function employed is defined by $h(key) = key$ mod 256. Under these assumptions each key is hashed into a nonnegative integer that is referred to as the *pseudokey* of the logical record, which, in this case, requires exactly 8 bits to be represented as an unsigned binary integer. The number of bits that are required to represent the pseudokey is known as the *length of the pseudokey (lp).* In our example, $lp = 8$.

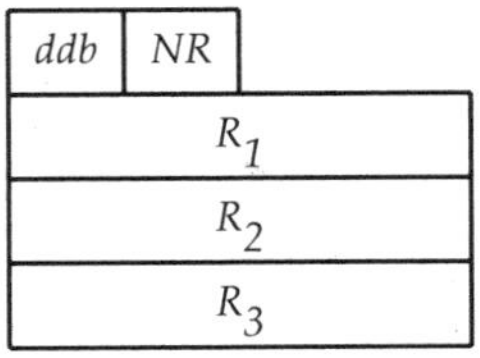

Figure 5.18 The physical structure of a data block with a blocking factor of 3.

The retrieval of any logical record requires exactly four steps, which are outlined below, in which the logical record to be retrieved is the one with key 1029:

1. Hash the key to the pseudokey. Using our hashing function the key will be mapped to the pseudokey with a decimal integer value of 5 and binary representation of %00000101.

2. Extract from the binary representation of the pseudokey a number equal to the one indicated by the *depth of the index set* of its most significant bits.[11] This *sid*-bit binary number is referred to as the *shifted pseudokey*. The decimal integer equivalent, i, of the shifted pseudokey is used as an index to the index set and is referred to as the *index*. In our example, since *dis*=3, we extract the three leftmost bits from the pseudokey, which leads to %000 as the shifted pseudokey. Therefore, the decimal integer i=0 is the index.

3. The ith entry (block pointer) of the index table is extracted. In our case, the pointer points to data block 1.

4. Finally, the indicated data block is accessed and read into main memory. The contents of the buffer are examined, and the record in question is retrieved.

These steps are illustrated in Figure 5.19. According to our earlier discussions we may assume, as we will from now on, that the index set is resident in main memory at all times and that it has been declared as an array, *Index_Set*, with its first element (block pointer) addressed via the index equal to zero. The *Retrieve_One* algorithm is given in Table 5.8; due to its simplicity, further discussion is omitted.

Closer examination of the pseudocode of the *Retrieve_One* algorithm reveals that all steps except step [5] require internal execution; our previous discussions suggest that under extendible hashing the logical record is *guaranteed* (if it exists) to be in the block pointed to by the block pointer of the index set.[12] Therefore, the cost of this operation, in terms of physical block accesses, is equal to one random block access required to access the target block.[13] The cost of accessing the ith component of the index set is negligible, since we have assumed that this set is resident in main memory.

The Insert_One Operation.   At the outset let's indicate the significance of the *ddb* field. Recall that the physical address of the data block where a logical record resides is stored in the pointer position within the index set indicated by

---

[11] This operation is equivalent to a right logical shift of the binary representation of the pseudokey by an amount equal to $lp - dis$.

[12] If the record is not in the target block, the record does not exist in the file either.

[13] Notice that if the entire index set cannot be accommodated in main memory at once, an extra overhead must be added equal to the cost of accessing the index component of the index set. From now on we will assume that the entire index set is resident in main memory.

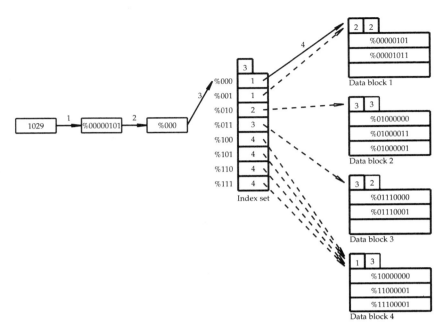

Figure 5.19 The step-by-step (solid arrows) accessing of the logical record with key 1029. Notice that only the pseudokeys of the logical records are shown.

TABLE 5.8 The *Retrieve_One* algorithm.

```
Retrieve_One(key,dis);
[1]    pseudokey ← h(key);
[2]    shifted_pseudokey ← logical_shift_right(pseudokey,lp-sid);
[3]    index ← unsigned_integer_representation(shifted_pseudokey);
[4]    block_pointer ← Index_Set(index);
[5]    read_block(block_pointer,data_block_buffer);
[6]    If data_block_buffer.NR=0 then write('record not found')
                else
                    { found ← false;
                      i ← 1;
                      while ((i ≤ data_block_buffer.NR) and not(found)) do
                          if (key = key_of_record_R_i then found ← true
                                                      else i ← i+1 };
[7]    if found then write ('record found')
                else write ('record not found);
[8]    exit;
```

the *dis* most significant bits of the pseudokey. The value of the *ddb* field attached to the data block indicates that this block contains all logical records whose *ddb* + *i* most significant bits of the pseudokey are identical to the *ddb* + *i* most significant keys of the pseudokey for all nonnegative values of the integer

$i = 0, 1, ..., n$ such that $ddb + n = dis$. To illustrate these notions with an example, observe that in Figure 5.19 the %000 pointer of the index table points to data block 1. The ddb field of this block is set to 2, indicating that this block contains all records whose pseudokey begins with either %00 or %000. In addition, the %010 pointer points to data block 2 whose ddb field is set to 3; therefore, this block contains all records whose pseudokey starts with %010. At the other extreme, the ddb field of data block 4 pointed to by the %101 pointer is set to 1, which indicates that this block contains all records whose pseudokeys begin with the binary digit 1 (i.e., %100, %101, %110, and %111).

The algorithm for an insertion can now be explained. The target block is located (subject to the *Retrieve_One* algorithm). There are two cases that could arise. The block is not full and the record is simply written there or the block is full so the record becomes an overflow record. In the latter case the mechanism of inserting the record depends on the relationship between the values of the *dis* and *ddb* fields. Roughly speaking, if their values are different, then the data block is split; otherwise, both the index set and the data block are split. Each such case is discussed in detail via the two examples below. Assume the situation as in Figure 5.19.

Insert Record with key = 464. According to our hashing function the key is hashed to 464 mod 256 or 208. The pseudokey is, therefore, %11010000 and the shifted pseudokey (since $dis = 3$) is %110. The %110 pointer points to data block 4; but the number of records field has been set to 3, indicating that the block is full. Therefore, the new record is an overflow record. Since $ddb = 1 < 3 = dis$, data block 4 splits into two; the block pointers in the index set are adjusted to reflect this fact; and the ddb field of both blocks (4 and 5) is incremented by one. All records in the old block (4) and the new record are distributed so that block 4 receives all records whose pseudokey begins with %10 (i.e., %100 or %101), while block number 5 receives all records whose pseudokey begins with %11 (i.e., %110 or %111). Figure 5.20 illustrates the new file structure after insertion of the new record.

The algorithm that performs the splitting of the block pointed to by the *index* and which updates the pointers of the index set is given in Table 5.9. Notice that the number of pointers that must be updated is a function of the difference $sid - ddb$.

TABLE 5.9   Splitting the data block pointed to by the *index* and updating the block pointers of the index set.

```
algorithm block_split(index_set,sid,ddb,index,new_block_pointer);
[1].   steps ← (2^(sid-ddb-1))-1;
[2].   if (((index-1) mod 2) = 0) then
                              { for k := index to (index+steps) do
                                    index_set[k] ← new_block_pointer}
                       else
                              { for k := index downto (index-steps) do
                                    index_set[k] ← new_block_pointer};
[3].   exit;
```

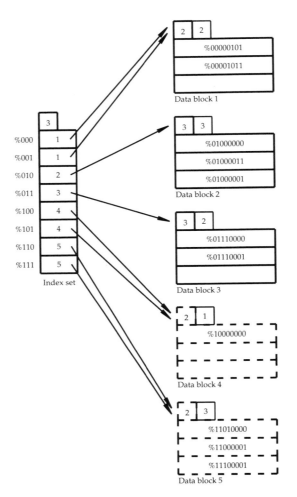

Figure 5.20 The physical structure of Figure 5.19 after insertion of the record with key 464 (pseudokey %11010000).

Insert Record with key = 792. Similar to the example above, the pseudokey of this record is %01010000 and the shifted pseudokey (since $dis = 3$) is %010. The %010 pointer points to data block 2; since that block is full, the new record becomes an overflow record. Since $ddb = 3 = dis$, data block 2 splits into two (blocks 2 and 5); the index set is split into two by doubling its size to 2^4; the block pointers in the index set are adjusted to reflect this fact; and the ddb field of both blocks (2 and 5) is incremented by one. All records in the old block (2) and the new record are distributed so that block 2 receives all records whose pseudo-keys start with %0100, while block 5 receives all records whose pseudokeys start with %0101. Figure 5.21 illustrates the new file structure after the insertion of the new record.

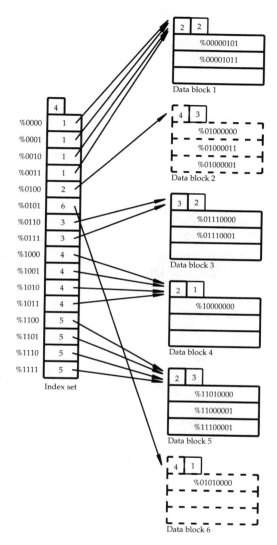

Figure 5.21 The physical structure of Figure 5.20 after insertion of the record with key 792 (pseudokey %01010000).

The algorithm that splits the data block pointed to by the *index* and the index set and thereafter updates the block pointers is given in Table 5.10.

It is important to notice that insertion of a new record that is also an overflow record could possibly require *multiple* splits. Observe that the insertion of a record whose pseudokey is %01000010 will require two splits. Therefore, when an overflow record must be inserted, the corresponding data block must be read; all its records together with the new one must be moved to a temporary

TABLE 5.10 Splitting the data block pointed to by the *index,* and splitting
the index set and updating the block pointers of the index set.

```
algorithm set_and_block_split(sid,index_set,index,new_block_pointer);

[1].  for j :=2^sid to (index+1) do
         { index_set[2*j] ← index_set[j];
           index_set[2*j-1] ← index_set[j]};
      index_set[2*index] ← new_block_pointer;
      index_set[2*index-1] ← index_set[index];
      for j := (index-1) downto 1 do
         { index_set[2*j] ← index_set[j];
           index_set[2*j-1] ← index_set[j]};
[2].  sid ← sid + 1;
[3].  exit;
```

area, *temp.* The overflow block, as well as the newly allocated block, are
rewritten with the same ddb and NR fields. In particular, the *ddb* field's setting is
one larger than the previous setting, whereas the *NR* field's setting is equal to
zero. Finally, each record from the temporary area must be reinserted via the
same sequence of steps into the file. The pseudocode for this algorithm is given
in Table 5.11.

TABLE 5.11 The *Insert_One* algorithm (extendible hashing).

```
Insert_One(key,dis,index_set);

[1]  pseudokey ← h(key);
[2]  shifted_pseudokey ← logical_shift_right(pseudokey,lp-sid)
[3]  index ← unsigned_integer_representation(shifted_pseudokey);
[4]  block_pointer ← index_set(index);
[5]  read_block(block_pointer,data_block_buffer);
[6]  If data_block_buffer.NR<Blocking_Factor
     then
         {data_block_buffer.NR ← data_block_buffer.NR +1;
          move record into the NR position in the data_block_buffer;
          write_block(block_pointer,data_block_buffer); }
     else
         { new_block_pointer ← allocate_new (block_pointer);
           for i:=1 to data_block_buffer.NR do
              temp[i] ← data_block_buffer.R[i];
           temp[i+1] ← new_logical_record;
           data_block_buffer.NR ← 0;
           data_block_buffer.ddb ← data_block_buffer.ddb + 1;
           if data_block_buffer.ddb <= sid
             then block_split(index_set,sid,ddb,index,new_block_pointer)
             else set_and_block_split(sid,index_set,index,new_block_pointer);
           write_block(block_pointer,data_block_buffer);
           write_block(new_block_pointer,data_block_buffer);
           repeat
                 insert(temp[i].key,dis);
           until (no more records in temp);
[8]  exit;
```

Notice that the algorithm Table 5.11 performs a considerably greater number of physical reads and writes than is required. Modification of this algorithm in order to obtain a minimal number of physical I/O operations is left as an exercise for the reader.

The Delete_One Operation.   Deletion of a record can be done simply by adjusting the *NR* field of the target block by possibly moving the records up in the data block. The cost of this operation is equal to two random accesses. Notice that a large number of deletions could yield a file structure with an unacceptably small loading factor. In this case one could "shrink" the size of the index of the table and merge the physical blocks. The algorithm that performs this task parallels that of the *Insert_One* algorithm and is left as an exercise for the reader.

5.3.4.4 Linear Hashing.

We remarked earlier that the cost of one random access for the retrieval of a record is attained if and only if the index set can be maintained in main memory at all times. Therefore, the size of the index set must be relatively small. Even in this ideal case, the index must be loaded in main memory when the file is opened and it must be written back onto the disk when the file is closed. Furthermore, the reader should have noticed that there are cases in which the number of logical records in the file could be small, whereas the index set (given that one of its splits forces its size to double), could be very large. In this case, the index set must be on the disk and, consequently, the search length for the retrieval of the record could increase by an amount equal to the cost of accessing the target index of the index set. That cost depends on the file structure employed to store the index, but it is definitely larger than 1. In this section we present a variation of the extendible hashing technique, the *linear hashing* technique, which will eliminate the need for an index set.

Linear hashing is similar to the extendible hashing technique in two respects. First, whenever an overflow record is generated, the address space increases via data block *splitting;* second, a dynamic *rehashing* technique is employed to rearrange the records of the block that was split and the overflow record by using a set of special functions whose elements are referred to as *split* functions. The difference between the extendible and the linear hashing techniques lies primarily in the fact that under the latter method, whenever a block splits, allocation of a new block is done in a *predetermined* linear fashion. A direct consequence of the previous remark is that there is *no* need for maintainance—or even the existence, for that matter—of the index set. Therefore, this method performs significantly better in terms of both average search length and storage than that of extendible hashing. The improvement in performance increases as the file enlarges.

We will illustrate the technique employed by linear hashing via a specific example. We will assume an initially empty hash file of address space $R = 100$, $BF = 5$, a hashing function h_0 defined by $h_0(key) = key \bmod R$ used in the initial loading of the file, and a collection of hashing functions, $\{h_i\}_{i=1}$, referred to as *split functions of h_0*, defined[14] for each $i = 1, 2, 3, ...,$ by

$$h_i(key) = key \bmod (2^i \cdot R)$$

To simplify this discussion we will adopt the policy that an overflow record will be generated whenever the corresponding block is full. In other words, we are not concerned with the value of the loading factor or any other parameter for that matter.

Initially, when a record must be inserted, each key will be hashed via the function h_0 defined by

$$h_0(key) = key \bmod R$$

This same function will be employed unless an overflow record is generated. For example, our hashing function h_0 will yield a number of collisions when we insert the logical records with keys 800, 3900, 1800, 700, 3400, 34601, 1201, 601, 1701, 2901, 102, 202, 1402, 5202, 65302, 103, 203, 1403, 52850, 2450, 250, 450, 650, 45199, 5499, 34199, and 2099 into our initially empty hash file, but it will not generate any overflow records. The file structure, after the insertion of all of these records and any number of other records that are not overflow records, is illustrated in Figure 5.22.

Closer examination of Figure 5.22 reveals the existence of a pointer field, the *split block (sb)* pointer, and a nonnegative integer field, the *file level (fl)* field. The *sb* pointer, which initially points to the first block of the hash file, *always* points to the block that must be split *next* as soon as an overflow record is generated irrelevant of the hashing address of that record. The value of the *fl* field, which is initially set to zero, is *always* equal to the highest index of a split function currently being used. Also note that the structure of each data block is similar to that used in extendible hashing except that the *ddb* field is absent in this case.

As a first example, notice that insertion of the logical record with primary key 4900 leads to an overflow record. In this case the block pointed to by the *sb* pointer should be split. The fact that the key is hashed to the same address as the *sb* pointer is immaterial. At any rate, the split block is split by allocating a new block whose address is $R = 100$. All records of the split block 0, together with the overflow record, are rehashed via the split function h_1, which is defined by

$$h_1(key) = key \bmod (2^1 \cdot 100) = key \bmod 200$$

The *sb* is incremented by 1, and thus points to the second block.[15] Observe that the preceeding discussion indicates that the new file structure can be thought of as a hash file where the hashing function h employed is defined as

---

[14] A formal definition of these functions is given in the next section.

[15] When a block is split, the newly allocated block is appended to the last one. Hence, the term *linear* hashing is used.

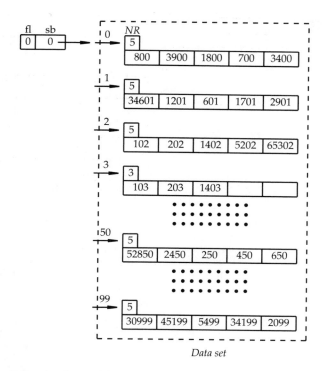

Figure 5.22   A physical hash file structure with no overflow records (only the keys of 28 records are shown) with linear hashing immediately after initial loading.

$$h(key) = \begin{cases} h_1(key) & \text{if } h_0(key) = 0 \\ h_0(key) & \text{otherwise} \end{cases}$$

Therefore, the fl field is set to 1. The new file structure is given in Figure 5.23.

Let's give one more definition. We will define the *upper bound (ub)* of the file to be the positive integer defined by $(2^{fl-1} \cdot R)$. The hashed address can then be computed via the algorithm presented in Table 5.12.

As an illustration, assume that we would like to retrieve the record with key 800 from the file structure of Figure 5.23. We have $fl = 1$, $R = 100$, and $ub = 2^0 \cdot 100 = 100$. Since $h_{fl}(key) = key \bmod (2^{fl} \cdot R)$, if the values $fl = 1$, $R = 100$, and key = 800 are substituted, we obtain that $h_1(800) = 800 \bmod (2^1 \cdot 100)$ or $h_1(800) = 0$. But $0 < 100 = ub$; therefore, 0 is the hashed address. On the other hand, if the record to be retrieved is the record with key 3900, then similar calculations indicate that $h_1(3900) = 100$. But $100 \geq ub$; therefore, the hashed address is given by $h_0(key) = 3900 \bmod (2^0 \cdot 100) = 100$.

As a second example, consider the file of Figure 5.23 and assume that we are ready to insert the record with key 3402. According to the *Retrieve_One*

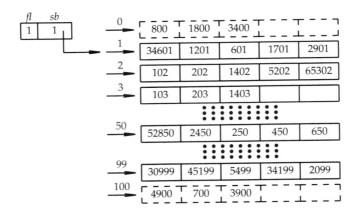

Figure 5.23 The hash file of Figure 5.22 (the *NR* field of each data block is not shown) after insertion of the logical record with key 4900. Notice that a new block (100) has been allocated; the records of the split block as well as the new record have been hashed via the h_1 function; and the *sb* pointer as well as the *fl* field have been adjusted.

TABLE 5.12 Calculating the hashed address under linear hashing.

```
algorithm hashed_address(key, fl,ub,R);
[1].   hashed_address ← h_fl(key);
[2].   if (hashed_address ≥ ub
           then hashed_address ← h_fl-1(key);
[3].   exit;
```

algorithm presented earlier, the key of the record is hashed to address 3402 mod 100 = 2; but that block is full. Therefore, the split block, block 1 in this case, is split. A new block with address $R + 1$ is allocated, and the new record together with all records of the split block are hashed via the function h_1. Figure 5.24 illustrates the resultant structure.

Notice that block splitting rearranged the records of the split block, but the new record is still an overflow record. Hence, the newly split block, block 2, is split; all records can be accommodated after this step. Figure 5.25 illustrates the structure of the file after insertion has been completed.

The discussion above suggests that whenever an overflow record is encountered, usually a number of splits are required to complete the process. But in each split the *sb* pointer is incremented by one. When the *sb* pointer points to the *R*th block and this block is ready to be split,[16] the function that used *h* has changed to $h = h_1$. At this point, h_1 plays the old role of h_0 whereas the split function h_2 plays the old role of h_1. Moreover, the *sb* pointer must be reset to point to block number 0. Continuing in this fashion after $2R$ splits, h_3 replaces h_2 and the latter replaces h_1. The *sb* pointer is reset and the process continues.

---

[16] This is equivalent to say that R splits have occurred.

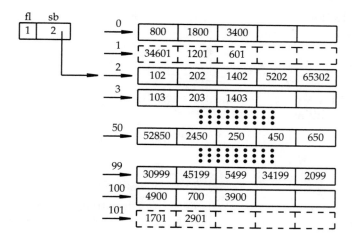

Figure 5.24 Block number 1 is split; its records are hashed via the hashing function h_1. But the new record with key 3402 is still an overflow record.

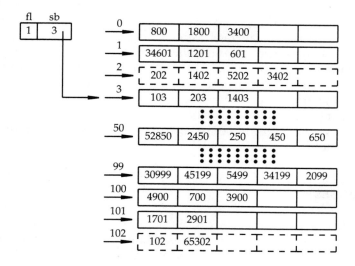

Figure 5.25 Block number 2 is split; and, its records together with the new record are rehashed via the split function h_1.

Split Functions.   We selected in our example a specific collection of functions to serve as our split functions. Despite the fact that it is true that there are a number of different collections of functions that could have been selected as split functions, it is not true that every collection of functions could qualify as split functions. In particular, if K denotes the key space, R the address space, and h_0 the hashing function used at the time of initial loading of the file, then a collection of functions $\{h_i\}_{i=0}$ is called a set of *split functions for h_0* if the following conditions are satisfied.

$$h_i : K \rightarrow \left\{0, 1, 2, 3, 4, ..., (2^i \cdot R-1)\right\} \text{ for each } i \geq 0$$

and for any key *key* and for any $i \geq 1$, one of the following two conditions must hold. Either

$$h_i(key) = h_{i-1}(key)$$

or

$$h_i(key) = h_{i-1}(key) + 2^{i-1} \cdot R$$

One should see that the collection of functions that were employed in the previous section satisfies the above requirements; therefore, they form a collection of split functions.

5.3.5 Load and Average Search Length Control

A number of the methods and, in particular, the *linear* and *extendible methods*, permit a certain degree of control of certain parameters of the performance such as load factor and average search length.

Load control requires that the load factor be approximately equal to a desirable constant value. The way that this is accomplished is by considering a record that must be inserted as an overflow record as soon as a collision occurs and the load factor is superior to some threshold; in this case, a split is in order. Average search length control, on the other hand, is attained by splitting whenever a collision occurs and the average search length is superior to some threshold.

5.4 EXERCISES

1. Consider a set of $NR = 7500$ logical records, an address size of $B = 1$, and an address space of $R = 10000$. Moreover, assume that the hashing function h employed generates a random distribution of the addresses.
   a. Find the number of overflow records.
   b. Find the load factor.
   c. Assuming that the overflow technique used is coalesced chaining and that the chains are not repaired (except the *free_chain*), find the average search length for the operation *Retrieve_One* immediately after initial *direct* loading.

2. Consider a set of $NR = 10000$ logical records, an address size of $B = 2$, and an address space of $R = 10000$. The intention is to implement a hash file

that employs the separate overflow area technique. The overflow area has been allocated blocks 8000 to 9999. Assume that the hashing function employed generates a random distribution of the addresses; also assume that the overflow blocks are reserved exclusively for the overflow records of the same home address and that all chains are repaired.

a. Find the average search length for the operation *Retrieve_One* immediately after the initial loading.

b. Find the average search length for the operation *Retrieve_One* at a time in which the number of records in the file is equal to 18000.

3. Consider the hash file in Figure 5.14(a).

a. Redraw this figure so that all *flag* and *pointer* fields are shown.

b. Write the algorithms *Insert_One*, *Delete_One*, and *Retrieve_One* (in pseudocode form) for this case.

4. Consider the hash file in Figure 5.14(b).

a. Redraw this figure so that all *flag* and *pointer* fields are shown.

b. Write in pseudocode form the algorithms *Insert_One*, *Delete_One*, and *Retrieve_One* for this case.

5. Verify the file structures of Figure 5.13 and also verify that the average search length improves from 2.1 to 1.4 by maintaining ordered chains.

6. Derive the minimum average search length assuming an address size greater than one and coalesced chaining. State all your assumptions.

7. Assume a hash file with address space R, which employs the separate file overflow area technique and which has an address size for both the primary and overflow file equal to B; assume that the hashing function h will generate a distribution given by D_h. The worst case occurs when, as a result of a large number of insertions and deletions, the records are stored so that the home address is full, whereas all other synonyms can be found in the overflow area. In particular, in this case there will be *just* one overflow record per address. Compute the average search length for this case.

8. Suggest a file structure that facilitates both random access to the logical records via the hashing function h and that also facilitates sequential processing of the logical records in increasing order of their keys. In addition, discuss the performance of the three basic operations under your file structure.

9. Compare the performances of *direct* versus *sequential* loading of a hash file.

10. Consider an initially empty hash file where extendible hashing is employed. The primary keys of the logical records are nonnegative integers; the hashing function is defined by $h(key) = key \bmod 256$; and the blocking factor of the data blocks is equal to 2. Indicate via a series of diagrams the physical file structure after insertion of the records (in this order) with keys 767, 968, 461, 132, 312, 320, 579, 43, 1102.

11. Give the pseudoalgorithm that performs the deletion of a record from a hash file (with extendible hashing) so that the resulting file structure occupies the minimal amount of storage.

12. Consider an initially empty hash file where linear hashing is employed. The primary keys of the logical records are nonnegative integers; the address space is $R = 10$; the hashing function is defined by $h_0(key) = key$ mod 10; the split functions are defined by $h_i(key) = key$ mod $(2^i \cdot R)$; and the blocking factor of the data blocks is equal to 4.

    a. Indicate via a series of diagrams the physical file structure after insertion of the records (in this order) with keys 800, 3900, 1800, 700, 34800, 34601, 1201, 601, 1701, 2901, 102, 202, 1402, 5202, 65302, 103, 203, 1403, 52850, 2450, 250, 450, 650, 45199, 5499, 34199, and 2099.

    b. Calculate the load factor for this file.

    c. Calculate the average search length for the operation *Retrieve_One* for this file.

13. Consider an initially empty hash file where linear hashing is employed. The primary keys of the logical records are nonnegative integers; the address space is $R = 10$; the hashing function is defined by $h_0(key) = key$ mod 10; the split functions are defined by $h_i(key) = key$ mod $(2^i \cdot R)$; and the blocking factor of the data blocks is equal to 4.

    a. Assuming that we would like to maintain a load factor close to 50%, indicate via a series of diagrams the physical file structure after insertion of the records (in this order) with keys 800, 3900, 1800, 700, 34800, 34601, 1201, 601, 1701, 2901, 102, 202, 1402, 5202, 65302, 103, 203, 1403, 52850, 2450, 250, 450, 650, 45199, 5499, 34199, and 2099.

    b. Calculate the average search length for the operation *Retrieve_One* for this file.

14. Consider an initially empty hash file where linear hashing is employed. The primary keys of the logical records are nonnegative integers; the address space is $R = 10$; the hashing function is defined by $h_0(key) = key$ mod 10; the split functions are defined by $h_i(key) = key$ mod $(2^i \cdot R)$; and the blocking factor of the data blocks is equal to 4.

    a. Assuming that we would like to maintain an average search length less than or equal to 1.3, indicate via a series of diagrams the physical file structure after insertion of the records (in this order) with keys 800, 3900, 1800, 700, 34800, 34601, 1201, 601, 1701, 2901, 102, 202, 1402, 5202, 65302, 103, 203, 1403, 52850, 2450, 250, 450, 650, 45199, 5499, 34199, and 2099.

    b. Calculate the load factor for this file.

15. Consider an initially empty hash file where linear hashing is employed. The primary keys of the logical records are nonnegative integers; the

address space is $R = 10$; the hashing function is defined by $h_0(key) = key$ mod 10; the split functions are defined by $h_i(key) = key$ mod $(2^i \cdot R)$; and the blocking factor of the data blocks is equal to 4.

a. Assuming that we would like to maintain an average search length less than or equal to 1.3 and that we permit the existence of overflow blocks with the same blocking factor as the primary data blocks, derive a strategy for deciding when a split should occur. Illustrate via a series of diagrams the physical file structure (subject to your strategy after insertion of the records (in this order) with keys 800, 3900, 1800, 700, 34800, 34601, 1201, 601, 1701, 2901, 102, 202, 1402, 5202, 65302, 103, 203, 1403, 52850, 2450, 250, 450, 650, 45199, 5499, 34199, and 2099).

b. Calculate the load factor for this file.

16. Give the pseudoalgorithm that performs the insertion of a record into a hash file (with linear hashing). State your assumptions.

17. Give the pseudoalgorithm that performs the deletion of a record from a hash file (with linear hashing) in such a way that the resulting file structure occupies the minimal amount of storage.

5.5 HOST LANGUAGE: PL/1

The PL/1 data sublanguage permits the creation and manipulation of direct files via REGIONAL files. Despite the fact that there are three types of REGIONAL file organizations, REGIONAL(1), REGIONAL(2), and REGIONAL(3), all three of them share a number of common properties:

- First, each block of the file referred to as a *relative block*, or *region*, is assigned a unique address by the file system *relative* to the very first region of the file which is assigned the address 0. In other words the fourth region of the file is assigned the address 3, the tenth the address 9, and so on. The addresses of these regions are referred to as *region numbers*. The number of the regions that may be allocated varies; in particular up to $2^{15} - 1$ (32,767) regions are allowed under both REGIONAL(2) and REGIONAL(3) organizations whereas up to $2^{24} - 1$ (16,777,215) regions are allowed under REGIONAL(1).

- These file organizations support both *sequential* and *direct* access modes of processing.

- The physical file structure resembles that of CONSECUTIVE files in that the regions(blocks) are contiguous in external storage. As a matter of fact, only one extend is allocated to a file in the case in which the access mode was *direct* at the time of initial creation of the file; otherwise, up to 15 extends can be allocated.

- Only fixed-length and unblocked logical records may be employed with REGIONAL(1) and REGIONAL(2) organizations. In other words, the access methods associated with the former two organizations *do not* block and deblock logical records. On the other hand, REGIONAL(3) organizations also permit variable-length and blocked records.

- Each region can be accessed by the application program via its region number. In addition, under REGIONAL(2) organizations a logical record can be addressed primarily by a region number and secondarily by its primary key value. For example if the retrieval of a logical record is requested, then the region number may not be enough to locate the record in the case in which the latter is an overflow record.

    It should be pointed out here that the remark previously made indicates one distinct advantage of REGIONAL(2) files over the other organizations. The reason for this is that the location of the target record is done under the supervision of the disk controller and *not* of the application program. In particular, the access method, in response to a logical *READ* request, uses the supplied region number and accesses the corresponding block. The disk controller uses the supplied key information to examine the *key* field of the count subblock of the accessed block where the record had been written via low-level routines of the file system at the time when the record was initially written (the format used with REGIONAL(2) files is count-key[17]). If a match is found, then the logical record from that region is delivered to the buffer. Otherwise, the record is assumed to be an overflow record and the overflow management technique is to be open addressing with linear search; hence, a linear search is initiated by examining the *key* field of each and every subsequent block[18] for a possible match or unsuccessful search. Notice that since the checking is done by the disk controller, the intermediately accessed blocks do *not* transfer in main memory; therefore, at most one data transfer is required. At the same time, there is a distinct disadvantage associated with REGIONAL(2) files! Namely, if logical records were to be blocked and/or deblocked by the application program, the search could not be performed. Hence this scheme works only with unblocked records; that obviously leads to an unacceptably low utilization.[19]

- The direct organization of the data set must always be indicated to the file system; this is accomplished via coding DSORG=DA in the JCL statement that defines the DCB parameter.

---

[17]See Chapter 2 for details.
[18]The exact mechanism will be discussed shortly.
[19]Unless, of course, the size of the logical records is sufficiently large.

5.5.1 REGIONAL(1) Files

5.5.1.1   Data Definition Language.   In the case of a REGIONAL(1) disk file, the block format is count-data;[20] therefore, for all practical purposes the physical structure is the same as that of a physical sequential file.

Declaring a REGIONAL(1) File.   The declare statement resembles that used in CONSECUTIVE files; its format is given below:

```
DCL (logical_filename) FILE RECORD ENV(REGIONAL(1));
```

As in the case of CONSECUTIVE files, the file attributes could be supplied either by the DCL statement or by the *JCL* statements. If these parameters are to be declared in the declaration statement, they must be placed after the keyword RE-GIONAL(1) and inside the parentheses. The allowable parameters, their syntaxes, and meanings are given in Table 5.13.

TABLE 5.13   The allowable DCB parameters in PL/1 under OS/MVS.

PARAMETER	MEANING
F	Fixed size, unblocked records
BLKSIZE(S)	Data sublock of size S bytes
BUFFERS(N)	Allocate N buffers to the file

For example, if each data subblock (region) is to have a size of 100 bytes, the following declare statement suffices.

```
DCL (FILE2) FILE RECORD ENV(REGIONAL(1) F BLKSIZE(100));
```

5.5.1.2   Data Manipulation Sublanguage

Opening a REGIONAL(1) File.   Recall that in order to perform an operation on a file that file must first be opened. The format of the PL/1 statement that accomplishes this task follows.

```
OPEN FILE (logical_filename) ACCESS OPTION [PARMS]
```

ACCESS indicates the *access mode* to be employed, i.e., either SEQUENTIAL or DIRECT. OPTION indicates the *type* of operation to be performed in the file, i.e., INPUT, OUTPUT, or UPDATE. Finally, whether or not the last keyword KEYED must be present depends on the values of ACCESS and OPTION. Table 5.14 indicates the available combinations of valid OPEN statements and the allowable operations.

Examination of Table 5.14 indicates the following:

---

[20]See the relevant discussion in Chapter 2.

TABLE 5.14 The allowable ACCESS modes, OPTION, KEYED attribute, and operations.

REGIONAL(1) ORGANIZATION					
ACCESS	OPTION	KEYED	OPERATIONS		
			READ	WRITE	DELETE
SEQUENTIAL	INPUT	Optional	Yes	No	No
	OUTPUT	Required	No	Yes	No
	UPDATE	Optional	Yes	Yes	Yes
DIRECT	INPUT	Required	Yes	No	No
	OUTPUT	Required	No	Yes	No
	UPDATE	Required	Yes	Yes	Yes

- Under a SEQUENTIAL access mode, the retrieval of regions is done in a sequential fashion; this implies that in order to access any region j, all $j-1$ predecessor regions must be accessed. Moreover, despite the fact that each region is individually addressable, the access of a predecessor region of the currently accessed region is impossible. At the other extreme under DIRECT access mode, regions can be accessed randomly.

- A file opened for INPUT can only be read. It is the responsibility of the application program to ensure that the region currently accessed does not contain a *dummy* record. The mechanism is straightforward; the application programmer must attach at the *beginning* of each logical record a 1-byte-wide FLAG field. The access method as well as the application program can detect an empty region (one that is occupied by a dummy record) from the contents of this FLAG field. The value of the contents FF (hex) indicates an empty region, whereas the value 00 indicates a full region. For example, when a *DELETE* of a logical record is issued, then the access method just overwrites the contents of the FLAG field of the corresponding region with FF.

- A file opened for OUTPUT can only be written to. No reads are permitted. Therefore, this OPTION is selected *only* when one or more logical records are to be *overwritten*. It is important to notice that at the time of *initial* creation of the file if the mode employed is DIRECT then the access method will set the first byte (the FLAG) field of each region in the file to FF to indicate that all logical records are dummy. On the other hand, if the access mode is SEQUENTIAL, then the file space is cleared, but the regions *are not* marked as containing dummy records.[21] The previous remarks should convince the reader that this OPTION is selected *only* in the case in which the file is to be created or its entire contents are to be *overwritten*. Finally, when a logical record is ready to be written out to a nonempty region, then the KEY condition is raised, and the application program must be prepared to handle it.

---

[21] For the exact mechanism employed in this case, see the section about a logical *WRITE*.

- A file opened for UPDATE can be read and written to. It must be pointed out that when a logical record is to be written out to either an empty or nonempty region, the new record overwrites the contents of the region; *but*, the KEY condition is not raised.

- The presence of the KEYED attribute is required whenever the application program wants to know, or for that matter indicate to the file system, a region address. The region number is obtained or returned via a string program variable. The length of the string, consisting of alphabetic characters and (possibly) leading blanks (interpreted as numeric zeros) must be equal to 8. If the length of the string is less than 8 characters, the string is padded to the left with blanks to bring it up to size. If the string has more than 8 characters, then only the rightmost 8 characters are used to form the region address.[22] For example, we stated that the region number of the first block is 0; therefore, its address will be specified by the string 40404040404040F0 (hex).

The Logical READ Request.   The format of the allowable *READ* statement depends on the access mode. Before access modes are discussed, recall that the region address can be passed from and to the file system from the application program via a string variable. Therefore, it can be assumed in the sequence that the variable REGION has been declared in the application program as a string variable of length 8 and also that FILE1 has been declared to be a REGIONAL(1) file.

- **Sequential access mode.** There are two statements that perform logical *READs*. They are presented below.

```
READ FILE (FILE1) INTO (program_variable) [IGNORE (number)]
```

Program_variable is the storage area where the logical record just read is to be delivered;[23] and, number is a positive integer or an integer variable. The last field, IGNORE (number), is optional. If it is present, then the access method will deliver to the program_variable the logical record that is stored in the (*number* + 1)st region past the currently accessed region.

The next form of the *READ* statement can be issued if and only if the file was opened with the KEYED attribute.

```
READ FILE (FILE1) INTO (program_variable) KEYTO (REGION)
```

The above statement also causes, in addition to the fact that the logical record in the current region is delivered to the program_variable, the region number of the current region to be delivered to the REGION variable.

---

[22] If the number specified by the string is greater than $2^{24}-1$, then a division modulo 172777216 takes place, and the address is formed by the result.

[23] See Chapter 4 for more details.

- **Direct access mode.** There is only one statement that can be issued in this case and its format is presented below:

```
READ FILE (FILE1) INTO (program_variable) KEY (REGION)
```

The effect of this statement is that the access method will access in a random fashion the region whose region number is specified by the string variable REGION;[24] it will deliver the logical record stored there to the pro-gram_variable.

The Logical WRITE Request.   The format of the allowable WRITE statement depends primarily on the access mode and secondarily on whether the file has been opened for OUTPUT or for UPDATE. At the outset it is assumed as before that a string variable REGION of length 8 has been declared in the application program and also that FILE1 has been declared to be a REGIONAL(1) file.

- **Sequential access mode.** There are two statements that perform a logical *WRITE.*

```
WRITE FILE (FILE1) FROM (program_variable) KEYFROM(REGION);
          REWRITE FILE (FILE1) FROM (S);
```

Both statements can be used if the file has been opened for OUTPUT whereas only the second can be used in the case of a file opened for UPDATE. Recall that in this case the blocks can be accessed only *forward.* Moreover, at the time of opening of an OUTPUT file, all file space is cleared *without,* as of yet, the flagging of empty regions. The mechanism of flagging these regions is explained below.

Assume that the first two logical *WRITE* statements are the following.

```
WRITE FILE (FILE1) FROM (program_variable) KEYFROM('0');
WRITE FILE (FILE1) FROM (program_variable) KEYFROM('105');
```

Upon encountering the first statement, the access method will deliver the first logical record from the program_variable to the very first region. On the other hand when the second statement is encountered, the access method, being aware of the sequential access mode, understands that no logical records are to be written in the intervening regions (region numbers 1 to 104). While all these regions are being accessed, the first byte of their data subblock is set to FF (hex) to indicate dummy records; and, then the logical record is written to the data subblock of region number 105. In

---

[24] It is the responsibility of the application program to store the address of the region that is to be accessed in the **REGION** program variable.

addition, the access method, immediately after the closing of the file, sets the **FLAG** fields of all subsequent regions after the last one was accessed. Finally, the **REWRITE** statement is used to write the updated version of the logical record currently in the buffer[25] (as a result of the previous *READ* request) in the region that was read from.

- **Direct access mode.** There is only one statement that can be issued in this case independent of the applied **OPTION** and its format is presented below.

```
WRITE FILE (FILE1) FROM (program_variable) KEYFROM (REGION)
```

The effect of this statement is that the access method will deliver the contents of the **program_variable** to the data subblock of the region whose region number is specified by the string variable **REGION**;[26] and, the access takes place in a random fashion.

The Logical DELETE Request.   Whenever a file is opened for **UPDATE**, a record can be deleted via the following statement.

```
DELETE FILE (FILE1) FROM (program_variable) KEYFROM (REGION)
```

Notice that deletion of a record is done by rewriting the **FLAG** to FF (hex).

5.5.2 REGIONAL(2) Files

This particular organization permits the application programmer to implement certain hash files with minimal programming effort. In addition the retrieval of a logical record is done via a minimum number of data transfers. The particular details are noted below.

- The address size must be equal to 1. In addition, for reasons that will become apparent shortly, the application program, unlike the case of **REGIONAL(1)** organization, should not block and deblock records.
- The access method inserts and retrieves a specified logical record based primarily on the primary key value (in **REGIONAL(2)** terminology this is referred to as the *recorded key*) and the *region number*. The overflow management technique used is open overflow, which is furnished with a search mechanism that resembles a linear search. The exact mechanisms differ according to whether the mode is *sequential* or *direct*. In this case, the discussion is restricted for the time being to *direct* files and to the mechanism

---

[25] Sequential access modes use double buffers by default. As a matter of fact, under this mode the **SET** and **LOCATE** options can be used in conjunction with *READ* and *WRITE* statements.

[26] It is the responsibility of the application program to store the address of the region that is to be accessed in the REGION program variable.

employed by the access method for the three operations *Insert, Retrieve,* and *Delete.* These mechanisms are presented below in terms of a pseudoalgorithm. Notice that the application program must supply to the access method the region number to which the key is hashed, along with the primary key.

```
Algorithm Insert(region_number,recorded_key);

Access the track which contains the region_number region;
block_number ← region_number of the first region in the track accessed;
while block_number.FLAG = '00' (hex) do
block_number ← block_number+1;
write recorded_key in key field of count subblock;
write logical record in data subblock;
exit;


Algorithm Retrieve(region_number,recorded_key);

Access the track which contains the region_number region;
block_number ← region_number of the first region in the track accessed;
while block_number.key ≠ recorded_key do
block_number ← block_number+1;
Retrieve logical record;
exit;

Algorithm Delete(region_number,recorded_key);

Access the track which contains the region_number region;
block_number ← region_number of the first region in the track accessed;
while block_number.key ≠ recorded_key do
block_number ← block_number+1;
block_number.FLAG ← 'FF' (hex)
exit;
```

Note that if the mode were *sequential,* an attempt to insert a logical record into a nonempty region would cause the **KEY** condition to be raised, and the application program should be prepared to handle the overflow record in some other fashion.

5.5.2.1 Data Definition Language.   In the case of a **REGIONAL**(2) disk file, the block format is count-key;[27] therefore, for all practical purposes the physical structure is the same as that of a physical sequential file.

Declaring a REGIONAL(2) File.   The declare statement resembles that used in **REGIONAL**(1) files; its format is given below:

```
DCL (logical_filename) FILE RECORD ENV(REGIONAL(2));
```

---

[27] See the relevant discussion in Chapter 2.

There is one more attribute that is *required* to be specified, namely, the KEYLEN attribute that indicates the length of the recorded key. This parameter can either be specified in the appropriate *JCL* statement or in the ENV attribute. The allowable parameters, their syntaxes, and meanings are given in Table 5.15.

TABLE 5.15 The allowable DCB parameters in PL/1 under OS/MVS. The LIMCT parameter must be indicated in the *JCL* statement.

PARAMETER	MEANING
F	Fixed size, unblocked records
BLKSIZE(S)	Data subblock of size S bytes
KEYLEN	Recorded key's length in bytes
LIMCT	Limit the search to LIMCT tracks
BUFFERS(N)	Allocate N buffers to the file

For example, if each block (region) is to have a size of 100 bytes and the primary key has a length of 10 bytes, then the following declare statement suffices.

```
DCL (FILE2) FILE RECORD ENV(REGIONAL(2) F BLKSIZE(100) KEYLEN(10));
```

Note here that the LIMCT parameter limits the search to the indicated number of tracks for retrieval and/or insertion of a logical record from the track containing the region to which the key of the logical record is hashed.

5.5.2.2 Data Manipulation Sublanguage.

Opening a REGIONAL(2) File.   The format of the PL/1 statement that opens a file is identical to that of REGIONAL(1) files. That is,

```
OPEN FILE (logical_filename) ACCESS OPTION [PARMS]
```

where ACCESS indicates the *access mode* to be employed, i.e., either SEQUENTIAL or DIRECT. OPTION indicates the *type* of operation to be performed on the file, i.e., INPUT, OUTPUT, or UPDATE. Finally, whether or not the last keyword KEYED must be present depends on the values of ACCESS and OPTION. The valid combinations are identical to those of REGIONAL(1) files.[28]

The Logical READ, WRITE, and DELETE Requests.   The format of the allowable READ, WRITE, REWRITE, and DELETE statements is identical to that of REGIONAL(1) files. There is only one fundamental difference between those two organizations that relates to the way the recorded key and the region number are passed to the access method. Recall that in a REGIONAL(1) organization only the

[28]Refer to Table 5.14.

region number was passed via the string variable REGION that appeared in the KEY and KEYFROM options.

In the case of REGIONAL(2) files, the recorded key and the region number are passed to the access method via a string variable that appears in the KEY and KEYFROM options. The new string variable is referred to as the *Source Key.*

When the access method receives the *Source Key* string variable, it decodes it as though it were a concatenation of two strings.

```
Source_Key = Recorded_Key | | Region_Number.
```

The Recorded_Key's length is known to the access system via the required KEYLEN parameter; therefore, the string of length KEYLEN is extracted starting from the leftmost position of the Source_Key. On the other hand, the Region_Number string conforms to the same syntax and semantics conventions described for REGIONAL(1) files so this string is formed by the rightmost 8 characters of the string Source_Key.

As an example consider the statement

```
WRITE FILE(FILE1) FROM (AREA) KEYFROM('987-32-4567A147bbbb1234');
```

where *b* denotes the blank character. Assuming the declaration KEYLEN = 11, the recorded key is 987-32-4567, whereas the region number is 00001234, with the string A147 is disregarded.

5.5.3 Examples

In the following paragraphs the PL/1 code required for the creation and update of a hash file, implemented via the REGIONAL(1) organization, is given. Recall that this organization requires unblocked logical records. *But* to the access method, a logical record is nothing more than a string of bytes; therefore, the application program can declare a logical record as an *array* of logical records. In this case, the unit of transfer will be the entire array of logical records; thus, the application program will be responsible for blocking and deblocking the logical records. Each of these two cases will be examined in turn.

5.5.3.1 Unblocked Logical Records.

The Creation of the Hash CHECKS File. Assume now that each customer's record has been punched on an 80-column card. Below the code is presented that is required to create the CHECKS file as a hash file. The address space consists of 1000 addresses; the address size is equal to 1; the hashing function maps the ACCOUNT number to the address formed by its three rightmost numeric digits; and the overflow management technique employed is open addressing with linear search. The loading method used in this example is *direct.*

```
      LINHASH:PROC OPTIONS(MAIN);
      DCL BEOF BIT(1) INIT('1'B);
/*
**    Declaration of a pointer that will allow the overlaying of a picture
**    field on a character string which will facilitate incrementing
**    the character string as a number.
*/

      DCL LOC  POINTER;
/*
**    The built-in function SUBSTR is used to extract part of the key.
*/
      DCL (ADDR,SUBSTR) BUILTIN;
      DCL SYSPRINT OUTPUT;
/*
**    Declaration of the file that will hold the records to be inserted into
**    the hash file.
*/
      DCL CARDS FILE RECORD ENV(CONSECUTIVE F RECSIZE(80)),
            1 CARDSAREA,
                  2 ACCOUNT  CHAR(11),
                  2 NAME     CHAR(20),
                  2 ADDRESS  CHAR(15),
                  2 BALANCE  PIC'999999V.99',
                  2 FILLER   CHAR(25);
/*
**    Declaration of CHECKS hash file.  The field BLKFLAG denotes
**    whether the block (region) is empty or not;  a value of '11111111'B
**    indicates the block is empty, while '00000000'B indicates there
**    is a record present.  The field DELFLAG denotes whether a record
**    as been deleted or not.  If BLKFLAG = '11111111'B and
**    DELFLAG = '11111111'B, then no record was ever inserted in that
**    block; but if DELFLAG = '00000000'B, then a record was there but
**    it was deleted.
*/
      DCL CHECKS FILE RECORD ENV(REGIONAL(1) F BLKSIZE(56)),
            1 CHECKSAREA,
                  2 BLKFLAG  BIT(8),
                  2 DELFLAG  BIT(8),
                  2 ACCOUNT  CHAR(11),
                  2 NAME     CHAR(20),
                  2 ADDRESS  CHAR(15),
                  2 BALANCE  FLOAT DECIMAL(16);
/*
**    Declaration of OVFLOW file to hold records that collide during the
```

```
**   initial insertion pass.
*/
      DCL OVFLOW FILE RECORD ENV(CONSECUTIVE F RECSIZE(80));
/*
**   FILSIZE will have the number of blocks the file contains.  REGN is
**   a string that will hold the region number of a block; it is a
**   character string so OVERLAY must be declared and overlaid on
**   REGN so the region number can be incremented as a number.
*/
      DCL FILSIZE,I,J FIXED BIN(31);
      DCL REGN CHAR(8);
      DCL OVERLAY PIC'99999999' BASED(LOC);
/*
**   Set LOC to be the address of REGN to cause overlay of picture
**   field and set FILSIZE to 1000.
*/
      LOC = ADDR(REGN);
      FILSIZE = 1000;
      ON ENDFILE(CARDS) BEOF='0'B;
      OPEN FILE(CARDS) INPUT, FILE(CHECKS) DIRECT OUTPUT KEYED;
/*
**   This block will initialize each block of the file.  The BLK and DEL
**   flags are both set to denote that each block is empty and no deletions
**   have occurred.
*/
      REGN = '      0';
      CHECKSAREA.BLKFLAG = '11111111'B;
      CHECKSAREA.DELFLAG = '11111111'B;
      DO I = 0 TO FILSIZE-1;
          WRITE FILE(CHECKS) FROM(CHECKSAREA) KEYFROM(REGN);
          CALL INCREGN;
      END;
      CLOSE FILE(CHECKS);
      OPEN FILE(CHECKS) DIRECT UPDATE KEYED;
      READ FILE (CARDS) INTO (CARDSAREA);
/*
**   While not end of cards file, write all records that do not collide
**   to CHECKS file and all records that do collide to the
**   OVFLOW file.  First the hashing function extracts the last
**   3 digits of the account number;  that represents the region number.
**   If that region's BLKFLAG denotes empty, then write the record
**   to that region;  otherwise write it to the OVFLOW file.
*/
      DO WHILE (BEOF);
```

```
            REGN = '       '  |   | SUBSTR(CARDSAREA.ACCOUNT,9);
            READ FILE(CHECKS) INTO(CHECKSAREA) KEY(REGN);
            IF CHECKSAREA.BLKFLAG = '11111111'B
            THEN DO;
                    CHECKSAREA.BLKFLAG = '00000000';
                    CHECKSAREA.DELFLAG = '00000000';
                    CHECKSAREA.ACCOUNT = CARDSAREA.ACCOUNT;
                    CHECKSAREA.NAME    = CARDSAREA.NAME;
                    CHECKSAREA.ADDRESS = CARDSAREA.ADDRESS;
                    CHECKSAREA.BALANCE = CARDSAREA.BALANCE;
                    WRITE FILE(CHECKS) FROM(CHECKSAREA) KEYFROM(REGN);
                    END;
            ELSE WRITE FILE(OVFLOW) FROM(CARDSAREA);
            READ FILE (CARDS) INTO (CARDSAREA);
        END;
/*
**   Close OVFLOW file and now open it for input so all the records that
**   collided can be inserted.  The same hash function is used.
*/
      CLOSE FILE(OVFLOW);
      OPEN FILE(OVFLOW) INPUT;
      BEOF = '1'B;
      ON ENDFILE(OVFLOW) BEOF='0'B;
      READ FILE(OVFLOW) INTO(CARDSAREA);
/*
**   While not end of OVFLOW, extract the region number and continue
**   incrementing it until the blocks specified are empty.  Once an empty
**   block is found, write the record and repeat for the next record.
*/
      DO WHILE(BEOF);
            REGN = '       '  |   | SUBSTR(CARDSAREA.ACCOUNT,9);
            CALL INCREGN;
            READ FILE(CHECKS) INTO(CHECKSAREA) KEY(REGN);
            DO WHILE(CHECKSAREA.BLKFLAG = '00000000'B);
                  CALL INCREGN;
                  READ FILE(CHECKS) INTO(CHECKSAREA) KEY(REGN);
            END;
            CHECKSAREA.BLKFLAG = '00000000';
            CHECKSAREA.DELFLAG = '00000000';
            CHECKSAREA.ACCOUNT = CARDSAREA.ACCOUNT;
            CHECKSAREA.NAME    = CARDSAREA.NAME;
            CHECKSAREA.ADDRESS = CARDSAREA.ADDRESS;
            CHECKSAREA.BALANCE = CARDSAREA.BALANCE;
            WRITE FILE(CHECKS) FROM(CHECKSAREA) KEYFROM(REGN);
```

```
              READ FILE(OVFLOW) INTO(CARDSAREA);
      END;
      CLOSE FILE(CHECKS);
      RETURN;
/*
**    This procedure will increment the region number as a number using the
**    overlaid picture field. If the current region number is 999,
**    then it will wrap around to zero.
*/
      INCREGN:PROC;
      IF OVERLAY < '    999'
          THEN OVERLAY = OVERLAY + 1;
          ELSE OVERLAY = 0;
      RETURN;
      END;
      END;
/*
//SYSPRINT DD SYSOUT=A
//GO.CHECKS DD DSNAME=UF.B0069143.S1.CHECKS,DISP=(NEW,CATLG),
//    UNIT=SYSDA,SPACE=(TRK,(2,1))
//GO.OVFLOW DD DSNAME=UF.B0069143.S1.OVFLOW,DISP=(NEW,CATLG),
//    UNIT=SYSDA,SPACE=(TRK,(1,1))
//GO.CARDS DD *
Data cards go here.
/*
```

Batch Mode Update of the Hash CHECKS File.   The following PL/1 code performs a *batch mode update* of the hash file CHECKS that was created in the previous section. Specifically, a set of requests, one per card, has been punched on a set of cards. The first field, COMMAND, on each card indicates the type of request. In particular, the field COMMAND will contain either an R, D, or I that corresponds to a request for *retrieval, deletion,* or *insertion,* respectively, of the indicated record. Notice that the ACCOUNT field is the only other required field that is present in the case of either a retrieval or a deletion operation.

```
LHSHUP:PROC OPTIONS(MAIN);
     DCL BEOF BIT(1) INIT('1'B);
     DCL LOC  POINTER;
     DCL (ADDR,SUBSTR) BUILTIN;
     DCL SYSPRINT OUTPUT;
/*
**    Declaration of a file that contains the update requests to be
**    performed on the hash file CHECKS. The field COMMAND will contain
**    either an R, D, or I corresponding to a retrieval, deletion
**    or insertion. The ACCOUNT field will be the only other field
```

```
**    present for a retrieval or deletion.
*/
        DCL CARDS FILE RECORD ENV(CONSECUTIVE F RECSIZE(80)),
            1 CARDSAREA,
                2 COMMAND CHAR(1),
                2 ACCOUNT CHAR(11),
                2 NAME    CHAR(20),
                2 ADDRESS CHAR(15),
                2 BALANCE PIC'999999V.99',
                2 FILLER  CHAR(24);
/*
**    Declaration of CHECKS file to be updated.
*/
        DCL CHECKS FILE RECORD ENV(REGIONAL(1) F BLKSIZE(56)),
            1 CHECKSAREA,
                2 BLKFLAG BIT(8),
                2 DELFLAG BIT(8),
                2 ACCOUNT CHAR(11),
                2 NAME    CHAR(20),
                2 ADDRESS CHAR(15),
                2 BALANCE FLOAT DECIMAL(16);
        DCL I,J FIXED BIN(31);
        DCL (REGN,STARTPOS) CHAR(8);
        DCL OVERLAY PIC'99999999' BASED(LOC);
        LOC = ADDR(REGN);
        ON ENDFILE(CARDS) BEOF='0'B;
        OPEN FILE(CARDS) INPUT, FILE(CHECKS) DIRECT UPDATE KEYED;
        READ FILE (CARDS) INTO (CARDSAREA);
/*
**    While not end of CARDS file process each command.  Extract region
**    number and read that block.
*/
        DO WHILE (BEOF);
            REGN = '      ' | | SUBSTR(CARDSAREA.ACCOUNT,9);
            READ FILE(CHECKS) INTO(CHECKSAREA) KEY(REGN);
/*
**    If COMMAND = 'D' or 'R' then process deletion or retrieval.
*/
            IF (CARDSAREA.COMMAND = 'D') | (CARDSAREA.COMMAND = 'R')
            THEN DO;
/*
**    STARTPOS is set to a flag value to allow entry into while loop if
**    necessary.  While loop will increment region number until one of the
**    following occurs: The CHECKSAREA.ACCOUNT = target account, a
```

```
**  region is read that is empty but not as a result of a deletion, or
**  all regions have been checked (REGN = STARTPOS).
*/
                STARTPOS = '-9999999';
                DO WHILE((((CHECKSAREA.ACCOUNT ^= CARDSAREA.ACCOUNT)&
                        (CHECKSAREA.BLKFLAG='00000000'B)) |
                        ((CHECKSAREA.BLKFLAG='11111111'B) &
                        (CHECKSAREA.DELFLAG='00000000'B))) &
                        (STARTPOS ^= REGN));
                    IF STARTPOS = '-9999999' THEN STARTPOS = REGN;
                    CALL INCREGN;
                    READ FILE(CHECKS) INTO(CHECKSAREA) KEY(REGN);
                END;
/*
**   If all regions were checked or an empty region(not via a deletion)
**   stops search, then record is not in file.
*/
                IF ((STARTPOS = REGN) | ((CHECKSAREA.BLKFLAG='11111111'B) &
                        (CHECKSAREA.DELFLAG='11111111'B)))
                THEN
                  PUT SKIP LIST('RECORD WITH KEY ',CARDSAREA.ACCOUNT,
                        ' NOT FOUND');
/*
**   Else if retrieval then write out record (or process it).
*/
                ELSE IF (CARDSAREA.COMMAND = 'R')
                    THEN PUT SKIP EDIT('RECORD RETRIEVED IS ',
                        CHECKSAREA.ACCOUNT,CHECKSAREA.NAME,
                        CHECKSAREA.ADDRESS,CHECKSAREA.BALANCE)
                        (A,A(11),A(20),A(15),E(8,2));
/*
**   Else it is a deletion, so flag the record as deleted and write it back
**   out.  Remember if BLKFLAG = '11111111'B and DELFLAG = '00000000'B,
**   then this denotes the record was deleted.
 */
                ELSE DO;
                    CHECKSAREA.BLKFLAG = '11111111'B;
                    WRITE FILE(CHECKS) FROM(CHECKSAREA)
                        KEYFROM(REGN);
                    END;
            END;
            ELSE DO;
/*
**   Record must be inserted so check if region is occupied;  if so, then
```

```
**    search for empty region. Once found assign fields from CARDS
**    record and write to CHECKS.
*/
                    IF CHECKSAREA.BLKFLAG = '00000000'B
                    THEN
                        DO WHILE (CHECKSAREA.BLKFLAG = '00000000'B);
                            CALL INCREGN;
                            READ FILE(CHECKS) INTO(CHECKSAREA) KEY(REGN);
                        END;
                    CHECKSAREA.BLKFLAG = '00000000'B;
                    CHECKSAREA.DELFLAG = '00000000'B;
                    CHECKSAREA.ACCOUNT = CARDSAREA.ACCOUNT;
                    CHECKSAREA.NAME    = CARDSAREA.NAME;
                    CHECKSAREA.ADDRESS = CARDSAREA.ADDRESS;
                    CHECKSAREA.BALANCE = CARDSAREA.BALANCE;
                    WRITE FILE(CHECKS) FROM(CHECKSAREA) KEYFROM(REGN);
                    END;
/*
**    Read next update request and continue.
*/
            READ FILE (CARDS) INTO (CARDSAREA);
        END;
        CLOSE FILE(CHECKS);
        RETURN;
        INCREGN:PROC;
        IF OVERLAY < '    999'
            THEN OVERLAY = OVERLAY + 1;
            ELSE OVERLAY = 0;
        RETURN;
        END;
        END;
/*
//SYSPRINT DD SYSOUT=A
//GO.CHECKS DD DSNAME=UF.B0069143.S1.CHECKS,DISP=(OLD,KEEP),
//    UNIT=SYSDA
//GO.CARDS DD *
Data cards go here.
/*
```

5.5.3.2 Blocked Logical Records.   As mentioned earlier the application program could block and deblock records. An example is given below that indicates how this is accomplished. In particular the code that will be presented performs the same task as the one demonstrated earlier; specifically, the CHECKS file is created as a hash file.

As before the address space consists of 1000 addresses; the hashing function maps the ACCOUNT number to the address formed by its three rightmost numeric digits; the overflow management technique employed is open addressing with linear search; and, the loading method is *direct*. But, unlike the previous case, the address size is equal to 10.

Using the above assumptions, the declaration of each block[29] of the hash file CHECKS is as follows:

```
DCL 1 CHECKSAREA,
       2 BLKFLAG  BIT(8),
       2 COUNT    FIXED BIN(31),
       2 BLKAREA(10),
           3 RECFLAG  BIT(8),
           3 ACCOUNT  CHAR(11),
           3 NAME     CHAR(20),
           3 ADDRESS  CHAR(15),
           3 BALANCE  FLOAT DECIMAL(16),
           3 PAD      CHAR(1);
```

Observe that each of the 10 logical records of the array BLKAREA has been furnished with the flag field RECFLAG; this flag is raised whenever a record that occupies that slot is deleted.[30] The PAD field is required under MVS/OS to force proper alignment. The BLKFLAG field is used to indicate whether or not the region is empty. Finally, the COUNT field records the number of logical records currently in this block. There are two distinct values, -1 and 0, of this field that indicate that no records are present but that have different meanings; a value of -1 indicates that no records have ever been inserted into this region, whereas a value of 0 indicates that the region has become empty via the deletions of some previously inserted records. Observe that this distinction will facilitate successful future *Retrieve_One* operations.

The Creation of the Hash CHECKS File.   The PL/1 code is given below.

```
BLKDHSH:PROC OPTIONS(MAIN);
       DCL BEOF BIT(1) INIT('1'B);
       DCL LOC  POINTER;
       DCL (ADDR,SUBSTR) BUILTIN;
       DCL SYSPRINT OUTPUT;
/*
**    Declaration of the file that consists of the input records.
```

[29]Notice that the declaration of the REGIONAL(1) CHECKS file indicates, as required, unblocked records.
[30]The *DELETE* statement (provided by PL/1) can not be employed in this case. All deletions must be done by the application program.

```
*/
      DCL CARDS FILE RECORD ENV(CONSECUTIVE F RECSIZE(80)),
          1 CARDSAREA,
                2 ACCOUNT  CHAR(11),
                2 NAME     CHAR(20),
                2 ADDRESS  CHAR(15),
                2 BALANCE  PIC'999999V.99';
                2 FILLER   CHAR(25);
/*
**  Declaration of the CHECKS file that will simulate blocked records
**  via an array structure that will hold the records.  The BLKFLAG
**  field is the same as before while the COUNT field will denote
**  how many records are currently in that particular region.  The COUNT
**  field is set to -1 initially to denote that no records have been
**  inserted; and, if decremented to 0 via a deletion, it will serve the
**  same purpose as the DELFLAG in the previous example.  Each
**  record will have a flag to denote whether or not that particular
**  position
**  of the array has a record in it.
*/
      DCL CHECKS FILE RECORD ENV(REGIONAL(1) F BLKSIZE(565)),
          1 CHECKSAREA,
                2 BLKFLAG        BIT(8),
                2 COUNT          FIXED BIN(31),
                2 BLKAREA(10),
                    3 RECFLAG BIT(8),
                    3 ACCOUNT CHAR(11),
                    3 NAME    CHAR(20),
                    3 ADDRESS CHAR(15),
                    3 BALANCE FLOAT DECIMAL(16),
                    3 PAD     CHAR(1);
      DCL OVFLOW FILE RECORD ENV(CONSECUTIVE F RECSIZE(80));
      DCL FILSIZE,I,J FIXED BIN(31);
      DCL REGN CHAR(8);
      DCL OVERLAY PIC'99999999' BASED(LOC);
      LOC = ADDR(REGN);
      FILSIZE = 1000;
      ON ENDFILE(CARDS) BEOF='0'B;
      OPEN FILE(CARDS) INPUT, FILE(CHECKS) DIRECT OUTPUT KEYED;
/*
**  Set the BLKFLAG and COUNT field of each physical record to the
**  appropriate values and write them to each region.
*/
      REGN = '        0'
```

```
      CHECKSAREA.BLKFLAG = '11111111'B;
      CHECKSAREA.COUNT   = -1;
      DO I = 1 TO 10;
            CHECKSAREA.BLKAREA(I).RECFLAG = '11111111'B;
      END;
      DO I = 0 TO FILSIZE-1;
            WRITE FILE(CHECKS) FROM(CHECKSAREA) KEYFROM(REGN);
            CALL INCREGN;
      END;
      CLOSE FILE(CHECKS);
      OPEN FILE(CHECKS) DIRECT UPDATE KEYED;
      READ FILE (CARDS) INTO (CARDSAREA);
      DO WHILE (BEOF);
            REGN = '      '||SUBSTR(CARDSAREA.ACCOUNT,9);
            READ FILE(CHECKS) INTO(CHECKSAREA) KEY(REGN);
```
```
/*
**    If the COUNT field is less than 10, then there is room in that
**    region for the record; update COUNT; find the first available
**    position in the array; set the appropriate fields; and write the
**    record to the CHECKS file.
*/
```
```
            IF CHECKSAREA.COUNT < 10
            THEN DO;
                  IF CHECKSAREA.BLKFLAG = '11111111'B
                  THEN DO;
                        CHECKSAREA.BLKFLAG = '00000000';
                        CHECKSAREA.COUNT = 1;
                        END;
                  ELSE CHECKSAREA.COUNT = CHECKSAREA.COUNT + 1;
                  I = 1;
                  DO WHILE(CHECKSAREA.BLKAREA(I).RECFLAG = '00000000'B);
                        I = I + 1;
                  END;
                  CHECKSAREA.BLKAREA(I).RECFLAG = '00000000'B;
                  CHECKSAREA.BLKAREA(I).ACCOUNT = CARDSAREA.ACCOUNT;
                  CHECKSAREA.BLKAREA(I).NAME    = CARDSAREA.NAME;
                  CHECKSAREA.BLKAREA(I).ADDRESS = CARDSAREA.ADDRESS;
                  CHECKSAREA.BLKAREA(I).BALANCE = CARDSAREA.BALANCE;
                  WRITE FILE(CHECKS) FROM(CHECKSAREA) KEYFROM(REGN);
                  END;
```
```
/*
**    Else write it to the overflow file.
*/
```
```
            ELSE WRITE FILE(OVFLOW) FROM(CARDSAREA);
```

```
            END;
            READ FILE (CARDS) INTO (CARDSAREA);
            END;
            CLOSE FILE(OVFLOW);
            OPEN FILE(OVFLOW) INPUT;
            BEOF = '1'B;
            ON ENDFILE(OVFLOW) BEOF='0'B;
            READ FILE(OVFLOW) INTO(CARDSAREA);
            DO WHILE(BEOF);
                REGN = '        '||SUBSTR(CARDSAREA.ACCOUNT,9);
                CALL INCREGN;
                READ FILE(CHECKS) INTO(CHECKSAREA) KEY(REGN);
/*
**      When the COUNT of the current region is equal to 10 go to the next
**      region.
*/
                DO WHILE(CHECKSAREA.COUNT = 10);
                    CALL INCREGN;
                    READ FILE(CHECKS) INTO(CHECKSAREA) KEY(REGN);
                END;
/*
**      If the region is empty, then set BLKFLAG to denote that it is now
**      occupied;  and, set COUNT to 1.
*/
                IF CHECKSAREA.BLKFLAG = '11111111'B
                THEN DO;
                    CHECKSAREA.BLKFLAG = '00000000'B;
                    CHECKSAREA.COUNT = 1;
                END;
/*
**      Else increment COUNT, find the first available position in the
**      array, and insert the record.
*/
                ELSE CHECKSAREA.COUNT = CHECKSAREA.COUNT + 1;
                I = 1;
                DO WHILE(CHECKSAREA.BLKAREA(I).RECFLAG = '00000000'B);
                    I = I + 1;
                END;
                CHECKSAREA.BLKAREA(I).RECFLAG = '00000000';
                CHECKSAREA.BLKAREA(I).ACCOUNT = CARDSAREA.ACCOUNT;
                CHECKSAREA.BLKAREA(I).NAME    = CARDSAREA.NAME;
                CHECKSAREA.BLKAREA(I).ADDRESS = CARDSAREA.ADDRESS;
                CHECKSAREA.BLKAREA(I).BALANCE = CARDSAREA.BALANCE;
                WRITE FILE(CHECKS) FROM(CHECKSAREA) KEYFROM(REGN);
```

```
          READ FILE(OVFLOW) INTO(CARDSAREA);
     END;
     CLOSE FILE(CHECKS);
     RETURN;
     INCREGN:PROC;
     IF OVERLAY < '      999'
          THEN OVERLAY = OVERLAY + 1;
          ELSE OVERLAY = 0;
     RETURN;
     END;
     END;
/*
//SYSPRINT DD SYSOUT=A
//GO.CHECKS DD DSNAME=UF.B0069143.S1.CHECKS,DISP=(NEW,CATLG),
//    UNIT=SYSDA,SPACE=(TRK,(30,10))
//GO.OVFLOW DD DSNAME=UF.B0069143.S1.OVFLOW,DISP=(NEW,CATLG),
//    UNIT=SYSDA,SPACE=(TRK,(5,1))
//GO.CARDS DD *
Data cards go here.
/*
```

6

Indexed Files

In Chapter 4 it was demonstrated that *sequential* file organizations facilitate relatively *fast ordered* sequential processing, whereas random accesses are considerably slower. On the other hand, in Chapter 5 we demonstrated how *direct* files facilitate *fast* random accesses, whereas *ordered* sequential processing is extremely slow. In this chapter we will present *indexed file* organizations, which on the average permit both relatively fast random accesses and *ordered* sequential processing.

Indexed file organizations incorporate the basic features of both sequential and direct files. Specifically, in order to facilitate sequential processing, logical records are arranged in such a way that the resulting physical structure resembles that of an ordered sequential file; the collection of all logical records will be referred to as the *data set*. On the other hand, random accessing of a logical record is done via its address; but unlike the case of direct files, the address of a logical record is not computed. Instead, its address, which depends on the *position* of the logical record within the data set, is stored alongside its primary key in a new record referred to as the *index record* or just simply the *index*. Alternatively, the *index* is a record with a minimum[1] of two fields, the primary key and the physical address of the record. The collection of all indexes is referred to as the *index set*. Figure 6.1 illustrates the structure of an index record.

---
[1] We will see that certain indexes contain more than two fields.

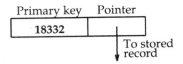

Figure 6.1 The index logical record type. Notice that the pointer points to the block in external storage where the logical record with key **18332** is stored.

The above discussion indicates that logically an indexed file consists of two file levels. In the lower level there is the collection of logical records, the *data set*, and in the upper level there is the collection of index records, the *index set*, as illustrated in Figure 6.2.

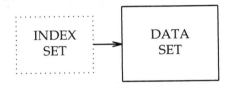

Figure 6.2 The two logical levels of an indexed file.

It should be noted here that even though an indexed file is viewed as a collection of two files, Data and Index, at the physical level, it can be implemented as a single file.[2] We begin our discussion with, conceptually, the simplest possible indexed file structure.

6.1 FULL INDEX ORGANIZATION

The indexed file organization, in which an index record is associated with each and every logical record, is referred to as a *full index* organization. Figure 6.3 illustrates one such structure.

Notice that in our example both the logical and index records are blocked; moreover, the blocking factor employed for the logical records of the index set is larger than that of the logical records of the data set. This is a direct result of the fact that in practice the size of the former records is considerably less than that of the latter.

The last remark explains why *random accesses* are performed considerably faster using this file organization than under a sequential file organization. To understand this more clearly, consider a sequential file of 100,000 records each of size 500 bytes. Assuming a selected data block size of 2,000 bytes we can see that

---

[2] Refer to the ISAM file organization discussed at the end of this chapter.

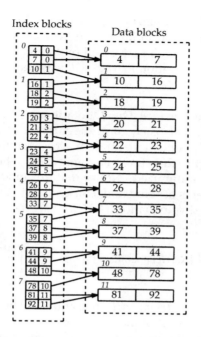

Figure 6.3 Full index organization. Notice that different blocking factors are employed for the index blocks (3) and data blocks (2).

the total number of blocks required[3] is 25,000. We can then see that the operation *Retrieve_One* requires, on the average, 12,500.5 sequential accesses. If it is assumed that an index record has a size of 20 bytes (primary key and address), then with the same blocksize we can see that the number of index blocks required is equal to 1000. Hence, with a full index organization the same operation *Retrieve_One* for an existing record would require only 500.5 sequential accesses to access the target index plus one extra random access to access the target data block.

6.1.1 The Operations

The performance of such a file organization depends on the physical structure of the file; as the reader should have noticed, there are a number of different physical structures that could represent the logical structure of Figure 6.3. For our purposes the following model will be considered.

Our physical structure consists of a physical sequential file of m blocks.[4] The index records are stored in an ordered sequential fashion in the first m_1 blocks, whereas the logical records comprise again an ordered set and occupy the

[3] Assume no block overhead.

[4] If different block sizes for the data and index set are desired, then two files must be allocated.

remaining $m_2 = m - m_1$ blocks. The access technique employed for accessing the "target" index (i.e., the index record whose primary key is that of the target record) is a binary search performed on the first m_1 blocks; the access technique employed for the operation *Retrieve_All* is sequential and is performed on the last m_2 blocks.

6.1.1.1 The *Retrieve_One* Operation.   The average search length for the operation *Retrieve_One* is equal to the number of accesses required to locate the "target" index plus one more random access required to access the stored record. The search length, therefore, is minimized when the search length for the "target" index is minimized. Notice that this model yields optimal performance, since the index set is ordered and, consequently, the binary search can be used.

With the aid of equation [4.3] we can see that the *average search length* is given by

$$ASL[Retrieve\_One, S] = \text{clg} \left[\log_2 \left(\frac{m_1}{2} \right) \right] \; rba \; + 1 \; rba \qquad [6.1]$$

6.1.1.2 The *Retrieve_All* Operation.   The average search length for this operation is *independent* of the index set structure but dependent on the structure of the data set. In this case, with the aid of equation [4.1], it can be seen that

$$ASL[Retrieve\_All, S] = m_2 \; sba + 1 \; rba \qquad [6.2]$$

where the one extra access in the above equation is required to access the $m_1 + 1$ block of the physical structure.

6.1.1.3 The *Delete_One* Operation.   The *Delete_One* operation consists of flagging both the logical record and its corresponding *index* record. Therefore, the average search length for this operation is the same as that of the operation *Retrieve_One* plus two more sequential accesses required to rewrite the flagged index and record.

6.1.1.4 The *Insert_One* Operation.   The cost of this operation is that this file organization is used only in the case of static files.[5] Notice that frequent insertions of records will yield *overflow* records whose handling requires complete reorganization of both the index (since an index record must be inserted) as well as the data set if we are to expect the highest possible performance of the other operations that require *ordered* index and data sets. However, the cost is considerable. In the best case, one in which there are empty slots in both the "target" index and data blocks, the average search length is equal to that of the operation *Delete_One*.

[5] The selection of a physical linked structure is possible but undesirable, since it prohibits the binary search option.

6.2.2 Storage Requirements

Assume a number of NR logical records with a blocking factor of BF_{dat} and an assumed blocking factor for the index records of BF_{ind}. Then the number of data blocks $NBLK_{dat}$ is given by

$$NBLK_{dat} = clg \left\lceil \frac{NR}{BF_{dat}} \right\rceil$$

while the number of index blocks $NBLK_{ind}$ is given by

$$NBLK_{ind} = clg \left\lceil \frac{NR}{BF_{ind}} \right\rceil$$

Therefore, the storage requirements in bytes for this file organization is given by

$$NBLK_{ind} \cdot BS_{ind} + NBLK_{dat} \cdot BS_{dat} \qquad\qquad [6.3]$$

where BS_{ind} and BS_{dat} are the block sizes (in bytes) of the index and data blocks, respectively.

6.2 INDEXED SEQUENTIAL FILES

In the previous section, it was shown that the cost of the operations *Insert_One, Delete_One, Update_One,* and *Retrieve_One* depends on the search length required to access the target index. Moreover, this search length depends in turn on the number of blocks, according to equation [6.1], in the index file. Therefore, decreasing the number of index blocks will improve the search length. Indexed sequential organizations are based on this principle. In particular, the significance of each index record is modified so that an index record is associated with each logical (physical) *block.* This modification further requires that the contents of the primary key field of each index reflect the *largest* key in the physical block pointed to by the pointer field of the index, as Figure 6.4 illustrates. One should also observe another welcomed side effect; namely, the storage requirements for

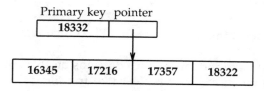

Figure 6.4   The indexed logical record type. Observe that the pointer points to the data block (with an assumed blocking factor of 4) in external storage where the logical record with key **18332** is stored and that the primary keys of the other records are smaller than **18322**.

this structure are considerably less than those of the associated full index organization. Figure 6.5 illustrates a *one*-level indexed sequential structure.

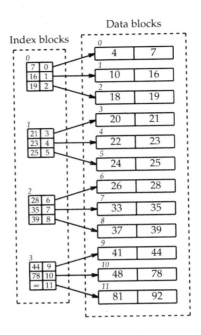

Figure 6.5   The indexed sequential organization over the same file as in Figure 6.2 with the same blocking factors for the index blocks (3) and data blocks (2). Notice the reduced number of index blocks.

To evaluate the improvement in performance of the file structure in Figure 6.5 over that in Figure 6.3, assume a sequential access technique for both the index and data sets. One should then be able to see that the average search length, in order to access the target index, falls from 4.5, required by the structure in Figure 6.3, to 2.5, required by the structure in Figure 6.5. Of course the improvement is not very significant, but this is due to the unrealistically small size of the file in these examples.

6.2.1 Multilevel Indexed Sequential File Organizations

Since the cost of random accesses depends on the search length required for accessing the target index, it is clear that trimming the search length will lead to better performance. This is accomplished by modifying the logical structure of the index set. In particular, that logical structure is often a tree-based structure. To be consistent with the bibliography, we define a k-level indexed sequential structure to be a multiway tree structure with the following properties:

1. The logical structure of the file is a $(k+1)$-level, n-ary tree structure, where n is the blocking factor of the index blocks.

2. The data blocks of the data set occupy the leaf positions (level k) of the structure.

3. The branch nodes of the structure are occupied by index blocks.

4. The index set is *static* in the sense that neither are there any new index blocks allocated nor are their contents altered during the lifespan of the file.[6] Furthermore, the index records are arranged in increasing order of their keys at each level of the structure.[7]

5. The index blocks at level k (the leaves of the index set) are referred to as the *sequence set*.

6. The semantics of the index are modified in such a way so that its pointer field points to a data block if and only if the index belongs to the sequence set; otherwise, the pointer points to an index block in the next lower level. In any case, the key value in an index at any level l represents the highest key value in the block that it points to in the next lower level.

Two-level and three-level indexed sequential structures are presented in Figures 6.6 and 6.7, respectively. The pseudoalgorithm that is required to access a specific (existing) record in such a structure is given in Table 6.1.

TABLE 6.1   The *Retrieve_One* algorithm for a multi-level indexed sequential structure.

```
Algorithm Retrieve_One;

[1]   Next ← 0;
[2]   Transmit Index_Block(Next) to Index_Buffer;
[3]   Find key kⱼ in the Input_Buffer such that
              kⱼ ≥ key of the target record;
[4]   Next ← pointer attached to kⱼ;
[5]   If at sequence set then transmit Data_Block(Next) to Data_Buffer
                      else go to step [2];
[6]   exit;
```

6.2.1.1 Overflow Records.   One should have noticed that the records in the data set are arranged in such a way that sequential processing is facilitated. The physical structure resembles that of a sequential file. In addition, at initial loading a fixed number of blocks is allocated with the provision that the effective blocking factor EBF_{dat} is less than BF_{dat} so that future insertions can be facilitated. One should also note that a highly volatile file will cause future insertions to generate *overflow records*. Clearly, one way to handle these records would have been,

---

[6]Certain system supported organizations do alter the contents of some indexes in the sequence set as well as the contents of a few indexes in the higher levels.

[7]Assuming the natural left to right order.

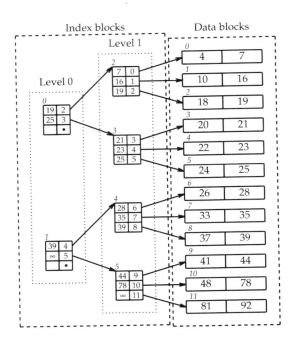

Figure 6.6   The indexed sequential organization over the same file as in Figure 6.3 with the same blocking factors for the index blocks (3) and data blocks (2). Note the two levels of indexes.

as in the case of full indexed organizations, to reorganize the file. But the cost of this operation is prohibitive, so another possible method of managing these records is outlined below.

At the time of creation of a file, extra blocks are allocated in order to facilitate these overflow records. In order that we may distinguish between these two sets of blocks, we will refer to the former collection as the *primary blocks*, whereas the latter will be referred to as the *overflow blocks*. Moreover, the collection of primary blocks will be referred to as the *primary area*, while that of the overflow blocks will be known as the *overflow area*. Despite the fact that there are a number of schemes that handle overflow records, most of these are similar to that of chained progressive overflow. In other words, overflow records are linked in a logical, *ordered*, chained fashion with the primary block to which they belong. Note that the pointer field of any index in the sequence set points to the primary block irrelevant of the existence of overflow records. In conclusion, it should be noted that usually overflow records are not blocked. Figure 6.8 illustrates how overflow records are handled.

The *Retrieve_One* algorithm shown in Table 6.1 must be modified in order to take into account the existence of overflow records; this pseudocode can be seen in Table 6.2.

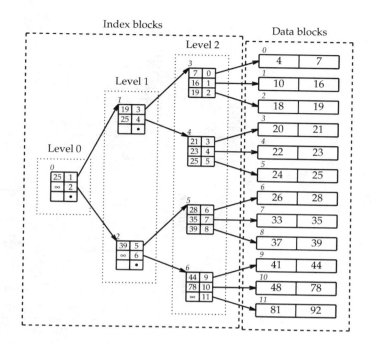

Figure 6.7   The indexed sequential organization over the same file as in Figure 6.4 with the same blocking factors for the index blocks (3) and data blocks (2). Notice the three levels of indexes.

6.2.2 Performance Analysis

The performance of such a file organization, as was mentioned earlier, depends on the physical structure of the file. Particularly, all random accesses depend primarily on the search length required to access the target index. Since the target index resides in a block of the sequence set, it follows that the number of random accesses needed to access a *target* primary block is equal to the height of the tree structure. The height of this structure in turn depends on the $NBLK_{dat}$ and the chosen BF_{ind}, as we will see in the next section.

6.2.2.1   The Height of an Indexed Sequential Structure.   Consider the indexed sequential organization of Figure 6.9. Assume that the number of primary blocks is equal to $NBLK_{dat}$, whereas the blocking factor of the index blocks is $EBF_{ind} = n$. If we also assume that no overflow records exist and that all index nodes are full, the height of this structure will be computed.

At the outset notice that from Figure 6.9 it follows that at the first level (level 0) there is only one node; in the second level there are n nodes. Each of the nodes at this level contributes n nodes to the next level; therefore, the

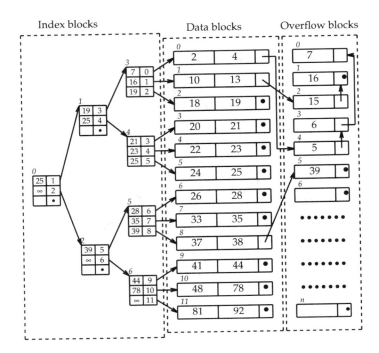

Figure 6.8 The modified indexed sequential organization over the same file as in Figure 6.5 with the same blocking factors for the index blocks (3) and data blocks (2), after the arrival (in this order) of logical records with keys 2, 13, 15, 6, 5, 39. Notice that the overflow blocks are chained (in order of their key value) to the primary data block.

number of nodes in the third level is equal to n^2. Inductively, we can show that at each level i we have n^i nodes, as Table 6.3 illustrates.

TABLE 6.3

Level	Number Of Nodes
0	1
1	n
2	n^2
3	n^3
.	.
.	.
.	.
j	n^j
.	.
.	.
.	.
$h-1$	$n^{(h-1)}$

TABLE 6.2   The *Retrieve_One* algorithm for a multilevel Index Sequential Structure.

```
Algorithm Retrieve_One;

[1]  Next ← 0;
[2]  Transmit Index_Block(Next) to Index_Buffer;
[3]  Find key kⱼ in the Input_Buffer such that
                  kⱼ ≥ key of the target record;
[4]  Next ← pointer attached to kⱼ;
[5]  If at sequence set then transmit Data_Block(Next) to Data_Buffer
                      else go to step [2];
[6]  If record not in the Data_Buffer
        then
            { Next ← Data_Buffer pointer to overflow chain;
              Found ← false;
              While ((Next ≠ Nil) and (not(Found)))
                    {Transmit Overflow_Block to Overflow_Buffer;
                     If logical record there
                        then
                            {write Overflow_Buffer;
                                 Found ← True}
                        else
                            Next ← Overflow_Buffer.pointer;}
[7]  If not(Found) then write ('record does not exist');
[8]  exit;
```

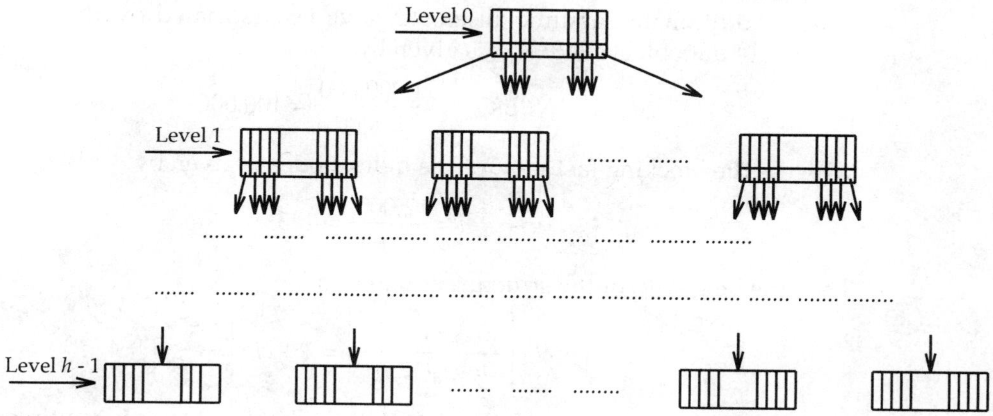

Figure 6.9   An indexed sequential structure of height h. Notice that the data nodes are the leaves (level $h - 1$), that the keys appearing in the index nodes are not shown, and that overflow records are absent.

But the number of nodes at the leaf level (level $h - 1$) must be equal to the number of primary blocks $NBLK_{dat}$; therefore,

$$NBLK_{dat} = n^{(h-1)}$$

It follows that the height h of the structure is given by

$$h = 1 + \log_n(NBLK_{dat}). \qquad [6.4]$$

In addition, the *total number of index blocks*, $NBLK_{ind}$, of the above structure can be computed. With the aid of Table 6.3, again one can see that the total number is given by

$$1 + n + n^2 + \dots + n^{(h-2)}$$

Therefore, $NBLK_{ind}$ is given by

$$NBLK_{ind} = \sum_{k=0}^{h-2} n^k = \frac{1 - n^{(h-1)}}{1 - n} \qquad [6.5]$$

Equation [6.4] was derived under the assumption that all index blocks were full. It is not difficult to show that the equation derived above can be replaced by

$$h = 1 + clg\,[\log_n(NBLK_{dat})] \qquad [6.6]$$

for the general case. As an example, consider the case of an indexed sequential file with 1,000,000 logical records of size 200 bytes each; moreover, assume that the primary key is of size ten bytes and that the pointer field has a size of six bytes. Additionally, assume all blocks have no associated overhead. Then, the number of data blocks $NBLK_{dat}$ is given by

$$NBLK_{dat} = \frac{1,000,000}{2,0000} = 100,000$$

whereas the blocking factor, n, of the index nodes is given by

$$n = \frac{2,000}{10 + 6} = 125$$

Then the height, h, of the structure is equal to

$$h = 1 + clg\left\lceil \frac{\log_{10}(10 \cdot 5)}{\log_{10}(125)} \right\rceil = 1 + clg\left\lceil \frac{5}{2.09} \right\rceil = 4$$

This section closes with the note that since the h accesses required to access the primary block are generally random, the height of the tree is chosen in most applications so that it does not exceed four.

6.2.3 A Simple Model

From now on we will assume an indexed sequential structure of height h and a data set comprising an ordered physical sequential file consisting of $NBLK_{dat}$.

The management technique employed for the handling of overflow records is that of chained progressive overflow, as has been outlined earlier.

At the time of initial loading, care is taken so that the primary blocks are not full (by choosing an appropriate *EBF* less than 1.0) and that no overflow records are present. During the lifespan of the file, overflow records will be created that undoubtedly will adversely affect the performance of the file. A number of overflow records can be accepted as long as the performance of the file remains lower than a predefined tolerance level. When that level is exceeded, then the file must be reorganized. As we will see later, this point of reorganization can be predicted.

Of course the performance of the file depends not only on the number but also on the distribution of the overflow records. Since our analysis is restricted to the average case, it will be assumed that the overflow records are distributed equally among the primary blocks. In other words, if we denote the length of the overflow chain associated with the primary block i, $(1 \leq i \leq NBLK_{dat})$, to be $l(i)$, then we denote by L the *average length of an overflow chain* defined by

$$L = \frac{\sum_{i=1}^{NBLK_{dat}} l(i)}{NBLK_{dat}} \qquad [6.7]$$

With this notation, the average search lengths of the main operations to be performed on this indexed sequential file will be derived.

6.2.3.1   The Initial Loading Operation.

At the outset, notice that the first task is to write out the logical records in the primary blocks. At the same time, when a block is to be written out, the key of the rightmost logical record in this block must be "promoted" to the parent node in the sequence set. When a block in the sequence set becomes full, the contents of the key field of the rightmost index in this block must be promoted to its parent node in the next upper level.

Although this operation seems innocent, there are some problems that may occur caused by the nature of the keys of the records. We will explain this problem with an example. For simplicity, assume a blocking factor *BF* of 2, an initial loading density *ILD* of 0.5, and that the keys of the logical records of the file are numeric.

Consider now the situation in which the values of the first three keys are 1, 2, and 3.[8] Under our assumptions the records with keys 1 and 2 will be written to the first block, whereas the record with key 3 will be written to the second block. Moreover, the fact that the loading density is 0.5 indicates that we *must* write four records per block; therefore, our application program is required to generate two dummy records and write them out to the first block before it starts writing records in the second block.

---

[8] Recall that the logical records of the data set must be presented in increasing sequence of their key values.

File systems that support such an organization *require* all records, dummy or not, to be presented in strict increasing order of their keys.[9] The question, then, is how can this problem be handled. Notice that if the third record had a key value of 20, there would be no problem relative to those three records; we would simply generate two dummy records with keys 3 and 4, respectively. The reason for which the latter case could be handled was that there were enough values that could separate two consecutive keys. This observation suggests that the desired solution is for the application program to map the given keys into a new set of keys in such a way so that two consecutive keys could be separated by as many values as necessary. The definition of the mapping requires that the designer be aware of the *largest* number of dummy records, d, that must be introduced in the data blocks.

Notice now the mapping

$$Old\_Key \rightarrow New\_Key$$

defined by

$$New\_Key = Old\_Key \cdot 10^k$$

where k is a positive integer, forces any two consecutive old keys to be mapped to two new keys that will be separated by at least $(10^k - 1)$ key values. For example, for $k = 1$ and $n = 2$, the two consecutive keys 32 and 33 are mapped into 320 and 330, respectively; that allows for 9 dummy keys, 321 through 329. Hence, one chooses the value of k to be the smallest integer satisfying

$$(10^k - 1) \geq n \qquad [6.8]$$

Finally, after the last no-dummy record with key k_l has been written to the current data block, n dummy records are generated with keys defined by $k_l + i$ where i represents the ith dummy record.[10]

The application program is therefore responsible for passing to the access method the new key value of any subsequent operations and also for passing to the user the old key value.

6.2.3.2 The *Retrieve_All* Operation.
Consider the ith data node. Then the number of accesses required to retrieve each record of that node is 1. Since there are L overflow records associated with that data node, L accesses will be needed to retrieve them. Hence, the average search length of this operation is clearly a function of L, since the number of primary blocks is fixed and is denoted by $SL[Retrieve\_All,IS](L)$. It is apparent then that

$$SL[Retrieve\_All, IS](L) = NBLK_{dat} \cdot L\ rba + NBLK_{dat}\ sba + 1\ rba \qquad [6.9]$$

---

[9] Otherwise, in the presence of duplicate keys the system would not be able to differentiate between them.
[10] It is possible to select a larger step than one by an appropriate choice of the integer k in equation [6.8].

where one extra random block access is required to access the *first* block in the data set.

Immediately after loading the file no overflow records are expected; therefore, in this case (since $L = 0$), the search length of the operation is

$$SL[Retrieve\_All, IS](0) = NBLK \; sba + 1 \; rba$$

6.2.3.3 The *Retrieve_One* Operation.

Recall that the average search length for the *Retrieve_One* operation is defined as the ratio of the total number of accesses required to access all records independently to the number of records. Since it is assumed that all overflow chains have the same length and that the primary blocks have the same number of records, the average search length can be found as the ratio of the total number of accesses required to access all records in a primary block and in its associated overflow chain to the number of these records.

Notice that exactly h random accesses are required to access each record in the primary block, while $h + i$ accesses are required to access the ith record of the overflow chain. Hence, the total number of accesses, τ_{tot}, is given by

$$\tau_{tot} = \left[h \cdot BF_{dat} \right] + \left[(h + 1) + (h + 2) + \cdots + (h + L) \right] \; rba$$

where the first term represents the number of accesses required to access all records in the primary block and the second term represents the total number of accesses to access all records in the overflow chain independently. The above equation can be rewritten as

$$\tau_{tot} = h \cdot BF_{dat} + \sum_{i=1}^{L} (h + i)$$

or

$$\tau_{tot} = h \cdot BF_{dat} + h \cdot L + \sum_{i=1}^{L} i = h \cdot (BF_{dat} + L) + \frac{L \cdot (L + 1)}{2}$$

Hence, the average search length is derived by dividing by the number of records $(BF_{dat} + L)$. That is,

$$ASL[Retrieve\_One, IS](L) = h + \left[\frac{1}{BF_{dat} + L} \cdot \frac{L \cdot (L + 1)}{2} \right] \; rba \qquad [6.10]$$

Note that immediately after loading the file no overflow records are expected; therefore, in this case (since $L = 0$) the average search length is

$$ASL[Retrieve\_One, IS](0) = h \; rba$$

as was expected.

6.2.3.4   The *Insert_One* Operation.   The cost of the *Insert_One* operation varies considerably according to the algorithm employed. The algorithm employed here is the one that provides us with ordered and full chains. In particular,

- If there are no overflow records and if there is an empty slot in the target primary block, the record is inserted there so that the records maintain their order (Figure 6.10(a)). Otherwise, the record with the largest key is pumped off the primary block, the new record is inserted in the primary block, and the old record is inserted in the overflow area and is linked appropriately to its primary block (Figure 6.10(b)). The cost of this operation varies according to which case is encountered. In the former case, the cost is only h random accesses required to access the primary block plus one extra sequential access required for rewriting this block. In the latter case, there is an extra overhead consisting of one random access required to access the overflow block and one sequential access to rewrite it.

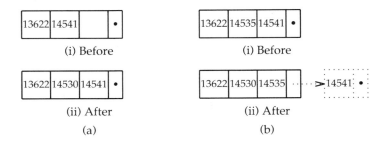

Figure 6.10   The effect of inserting a logical record with key 14530 in the file structure. Notice the absence of overflow records before the insertion operation in both cases.

- In the presence of overflow records, a new record could be placed either in the primary block or in any position in a chain of length L. Figure 6.11 illustrates the former case.

We are now ready to derive the search length of an inserted record that is also an overflow record. To insert the record the chain must be traversed until a record is found with a key greater than that of the inserted record. Assuming that the record which is found occupies the ith position within the chain, then $h + 1$ random accesses are required. In addition, a new block must be allocated, the block must be rewritten; and the predecessor block must be rewritten. It is clear then that the search length is given by $(h + i + 1)$ random accesses plus two sequential block accesses. Summarizing the preceding discussion, it can be seen that the search length is given by the following general formula:

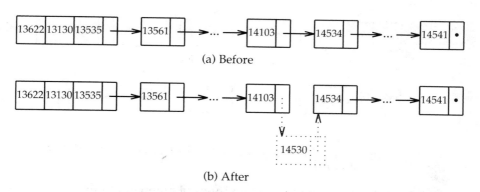

(a) Before

(b) After

Figure 6.11   The effect of inserting a logical record with key 4530 in the file structure. Notice the chain of the L overflow records.

$$SL\,[Insert\_One\,,\,IS\,] = \begin{cases} h & rba + 1 & sba & L = 0 \text{ and primary block not full} \\ (h + j + 1) & rba + 2 & sba & \text{otherwise} \end{cases}$$

where j indicates the position within the chain where the record must be inserted. With this notation, the primary block is considered block 0; the first overflow block, block 1; and so on.

6.2.3.5   The *Delete_One* Operation.   In order to maintain orderly chains, the cost of the *Delete_One* operation depends on the method used. In particular, if a deleted record is stored in the primary block, then the record is simply flagged. In addition, in the case in which overflow records exist, the first overflow record is moved in the primary block, which is rewritten; the overflow block is deallocated; and the chain is repaired. Figure 6.12 illustrates the latter case. When the record to be deleted is an overflow record, then its block must be deallocated and the chain must be repaired. Figure 6.13 illustrates this case. Notice that the search length depends on the position of the overflow record within the chain; this derivation is left as an exercise for the reader.

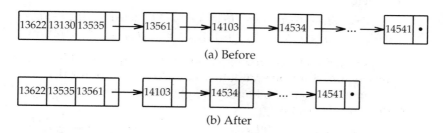

(a) Before

(b) After

Figure 6.12   The effect of deleting the logical record with key 13130 in the file structure.

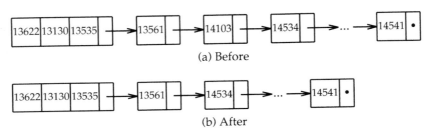

Figure 6.13 The effect of deleting the logical record with key 14103 in the file structure.

6.2.4 Reorganization Points of an Indexed Sequential File

As we mentioned before, the number of overflow records does affect the performance of an indexed sequential file. Therefore, after a certain amount of time the file must be reorganized. Empirical studies indicate that the reorganization point can be determined by the point at which the performance of the file has deteriorated by 50% (or more) relative to its initial performance (after initial loading).

This performance is measured in terms of the average search length during retrievals. In particular, let n_1 and n_2 be the number of *Retrieve_All* and *Retrieve_One* operations per unit of time[11], respectively. Then, according to equation [1.5], we obtain for the average search length $SL(L)$

$$SL(L) = \frac{n_1 \cdot SL[Retrieve\_One, IS](L) + n_2 \cdot SL[Retrieve\_All, IS](L))}{n_1 + n_2} \quad [6.11]$$

Hence reorganization should occur when

$$\frac{SL(L)}{SL(0)} = 1.5 \quad [6.12]$$

By letting $f_1 = \dfrac{n_1}{n_1 + n_2}$ and $f_2 = \dfrac{n_2}{n_1 + n_2}$, equation [6.12], in view of equation [6.11], yields

$$\frac{f_1 \cdot SL[Retrieve\_One, IS](L) + f_2 \cdot SL[Retrieve\_All, IS](L))}{f_1 \cdot SL[Retrieve\_One, IS](0) + f_2 \cdot SL[Retrieve\_All, IS](0))} = 1.5 \quad [6.13]$$

If it is assumed that the time required for one sequential block access is equal to the time required for one random block access, and if, for the sake of simplicity, it is assumed that $f_1 \approx f_2$, then by taking into account equations [6.9] and [6.10], equation [6.13] becomes

$$\frac{NBLK_{dat} \cdot L + NBLK_{dat} + 1 + h + \left[\dfrac{1}{BF_{dat} + L} \cdot \dfrac{L \cdot (L+1)}{2} \right]}{NBLK_{dat} + 1 + h} = 1.5$$

---

[11] A unit of time in this case could be a day, a week, a month, etc.

In rearranging the terms of the above equation, we obtain

$$\left[\frac{1}{BF_{dat} + L} \cdot \frac{L \cdot (L+1)}{2} \right] + NBLK_{dat} \cdot L - 0.5NBLK_{dat} - 0.5h - 0.5 = 0$$

Letting

$$\delta = 0.5NBLK_{dat} + 0.5h + 0.5$$

the above equation yields

$$\left[\frac{1}{BF_{dat} + L} \cdot \frac{L \cdot (L+1)}{2} \right] + NBLK_{dat} \cdot L - \delta = 0$$

This equation, after simplification, yields

$$L^2 + L + 2LBF_{dat}NBLK_{dat} + 2L^2NBLK_{dat} - 2\delta BF_{dat} - 2L\delta = 0$$

Letting

$$\alpha = 1 + 2NBLK_{dat}, \quad \beta = 1 + 2BF_{dat}NBLK_{dat} - 2\delta, \quad \gamma = 2BF_{dat}\delta$$

we obtain the second-degree equation

$$\alpha L^2 + \beta L - \gamma = 0$$

Solving for L, it can be seen that the file must be reorganized at the point at which the chain length L becomes equal to L_t, where

$$L_t = \frac{-\beta + \sqrt{\beta^2 + 4\alpha\gamma}}{2\alpha}$$

According to the definition of the average search length, the time t at which the length will assume the value L_t will be that point at which the number of logical records NR_t in the file has grown to

$$NR_t = NBLK_{dat} \cdot BF_{dat} + L_t \cdot NBLK_{dat}$$

If we now assume a positive *growth*[12] of g records per unit of time, the reorganization time t is given from the equation

$$g \cdot t + NR_{init} = NR_t$$

as

$$t = \frac{NR_t - NR_{init}}{g} \quad \text{units of time}$$

where NR_{init} denotes the number of actual (no-dummy) logical records that were written at the initial loading time.

[12] Growth is defined as the number of insertions minus the number of deletions.

6.3 EXERCISES

1. The primary keys of the logical records of a file are: 8, 9, 11, 14, 15, 17, 23, 25, 29, 35, 40, 48, 58, 70, 99. The blocking factor of the primary, overflow, and index blocks is equal to 3. If the initial loading factor is 100%, calculate the following.

    (a) Draw the indexed sequential structure for this file.

    (b) Draw the structure after the following operations are performed: insert 20, insert 96, delete 35, insert 16, and delete 23.

2. An indexed sequential file contains 2300 logical records. Each record is 70 bytes long with an embedded key of length 8 bytes. The length of a block pointer is equal to 6 bytes. Assuming that the block size of all blocks is 512 bytes and that the initial loading factor requires 6 records per data level block, calculate the following.

    (a) Find the blocking factors of the primary blocks and of the index blocks.

    (b) Find the height of the structure (assuming no overflow blocks).

    (c) If the growth of the file is 200 records per week, determine when the first file reorganization should occur if we reorganize when the cost of the *Retrieve_One* operation becomes 30% greater than it was initially.

3. A file consists of 40,000 records. Each record is 235 bytes long while the primary key is of length 10 bytes. You are to design an indexed sequential file to reside on a sector addressable magnetic disk device according to the following specifications.

    The disk's characteristics are as follows. 411 cylinders, 19 tracks per cylinder, 22 sectors per track, 512 bytes per sector, block pointers require 6 bytes. Storage on the disk is allocated by individual cylinders. The index set resides on a group of cylinders; the data set resides on the remaining cylinders. In each "data" cylinder some space is allocated for overflow records. The inital loading factor is 100%. The growth of this file is estimated at 200 records per week. Each week 12,000 *Retrieve_One* and 8 *Retrieve_All* operations are performed.

    (a) What is the blocking factor of the primary blocks and of the index blocks?

    (b) How many cylinders must be allocated?

    (c) How many overflow tracks should be allocated per cylinder?

    (d) Would you recommend the use of one extra cylinder for overflow? Why or why not?

    (e) When should the first file reorganization occur if the deterioration in performance is 25% since the file was created?

6.4 ISAM FILE ORGANIZATION

Under the IBM file system there are two ways that indexed sequential files can be implemented, namely, via either the *indexed sequential access method (ISAM)* or the *virtual sequential access method (VSAM)*. The fundamental difference between these two organizations is the way that overflow records are managed. In particular, *ISAM* uses the method of chaining overflow records to their primary blocks, whereas *VSAM* uses the method of block splitting to handle overflow records. It is apparent that this fundamental difference suggests that the tree structure formed by the indexes is different. Specifically, the index set maintained by the *VSAM* organizations is that of a B^+ tree; therefore, as will be seen, the index structure is *dynamic*, whereas under *ISAM* the index structure is *static*. Therefore, the discussion of *VSAM* organization is delayed to the next chapter; in the following paragraphs the discussion will be restricted to *ISAM* organization.

6.4.1 The File Structure

6.4.1.1 Primary Area.   The records of such an organization could be either of a fixed or of a variable length and either blocked or unblocked, depending on the declaration. The logical records are maintained in increasing order of their keys; and the largest key, the *recorded key*, is inserted in the key field of the count subblock. The last remark indicates that the format employed is count-key; moreover, according to the declaration, the keys could be either embedded or nonembedded.

The *primary area*[13] constitutes the collection of all *primary blocks (control intervals)*. A primary block is always an *entire*[14] track. For example, Figure 6.14 illustrates the portion of an *ISAM* file consisting of only one primary area and three primary blocks, with unblocked records assuming a disk in which each cylinder consists of 7 tracks.

Low-level data-management routines construct a set of *index records*, referred to as the *track index*, for each primary area that is placed in track 0 of the cylinder in which the primary area resides. Therefore, the number of index records of the track index is equal to the number of primary blocks in the primary area. In our case there is only one primary area;[15] therefore, the track index contains three indexes.

Logically, each index consists of two "entries." The first entry, the *normal entry*, consists of two fields that describe the primary block to which the index points; specifically, the first field contains the *recorded key* of the associated track,

---

[13] *Prime area* in IBM terminology.

[14] With one possible exception that will be presented later.

[15] The number of primary areas, the blocking factor of the logical records, as well as other parameters that we will see, are specified explicitly by the user via the *JCL*. On the other hand, the number of primary blocks per primary area and the number of data blocks contained in each primary block are defined implicitly via the above-discussed parameters.

Track

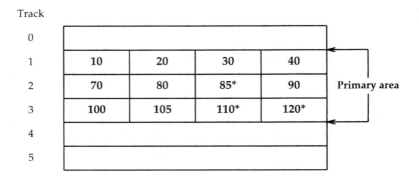

Figure 6.14 The primary blocks and the logical records of an *ISAM* file. Notice that only the keys of the logical records are shown and that an asterisk indicates a dummy record.

whereas the second field contains the pointer to the track. The second entry, the *overflow entry*, consists of three fields that describe the overflow chain[16] of the logical records associated with that primary block. The three fields, *First_Key*, *Track_Pointer*, and *Chain_Pointer*, will be explained shortly; but in this case (i.e., in the absence of overflow records) the *First_Key* field contains the recorded key, the *Track_Pointer* points to the primary block, and the *Chain_Pointer* is set to "nil." Figure 6.15 illustrates the *track index* and its relationship to the primary blocks.

Track

0	40	1	40	1	•	90	2	90	2	•	120	3	120	3	•	Track index
1	10		20			30			40								
2	70		80			85*			90								Primary area
3	100		105			110*			120*								
4																	
5																	

Figure 6.15 The track index, primary blocks, and logical records of an *ISAM* file. Only the keys of the logical records are shown; an asterisk indicates a dummy record.

At this point one should note that the size of the first track in certain instances is not large enough to accommodate the track index; in this case the file system routines allocate as many subsequent tracks as will be necessary.

[16] See the next section.

Moreover, if there is free space on the last track allocated to the track index and if its size is such that it permits the storage of an integral number of blocks (for blocked records) or an integral number of records (for unblocked records), then that free space is defined by the system as the first primary block of this area.

Physically, an index record is implemented as the collection of two consecutive blocks, the first of which records the normal component and the second, the overflow component. The format of each is count-key; the contents of the key field are placed in the key field of the count subblock;[17] and the contents of the pointer field are placed into a 10-byte data subblock. The above discussion indicates that if the size of the key is denoted by l_{key}, then the size of each block is equal to $(2 \cdot l_{key} + 277)$ bytes; therefore, the number of bytes allocated to each index record is equal to $2 \cdot (2 \cdot l_{key} + 277)$ bytes. Moreover, the set of index blocks is followed by a *dummy* index block that is not shown in any of the Figures 6.15 through 6.20. Its format is the same as that of an index block; but the contents of its key area consist of a binary string of ones; whereas its data subblock contains a binary string of zeroes. Hence, the total number of bytes required for the track index is equal to

$$(2 \cdot n + 1) \cdot (2 \cdot l_{key} + 277) \quad \text{bytes} \qquad [6.14]$$

where n denotes the number of primary blocks associated with this track index.

6.4.1.2 Overflow Area. Overflow records are placed in the *overflow area* that could reside, according to user specifications, either in the same cylinder as that of the primary area, referred to as the *cylinder overflow area,* or in another cylinder referred to as the *independent overflow area*[18]. In either case, the overflow records are unblocked and the block structure is count-key. In addition, since overflow records associated with each primary block are chained together, a pointer field 10 bytes wide is attached to the beginning of each overflow record pointing to the next element in the chain. The pointer of the very last record in a particular chain points to the track index of the associated primary block. We will see later that overflow records are placed in the indicated overflow area on a first-come, first-serve fashion. In other words, the overflow records are not stored according to their logical order. Their logical order is maintained via the presented system of pointers.

This section closes with the remark that in the case of the cylinder overflow area, the address of the last record in the overflow chain as well as the amount of storage available in the overflow area is recorded by the file system in the track descriptor word of track 0 of this cylinder.

6.4.1.3 Index Area. It was shown earlier that low-level data management routines build a track index for each cylinder. In addition, these routines are capable of building a *cylinder* index for each cylinder. Specifically each cylinder index contains in its key field a copy of the largest primary key of all

---

[17] See Chapter 2 for details.

[18] A user may request and receive both types of overflow areas.

records that reside in the cylinder that is associated with it.[19] Moreover, as a response to a user request, the low-level routines of the file system are capable of building a *master index*. Clearly the master index indexes the cylinder index. Figure 6.16 illustrates the above concepts.

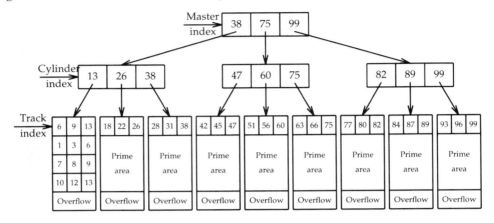

Figure 6.16 The logical ISAM structure. The file employs nine cylinders; each cylinder consists of five tracks; each prime area consists of three tracks; and one overflow track is allocated per cylinder.

Closer examination of Figure 6.16 reveals that the master index is a one-level index. In practice, the file system could build up to a three-level index to cut down on the search time required to access the target cylinder index. The height of this structure depends on user specifications.

We note here that the *index area*, which is the collection of cylinder and master indexes,[20] can be placed in an entirely different cylinder(s) as a result of a user request expressed via appropriate DD[21] statements. In the absence of such a request and in the case of a file that requests more than one cylinder, the file system will build a cylinder index anyway that will be stored at the end of the independent overflow area if one has been requested; otherwise, the cylinder index will be stored at the end of the prime area.

6.4.2 The Operations

6.4.2.1   The *Insert_One* Operation.   It will be assumed that the first few steps of the *Insert_One* algorithm have been executed to the point that the *index*

---

[19] The actual contents of the pointer field reflect the address of the track index associated with that cylinder.

[20] The format of each cylinder and master index is the same as that of the normal component of a track index.

[21] For more specific information on the format of the different DD statements refer to the section about PL/1 at end of this chapter.

of the target primary block has been found and that the file is as in Figure 6.15. We will show the mechanism followed by the *Insert_One* algorithm by considering a number of distinct cases that may arise:

1. *Insert record with key = 110.* The track index indicates via its normal component that the record must be inserted in primary block 3; examination of this block, by the access method, indicates that there is a *dummy* record with the *same* key as that of the record. Therefore, the record is inserted in this slot; no field of the track index is adjusted. Figure 6.17 indicates the file structure after the completion of this operation.

Track

0	40 1 40 1 •	90 2 90 2 •	120 3 120 3 •		Track index
1	10	20	30	40	
2	70	80	85*	90	Primary area
3	100	105	110	120*	
4					
5					

Figure 6.17   The *ISAM* file after insertion of the logical record with key 110.

2. *Insert record with key = 25.* Examination of the track index in Figure 6.17 indicates that the target primary block is track 1. But examination of this block indicates that the block is full. Since the key of the new record is *less* than the recorded key and, since the order of the logical records is maintained, the following steps are taking place:

   a. The last record in the block, in this case record 40, is pumped-off so room will become available in the primary block for the new record. The new record is inserted in this block; at the same time the key field of the normal component of the index is adjusted so that it will contain the largest key of the primary block, which in this case is equal to 30.

   b. If the pumped-off record is a *dummy* record, nothing else takes place; otherwise, as in this case, the pumped-off record is treated as an overflow record.

   c. The overflow record is placed in the first *available* slot of the overflow area; therefore, an overflow track could conceivably contain logical records that overflow from a number of primary blocks. When the overflow record is inserted in the overflow area, the fields of the overflow entry of the index are adjusted so that the following occur:

(i) The *Key* field *always* contains the key of the *very first* record that was pumped-off the track; in our example, this value is 40.

(ii) The *Track* field points to the track to which the *last* record pumped-off the primary block was inserted; in our example, this value is equal to 4.

(iii) The *Pointer* field points to the block in the overflow track, which now contains the *last* record that was pumped-off the primary block. This pointer indicates the *relative* position of the overflow block *within* the track; in our example, this value is equal to 1.

(iv) Finally, if there is a need, the overflow records are linked.

Figure 6.18 indicates the file structure after insertion of the record with key 25.

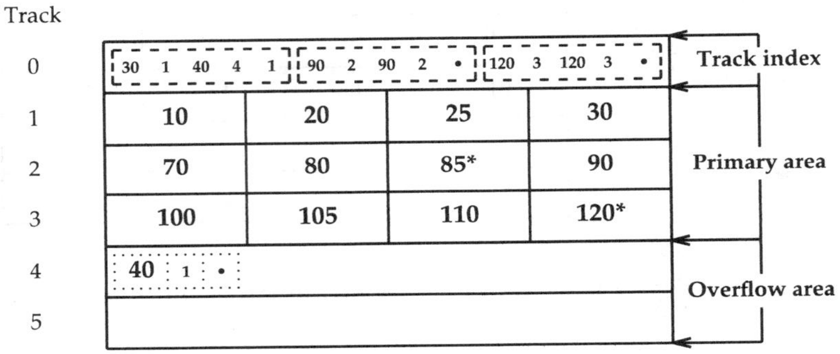

Figure 6.18 The ISAM file after insertion of the logical record with key 25.

3. *Insert record with key = 35.* Examination of the normal and overflow components of the track index in Figure 6.18 indicates that the new record must be inserted as an overflow record of the chain associated with primary block 1. In this case the following steps are taking place. The overflow record is placed in the first *available* slot of the overflow area; the chain is repaired so that it maintains the logical order of the records; and in the case in which the newly inserted record is the very first record of this chain, the *Track* and *Pointer* fields of the overflow component are adjusted so that they point to this block. Figure 6.19 indicates the file structure after the insertion of the logical record with key 35.

4. *Insert record with key = 125.* Examination of the normal and overflow components of the track index in Figure 6.18 indicates that the key of the new record is larger than any other key of the records in the *file*. In this case the file system attempts to put the new record into the last primary block. But since the block is full, the new record is treated as an overflow record; and the steps outlined in case [c] above are followed. Notice that in this case,

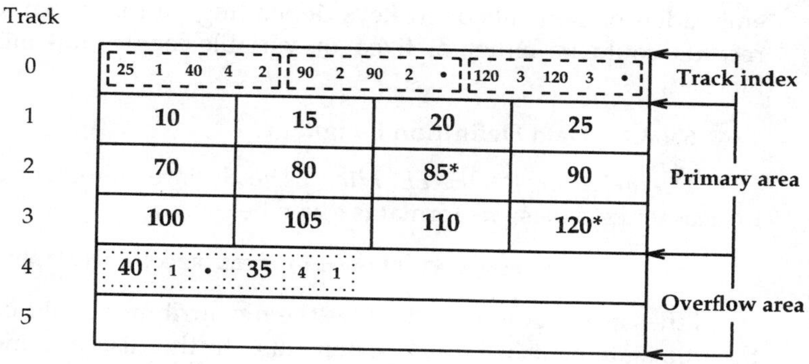

Track

Figure 6.19 The ISAM file of Figure 6.18 after insertion of the logical record with key 35.

the cylinder index (and its associated master index) corresponding to this cylinder are adjusted. Figure 6.20 indicates the file structure after the insertion of the logical record with key 125.

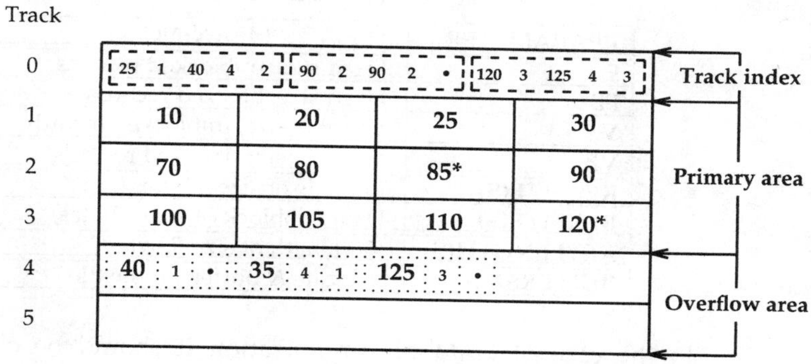

Track

Figure 6.20 The ISAM file of Figure 6.18 after insertion of the logical records with key 125.

6.4.2.2   The *Delete_One* Operation.   Deletion of a record consists of flagging the record. Specifically, each logical record is furnished by the application program with a byte field at the very beginning of the record. A record is marked as deleted by setting the contents of this field to FF (hex).

Notice that the index is never adjusted, records are not rearranged, and chains are not repaired.

6.4.3 HOST LANGUAGE: PL/1

The PL/1 data sublanguage permits the creation and manipulation of ISAM files via **INDEXED** files. Recall that the block format is count-key with either embedded or nonembedded keys depending on the declaration; moreover, the records could be either of fixed or variable length and either blocked or un-blocked.

6.4.3.1 Data Definition Language.

Declaring an INDEXED File.   The declare statement resembles that used in CONSECUTIVE files; its format is given below.

```
DCL (logical_filename) FILE RECORD ENV(INDEXED);
```

As in the case of CONSECUTIVE files the file attributes could be supplied either by the DCL statement or by *JCL* statements. In the case in which these parameters are to be declared in the declaration statement, they must be placed after the keyword INDEXED and inside the parentheses. Some of the allowable parameters, their syntaxes, and meanings are given in Table 6.4. The parameters F, FB, V, VB, RECSIZE, BLKSIZE, and BUFFERS have the same meaning as in our previous discussions, and they will not be discussed any further. The parameter KEYLENGTH indicates to the access method the size of the primary key in bytes.

TABLE 6.4   The allowable DCB parameters in PL/1 under OS/MVS.

PARAMETER	MEANING
F	Fixed size, unblocked records
FB	Fixed size, blocked records
V	Variable size, unblocked records
VB	Variable size, blocked records
RECSIZE(S)	Records of size S bytes
BLKSIZE(S)	Data Subblock of size S bytes
KEYLENGTH(S)	Keylength of size S bytes
BUFFERS(N)	Allocate N buffers to the file

In the case of ISAM file organization it should be clear that some new parameters should be indicated in the DCB at the time of *creation* of the file. Some of these parameters are discussed here; they are summarized in Table 6.5.

TABLE 6.5   The allowable DCB parameters for ISAM files.

PARAMETER	MEANING
RKP=	Key location
SPACE=(CYL(n,,m))	Allocate n cylinders for primary and m cylinders for index area
OPTCD=	Some possible settings Y,I,M
CYLOFL=n	Allocate n tracks per cylinder for overflow
NTM=m	Allocate m tracks for the master index

First of all, the position of the primary key within the record is specified via the RKP parameter. The value of this parameter indicates the offset, in bytes, of the initial byte of the embedded key. For example, a setting of the parameter RKP to 3 indicates that the key field begins at the fourth byte of the logical record. We will assume from now on that the offset is greater than or equal to one[22] and that the logical records are blocked.

As was mentioned earlier, the user may request from the file system a number of cylinders for the file as well as a request that the index area (cylinder and master index) build in an entirely different set of cylinders. This request is issued via the SPACE parameter. Requests for creation of a master index, for independent overflow areas, for allocation of overflow tracks, and for the detection and deletion of dummy records are indicated via the OPTCD parameter. Finally, the number of cylinder overflow tracks and the number of tracks that are to be used for storage of the index area are specified via the CYLOFL and NTM parameters, respectively. We will briefly discuss these parameters below.

- If OPTCD=Y has been coded, the number of overflow tracks per cylinder must be specified via the CYLOFL parameter. For example, the statement CYLOFL=3 causes the access method to allocate three tracks per cylinder for overflow records.

- If OPTCD=I has been coded, the number of independent overflow cylinders must be specified via a new DD statement that must follow the DD statement defining the file.

- If OPTCD=M has been coded, the file system will create a master index that will physically follow the cylinder index in the index area. The number of tracks that will be allocated to this master index is defined via the NTM parameter. Setting NTM=4 will cause the access method to create a master index and to store it in the first four tracks that follow the cylinder index in the index area.

6.4.3.2   Data Manipulation Sublanguage.

Opening an INDEXED File.   Recall that in order to perform an operation on a file that file must first be opened. The format of the PL/1 statement that accomplishes this task follows.

```
OPEN FILE (logical_filename) ACCESS OPTION [PARMS]
```

ACCESS indicates the *access mode* that will be employed, i.e., either SEQUENTIAL or DIRECT. OPTION indicates the *type* of operation that will be performed on the file, i.e., INPUT, OUTPUT, or UPDATE. Finally, whether or not the last keyword KEYED must be present depends on the values of ACCESS and OPTION. Table 6.6 indicates the available combinations of valid OPEN statements and the allowable operations.

Examination of Table 6.6 indicates the following.

---

[22] This is ensured in our case by the presence of the **FLAG** byte.

TABLE 6.6 The allowable **ACCESS** modes, **OPTION**, **KEYED** attribute, and operations allowable for ISAM organizations.

INDEXED ORGANIZATION					
ACCESS	**OPTION**	**KEYED**	OPERATIONS		
			READ	*WRITE*	*DELETE*
SEQUENTIAL	**INPUT**	Optional	Yes	No	No
	OUTPUT	Required	No	Yes	No
	UPDATE	Optional	Yes	Yes	Yes
DIRECT	**INPUT**	Required	Yes	No	No
	UPDATE	Required	Yes	Yes	Yes

- Under a **SEQUENTIAL** access mode, the retrieval of records is done in an ordered sequential fashion; this implies that to access a record with k_0, all[23] j predecessor records with keys k_i satisfying $k_i \leq k_0$ must be accessed. At the other extreme under **DIRECT** access mode, records can be accessed randomly.

- A file opened for **INPUT** can only be read. It is the responsibility of the application program to ensure that the record currently accessed does not contain a *dummy* record. The mechanism is straightforward; the application programmer must attach at the *beginning* of each logical record a 1-byte-wide **FLAG** field. The access method, as well as the application program, can detect a dummy record from the contents of this **FLAG** field; the value of the contents FF (hex) indicates a dummy record. When a DELETE of a logical record is issued, the access method overwrites the contents of the **FLAG** field of the corresponding record with FF. We must stress the fact that the access method will detect dummy records and delete the requested records, if and only if, at the time of creation of the file the parameter **OPTCDL=L** has been included in the JCL statements.

- A file opened for **OUTPUT** can only be written to. No reads are permitted. This **OPTION** **is selected in** *only* two cases, when a file is created and in the case in which one wishes to insert records at the *end* of the data set and these logical records are of a fixed length. Furthermore, in either case the records must be presented in increasing order of their keys; and in the latter case they should be greater than those of the records in the dataset.

- A file opened for **UPDATE** can be read and written to.

- It has been pointed out that certain operations can raise the **KEY** condition. The reason can be found by examining its value. Specifically, an **ONCODE** value of 51 indicates that the record was not found; a value of 52 indicates a duplicate record; a value of 53 indicates that the record can not be inserted given that it is out of sequence; and finally, a value of 57 indicates

---

[23]If **OPTCD=L** has been coded, dummy records are not retrieved, and the KEY condition is raised in this case.

that there is no room to insert the record. In those cases the application program should be ready to take appropriate action.

- The presence of the **KEYED** attribute is required whenever the application program wants to know, or for that matter indicate to the file system, the primary key of a record. The primary key is obtained or returned via a string program variable. The length of the string, consisting of alphabetic characters and possibly leading blanks (interpreted as numeric zeros) must be equal to the one indicated by the **KEYLENGTH** parameter. If the length of the string is less than the one indicated by the **KEYLENGTH** attribute, the string is padded to the right with blanks to bring it up to size. If the string has more than **KEYLENGTH** characters, then only the leftmost **KEYLENGTH** characters are used to form the primary key.

The Logical **READ** ***Request.***   The format of the allowable *READ* statement depends on the access mode. Before access modes are discussed, we note here that the primary key of a record can be passed from and to the file system from the application program via a string variable. Therefore, it can be assumed in the sequence that the variable **expression** has been declared in the application program as a string variable of length S and also that **FILE1** has been declared to be an **INDEXED** file.

- **Sequential access mode.** There are three statements that perform logical *READ*s. They are presented below.

  ```
  READ FILE (FILE1) INTO (program_variable) [IGNORE (number)]
  ```

  Program_variable is the storage area where the logical record will be delivered;[24] **number** is a positive integer or an integer variable. The last field, **IGNORE (number)**, is optional. If it is present, the access method will deliver to the **program_variable** the logical record that is stored in the (*number* + 1)st record past the currently accessed record.

The next two forms of the *READ* statement can be issued if and only if the file was opened with the **KEYED** attribute.

  ```
  READ FILE (FILE1) INTO (program_variable) KEYTO (expression)
  ```

The above statement also causes the key of the current record to be delivered to the **expression** variable. Instead, one could use

  ```
  READ FILE (FILE1) INTO (program_variable) KEY (expression)
  ```

The above statement also causes the logical record with the key indicated by the value of the expression to be delivered to the **program_variable.**

[24] See Chapter 4 for more details.

• **Direct access mode.** There is only one statement that can be issued in this case:

```
READ FILE (FILE1) INTO (program_variable) KEY (expression)
```

This statement causes the access method to access in a random fashion the record whose primary key is specified by the string variable `expression`; it will deliver the logical record stored there to the `program_variable`.

The Logical WRITE *Request.* The format of the allowable *WRITE* statement depends primarily on the access mode and secondarily on whether the file has been opened for OUTPUT or for UPDATE. At the outset it is assumed, as before, that a string variable `expression` of length S has been declared in the application program and also that FILE1 has been declared to be an INDEXED file.

• **Sequential access mode.** There are two statements that perform a logical *WRITE*:

```
WRITE FILE (FILE1) FROM (program_variable) KEYFROM (expression);
    REWRITE FILE (FILE1) [FROM (program_variable)];
```

The first statement can be used if the file has been opened for OUTPUT, whereas only the second can be used in the case of a file opened for UPDATE. The WRITE statement causes the record contained in the `program_variable` to be written in the appropriate position (unless the record is duplicate) specified by its key. The REWRITE statement is used to write the updated version of the logical record previously accessed[25] as a result of the previous *READ* request.

• **Direct access mode.** There are two statements that can be issued in this case given that the selected OPTION is UPDATE; their format is presented below.

```
WRITE FILE (FILE1) FROM (program_variable) KEYFROM (expression)
 REWRITE FILE (FILE1) FROM (program_variable) KEY (expression)
```

As a result of the first statement the access method will deliver the contents of the `program_variable` to the appropriate position in the data set (possibly by shifting of the records or placement in the overflow area) given that the record is not duplicate.[26] In the latter case the KEY condition will be raised. At the other extreme the REWRITE statement will cause the new record to be rewritten over the stored record whose key is indicated by the string variable `expression`.

---

[25] Under this mode, the SET and LOCATE options can be used in conjunction with *READ* and *WRITE* statements.

[26] If the new record is duplicate but the stored record is dummy, the new record will override the stored record.

The Logical DELETE Request.   Whenever a file is opened for UPDATE, a record can be deleted via the following statement.

```
DELETE FILE (FILE1) FROM (program_variable) KEY (expression)
```

Notice that deletion of a record is done by rewriting[27] the FLAG to FF (hex).

6.4.3.3 Examples.

The Creation of an ISAM file.   It is apparent now that if we know enough about the physical file structure, the applicable access methods, and the characteristics of the storage medium, a strategy can be developed for storing the logical records in such a way that will lead to a significant savings in response time. In the following paragraphs, we will develop such a strategy for the creation of an ISAM file.

At the outset we agreed that our device is an IBM 3350.[28] Moreover, we assume that the file is relatively small; therefore, only one cylinder is required. Assume the following logical record structure

```
DCL 1 CHECKSAREA,
      2 FLAG        BIT(8),
      2 ACCOUNT     CHAR(11),
      2 NAME        CHAR(20),
      2 ADDRESS     CHAR(18);
```

And assume initially 5500 records. It can be seen that the parameter KEYLENGTH must be set to 11, RKP must be set to 1, the parameter RECSIZE must be set to 50, and if a blocking factor of 40 is considered, we can see that the parameter BLKSIZE must be set to 2000. Hence, the declaration of the file follows.

```
DCL CHECKS FILE RECORD ENV(INDEXED FB RECSIZE(50)
                    BLKSIZE(2000)), KEYLENGTH(11)),
      1 CHECKSAREA,
          2 FLAG        BIT(8),
          2 ACCOUNT     CHAR(11),
          2 NAME        CHAR(20),
          2 ADDRESS     CHAR(18);
```

We must now decide on a number of additional parameters. Assume that our initial analysis indicates that approximately 200 overflow records are anticipated

---

[27] If OPTCD=L has not been coded, this statement cannot be used; in this case the application program is responsible for the deletion.

[28] This is the major drawback of this file organization. The structure is *device dependent*, which makes portability impossible.

before the reorganization point. Since overflow records are unblocked, it can be seen that the total storage requirements for such a record is equal to 267 bytes (block overhead) plus 22 bytes (key overhead) plus 10 bytes (pointer overhead) plus 50 bytes (the record itself). Hence, 349 bytes per overflow record are needed. Given that in each track 19,069 bytes are available to the user, it can be seen that 54 overflow records per track can be accommodated. Therefore, four overflow tracks should be allocated; to accomplish this, we will code CYLOFL=4, OPTCD=YL, which will force the file system to detect dummy records and to delete the requested ones. Finally SPACE=(CYL(1,,0)) should be coded, since the file occupies only one cylinder; there is no need for either a cylinder or a master index.

The next question that must be resolved is how many primary blocks are available. If we assume that there are 30 tracks per cylinder and that already 4 overflow tracks have been allocated, this implies that the number of primary blocks can not be greater than 26; the exact number, of course, depends on the storage requirements of the track index. We are now ready to derive these storage requirements.

According to equation [6.14] the storage requirements for each index record is given by $2 \cdot (22 + 277)$, or 598 bytes. Given that we know that no more than 26 primary blocks must be indexed from equation [6.14] it can be derived that the total storage requirements for the track index is $53 \cdot 299$, or 15,847 bytes.

But the storage requirement for each data block (including the block overhead) is equal to $267 + 2 \cdot 11 + 2000$, or 2,289 bytes.[29] Hence, in the first track $flr \left\lceil \dfrac{19,069 - 15,847}{2289} \right\rceil$, or 1 block, can be accommodated, whereas in each of the remaining 25 tracks, $flr \left\lceil \dfrac{19,069}{2289} \right\rceil$, or 7 blocks, can be accommodated. Hence, in the first primary block exactly 40 records can be stored, whereas 280 records can be stored in each of the remaining 25 primary blocks. Equivalently, one can see that the primary area has a maximum capacity of 7040 records.

The above discussion indicates that at initial loading 7040 logical records must be written, 1540 of which are dummy. To minimize the number of overflow records, those dummy records must be distributed among the primary blocks; in particular, they must be written at the physical end of the primary blocks. One possible strategy that could be followed is to distribute the dummy records so that each primary block contains the same percentage of dummy records. Since the percentage of dummies is (1540/7040)%, or 21.875 %, the first primary block will receive $21.875 \cdot 40$, or 8.75 dummies, while each of the other primary blocks will receive $21.875 \cdot 280$, or 61.25 records. Therefore, the distribution scheme dictates that the first primary block will receive 15 dummies, while each of the remaining 25 primary blocks will receive 61 dummies.

Below the code is presented that is required to create the **Checks** file as an *ISAM* file. This algorithm does not attempt to place the logical records according

---

[29] Recall that the format is count-key with embedded records.

to the strategy outlined above; instead the reader is encouraged to modify the algorithm presented below to accomplish this task.

At any rate, we assume that each customer's record has been punched on 80-column cards. The blocking factor is 10, one cylinder is allocated to the file, and two tracks are allocated for overflow area. The primary key is assumed to be the four-digit integer formed by the four rightmost digits of the **Account** field.

```
CREATE:PROC OPTIONS(MAIN);
     DCL BEOF BIT(1) INIT('1'B);
     DCL (SUBSTR) BUILTIN;
/*
**   Declaration of the file that holds the logical records to be inserted
**   in the file.
*/
     DCL CARD FILE RECORD ENV(CONSECUTIVE F RECSIZE(80)),
          1 CARDAREA,
               2 ACCOUNT  CHAR(11),
               2 NAME     CHAR(20),
               2 ADDRESS  CHAR(15),
               2 BALANCE  PIC'999999.99',
               2 FILLER   CHAR(25);
/*
**   Declaration of the CHECKS file follows.
*/
     DCL CHECKS FILE RECORD SEQUENTIAL KEYED ENV(INDEXED RECSIZE(58)),
          1 CHECKSAREA,
               2 ACCOUNT  CHAR(11),
               2 NAME     CHAR(20),
               2 ADDRESS  CHAR(15),
               2 BALANCE  FLOAT DECIMAL(16);
/*
**   Declaration of a four-character field that will hold the primary key
**   of the logical record.
*/
     DCL REGN CHAR(4);
     ON ENDFILE(CARD) BEOF='0'B;
/*
**   The CHECKS file to be created must be opened for OUTPUT.
*/
     OPEN FILE(CARD) INPUT, FILE(CHECKS) OUTPUT;
/*
**   The main loop. Each logical record is read from the sorted CARD file;
** its required fields are moved to the CHECKSAREA structure;  the key is
** placed into the REGN string variable and the logical record is
```

```
** written in each appropriate position in the CHECKS file via the
** WRITE statement.
*/
      READ FILE (CARD) INTO (CARDAREA);

      DO WHILE (BEOF);
            CHECKSAREA.ACCOUNT = CARDAREA.ACCOUNT;
            CHECKSAREA.NAME    = CARDAREA.NAME;
            CHECKSAREA.ADDRESS = CARDAREA.ADDRESS;
            CHECKSAREA.BALANCE = CARDAREA.BALANCE;
            REGN = SUBSTR(CHECKSAREA.ACCOUNT,8,4);
            WRITE FILE (CHECKS) FROM (CHECKSAREA) KEYFROM(REGN);
            READ FILE (CARD) INTO (CARDAREA);
      END;
      CLOSE FILE (CHECKS);
END;
/*
//SYSPRINT DD SYSOUT=A
//GO.CHECKS DD DSN=U.B0069143.S1.CHECKS(INDEX),UNIT=SYSDA,
//              DCB=(RECFM=FB,BLKSIZE=580,DSORG=IS,KEYLEN=4,OPTCD=LIY,
//              CYLOFL=2),SPACE=(CYL,1),DISP=(NEW,CATLG,DELETE)
//         DD DSN=U.B0069143.S1.CHECKS(PRIME),UNIT=SYSDA,
//              DISP=(NEW,KEEP),DCB=DSORG=IS,SPACE=(CYL,1)
//         DD DSN=U.B0069143.S1.CHECKS(OVFLOW),UNIT=SYSDA,
//              DISP=(NEW,KEEP),DCB=DSORG=IS,SPACE=(CYL,1)
//GO.CARD DD *
Data cards go here.
/*
```

The Update of the CHECKS file. The following PL/1 code performs a *Batch Mode Direct Update* of the *ISAM* file CHECKS that was created in the previous section. Specifically, a set of requests, one per card, has been punched on a set of cards. The first field, COMMAND, on each card indicates the type of request. In particular, the field COMMAND will contain either an R, D, or I that corresponds to a request for a *replacement, deletion,* or *insertion,* respectively, of the indicated record. Notice that the ACCOUNT field is the only other required field that is present in the case of either a replace or a deletion operation.

```
UPDATE:PROC OPTIONS(MAIN);
      DCL BEOF BIT(1) INIT('1'B);
      DCL SYSPRINT OUTPUT;
      DCL (SUBSTR) BUILTIN;
/*
**    Declaration of the file that contains the update requests to be
**    performed on the ISAM file CHECKS.  The field COMMAND
```

```
**    will contain the operation request; R, D, I correspond to a
**    replace, delete,  and insert a logical record, respectively.
*/
      DCL CARD FILE RECORD ENV(CONSECUTIVE F RECSIZE(80)),
          1 CARDAREA,
              2 ACCOUNT  CHAR(11),
              2 NAME     CHAR(20),
              2 ADDRESS  CHAR(15),
              2 BALANCE  PIC'999999.99',
              2 COMMAND  CHAR(1),
              2 FILLER   CHAR(24);
/*
**    Declaration of the CHECKS file.
*/
      DCL CHECKS FILE RECORD KEYED ENV(INDEXED RECSIZE(58)),
          1 CHECKSAREA,
              2 ACCOUNT  CHAR(11),
              2 NAME     CHAR(20),
              2 ADDRESS  CHAR(15),
              2 BALANCE  FLOAT DECIMAL(16),
          ONCODE BUILTIN;
      DCL REGN CHAR(4);
/*
**    The ON KEY condition.  Write appropriate diagnostics whenever
**    the record is not found (ONCODE is set to 51) or a duplicate
**    record is encountered (ONCODE is set to 51).
*/
      ON ENDFILE(CARD) BEOF='0'B;
      ON KEY(CHECKS)
        BEGIN;
            IF ONCODE=51
              THEN PUT FILE(SYSPRINT)
                  SKIP EDIT ('NOT FOUND:',CARDAREA.ACCOUNT)(A(15),A);
            IF ONCODE=52
              THEN PUT FILE(SYSPRINT)
                  SKIP EDIT ('DUPLICATE:',CARDAREA.ACCOUNT)(A(15),A);
END;
/*
**    Open the files.
*/
      OPEN FILE(CARD) INPUT;
      OPEN FILE(CHECKS) DIRECT UPDATE;
/*
**    The main loop.  Read a logical record and perform the indicated operation.
```

```
*/
      READ FILE (CARD) INTO (CARDAREA);

      DO WHILE (BEOF);
            REGN = SUBSTR(CHECKSAREA.ACCOUNT,8,4);
            IF CARDAREA.COMMAND='I'
               THEN WRITE FILE(CHECKS) FROM(CARDAREA) KEYFROM(REGN);
               ELSE IF CARDAREA.COMMAND='R'
                    THEN REWRITE FILE(CHECKS) FROM(CARDAREA) KEY(REGN);
                    ELSE IF CARDAREA.COMMAND='D'
                         THEN DELETE FILE(CHECKS) KEY(REGN);
                         ELSE PUT FILE(SYSPRINT)
                              SKIP EDIT('INVALID CODE:',CARDAREA.ACCOUNT)(A(15),A);
      END;
      CLOSE FILE(CHECKS);
END;
/*
//SYSPRINT DD SYSOUT=A
//GO.CHECKS DD DSN=U.B0069143.S1.CHECKS(INDEX),UNIT=SYSDA,
//              DISP=(OLD,KEEP)
//           DD DSN=U.B0069143.S1.CHECKS(PRIME),UNIT=SYSDA,
//              DISP=(OLD,KEEP)
//           DD DSN=U.B0069143.S1.CHECKS(OVFLOW),UNIT=SYSDA,
//              DISP=(OLD,KEEP)
//GO.CARD DD *
Data cards go here.
/*
```

7

Tree-Based Files

7.1 BINARY SEARCH TREES

Recall from Chapter 4 that the binary search technique employed in a sequential file yields the best performance for a random access. Unfortunately this technique cannot be used for linked physical sequential files, since midpoint addresses cannot be computed. A structure that eliminates that limitation is a *Binary Search Tree.*

Logically, when a *binary search* tree organization is employed, a file of *NR* records with primary keys k_i, for $i = 1, 2, ..., NR$, is viewed as a binary tree satisfying the following two properties.

1. Each node of the tree contains, minimally, either three or four fields, depending on the implementation. In either case two of the fields are occupied by two pointers, *lptr* and *rptr,* pointing to the left and right child of this node, respectively. If three fields are used, the third field is occupied by the logical record; otherwise, the third field contains the primary key of the logical record, while the fourth field is used as a record pointer pointing to the data block where the logical record is stored. Figure 7.1 illustrates the two possible node types.

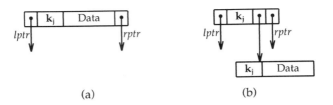

(a)   (b)

Figure 7.1   The two possible node types.

From now on, unless otherwise noted, we will assume the structure of Figure 7.1(a), and we will use the representation appearing in Figure 7.2 for such a node of a binary search tree.

Figure 7.2

2. If k_j is the key of a logical record, the keys of all records occupying the nodes of its left subtree are less than k_j, whereas the keys of all records occupying the nodes of its right subtree are larger than k_j. Figure 7.3 illustrates a binary search tree.

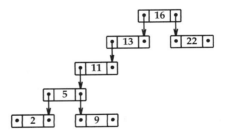

Figure 7.3   A binary search tree.

It is simple to see that an *inorder traversal*[1] performed on a binary search tree will visit the nodes in increasing order; therefore, this structure also permits an *ordered* sequential processing.

Physically the nodes of such a structure comprise a linked sequential file; Figure 7.4 represents a possible implementation of the logical structure of Figure 7.3. Closer examination of the physical structure reveals the existence of a *dummy*[2] block, block 0. The *lptr* field of this block points to the root node and

---

[1] The algorithm is presented later.

[2] The dummy block serves as a header node for the logical tree structure of Figure 7.3. In subsequent logical structure drawings, this node will not be shown.

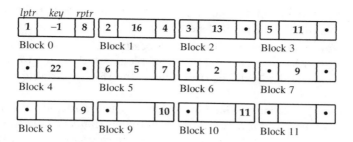

Figure 7.4   A possible implementation of the binary search tree logical organization of Figure 7.3. Notice that the *Free_Chain* is implemented as a singly linked physical structure.

aids the application program in detecting an empty tree and also in accessing the *Free_Chain*,[3] since the *rptr* field is used for this purpose.

7.1.1 The Operations

In this section the pseudocode will be developed for the application programs that perform a number of basic operations in a binary search tree *(BST)* file organization. A physical structure such as the one in Figure 7.4 will be assumed.

The pseudoalgorithms that will be developed utilize a number of program variables, procedures, and functions; their syntax as well as their significance is explained below.

- **Header, buffer.** The purpose of the first structure variable is to "hold" the header node (block number 0) in main memory at all times. In other words, this block is read in main memory only once at the opening of the file; it is updated as long as those operations are taking place; it is rewritten only at the closing of the file. The second structured variable indicates the buffer area where a block can be read to and written from as a result of the appropriate physical I/O request.
- **Parent, pointer, delete, next, previous, successor.** These are string variables that contain block pointers.
- **Read_Block(Buffer,Next).** This is a procedure that reads the block with region address **Next** into the **Buffer.**
- **Write_Block(Buffer,Next).** This is a procedure that writes the contents of the **Buffer** into the block with region address **Next.**
- **Write(Buffer).** This is a procedure that writes the logical record currently in the **Buffer** to the standard output.
- **Get_Free_Block(Header).** This is a function that returns the address of the first available block from the *Free_Chain.* In addition, it also deallocates the

---

[3] *Free_Chains* were discussed in Chapter 5.

first block, repairs the chain, and adjusts the *rptr* field of the **Header** variable that points to the *Free_Chain*.

- **Free_Block(Next).** This is a procedure that inserts the deallocated block with address **Next** as the first block of the *Free_Chain*, performs chain repair, and adjusts the *rtptr* field of the *Header* variable.

7.1.1.1 *Retrieve_One* Operation.   The algorithm is very simple. The root node is accessed and a comparison between the *New_Key* (the key of the target record) and the key of the record stored there takes place. If the keys are equal, the search terminates and the record already in the *Buffer* is written out; if the keys are not equal, either the left or the right child is accessed (according to the result of the test) and the same test is repeated. Notice that if a *Nil* pointer is encountered, the search should terminate unsuccessfully. The pseudoalgorithm is given in Table 7.1.

TABLE 7.1   The algorithm *Retrieve_One* on a *BST*.

```
Algorithm Retrieve_One(Header,New_Key);

[1]   Next ← Header.lptr;
[2]   If (Next = Nil) then {write ('record not found') and exit};
[3]   Read_Block(Buffer,Next);
[4]   If (Buffer.Key = New_Key) then {write ('Buffer') and exit};
[5]   If (Buffer.Key > New_Key) then Next ← Buffer.lptr
                                 else Next ← Buffer.rptr;
[6]   go to [2];
```

According to the presented algorithm, one can see that each unsuccessful comparison ([4]) leads to a new physical *Read* request ([5], [6], [3]). In other words, each unsuccessful comparison on a binary search tree corresponds to one access. Hence, the cost of this operation in terms of accesses depends primarily on the level where the requested record resides. If the record resides in the *k*th level[4], exactly $k + 1$ random accesses are needed under the assumption made earlier that the header node resides in main memory.

In terms of the *average search length*, the above discussion indicates that the optimal performance is obtained when the height of the tree is *minimal* and worst when the height of the tree is *maximal*. The two extremes are illustrated in Figure 7.5 by the two distinct logical binary search tree structures that could represent the *same* file with records 2, 5, 9, 13, 16, 11, and 22. The actual tree "shape" depends, as will be seen shortly, on the keys and on the order in which the logical records are inserted and deleted.

Returning now to the derivation of the average search length, Figure 7.5 illustrates the fact that the height of the tree is maximal whenever there is *only* one node at each level. In this case the tree has exactly *NR* levels and the average search length is given by

[4] The level of the root is assumed to be 0.

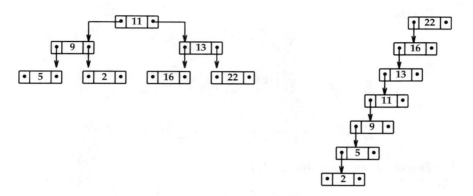

Figure 7.5   The two extremes.

$$ASL\,[Retrieve\_One\,,BST\,] = \dfrac{\displaystyle\sum_{k=1}^{NR} k}{NR}\; rba$$

or

$$ASL\,[Retrieve\_One\,,BST\,] = \dfrac{NR\cdot(NR+1)}{2\cdot NR}\; rba$$

and finally

$$ASL\,[Retrieve\_One\,,BST\,] = \dfrac{NR+1}{2}\; rba$$

On the other hand the height of the tree becomes minimal if at each level, k (except the last one), there are exactly 2^k nodes. Proceeding as in the case of Indexed Sequential files and under the assumption that the tree is full, one can see that $NR = (2^m - 1)$ for some nonnegative integer m and also that the number of levels in the tree is equal to m. Hence, the average search length is given by

$$ASL\,[Retrieve\_One\,,BST\,] = \dfrac{\displaystyle\sum_{k=1}^{m}\left[k\cdot 2^{(k-1)}\right]}{NR}\; rba$$

Our claim is that the above sum is given by

$$ASL\,[Retrieve\_One\,,BST\,] = \log_2(NR+1) - 1 \;\; rba \qquad\qquad [7.1]$$

To prove this, let

$$f(m) = \sum_{k=1}^{m}\left[k\cdot 2^{(k)}\right] \qquad\qquad [7.2]$$

It is simple then to see that

$$f(m+1) = f(m) + (m+1)2^{(m+1)} \qquad\qquad [7.3]$$

But then

$$2f(m) = 2\sum_{k=1}^{m}\left[k \cdot 2^k\right] = \sum_{k=1}^{m}\left[k \cdot 2^{(k+1)}\right] = \sum_{k=2}^{m+1}\left[(k-1) \cdot 2^k\right] = \sum_{k=2}^{m+1}\left[k \cdot 2^k\right] - \sum_{k=2}^{m+1}\left[2^k\right]$$

$$= \sum_{k=1}^{m+1}\left[k \cdot 2^k\right] - \sum_{k=1}^{m+1}\left[2^k\right] = \sum_{k=1}^{m+1}\left[k \cdot 2^k\right] - \left[\sum_{k=0}^{m+1}\left[2^k\right] - 1\right]$$

$$= \sum_{k=1}^{m+1}\left[k \cdot 2^k\right] - \left[\frac{1 - 2^{(m+2)}}{1 - 2} - 1\right] = \sum_{k=1}^{m+1}\left[k \cdot 2^k\right] - 2^{(m+2)} + 2$$

Therefore, we have shown that

$$2f(m) = f(m+1) - 2^{(m+2)} + 2 \tag{7.4}$$

Substituting the expression of $f(m+1)$ from equation [7.3] in equation [7.4] yields that

$$2f(m) = f(m) + (m+1)2^{(m+1)} - 2^{(m+2)} + 2 \tag{7.5}$$

or, by simplifying,

$$f(m) = (m-1)2^{(m+1)} - 2$$

Consequently,

$$\sum_{k=1}^{m}\left[k \cdot 2^{(k-1)}\right] = (m-1) \cdot 2^{(m+1)} + 1$$

Therefore,

$$ASL[Retrieve\_One, BST] = \frac{\sum_{k=1}^{m}\left[k \cdot 2^{(k-1)}\right]}{NR} = \frac{(m-1) \cdot 2^{(m+1)} + 1}{2 \cdot NR}$$

Replacing 2^m with its equal, $(NR+1)$, in the above equation,

$$ASL[Retrieve\_One, BST] = \frac{(m-1) \cdot (NR+1) + 1}{NR} = (m-1) + \frac{m}{NR}$$

$$= (m-1) + \frac{m}{2^m - 1}$$

The last term of the sum approaches zero for large values of m; therefore, it may be ignored. Using the fact that $\log_2(NR+1) = m$, the above equation yields the desired equation [7.1].

7.1.1.2 The *Insert_One* Operation. The algorithm for *inserting* a new record in a binary search tree is presented below. If the tree is empty, the insertion is trivial. If the tree is not empty and if the key of the new record is less than the key of the record stored at the root, the new record must be placed in the left subtree of the root; otherwise, it must be placed in its right subtree. The process is repeated until a Nil pointer is encountered. The above discussion implies that each new insertion forces the insertion of a leaf node. Figure 7.6 illustrates the structure of Figure 7.3 after insertion of the logical record with key 12.

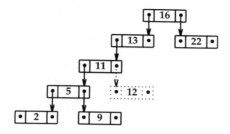

Figure 7.6   Inserting the logical record with key 12 in the binary search tree structure of Figure 7.3.

The algorithm that is presented in Table 7.2 examines first the case of an empty tree ([1]). If the test succeeds a new block is allocated, the *lptr* of the header points to this block, and its *rptr* is modified so that it points to the very first block of the *Free_Chain;* otherwise, a search is initiated.

This particular search consists of a loop in which the "next" block is read into the buffer ([2]). If the test of step [3] does not succeed, then in step [5] a check is made to the appropriate pointer to see if it is equal to *Nil*. If it is not, the "next" block pointed to by either the *lptr* or *rptr* (depending on the test of the first line of step [4]) of the buffer that contains the parent node is read, and the process is repeated (steps [2] through [5]). Otherwise, the appropriate pointer of the parent node, currently in the buffer, is adjusted so it will point to the newly allocated block via the *Get_Free_Block(Header)* procedure; and the updated parent node is rewritten in its old disk position via the variable *Parent* that had been saved in step [4] ([6]).

Finally, in step [7] the contents of the buffer are rewritten, and the new record is written in the allocated block whose address had been saved via the *Next* variable.

With respect to the average search length, it follows from the algorithm mentioned previously that a number of *ASL[Retrieve_One, BST]* random block accesses are required to access the "parent" record. Step [6] requires an extra sequential access, while one random access is required to access the first available free block (step [7]) plus one sequential access is required to rewrite it. Hence,

$$ASL[Insert\_One, BST] = ASL[Retrieve\_One, BST] \ rba + 1 \ rba + 2 \ sba$$

7.1.1.3 The *Delete_One* Operation.   The algorithm for *deletion* of a record from a binary search tree is slightly more complicated. When a node is deleted, the structural pointers of its parent and possibly its children must be readjusted so that the obtainable structure preserves the property that the inorder traversal will output the keys in increasing order. One should consider three distinct cases

TABLE 7.2 The algorithm *Insert_One* on a *BST*.

```
Algorithm Insert_One(Header,New_Key);

[1]   If Header.lptr = Nil then
                              {Next ←Get_Free_Block(Header);
                               Header.lptr ← Next;
                               go to [7]}
                         else
                               Next ← Header.lptr;
[2]   Read_Block(Buffer,Next);
[3]   If Buffer.Key= New_Key then {write ('Duplicate Record') and exit};
[4]   Parent ← Next;
[5]   If Buffer.Key > New_Key
         then
            {if Buffer.lptr = Nil then {Buffer.lptr←Header.rptr;
                                        go to [6]}
                            else
                                {Next←Buffer.lptr}}
         else
            {if Buffer.rptr = Nil then {Buffer.rptr←Header.rptr;
                                        go to [6]}
                            else
                                {Next←Buffer.rptr}};
      go to [2];
[6]   Write_Block(Buffer,Parent);
[7]   Next←Get_Free_Block(Header);
      Buffer.lptr←Nil;
      Buffer.Key←New_Key;
      Buffer.rptr←Nil;
[8]   Write_Block(Buffer,Next);
[9]   Exit;
```

according to the degree[5] of the node that will be deleted. Each such case will be discussed below.

Degree = 0. In the case degree = 0, the node may be removed and the new tree will still be a binary search tree. Figure 7.7 illustrates the new structure obtained from the one in Figure 7.6 after deletion of the record with key equal to 9.

Degree = 1. In the situation degree = 1, the tree will remain a binary search tree only if one "replaces" the node in question by its one and only child. By "replacement" it is meant that the pointer of its parent node is adjusted so that it points to the only child of the deleted node. Figure 7.8 illustrates the new tree structure that is obtained from the structure of Figure 7.7 after deletion of the record with key equal to 5.

Degree = 2. To preserve the property of the binary search tree, the node that is to be deleted should be "replaced" by its inorder successor.[6] By replacement it is meant that after the inorder successor has been found, its data record is rewritten over the record that is to be deleted; then the inorder successor is

[5] By the degree of a node we mean the number of its children.
[6] The same result can be accomplished by replacing the node with its inorder predecessor.

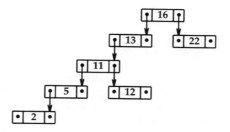

Figure 7.7   The first case. Deleting the logical record with key 9 from the binary search tree structure of Figure 7.6.

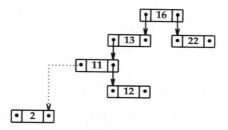

Figure 7.8   The second case. Deleting the logical record with key 5 from the binary search tree structure of Figure 7.7.

deleted. The inorder successor is the leftmost node in the right subtree of the node that is to be deleted. This ensures two things. First, no inorder traversal is required to locate that node; second, the deletion of the inorder successor falls into either the first or second case discussed above. Figure 7.9 illustrates the structure obtainable from the structure of Figure 7.6 after deletion of the node with key 11.

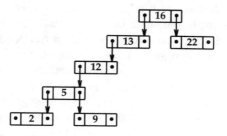

Figure 7.9   The third case. Deleting the logical record with key 11 from the binary search tree organization of Figure 7.6.

The algorithm required to perform the deletion will be developed shortly. The degree of the node to be deleted is irrelevant; one should first access both the node to be deleted and its parent node. The algorithm that is presented in Table 7.3 performs exactly that task.

TABLE 7.3 The algorithm *Search_Delete* in a *BST*.

```
Algorithm Search_Delete(Header,Parent,Delete,Delete_Key);

[1]   Read_Block(Del_Buffer,Delete);
[2]   If Del_Buffer.Key = Delete_Key then go to [4];
[3]   If Del_Buffer.Key > Delete_Key
      then
          {if Del_Buffer.lptr = Nil then
                                      {write('Record not found');
                                       exit}
                                 else
                                      {Parent ← Delete;
                                       Par_Buffer ← Del_Buffer;
                                       Delete←Del_Buffer.lptr}}
      else
          {if Del_Buffer.rptr = Nil then
                                      {write('Record not found');
                                       exit}
                                 else
                                      {Parent ← Delete;
                                       Par_Buffer ← Del_Buffer;
                                       Delete←Del_Buffer.rptr}};
      go to [1];
[4]   return;
```

The algorithm that assumes a nonempty tree initially accepts the address of the header via the *Parent* variable, the address of the root via the *Delete* variable, and the key value of the record that is to be deleted via the *Delete_Key* variable. Upon normal return from this procedure the address of the node to be deleted and that of its parent are reflected in the contents of the *Delete* and *Parent* variables, respectively. Moreover, the two buffers *Del_Buffer* and *Par_Buffer* contain the node to be deleted and its parent, respectively.

As an example consider the *BST* structure and its corresponding physical structure as in Figure 7.10. Assume that our task is to delete the record with key 20. The *Search_Delete* algorithm accepts the values 0 and 1 for the variables *Parent* and *Delete*, respectively. When the procedure returns, the values of those variables are 1 and 2, respectively, while the pointers *Previous* and *Successor* point to blocks 3 and 4 as required. A step-by-step trace of the *Search_Delete* algorithm over the structure of Figure 7.10 is presented in Table 7.4.

If the degree of the node to be deleted is equal to 2, a search must be initiated at the node to be deleted so that its inorder successor node, as well as the parent of the successor node, is found to "replace" the deleted node with its inorder successor. The procedure *Inorder_Successor* given in Table 7.5 performs this task. Notice that the algorithm returns the address of the *Inorder_Successor* and its parent node via the *Successor* and *Previous* variables, respectively.

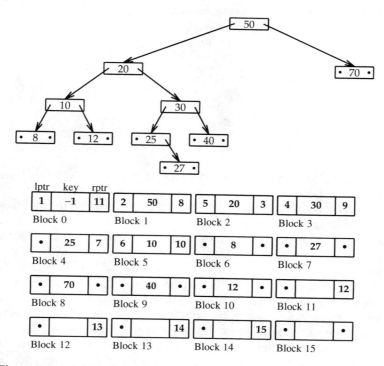

Figure 7.10   A binary search structure and its associated physical structure.

TABLE 7.4   The tracing of the *Search_Delete* algorithm over the physical structure of Figure 7.10. The record to be deleted is the one with key 27.

Step	Header	Par_Buffer			Del_Buffer			Parent	Delete
		lptr	Key	rptr	lptr	Key	rptr		
0	0	-	-	-	-	-	-	0	1
1	0	-	-	-	2	50	8	0	1
3	0	2	50	8	2	50	8	1	2
1	0	2	50	8	5	20	3	1	2
3	0	5	20	3	5	20	3	2	3
1	0	5	20	3	4	30	9	2	3
3	0	4	30	9	4	30	9	3	4
1	0	4	30	9	•	25	7	3	4
3	0	•	25	7	•	25	7	4	7
1	0	•	25	7	•	27	•	4	7
4	0	•	25	7	•	27	•	4	7

TABLE 7.5 The algorithm *Inorder_Successor* in a *BST*.

```
Algorithm Inorder_Successor(Delete,Previous,Successor);
[1] Successor ← Delete.rptr
[2] Previous ← Delete
[3] Read_Block(Succ_Buffer,Successor);
[4] while Succ_Buffer.lptr ≠ nil
         {Previous ← Successor
          Prev_Buffer ←Succ_Buffer;
          Successor ← Succ_Buffer.lptr;
          Read_Block(Succ_Buffer,Successor)};
[5] Return;
```

Moreover, the buffers *Suc_Buffer* and *Prev_Buffer* contain the former and latter nodes, respectively.

The complete algorithm required to perform the deletion of a requested record is given in Table 7.6. Initially a test is performed to handle the case of an empty tree; if the test fails, the *Parent* pointer is set to the header and the *Delete* pointer is set to the root([1]). In step [2] a call is made to the *Search_Delete* procedure, which sets the contents of the pointer variables *Delete* and *Parent* to the deleted node and its parent, respectively. Step [3] handles both cases in which the degree of the node is either 0 or 1. If that is not the case, then a call is issued to the *Inorder_Successor* ([4]), which eventually returns the address of the inorder successor of the node to be deleted and its parent node via the *Successor* and *Previous* variables, respectively. As soon as these two blocks are found, the node to be deleted is "replaced" by its *Successor* ([5]); the Inorder_Successor node is

TABLE 7.6 The algorithm *Delete_One* in a *BST*.

```
Algorithm Delete_One(Header,Delete_Key);

[1] If Header.lptr = Nil then {write('empty file') and exit}
                          else
                             {Parent ← Header;
                              Delete ← Header.lptr;}
[2] Search_Delete(Header,Parent,Delete,Delete_Key);
[3] If Del_Buffer.lptr=Nil
       then pointer ←Del_Buffer.rptr
       else if Del_Buffer.rptr=Nil then pointer ←Del_Buffer.lptr;
    Free_Block(Delete);
    Write_Block(Par_Buffer,Parent);
    go to [11];
[4] Inorder_Successor(Delete,Previous,Successor);
[5] Delete_Buffer.key ← Succ_Buffer.key
[6] If (Previous = Delete) then Del_Buffer.rptr ← Succ_Buffer.rptr
                          else Prev_Buffer.lptr ← Succ_Buffer.rptr;
[7] If (Previous ≠ Delete) Write_Block(Prev_Buffer,Previous);
[8] Write_Block(Par_Buffer,Parent);
[9] Write_Block(Del_Buffer,Delete);
[10]Free_Block(Successor);
[11]Exit.
```

deleted ([6], [7]); finally, the adjusted nodes are rewritten([8], [9]); and the Inorder Successor block is freed ([10]). A tracing of the algorithm over the file of Figure 7.10 is presented in Table 7.7, and the new tree structure is illustrated in Figure 7.11. Notice now that as a result of the write statements ([10] through [14]) the physical structure takes the form as in Figure 7.11.

TABLE 7.7 The tracing of the *Delete_One* algorithm over the physical structure of Figure 7.10. The record that is to be deleted is the one with key 20.

Step	Header	Par_Buffer	Del_Buffer	Parent	Delete	Prev_Buffer	Suc_Buffer	Previous	Successor
1	0	-	-	1	2	-	-	-	-
2	0	2-50-8	5-20-3	1	2	-	-	-	-
4	0	2-50-8	5-20-3	1	2	-	-	-	3
5	0	2-50-8	5-20-3	1	2	-	-	2	3
6	0	2-50-8	5-20-3	1	2	-	•-25-7	2	3
7	0	2-50-8	5-20-3	1	2	4-30-9	•-25-7	3	4
8	0	2-50-8	5-25-3	1	2	4-30-9	•-25-7	3	4
9	0	2-50-8	5-25-3	1	2	7-30-9	•-25-7	3	4

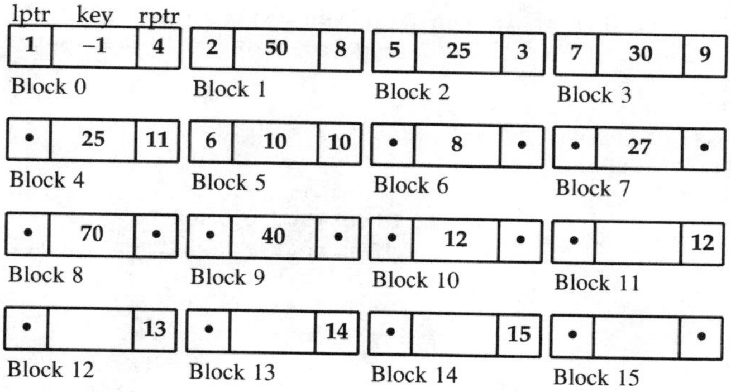

Figure 7.11 The physical structure of Figure 7.10 after deletion of the record with key 20.

In terms of the search length, at the outset a number of *ASL[Retrieve_One, BST]* accesses are required to access the record that is to be deleted. After the search is completed, in order to delete the record an additional overhead is required consisting of one random access; one sequential access is also required in order to rewrite the pointer of the parent node. Again, the additional overhead required to repair the free chain depends on the free chain structure; this point has been discussed in Chapter 5.

7.1.1.4 The *Retrieve_All* Operation. One might think that since the physical structure is linked sequential, all logical records can be retrieved by performing a sequential processing of the file. But such a processing will also retrieve previously deleted records. One could argue that we could associate a *delete* flag with each logical record and the application program would then be able to detect and ignore non-existent records. This technique will work but at considerable and unnecessary I/O time overhead. Specifically, the cost associated with all random operations will increase because those deleted blocks must be accessed; in the case of a highly volatile file, the cost of the operation *Retrieve_All* will be unacceptably large.

Instead an algorithm is used, which performs that task at a cost of exactly *NR* random accesses and is presented in Table 7.8. The idea is very simple; initially, the nodes on the *leftmost* branch of the tree are accessed and it outputs one by one. At the same time, when one of these nodes possesses a nonempty right subtree, the block address of the root of that subtree is saved (by pushing it into a stack **Stack**). When all nodes of the leftmost branch have been processed, an address is popped off the stack; and the leftmost branch of that subtree is traversed. Notice that the algorithm terminates whenever the stack is empty. A tracing of this algorithm over the physical structure of Figure 7.10 is given in Table 7.9.

TABLE 7.8   The algorithm *Retrieve_All* (unordered) in a *BST*.

```
Algorithm Retrieve_All(Header);

[1]   If Header.lptr = Nil then {write('empty file') and exit}
                          else Next ← Header.lptr;
[2]   Clear(Stack);
[3]   Push(Stack,Nil);
[4]   If ( not ((Empty(Stack)) and (Next ≠ Nil))
        then
             {while (Next ≠ Nil)
                  {Read_Block(Buffer,Next);
                   If Buffer.rptr ≠ Nil then Push(Stack,Buffer.rptr);
                   Write(Buffer.Record);
                   Next ← Buffer.lptr};
              if (not empty(Stack)) then
                                       {Next ← Pop(Stack);
                                        Next ← Buffer.rptr};
      go to [4]};
[5]   Exit.
```

The algorithm presented in Table 7.10 will output the records in their logical order only in the extreme and highly unlikely case in which the tree contains only either a leftmost branch or a rightmost branch. On the other hand, an inorder traversal of the tree structure guarantees that the logical records will be output in their logical order irrelevant of the "shape" of the tree. But this method requires an unacceptably large search length and internal storage requirements.

Observe that the first record that will be output is the leaf of the leftmost branch. But in order to accomplish this, all the ancestor nodes on this branch must first be accessed. For example, to access the logical record with key 2 from the tree of Figure 7.7, we must access but *not output* as of yet the nodes with keys 16, 13, 11 and 5. In addition, the disk addresses of those nodes must be saved to permit backtracking.

TABLE 7.9 The tracing of the *Retrieve_All* algorithm over the physical structure of Figure 7.10.

Step	Header	Next	Stack	Buffer			Output
				lptr	*Key*	*rptr*	
1	0	1					
3	0	1	•				
4	0	1	•-8	2	50	8	50
4	0	2	•-8-3	5	20	3	20
4	0	5	•-8-3-10	6	10	10	10
4	0	6	•-8-3-10	•	8	•	8
4	0	•	•-8-3-10	•	8	•	
4	0	10	•-8-3	•	12	•	12
4	0	•	•-8-3	•	12	•	
4	0	3	•-8-9	4	30	9	30
4	0	4	•-8-9-7	•	25	7	25
4	0	•	•-8-9-7	•	25	7	
4	0	7	•-8-9	•	27	•	27
4	0	•	•-8-9	•	27	•	
4	0	9	•-8	•	40	•	40
4	0	•	•-8	•	40	•	
4	0	8	•	•	70	•	70
4	0	•	•	•	70	•	
4	0	•		•	70	•	

TABLE 7.10 The algorithm *Inorder_Traversal* in a binary tree.

```
Algorithm Inorder_Traversal(Header);

[1]   If Header.lptr = Nil then {write('empty file') and exit}
                        else Next ← Header.lptr;
[2]   Clear(Stack);
[3]   Push(Stack,Nil);
[4]   If ( not ((Empty(Stack)) and (Next ≠ Nil))
      then
            {while (Next ≠ Nil)
                  {Push(Stack,Next);
                  Read_Block(Buffer,Next);
                  Next ← Buffer.lptr};
            if (not empty(Stack)) then
                              {Next ← Pop(Stack);
                              Read_Block(Buffer,Next);
                              Write(Buffer);
                              Next ← Buffer.rptr};
            go to [4]};
[5]   Exit.
```

There are two solutions to this problem: Either the addresses of these nodes or the entire blocks are stacked. The first solution indicates that every ancestor record must be accessed one more time, while the second solution indicates that a large amount of internal storage will be required. In a paged system, this indicates that we operate in disk and not main memory speeds.

Another more preferable solution to the case in which the frequency of the required *ordered* sequential processings is large is to store the records in another storage area. This can be accomplished by utilizing the index type of Figure 7.1(b). If this scheme is utilized, the resulting structure is viewed in the same way as an Indexed Sequential file; that is, it will consist of two levels, the *index set* and the *data set*. The fundamental difference will be that the logical structure of the index set will be a binary search structure and also a dynamic structure. It will be dynamic in the sense that indexes are inserted, deleted, etc. Physically the two levels usually comprise two physical sequential lists. The extra benefit is that the data set can be maintained in such a way so that the logical records maintain their order. Moreover, the data set can reside in a totally *different* file where the records can be blocked.

Independent of the solution, new overheads are introduced relative to the random operations. For example, a *Retrieve_One* operation requires an extra random access required to access the data block containing the target record, while the cost of the operation *Insert_One* increases considerably, since an insertion into a data set could lead to block splitting.

7.2 THREADED BINARY SEARCH TREES

We showed in the previous section that *ordered* sequential processing in a *BST* introduces either considerable I/O overhead or internal storage requirements. In some instances, one may extend the notion of the *BST* to that of a *threaded* binary search tree *(TBST)*. Such a tree is obtained from a *BST* by replacing the Nil pointers of each node[7] by block pointers, referred to as *threads*, so that the *lptr* points to the inorder predecessor and the *rptr* points to the inorder successor of that node. Figure 7.12 illustrates the threaded tree obtained from the binary search tree of Figure 7.7. Dotted arrows represent threads.

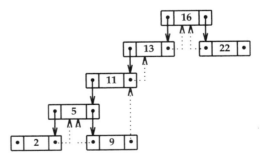

Figure 7.12   A threaded binary search tree. Dotted arrows represent threads, while solid arrows represent structural block pointers.

[7] Except the *lptr* of the first node and the *rptr* of the last node.

Physically a *TBST* is implemented in the same fashion as in the case of a *BST* with one exception. In order for the application program to be able to distinguish between threads and structural pointers, two extra 1-bit fields, a *lflag* and a *rflag*, are attached to the *lptr* and *rptr* fields of each node, respectively. The setting of such a field to 0 indicates that the associated pointer is a structural pointer, whereas a setting of such a field to 1 indicates a thread. Figure 7.13 indicates a possible implementation of the logical structure of Figure 7.12.

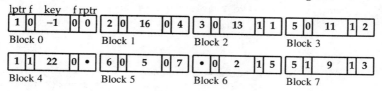

Figure 7.13 A possible implementation of the threaded binary search tree logical organization of Figure 7.12.

The presence of threads in this structure facilitates relatively fast performance for the operations *Retrieve_Previous* and *Retrieve_Next*.[8] To help one understand this point, we will develop the algorithm for the operation *Retrieve_Previous*.

Assume that the last record accessed is currently in the *Buffer*; let k_0 denote its key. The first step of the algorithm is to access the record (block) pointed to by the *lptr* of the node.[9] There are two possible cases depending on the nature of the *lptr*; each is outlined below.

1. If the *lptr* is a thread, the record pointed to by that pointer is the predecessor record, and the algorithm terminates. For example, to access the predecessor of the record with key 9 in Figure 7.12, we can see that its *lptr* is a thread; consequently, its predecessor is the record with key 5.

2. If the *lptr* is not a thread, key k_l of the record pointed to by that pointer as well as the keys k_{lj} of all descendants of the node with key k_l is smaller than k_0. Moreover, the keys of all other records are larger than k_0 (since they do not belong to its left subtree); therefore, the predecessor record to the one with key k_0 will be that record with the largest key among those with keys k_{lj}. But this record is the one whose *successor* is the record with key k_0. Hence, from that point we traverse the tree by examining the *rptr*; if it is a thread, the algorithm terminates; otherwise, the block pointed to by its right pointer is accessed and the process is repeated. To find the predecessor of the record with key 11 in Figure 7.2, we see that its *lptr* is a structural link, and the node (with key 5) is accessed. The *rptr* of the new record

---

[8] The operation *Retrieve_Previous* on a *BST* requires that a new search be initiated from the root of the tree. If the last (under inorder ordering) record has been accessed, then in order to access the previous record an inorder traversal of the entire tree must be performed.

[9] If this pointer is Nil, then the algorithm terminates.

is a structural link so the record pointed to by this pointer (with key 9) is accessed. Now the *rptr* of this record is a thread, which indicates that this record is the required predecessor.

The algorithm *Retrieve_Previous* is presented in Table 7.11.

TABLE 7.11   The algorithm *Retrieve_Previous* on a *TBST*.

```
Algorithm Retrieve_Previous(Buffer);

[1]   If Buffer.lflag = Nil then
                              {write('first record);
                               exit};
[2]   If Buffer.lflag = B'1' then
                              {Read_Block(Buffer,Buffer.rptr);
                               exit}
                       else
                              Read_Block(Buffer,Buffer.rptr);
[3]   If Buffer.rflag = '0' then exit
                       else Read_Block(Buffer,Buffer.lptr);
[4]   go to [2];
```

Observe that an ordered sequential processing is now possible via repeated calls to the *Retrieve_Next* algorithm, which is similar to *Retrieve_Previous;* it does not require maintenance of a stack. Of course, as should be clear by now, nothing is gained for free. The price that must be paid is that extra overhead is encountered in the cases of the *Insert_One* and *Delete_One* operations, since not only must the structural pointers be adjusted but also the threads will need adjustment. Even though these algorithms are simple, we will present the algorithm for inserting a new record in such a structure in Table 7.12. The reader is encouraged to read and trace it.

7.3 HEIGHT-BALANCED (*AVL*)-TREES

In the previous sections we demonstrated that the average search length for random operations depends on the shape of the binary search tree. In particular, we described how the cost of these operations would be minimal whenever the length of all paths from the root to the leaves is minimal. In this section one method, which permits the maintenance of the height of a binary search tree structure that *approximates* the ideal case, will be discussed.

Some definitions are necessary before we begin. Let n_i be a node of a binary tree. Denote by d_i^L and by d_i^R the heights of its left and right subtree[10] respectively. The *balance indicator (BI)* of a node n_i, denoted by $BI(n_i)$, is defined to be the integer given by $d_i^R - d_i^L$. This definition allows the nodes of a binary

---

[10] The height of an empty tree is defined to be equal to zero.

TABLE 7.12   The algorithm *Insert_One* in a *TBST*.

```
Algorithm Insert_One(Header,New_Key);

[1]   If Header.lptr = Nil then
                                 {Next ←Free_Block(Free_Chain,Header);
                                  Header.lptr ← Next;
                                  go to [7]};
                              else
                                    Next ← Header.lptr;
[2]   Read_Block(Buffer,Next);
[3]   If Buffer.Key = New_Key then {write ('Duplicate Record') and exit};
[4]   Previous ← Next;
[5]   If Buffer.Key< New_Key
         then
             {if ((Buffer.lflag = B'1') or (Buffer.lflag = Nil))
                then
                    {Next←Free_Block(Free_Chain,Header);
                     Save.lptr← Buffer.lptr;
                     Save.lflag← Buffer.lflag;
                     Buffer.lptr←Next;
                     Buffer.lflag←B'0';
                     go to [6]}
                else
                    {Next←Buffer.lptr}}
         else
             {if ((Buffer.rflag = B'1') or (Buffer.rflag = Nil))
                then
                    {Next←Free_Block(Free_Chain,Header);
                     Save.rptr← Buffer.rptr;
                     Save.rflag← Buffer.rflag;
                     Buffer.rptr←Next;
                     Buffer.rflag←B'0';
                     go to [6]}
                else
                    {Next←Buffer.rptr}};
         go to [3];
[6]   Write_Block(Buffer,Previous);
[7]   If Buffer.lptr=Next then
                              {Buffer.lptr←Save.lptr;
                               Buffer.lflag←Save.lflag;
                               Buffer.rptr←Previous;
                               Buffer.rflag←B'1'}
                           else
                              {Buffer.rptr←Save.lptr;
                               Buffer.rflag←Save.lflag;
                               Buffer.lptr←Previous;
                               Buffer.lflag←B'1';
                               Buffer.Key←New_Key};
[8]   Write_Block(Buffer,Next);
[9]   Exit;
```

tree to be partitioned into four disjoint sets, *LH, RH, B,* and *U,* according to the value of their *BI.* These four sets are defined below.

1. The set *LH* is the set of all nodes n_i for which $BI(n_i) = -1$. In addition, if a node belongs to this set, the node is said to be *left heavy*.
2. The set *RH* is the set of all nodes n_i for which $BI(n_i) = 1$. In addition, if a node belongs to this set, the node is said to be *right heavy*.
3. The set *B* is the set of all nodes n_i for which $BI(n_i) = 0$. In addition, if a node belongs to this set, the node is said to be *balanced*.
4. The set *U* is the set of all nodes n_i for which $|BI(n_i)| > 1$. In addition, if a node belongs to this set, the node is said to be *unbalanced*.

Figure 7.14 illustrates a binary tree together with each node's *balance indicator*.

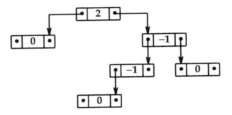

Figure 7.14   The balance indicators.

One more definition follows. A *height-balanced tree (HBT)* is a binary tree in which the set *U* is empty. In the binary tree of Figure 7.14 the root node is unbalanced; therefore, the tree is not a *HBT*. Finally, an *AVL-tree (AVLT)* is defined as a binary search tree, which is also a *HBT*. Figure 7.15 illustrates three binary search trees, only two of which are *AVL* trees. An AVL-tree could become unbalanced[11] after either a deletion or an insertion. For example, observe that the insertion of the record with key 22 in the *AVL*-tree of Figure 7.15(a) does not upset the balance of the tree (Figure 7.15(b)), but the insertion of the record with key 14 leads to the unbalanced tree of Figure 7.15(c). In that case the unbalanced tree can become an AVL-tree again through a number of successive *rotations*.

The above discussion can be summarized as follows. An *AVL-tree* is a binary search tree with the additional feature that if any node of the tree is taken, the difference in height between its left and right subtree is at most one.

7.3.1 The Rotations

A *rotation* is a transformation that maps a binary tree onto another in such a way that the inorder traversal is preserved; therefore, a rotation of a *BST* will yield another *BST*. There are only two such mappings, *left* and *right* rotations. Both rotate a given subtree (tree) *about* its root.

Consider the tree of Figure 7.16(a) rooted at **A**. Note that a *left* rotation *about* its root **A** is possible if and only if the right subtree is nonempty. Using this

---

[11] By unbalanced, it is meant that the tree is not an *AVL tree*.

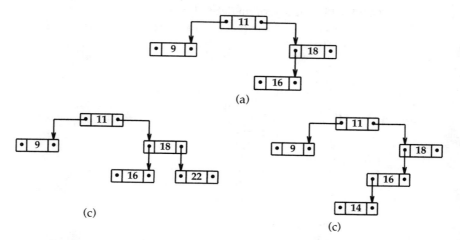

(a)

(c)

(c)

Figure 7.15   Trees (a) and (b) are *AVL*-trees but tree (c) is not.

assumption the "old" tree (subtree) of Figure 7.16(a) will be mapped to a "new" tree so that the new tree is rooted at the right child, **C**, of the old root (**A**) and that the left subtree (in the old tree) of the new root, *l_C*, becomes the right subtree of the old root. The new tree is illustrated in Figure 7.16(b). It should be mentioned that all subtrees *l_A*, *l_C*, and *r_C* could be empty.

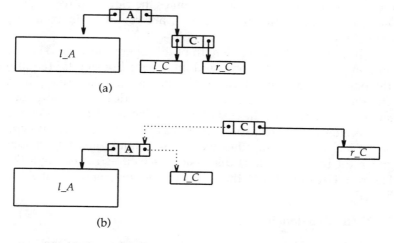

(a)

(b)

Figure 7.16   Performing a left rotation about **A**.

The algorithm presented in Table 7.13 that will perform a left rotation about a node **A** initially accepts the pointer to its root and the address of its Parent via the *Old_Pointer* and *Parent* variables, respectively. In addition, both of these nodes, the root and its parent, have already been read into the buffers *Old_Buffer* and *Par_Buffer*, respectively. In step [1] a test is performed to examine the case in

TABLE 7.13   The algorithm *Rotate_Left*.

```
Algorithm Rotate_Left(Parent,Par_Buffer,Old_Root,Old_Buffer);

[1]    If (Header.lptr = Old_Root)
          then Header.lptr ← Old_Buffer.rptr
          else
              {if (Par_Buffer.rptr = Old_root)
                  then Parent_Buffer.rptr ← Old_Buffer.rptr
                  else Parent_Buffer.lptr ← Old_Buffer.lptr;
              Write_Block(Par_Buffer,Parent)};
[2]    Read_Block(New_Buffer,Old_Buffer.rptr);
[3]    Save1 ← New_Buffer.lptr;
[4]    New_Buffer.lptr ← Old_Root;
       Save2 ← Old_Buffer.rptr
       Old_Buffer.rptr ← Save1;
[5]    Write_Block(New_Buffer,Save2);
       Write_Block(Old_Buffer,Old_Root);
[6]    exit;
```

which the rotation is about the root of the structure; if it is successful, the *lptr* of the Header is set to the right child of the old root. Otherwise, the appropriate pointer field of the *Parent* node is adjusted and the parent block is rewritten. In step [2] the right child of the old root is read into the *New_Buffer*[12] and the address of its left subtree is saved via the *save1* variable([3]). Its *lptr* field is adjusted so that it points to the old root; its address is saved via the *save2* variable; and the left subtree of the new root becomes the right subtree of the old root([4]). Finally, both nodes, the new and old, are rewritten in their original disk positions([5]).

In terms of the search length of this operation, step [1] requires at most one random access; step [2], one random access; but step [5] requires one sequential and one random access if the writing is done in this order. The reader is warned that the derived search length, 3 *rba* + 1 *sba*, deals with only the operation of rotation. As we will see the cost of *maintaining* an *AVL* tree is considerably higher.

Note that the *right* rotation about the root of the tree is symmetric with that of the left rotation. In other words, one should just interchange the words left and right in the previous discussion as well as in the algorithm of Table 7.13. Figure 7.17(b) illustrates the result of rotating right about **A** the tree of Figure 7.17(a).

7.3.2 The Rebalancing Operation

As we discussed earlier, after a node has been inserted the tree could cease to be an AVL-tree. An insertion will affect the balance indicator of *only* those nodes that lie along the path from the root of the tree to the leaf that was just inserted. One can see that the insertion of the record, **N**, in either of the *AVL*-trees of Figure 7.18 will cause an adjustment to the balance indicators of the nodes along the

---

[12] The *New_Buffer* could really be the *Par_Buffer*; we use this notation for clarity.

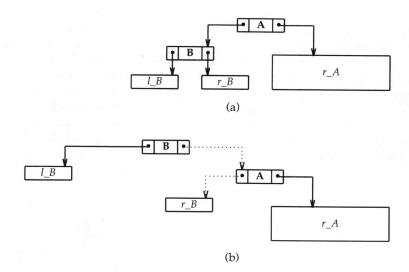

(a)

(b)

Figure 7.17   Performing a right rotation about **A**.

path (marked with dotted segments) from the root **A** to **N**. The question that now arises is how either of these two trees must be treated. As a first step the *youngest ancestor* (**YA**) of the inserted node that becomes unbalanced *after* the insertion must be determined. In Figure 7.18 the balance indicators of each node are shown adjacent to it; moreover, the new balance indicators of the affected nodes after the insertion are shown between the brackets. The **YA** of node **N** is pointed to by an arrow in the former figure.

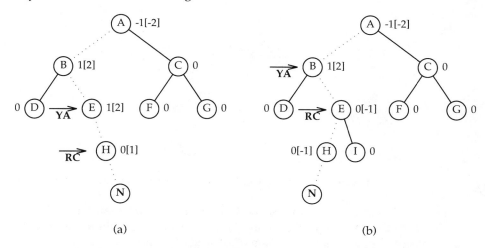

(a)   (b)

Figure 7.18   The tree becomes unbalanced after the insertion of the new node.

The type of treatment depends on whether the **YA** was *LH* or *RH* before the insertion. In our case the **YA** was *RH*; therefore, we will examine this case first. The treatment now depends on the balance indicator of the *right child* **(RC)** of the **YA** node. Specifically, if the balance indicator of the **RC** has the same sign as that of the **YA**, then only one *left* rotation of the subtree rooted at **YA** is needed. Figure 7.19 illustrates the tree obtained from the one of Figure 7.18(a) after this rotation is performed. But in the case in which the balance indicators of the **YA** and of its right child have opposite signs, then two rotations are needed. First, the subtree rooted at the **RC** is rotated right. Figure 7.20 illustrates the tree obtained after this first rotation is performed.

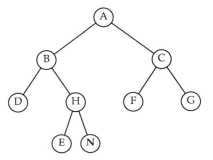

Figure 7.19   The tree of Figure 7.18(a) after rotating left about **YA**.

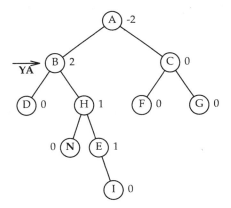

Figure 7.20   The tree of Figure 7.18(b) after rotating right about **RC**.

Upon examination of the new balance indicators, one will notice that the *BI*s of the **YA** and its right child have the same sign; therefore, the tree is treated as in the first case above—namely, the subtree rooted at **YA** is rotated left. Figure 7.21 illustrates the tree obtained after this rotation is performed on the tree of Figure 7.20.

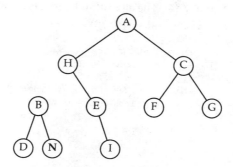

Figure 7.21   The tree of Figure 7.20 after rotating left about **YA**.

Since the other case (**YA** is *LH*) is symmetric to the one just examined, the treatment can be summarized as follows: If the unbalanced **YA** ancestor node was *RH (LH)* before the insertion of the new node, then if its **RC (LC)** is *RH (LH)*, a *left (right)* rotation of the tree rooted at the **YA** is required; otherwise, this rotation must be preceded by a *right (left)* rotation about the tree rooted at the **RC (LC)**.

7.3.3 The Insert Algorithm

The first step of the algorithm presented in Table 7.14 is to insert the new record via the algorithm *Insert_and_Store_Path* ([1]). This algorithm differs from the algorithm presented in Table 7.2 in one respect.

Given that the insertion will necessitate the adjustment of certain *BI*s of certain nodes along the path from the root, the addresses of all these nodes, as well as the direction *D* that we followed, should be saved by inserting them in their order of arrival into a double-linked list. Figure 7.23 illustrates the double-linked list structures that will be created as a result of the invocation of the procedure of step [1] for the three tree structures in Figure 7.22 (a), (b), and (c), respectively.

In the second step, we are trying to determine the youngest ancestor **YA** that becomes unbalanced, as was discussed in the previous section. The method that is followed is straightforward; the list that has been saved is traversed until a node that is not balanced (*before* the insertion) is found. We will refer to this node as the *critical node* (**CN**). If all nodes were balanced before the insertion, then the **CN** node would not be found. In either case it must be clear that the ancestors of the critical node will retain the same balance indicators, whereas the descendants' balance indicators will be affected. This is exactly the function of the third step.[13] Figure 7.24 illustrates the modification in the double linked lists of Figure 7.23 after the execution of steps [2] and [3].

---

[13] If the critical node is not found, the balance indicators of all ancestors of the inserted node should be adjusted.

TABLE 7.14   The algorithm *Insert_One_AVL*.

```
Algorithm Insert_AVL(Header);

[1]    Insert_and_store_Path;
[2]    Temp ← Front;
       Found ← False;
       while (not(Found) and (Temp ≠ Nil))
             {if Temp.BI = 0 then Temp ← Temp.lptr
                             else Found = True;}
[3]    CN ← Temp;
       Temp = Front;
       while (Temp ≠ CN)
             {Temp.BI ←Temp.BI+Temp.D;
              Temp ← Temp.lptr;}
[4]    if (CN = Nil) then exit_1;
[5]    if ((CN.D * CN.BI)<0) then
                                      {CN.BI ← 0;
                                       exit_2};
[6]    YA ← CN;
       P ← YA.lptr;
       if (YA.BI = 1) then RC ← YA.rptr
                      else LC ← YA.rptr;
[7]    Rotate_and_Adjust;
[8]    exit;
```

In step [4] the algorithm determines whether the "new" tree is still an *AVL*-tree; this would be the case if the **CN** node was not found, as in the tree of Figure 7.20(a). If this is the case, all blocks are rewritten via the procedure exit_1 and the algorithm terminates.

In the fifth step the algorithm examines to see in which subtree of the **CN** the insertion took place. If it occurred in the shorter (before the insertion) subtree, as in the case in Figure 7.22(b), then the **CN** is now balanced; therefore, the tree is an *AVL-tree*. The **CN**s *BI* is adjusted, and the required blocks are rewritten via the procedure exit_2. Otherwise, the subtree rooted at **YA = CN** should be rebalanced. The parent **P**, as well as the **RC** (or the **LC** depending on the case) of the **YA**, are known (Figure 7.24 (c)); the balance indicator of the child of **YA** is examined; and the appropriate rebalancing operation is selected as was discussed in the previous section. In Figure 7.22(c) two rotations are needed. Finally, the BIs of the appropriate descendants of **YA** are adjusted in step [7][14] and the algorithm terminates.

7.3.4 The Performance

At this point the reader should wonder whether the benefits outweigh the extra computational and I/O overhead required to maintain an *AVL*-tree. Recall that the search length for the operation *Retrieve_One* yields its highest value in the

---

[14] The pseudocode for this procedure is an exercise for the reader.

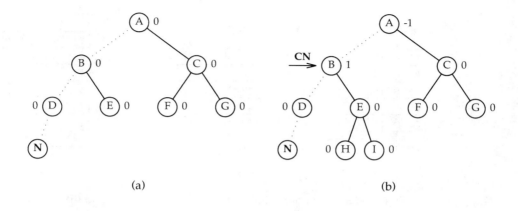

(a)   (b)

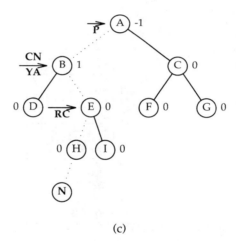

(c)

Figure 7.22   The next insertion of a record (**N**) into an *AVL* tree; three possible cases are shown.

case in which the target record resides in the leaf position of the *longest* path from the root to the leaves. We have shown that in the case of a *BST* the length can be as high as *NR*. Hence, in order to answer the question posed earlier of whether the benefits outweigh the cost, we must calculate the length of the longest path in an *AVL*-tree (in the worst case). The following paragraphs do exactly that.

If m represents the number of levels of the *AVL*-tree, one of the subtrees of the root must have $m - 1$ levels whereas the other should have $m - 2$ levels. In addition, the worst case that must be considered occurs when the number of records *NR* is *minimal,* and we will proceed to derive that number.

It is clear that if $m = 1$, then $NR = 1$; if $m = 2$, then $NR = 2$. If $m = 3$, then according to the observation made in the paragraph above, one subtree of the root must have $(m - 1) = 2$ levels and consequently two records, while the other

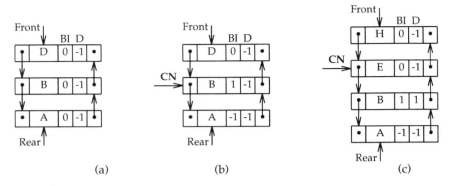

Figure 7.23 The double-linked lists for Figure 7.22 (a) and (b), respectively, where the path as well as the direction is stored.

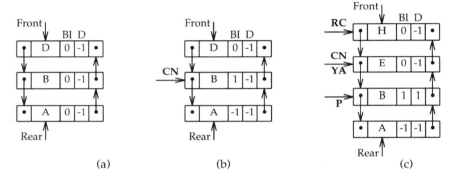

Figure 7.24 The double-linked lists for Figure 7.22 (a) and (b), respectively, where the path as well as the direction is stored.

subtree must have $(m-1)=1$ level and consequently one record. Figures 7.25 and 7.26 illustrate these concepts for the values of $m=0, 1, 2, 3$ and $m=5$, respectively. Therefore, the total number of records is equal to the number of records in the two subtrees plus one (the root); i.e., $NR = 2 + 1 + 1 = 4$. Inductively then, we can see that the minimal number of records in an AVL-tree of $(m+1)$ levels is given by

$$NR(m+1) = NR(m) + NR(m-1) + 1 \quad \text{for } m \geq 2 \text{ and with } NR(-1) = 0$$

Define a sequence, $\left\{ \chi_m \right\}_{m=0}^{\infty}$, of nonnegative integers by

$$\chi_m = \begin{cases} NR(m-2) + 1 & \text{if } m > 1 \\ 1 & \text{if } m = 1 \\ 0 & \text{if } m = 0 \end{cases} \qquad [7.5]$$

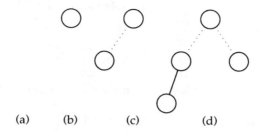

(a)   (b)   (c)   (d)

Figure 7.25   *AVLT* (a),(b),(c), and (d), of heights 0, 1, 2, and 3, respectively; notice the minimal number of nodes in each tree.

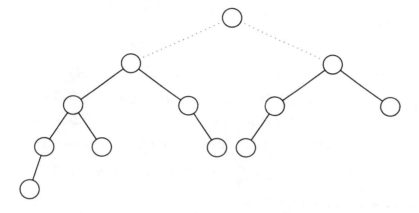

Figure 7.26   An *AVLT* of height $m = 5$ and with the minimal number of nodes.

But for $m > 3$, we have $\chi_m = NR\,(m - 2) + 1$. In view of equation [7.5], we obtain $\chi_m = NR\,(m - 3) + 1 + NR\,(m - 4) + 1$; therefore, $\chi_m = \chi_{m-1} + \chi_{m-2}$. Substituting in equation [7.5] we obtain

$$\chi_m = \begin{cases} \chi_{m-1} + \chi_{m-2} & \text{if } m > 1 \\ 1 & \text{if } m = 1 \\ 0 & \text{if } m = 0 \end{cases} \qquad [7.6]$$

The above equation indicates that the sequence at hand χ_m is none other than a Fibonacci sequence of order 2; a few of the terms of that sequence are

$$0, 1, 1, 2, 3, 5, 8, 13, 21, 34, 55, 89$$

From the above discussion we can conclude that

$$NR(m) = \chi_{m+2} - 1 \qquad \text{for all } m \geq 0$$

where $\left\{ \chi_i^m \right\}_{i=0}^{\infty}$ is the Fibonacci sequence of order 2. We will show that

$$m \leq 1.44 \cdot \log_2(NR + 2)$$

It is known that

$$\chi_m > \frac{\alpha^m - \sqrt{(5)}}{\sqrt{(5)}}$$

where $\alpha = (1 + \sqrt{5})/2$. Therefore, in view of equation [7.6] we obtain

$$NR(m) = \chi_{m+2} - 1 > \frac{\alpha^{m+2} - \sqrt{5}}{\sqrt{5}} - 1$$

$$NR(m) > \frac{\alpha^{m+2} - \sqrt{5}}{\sqrt{5}} - 1$$

$$(NR(m) + 2) > \frac{\alpha^{m+2}}{\sqrt{5}}$$

$$\log_\alpha(NR(m) + 2) > \log_\alpha(\frac{\alpha^{m+2}}{\sqrt{5}})$$

$$\log_\alpha(NR(m) + 2) > (m + 2) - \log_\alpha(\sqrt{5})$$

$$\log_2(NR(m) + 2) > (m + 2) \cdot \log_2(\alpha) - \log_2(\sqrt{5})$$

$$\log_2(NR(m) + 2) > (m + 2) \cdot 0.694 - 1.16$$

$$\log_2(NR(m) + 2) > 0.694 \cdot m + 0.228 > 0.694 \cdot m - 1.16$$

$$\frac{1}{0.694} \cdot \log_2(NR(m) + 2) > m$$

which leads to the desired equation.

Hence, if a file consists of 10,000 records, the number of accesses required for the *Retrieve_One* operation can be as large as 10,000 random accesses for the case of the *BST*, while it falls to at most $1.44 \cdot \log_2(10,000 + 2)$, or 19 random accesses, for the *AVL*-tree. Moreover, if the number of records is increased by a factor of 10 (i.e., if $NR = 100,000$), then the cost of the operation increases in the case of the *BST*; but, it increases to only 23 accesses in the case of an *AVL*-tree.

7.4 PAGED TREES

Up to this point a number of tree-based structures have been presented, but the issue of blocking the index nodes has not been discussed. In this section a *natural* technique is presented that enables one to block the index nodes. This technique can be applied to any of the binary tree structures that have been discussed so far. Whenever the index nodes of a tree structure are blocked, the resultant tree structure is referred to as a *paged tree* structure.

The technique of blocking records emanates from the observation that during any type of a random operation, one first accesses the root node and then possibly either its left or right child at a cost of one access. This access can be eliminated altogether if one blocks the index nodes so that each block contains the root node and both its children, as Figure 7.27 shows.

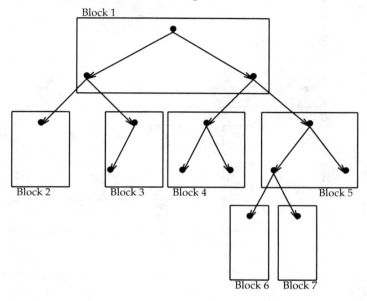

Block 1

Block 2   Block 3   Block 4   Block 5

Block 6   Block 7

Figure 7.27   A *paged tree* with a blocking factor of three. Notice that all blocks are actually the same size.

This technique can be extended naturally to permit one to obtain a higher blocking factor than three by blocking the index records so that each block contains a root node and both of its subtrees are of height h_b. Figure 7.28 illustrates the paged tree structure over the same binary tree as in Figure 7.27, but where h_b has been selected to be equal to three.

It is easy to see that the employed blocking factor BF that is induced by the selected value of h_b is given by the equation

$$BF = \sum_{i=0}^{h_b-1} 2^i = 2^{h_b} - 1$$

Each data block in addition to the BF key values should contain

$$2^{h_b}$$

block pointers that are needed to link the leaf nodes in each block with the blocks that contain their children.

The apparent gain that results from the blocking is that the height of the tree structure is reduced by a factor of $h_b - 1$; therefore, one can conclude that the search length of the operations will be reduced with the employment of a paged tree structure. Unfortunately, there are a number of major problems with such a structure and some are discussed below.

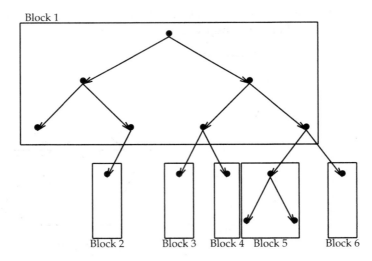

Figure 7.28 A *paged tree* with a blocking factor of seven. Notice that all blocks are actually the same size.

Utilization of the allocated storage area is reduced considerably. To see this, note that in Figure 7.27 three blocks are one-third full, one is two-thirds full, and only three blocks are full. In addition, increasing the blocking factor could lead to an even smaller utilization. As an example consider the structure of Figure 7.28; four blocks now are one-eighth full, one is three-eighths full, and only one block (out of six) is full. The fact that the structure of Figure 7.28 employs only six blocks versus the seven that are required by the structure of Figure 7.27 does not lead to any savings at all given that the size of each data block of the former structure is considerably larger than that of the latter.

Furthermore, the savings in the number of accesses are accompanied by considerable internal memory computational overhead. The application program should keep track of the right and left subtrees; and in the cases of deletion of a record, as well as in the case of insertions into an *AVL*-tree, it may be necessary to rearrange and rewrite the contents of entire blocks. In general, therefore, the maintenance of a paged tree structure is extremely complex and will not be discussed any further.

7.5 B-TREES

We have seen a number of structures that have been designed so that relatively fast random and sequential processing of the file in question is facilitated. But the performance of indexed sequential files deteriorates with the generation of overflow records; similarly, considerable I/O overhead is required to maintain the ''balance'' of the *AVL*-tree structure. What should have become clear by now is that blocking of the nodes of an *AVL*-tree structure, despite the fact that it is desirable, it is usually not implemented, since this would require an unreasonably large overhead to maintain. In this section a new tree-based structure will be presented that incorporates all the "nice" features but at the same time eliminates the "bad" features of the organizations mentioned earlier.

Logically a B-tree structure resembles an indexed sequential organization in that the file is comprised of two logical levels, the *index set* and the *data set* as illustrated in Figure 7.29. The difference between them is that the index set here is a B-tree structure of order m. From now on the notation B_m will be used to denote such a tree.

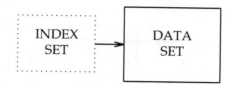

Figure 7.29   The two logical levels of a B-tree file organization. The index set comprises a B-tree of order m.

A B-tree of order m, B_m, is a $(2m + 1)$-way search tree where all nodes (with the exception of the root node) are at least half full and all leaves are at the same level. Each node of such a tree contains, minimally, $6m + 2$ fields, as Figure 7.30 illustrates. The first field, the *counter (c)*, is an integer field and reflects the number of keys presently in this node. As mentioned earlier, each node, except the root, is required to be *half* full; therefore, the value of the counter must be between m and $2m$. In the case of the root node, the value of c could be as small as one.

In addition, the key values k_j in each node should form an increasing sequence; in other words, we must have $k_i \le k_j$ for $i < j \le c$. As illustrated in Figure 7.30, each key k_j is "surrounded" by two pointer fields, p_j and r_j, for $j = 1, 2, ..., 2m$. The pair (p_j, k_j) serves as an index in the sense that it points to the index block in the next lower level whose keys are *less* than k_j. The pointer field r_j serves as a block pointer to the block in the external storage (Data Set) where the logical record with key k_j is stored. Finally, the last pointer field p_{2m+1} points to the block on the next level where the keys are *larger* than k_{2m}. The above discussion indicates that the number of structural pointers, p_j, in each node must be equal to $c + 1$; therefore, each node, except the root, has at least $m + 1$ children, while the root node can have as few as two.

From now on the simplified version of the node type, as illustrated in Figure 7.31, will be used. In other words, the fields c and r_i will not be shown; instead they will be implied.

The above discussion can be summarized as follows. A *B-tree* of order m is a $(2m + 1)$-way search tree with the following properties. ·

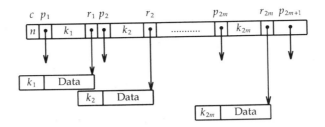

Figure 7.30 The node type of a B_m-tree.

Figure 7.31 The simplified notation node type.

1. All leaves are on the same level.
2. The root node has at least 2 children, while any other node has at least $m + 1$ children. The maximal number of the children of each node is $2m + 1$.
3. The number of keys in each node is one less than the number of children of that node.

Figure 7.32 is an example of a B-tree of order 1.

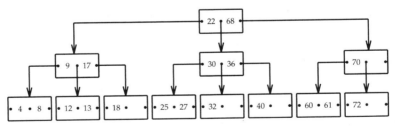

Figure 7.32 The logical B_1-tree structure.

7.5.1 The Operations

In this section the algorithms will be outlined that perform a number of basic operations in a B_m-tree file organization. To simplify the discussion it will be assumed that the logical records are unblocked; in order to facilitate fast, *ordered* sequential processing, the data set is implemented as an ordered physical linked sequential file.

7.5.1.1   The *Retrieve_One* Operation.   The algorithm presented in Table 7.15 is straightforward. If the tree is nonempty, the root node is accessed ([3]); it is transferred into the *Index_Buffer* ([4]); and a comparison is made between the *New_Key* (the key of the target record) and the keys stored there ([4]). If the *New_Key* is found to be equal to k_j for some j, the search terminates; the data block pointed to by the pointer p_j is accessed, transferred into the *Data_Buffer*, and written out. If during the comparison the *New_Key* is less than some k_i, the index block pointed to by the p_i is accessed via the pointer variable *Next*; otherwise, the block pointed to by p_{c+1} is accessed ([6]). If the key is not yet found, the same test is repeated. Notice that if a *Nil* pointer is encountered, the search should terminate unsuccessfully ([7]).

TABLE 7.15   The algorithm *Retrieve_One* in a B-tree.

```
Algorithm Retrieve_One(Header,New_Key);

[1]   Next ← Header.lptr;
[2]   If (Next = Nil) then {write ('record not found') and exit};
[3]   Read_Index_Block(Index_Buffer,Next);
[4]   i ← 1;
      found ← false;
      while ((i≤Index_Buffer.c) and (not (found))
          {if (Index_Buffer.Key[i] = New_Key)
             then
                 {Read_Data_Block(Data_Buffer,Index_Buffer.r[i]);
                  write ('Data_Buffer') and exit}
             else
                 {if (Index_Buffer.Key[i] > New_Key)
                     then
                         {Next ← Index_Buffer.p[i];
                          found ←true}
                     else
                         i ← i+1;}}
[6]   if (i = (c+1)) then Next ← Index_Buffer.p[c+1];
[7]   if Next ≠ Nil then go to [3]
                 else {write('record not found') and exit};
```

According to that algorithm, one can see that if the *New_Key* is not found in the current block, a new physical *Read* request is issued ([3], [4], [6], [7]). Hence, the search length for this operation depends primarily on the level where the key of the requested record resides. In particular if the key resides in the kth level,[15] one more random access is required. The above discussion can be summarized by the following equation.

$$2 \le SL[Retrieve\_One, B_m] \le h + 2 \quad rba$$

One can conclude that both the search length and the *average search length* become minimal whenever the height of the B_m-tree is *minimal* and maximal

---

[15] The level of the root is assumed to be 0.

whenever the height of the tree is *maximal*. In the following section an upper and a lower bound is derived for the height of the B_m-tree.

The Height of a B-tree. The actual tree shape depends primarily on the keys and on the order in which the logical records are inserted and deleted and secondarily on the respective algorithms. For example, the two extremes are illustrated in Figure 7.33 by the two distinct logical B_1-tree structures of order 1 that could represent the *same* file with records 4, 9, 12, 22, 30, 25, and 32.

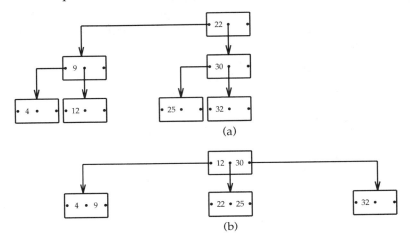

Figure 7.33 The maximal (a) and minimal (b) height of the B_1-tree over the same file of 7 records with keys 4, 9, 12, 30, 22, 25, and 32.

Figure 7.33(a) illustrates the fact that the height of a B_m-tree is maximal whenever each node has a minimum number of keys. In this case the root node should have only one key, but the root node should have two children. Since each child node is half full, the total number of keys in this level (level 1) should be equal to $2m$. Similarly, each of the nodes in this level has (according to our assumption) $m + 1$ children; therefore, the number of nodes in the next level (level 2) is equal to $2(m + 1)$. But each node has m keys; consequently, the total number of keys in this level is equal to $2m(m + 1)$. Inductively, we can conclude that the total number of keys in each level i for $2 \leq j \leq h - 1$ is given by $2m \cdot (m + 1)^{i - 1}$. Hence, the minimum number of keys, $t_{\min}$, in the entire tree structure is equal to

$$t_{\min} = 1 + 2m + 2m(m + 1) + 2m(m + 1)^2 + \cdots + 2m(m + 1)^{(h-2)}$$

The above equation can be rewritten as

$$t_{\min} = 1 + 2m \cdot \left[1 + (m+1) + (m+1)^2 + \cdots + (m+1)^{(h-2)} \right] = 1 + 2m \cdot \left[\sum_{i=0}^{h-2} (m+1)^i \right]$$

or

$$t_{\min} = 1 + 2m \cdot \frac{1 - (m + 1)^{(h-1)}}{1 - (m + 1)} = 2 \cdot (m + 1)^{(h-1)} - 1$$

But t_{min} represents the *minimum* number of keys that can be stored in that "sparse" tree; therefore, t_{min} must be less than or equal to NR. Hence,

$$NR \geq 2(m+1)^{(h-1)} - 1 \text{ or } \frac{NR+1}{2} \geq (m+1)^{(h-1)}$$

Taking logarithms of both sides of the above inequality we obtain

$$h - 1 \leq \left\lceil \log_{(m+1)} \left\lceil \frac{NR+1}{2} \right\rceil \right\rceil$$

The left side of the inequality represents an integer; therefore, the right size of the inequality can be replaced by its floor value and

$$h_{max} \leq 1 + flr \left[\log_{(m+1)} \left\lceil \frac{NR+1}{2} \right\rceil \right]$$

On the other hand, the height of the tree becomes minimal if and only if all nodes of the tree contain the maximal number of keys. In that case each root node contains $2m$ keys; the next level (level 1) has $2m + 1$ nodes; and each node has $2m$ keys. Therefore, the total number of keys in this level is $2m(2m + 1)$. Inductively one can conclude that at each level i, $0 \leq i \leq h - 1$, there are $2m(2m + 1)^i$ keys. Hence, the *maximum* number of keys in this tree structure, t_{max}, is given by

$$t_{max} = 2m + 2m(2m+1) + 2m(2m+1)^2 + \cdots + 2m(2m+1)^{(h-1)}$$

One can show that the above sum is equal to

$$t_{max} = (2m+1)^h - 1$$

But t_{max} represents the maximum number of keys that can be stored in this tree structure; therefore, we should have

$$NR \leq (2m+1)^h - 1$$

Solving for h we obtain

$$h_{min} \geq clg \left[\log_{(2m+1)} \left\lceil NR + 1 \right\rceil \right]$$

7.5.1.2 The *Retrieve_All* Operation.   According to our assumption, the *Retrieve_All* operation requires exactly NR random accesses since the Data Set is maintained as an ordered physical linked sequential file. Of course, there is a certain associated overhead relative to the maintenance of this ordered list.

7.5.1.3 The *Insert_One* Operation.   It should be noted at the outset that the target index block is *always* a leaf. In other words, the key of the new record is always inserted at a leaf node, *but* unlike the case of the binary search tree, the length of the path from the root to the target block may or may not increase. As will become apparent shortly, even if the length of this path increases, *all* the leaf nodes are still on the same level. The last remark is equivalent to the fact that the B_m structure remains fully balanced at all times.

Before the technique of insertion is discussed, the algorithm required for the location of the target block is presented in Table 7.16. In step [2] the case of an empty B_m tree is handled; the addresses of a new index and a new data block are obtained; the key of the new record is inserted into the index block; the new logical record is written into the *Data_Buffer;* and the two new blocks are written out in the disk positions with addresses indicated by the variables *Index_Header.lptr* and *Data_Header.lptr,* respectively. In steps [3] and [4], the tree structure is traversed until the target index block is found. The code resembles that of the *Retrieve_One* algorithm and it differs in only two respects—namely, the path from the root to the target leaf node is saved (by pushing the addresses of the nodes in this path into a stack), and the algorithm terminates when the current pointer value of *Next* is equal to *Nil* ([7]). At any rate, when the algorithm terminates, the address of the target block is at the top of the stack, while the target block resides in the *Input_Buffer.*

Observe that the search length for this operation is bounded below by one and above by $h + 1$ random accesses, where h denotes the height of a nonempty B_m-tree. Therefore,

$$1 \ rba \leq SL[Search\_and\_Store, B_{m]} \leq h + 1 \ \ rba$$

TABLE 7.16   The algorithm *Search_and_Store* in a B-tree.

```
Algorithm Search_and_Store(Index_Header,Data_Header,Stack,New_Key);

[1]   Next ← Index_Header.lptr;
[2]   If (Next = Nil)
         then
              {Index_Header.lptr ← Get_Free_Index_Block(Index_Header.rptr);
              Data_Header.lptr ← Get_Free_Data_Block(Data_Header.rptr);
              Index_Buffer ← New_Key;
              Data_Buffer ← New_Record;
              Write_Index_Block(Index_Buffer,Index_Header.lptr);
              Write_Data_Block(Data_Buffer,Data_Header.rptr);
              exit};
[3]   Read_Index_Block(Index_Buffer,Next);
[4]   i ← 1;
      found ←false;
      while ((i≤Index_Buffer.c) and not(found))
           {if (Index_Buffer.Key[i] = New_Key)
               then
                   {write ('Duplicate_Record') and exit}
               else
                   {Push(stack,Next)
                    if Index_Buffer.Key[i] > New_Key)
                       then
                           {Next ← Index_Buffer.p[i];
                            found ←true}
                       else
                           i ← i+1;}}
[6]   if (i = (c+1)) then Next ← Index_Buffer.p[c+1];
[7]   if Next ≠ Nil then go to [3]
                     else return;
```

If the tree was empty before the insertion, then the above algorithm does *perform* this insertion at an additional cost of two random accesses required to write out the index and data blocks.

In the following paragraphs the technique employed for an insertion in a B_m structure will be presented via a set of examples. With no loss of generality we will assume an initially empty B_2 structure and that the procedure *Search_and_Store* has been completed. The figures that follow will show that when a new block is allocated, the node will be presented by a dashed box; whenever pointers are adjusted they will be presented by dashed arrows; and whenever keys are either inserted or rewritten, they will be shown in boldface characters. The address (region number) of each block will be indicated below the southwest corner of each box that it represents. Finally, the discussion will be limited to the insertion of keys into the B_m structure; in other words, the insertion of records in the data blocks will be implied as well as the setting of the corresponding r pointers associated with the keys.

Insert 4. The tree is initially empty; therefore, this case has been handled by the *Search_and_Store* procedure. The first available index block (block 1^{16}) is allocated and the record is inserted there, as Figure 7.34 illustrates.

Figure 7.34   Inserting 4 into an initially empty B_2.

Insert 7, 22, 21. This is the first case that can be encountered in a nonempty tree—namely, the target block (block 1) is not full. In this case, the key is inserted in *order* into this node. Regardless of the order of arrival of these three keys, the B_2 structure will be as shown in Figure 7.35 after their insertion has been completed.

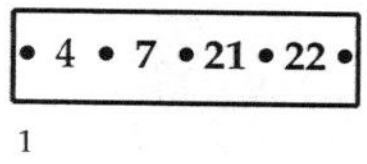

Figure 7.35   Inserting the records with keys 7, 22, and 21 into the B_2-tree of Figure 7.34.

Insert 35. This is the second type of situation that may occur. The target block (block 1) is full; this block is referred to as an *overflow* block. When dealing with an overflow block there are two methods that can be followed, *key redistribution* and *node splitting*. The former method is not always applicable; if it is, this is the preferred method. The circumstances under which this method is

---

^{16} Recall that block 0 is the *Header* block.

applicable as well as its technique are explained later; therefore, the discussion is limited here to the latter method, the only one applicable in this particular case.

The node-splitting technique consists of a number of steps that are outlined below and Figure 7.36 illustrates the B_2 structure that is obtained from the one in Figure 7.35 after insertion of this key has been completed.

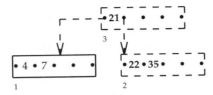

Figure 7.36   Inserting the record with key 35 into the B_2-tree of Figure 7.35.

First the *median* of the set consisting of the keys in the overflow block and the *New_Key* is determined; in this case the median is 21. The keys of this set are distributed so that only the keys that are *smaller* than the median are rewritten out to the overflow block at a cost of one sequential access. The keys that are *larger* than the median are written out to a newly allocated block (block 2) at a cost of one random access. Finally, the median is *promoted* to the parent node of the overflow block. In this case the parent node does not exist;[17] therefore, the median as well as the $p[1]$ and $p[2]$ pointer fields are written out to a newly allocated block (block 3) at a cost of one random access.

Note that the B_2 structure "grew" from the bottom up and that all leaves are in the same level. In addition, notice that the cost of the insert operation in this case is equal to 1 *sba* + 2 *rba*.

Insert 12, 23, 39, 16.   The target blocks are not overflow blocks; therefore, no splitting is required. Figure 7.37 illustrates the new tree structure.

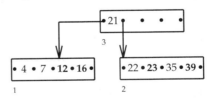

Figure 7.37   Inserting the records with keys 12, 23, 39, and 16, into the B_2-tree of Figure 7.36.

Insert 32.   The target block (block 2) is an overflow block. The only method applicable here is that of node splitting; the keys are distributed, as explained earlier, between the overflow block and the newly allocated block, block 4. The median is promoted to the parent block, block 3. This block is not an overflow

---

[17] The insert algorithm detects this event from the fact that the stack is empty.

block; therefore, the key is inserted in order there, the appropriate pointers are adjusted, and the block is rewritten.

As Figure 7.38 illustrates, the height of the tree did not increase; as a matter of fact, the general rule is that the height of the tree increases by one if and only if the promotion of the median *propagates* all the way to the root node *and* the root node splits.

In terms of the cost of this operation, it is the same as the one before if and only if the entire parent index block has been pushed into the stack. Otherwise, if only the parent's pointer has been pushed into the stack, an extra sequential access is needed in order to rewrite it.

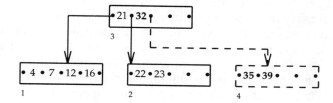

Figure 7.38   Inserting the record with key 32 into the B_2-tree of Figure 7.37.

Insert 29, 46, 28, 43. No node splitting is required (Figure 7.39).

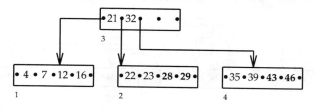

Figure 7.39   Inserting the records with keys 29, 46, 28, and 43, into the B_2-tree of Figure 7.38.

Insert 64, 9, 49, 53, 40, 42. Nothing here is new. As Figure 7.40 illustrates, along the way two nodes split, but the parent node is not an overflow block in either case, and the medians are simply inserted there. The reader is encouraged to trace the tree modification as a result of these insertions.

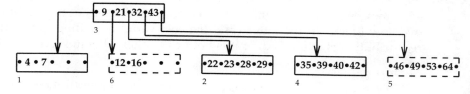

Figure 7.40   Inserting the records with keys 64, 9, 49, 53, 40, and 42, into the B_2-tree of Figure 7.39.

Insert 24. The target block (block 2) is an overflow block; moreover, block splitting will cause a new block splitting of the parent node; therefore, the height of the tree will increase. As we mentioned earlier, the first action (when an overflow block is encountered) should be to apply the *redistribution* method. This method is applicable in this case and is discussed below. The new structure obtained from the insertion of the key in the one in Figure 7.40 can be seen in Figure 7.41.

When the overflow block is encountered, the left sibling[18] of that block (block 6) is examined. If the block is not full, the corresponding key from the parent node of the two blocks, 21, is inserted into the left sibling block; the leftmost key of the overflow block 22 replaces the "moved" key in the parent block; and finally, the new key is inserted into the target block that is no longer an overflow block. Whenever this method is applicable, no key is promoted to the parent node; therefore, the height of the tree does not increase. Moreover, the *left* redistribution scheme employed here could be replaced by *right* redistribution or for that matter a combination of the two.[19]

Finally, the cost for this operation depends as before on the redistribution scheme and the contents of the stack. Assuming left distribution and that all the index blocks have been pushed in the stack, the cost of this operation is given by $3\ rba + 1\ sba$, where one random access is needed to access the sibling,[20] one sequential access is needed to rewrite it, one random access is needed to rewrite the parent block, and one random access is needed to rewrite the target block.

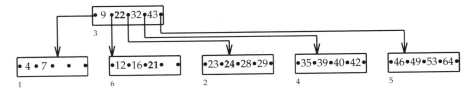

Figure 7.41   Inserting the record with key 24 into the B_2-tree of Figure 7.40.

Insert 60. This last example indicates the case in which the promotion of a key propagates all the way to the root and the root node is full. The reader is encouraged to justify the resultant tree structure, as illustrated in Figure 7.42.

The last example, as well as our discussion in the previous paragraphs, indicates that the search length of the operation *Insert_One* depends on a number of factors, such as the height of the tree and whether or not the target block is an overflow block. In the latter case, the cost varies according to whether or not redistribution is attempted; if it is not or the attempt is unsuccessful, the search

---

[18] If it exists.

[19] Of course, such an extension requires more accesses than a simple redistribution scheme; and, moreover, those accesses could be unnecessary in the sense that both siblings could be full.

[20] Assuming that it exists; otherwise, left distribution cannot be performed.

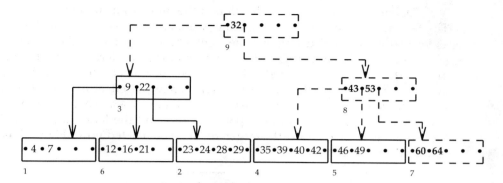

Figure 7.42   Inserting the record with key 60 into the B_2-tree of Figure 7.41.

length depends then on how many "splits" occurred. In the worst case, h splits are possible.

At any rate, one could incorporate the search lengths derived for each particular case and calculate the number of accesses in each case.

7.5.1.4   The *Delete_One* Operation.   Following the pattern that was established in the previous section we will present the techniques via examples. At the outset, note that there are two general cases to be considered; both deal with whether or not the target block is a branch or a leaf node. We will examine the latter case first. Assume a B_2 structure as is shown in Figure 7.42 and that the target index block has been located.

Delete 40.   This is the simplest case to handle. The target block (block 4) contains more than two keys. Hence, deletion of the key of the target record will not lead to an *underflow* node, since the node will remain half full. In that case the keys of the target block are "rearranged" (Figure 7.43) at an additional cost of one sequential access. Notice also that the associated data block must be deallocated.

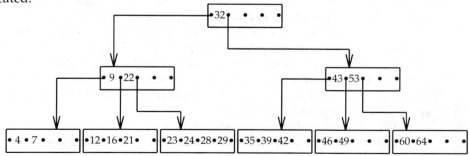

Figure 7.43   Deleting the record with key 40 from the B_2-tree of Figure 7.42.

Delete 7. In this case the deletion of the index leads to an underflow node. The first attempt should be to examine whether *redistribution* of the keys is possible; assume *right* distribution. The right sibling (block 6) of the target block is accessed; if the total number of keys in both blocks (underflow and its sibling) is greater than $2m$ (in our case 4), a key may be "borrowed" from the sibling. The key occupying the position k_1 of the right sibling in effect is deleted from that node; the key value is 12, as illustrated in Figure 7.43. That key replaces the corresponding key (key 9) in the parent node, and the latter key is inserted in the target block. Therefore, the target key may be deleted now. Figure 7.44 illustrates the resultant structure.

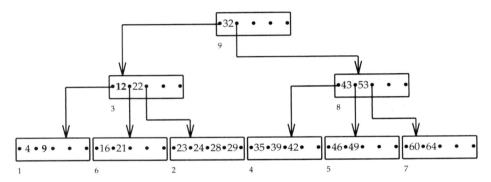

Figure 7.44   Deleting the record with key 7 from the B_2-tree of Figure 7.43.

In terms of the search length notice that 1 *rba* is needed to access the sibling; one sequential access is needed to rewrite it. Finally, two more random accesses are needed to rewrite the parent and target blocks.[21]

Delete 9. This case is similar to the one discussed previously with one exception. The similarity is that the underflow target node is a leaf node, and the difference is that redistribution is not possible. In this case, the remaining keys of the two nodes, target block and right sibling (blocks 6 and 2, respectively), as well as the corresponding key 12 of the parent node are inserted into the right sibling node (node 6). The *removal* of key 12 from the parent node requires rearrangement of the remaining keys in this node. There is a possibility that the parent node becomes an underflow node, as in this case. Therefore, the parent node must be "fixed"; fixing can be accomplished by either redistribution or concatenation. In our case only concatenation is possible; the resulting tree structure is illustrated in Figure 7.45.

The cost of a single concatenation is equal to 2 *rba* + 1 *sba*.

Delete 32. The only case that remains to be examined is the one in which the key to be deleted is in a branch node. (See Figure 7.46.) Here the key is deleted by "replacing" it with its inorder successor, as in the case of the binary

---

[21] Assuming that the sibling exists and that the entire index blocks are in main memory.

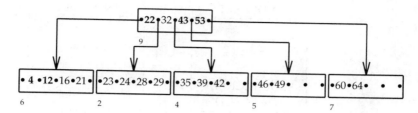

Figure 7.45   Deleting the record with key 9 from the B_2-tree of Figure 7.44.

search tree. With an argument similar to the one made in the case of the *BST*, one can see that the inorder successor key is the one occupying the k_1 position in the leftmost leaf node of the right subtree of that key. In this case, the inorder successor is key 35. In some instances the leaf node will be an underflow node; therefore, it must be treated via the techniques explained in the previous paragraphs.

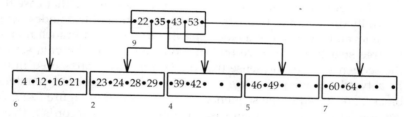

Figure 7.46   Deleting the record with key 32 from the B_2-tree of Figure 7.44.

7.6 B^+-TREES

In the previous section we indicated that in order to perform *ordered* sequential processing, the data set is implemented as an ordered sequential file. But as we saw in Chapter 4, the cost of maintaining such a structure is relatively high. Moreover, the data set and the index set are built *simultaneously* at a very high cost. For example, at initial loading of a file of 100,000 records, for each record both the index in the index set and also the data record in the data set should be inserted; in addition, the r_j pointers associated with the indexes must be rewritten whenever a block splits or keys are redistributed.[22] These problems can be eliminated with the use of a B_m^+-tree structure.

A B_m^+-tree structure is viewed as either a one- or two-level structure. Figure 7.47 illustrates the two distinct structures.

---

[22] The same adjustments of pointers should take place during deletion.

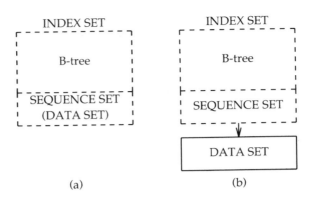

Figure 7.47 Two views of a B^+-tree file organization. The last level of the index set is the *sequence* set, while the upper levels comprise a B-tree. In (a) the sequence set *is* the data set, while in (b) the sequence set indexes the data set.

Closer examination of Figure 7.47 reveals that in either case the index set is naturally divided into two sets. The set consisting of leaf nodes, which are on the same level, is referred to as the *sequence set*; the set of branch nodes comprises a B_m-tree structure. Observe that in a one-level view the data set coincides with the sequence set in the sense that the *logical records* are stored in the leaf nodes. In a two-level view the *keys*, as well as their associated pointers to the data blocks, are stored in the sequence set as illustrated in Figure 7.48. The above discussion implies that in either case the pointers to the records r_i that were present in the branch nodes of the B-tree structures are no longer needed.

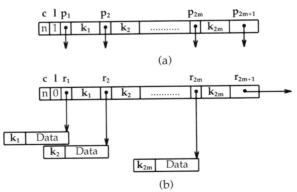

Figure 7.48 The node type of a branch node (i) and a leaf node (ii) of a B_m^+-tree structure.

The two-level implementation has a distinct advantage over a one-level implementation because in the former case the order of the tree is usually larger than that of the latter; therefore, the height of the tree structure is considerably reduced. To see this, consider a selected blocksize of 2000 bytes. Assuming a length of 10 bytes for the primary keys, a 6-byte block address, and logical records of length 190 bytes, we can see that a leaf node will contain no more than 10 records. Therefore, the number of keys in each index block should not exceed 10, which forces the order of the tree to be at most 5. In addition, notice that the utilization of the data blocks will fall to at most $(10 \cdot 10 + 11 \cdot 6)/2000$, or 8.3%; in the case of a half-full block, the utilization falls to 4.15%, far from the desired 50%. On the other hand, with the use of the two-level implementation, the data blocks could still have a size of 2000 bytes, but the order of the tree could increase to 125. For these reasons we will assume from now on a two-level implementation.

Formally a B_m^+-tree is a $(2m + 1)$-way search tree where all nodes (with the exception of the root node) are at least half full and all leaves are at the same level. Each node of such a tree contains, minimally, $4m + 3$ fields,[23] as Figure 7.48 illustrates, but the significance of the pointers differs. The first field, the *counter (c)*, is the same as the one utilized by a B_m structure; it records the number of keys presently in this node. Again, each node, except the root, is required to be at least *half* full; therefore, the value of the counter must be between m and $2m$. In the case of the root node, the value of c could be as small as one. The second field, the *leaf indicator (l)* is employed to permit the application program to differentiate between nodes that belong to the sequence set and branch nodes; in the former case, this bit is set (Figure 7.48(a)), while in the latter case it is reset (Figure 7.48(b)). The number of pointers as well as keys is the same in all nodes of the tree. But in the case of the branch nodes a pointer, p_i, points to the node in the next level where all keys are *less* than k_i, while the pointer p_{i+1} points to the node in the next level where all keys are *greater than or equal*[24] to the key k_i. In the case of the leaf nodes, all pointers r_i for $1 \leq 1 \leq 2m$ point to the block that contains the corresponding record, while the r_{2m+1} pointer points to the *next* node of the sequence set. Figure 7.49 illustrates a B_1^+ structure.

The above discussion can be summarized as follows. A B^+-*tree* of order m is a $(2m + 1)$-way tree with the following properties:

1. All leaves (the sequence set) are on the same level.
2. The root node has at least 2 children, while any other node has at least $m + 1$ children. The maximal number of children of each node is $2m + 1$.
3. The number of keys in each node is one less than the number of children in that node.
4. The tree formed by the branch nodes forms a B_m tree.[25]

---

[23] Comparing the number of fields of a node of a B_m^+ with that required by a B_n, $6n + 2$, we can see that the implied order m, for a selected blocksize, is considerably larger than that of n.

[24] The last definition suggests another difference between B and B^+ structures; the keys in the index set of the latter structure could be duplicates.

[25] Only the r_i pointer fields are absent.

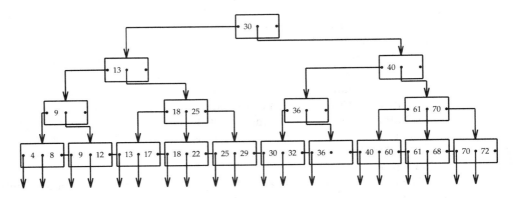

Figure 7.49 A B_1^+-tree structure. Compare with the B_1-tree structure of Figure 7.33.

    5. Every[26] key in a branch node is a duplicate of some key in the sequence set.

7.6.1 The Operations

The algorithms that perform the basic operations on B_m^+ structures are similar to those on B_m file organizations, and they are discussed briefly below.

    7.6.1.1 The *Retrieve_One* Operation.   This *Retrieve_One* algorithm is similar to the one that was presented in Table 7.15; the only difference is that this algorithm terminates only when a node in the sequence set is reached.

    The apparent difference suggests that unlike the case of B-tree structures, the search length for this operation does not vary. In particular the search length in random accesses is numerically equal to the height of the tree structure. One more random access is required in the case in which the record exists. The above discussion can be summarized by the following equation.

$$SL[Retrieve\_One, B_m^+] = h + 1 \quad rba$$

    One can now conclude that both the search length and the *average search length* become minimal whenever the height of the B_m^+-tree is *minimal* and maximal whenever the height of the tree is *maximal*. In the following section an upper and lower bound is derived for the height of this structure.

    The Height of a B^+-tree.   The actual tree shape depends, as in the case of B_m trees, primarily on the keys and on the order in which the logical records are inserted and deleted, and secondarily on the respective algorithms. Figure 7.50 illustrates two distinct logical B_1-tree structures of order 1 that could represent the *same* file with records 4, 9, 12, 22, 25, and 39.

---

[26] Unless deletion is done via flagging.

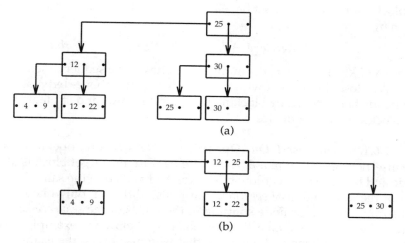

Figure 7.50 The maximal (a) and minimal (b) height of the B_1^+-tree over the same file of 6 records with keys 4, 9, 12, 22, 25, and 30.

Figure 7.50(a) illustrates the fact that the height of a B_m-tree is maximal whenever each node (and in particular the branch nodes) has the minimum number of keys. In this case we have seen[27] that in the last level, $h - 1$, the minimal number of keys is equal to $2m \cdot (m + 1)^{(h-2)}$. Therefore, we should have $NR \geq 2m \cdot (m + 1)^{(h-2)}$. Solving the last equation for h we find that the maximum height of the tree structure is bounded above by

$$h_{\max} \leq 2 + flr \left\lceil \log_{(m+1)} \left\lceil \frac{NR}{2m} \right\rceil \right\rceil$$

Similarly, when the nodes become full, the height of the tree attains its minimum value. In this case, one can see again that the maximal number of keys in the last level is equal to $2m \cdot (2m + 1)^{(h-1)}$. Hence, the number of records NR cannot exceed the previously derived number; therefore, we obtain the inequality $NR \leq 2m \cdot (2m + 1)^{(h-1)}$. Solving for h shows that

$$h_{\min} \geq 1 + clg \left\lceil \log_{(2m+1)} \left\lceil \frac{NR}{2m} \right\rceil \right\rceil$$

7.6.1.2 The *Retrieve_All* Operation. Recall that with the use of the sequence set, one can retrieve records in an *ordered* sequential fashion. To accomplish this one must access the leftmost node of the sequence set at a cost of exactly h random accesses. At this point all records with keys in this node can be accessed. The next node of the sequence set can then be accessed and, consequently, so can all records with keys in that node. The process is repeated until

---

[27] See section about the height of a B_m tree.

all blocks of the sequence set have been visited. The total cost of this operation is given by

$$SL[Retrieve\_All,\ B_m^+] = h + NBLK_{seq} + NR\ \ rba$$

where $NBLK_{seq}$ represents the number of nodes in the sequence set.

We close this section with the remark that the above-derived search length can be further reduced by blocking the logical records and strategic placement of the blocks in the disk device.

7.6.1.3 The *Insert_One* Operation.

The insertion operation is similar to the insertion operation in a B_m structure because the target block is always a leaf node and because the overflow blocks can be handled in the same way, *redistribution* of the keys and *node splitting*. But it also differs in only one respect, in the redistribution and/or node splitting of the nodes of the *sequence* set. The differences as well as the similarities are explained below via examples. We employ the same conventions and notations that were used with the examples given for B_m structures. It can be assumed that an algorithm similar to the *Search_and_Store* has been completed and the block at hand is the target block.

Insert 4, 7, 22, 21. The tree is initially empty; therefore, this case has been handled by the *Search_and_Store* procedure. The first available index block (block 1^{28}) is allocated and the keys are inserted in order there, as Figure 7.51 illustrates.

```
┌ ─ ─ ─ ─ ─ ┐
│ • 4 • 7 • 21 • 22 • │
└ ─ ─ ─ ─ ─ ┘
  1
```

Figure 7.51 Inserting the records with keys 4, 7, 22 and 21 into an initially empty B_2^+ structure.

Insert 35, 12. Notice that the target block (block 1) is an overflow block. Redistribution does not work here; therefore, *node splitting* must be performed. The keys of the set, consisting of the keys in the overflow block and the key of the new record that is *smaller* than the *median* (21), are rewritten into the overflow block as before. The keys that are *greater than or equal* to the median are written out to a newly allocated block (block 2) at a cost of one random access. Finally the median is *promoted* to the parent node of the overflow block. In this case the parent node does not exist;[29] therefore, the median as well as the $p[1]$ and $p[2]$ pointer fields are written out to a newly allocated block (block 3) at a cost of one random access. The discussion above exemplifies the difference between insertions in B_m and B_m^+ structures. In the latter case, when a *leaf* node is split, the median is not only promoted but is also written as the first key in the newly allocated block. Figure 7.52 illustrates the effect of insertion of that record.

---

[28] Recall that block 0 is the *Header* block.

[29] The insert algorithm detects this event from the fact that the stack is empty.

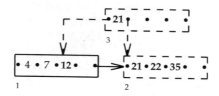

Figure 7.52 Inserting the records with keys 35 and 12 into the B_2^+ structure of Figure 7.51.

Insert 23, 39. The insertion of the first record (with key 23) is uneventful. The target block is not full so the key is inserted in order there. When the second record (with key 39) arrives, the target block (block 2) is an overflow block, but the left sibling is not. Hence, *left redistribution* is possible. This method again differs from the one that is used in B_m structures in one respect; namely, if redistribution is performed on a leaf node, the *promoted* key also remains in the overflow block. Figure 7.53 illustrates the tree structure after these insertions have been completed.

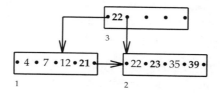

Figure 7.53 Inserting the records with keys 23 and 39 into the B_2^+ structure of Figure 7.51.

Figure 7.54 illustrates the structure after the insertion of the keys 16, 32, 29, 46, 28, 43, 64, 9, 49, 53, and 40. Left redistribution is utilized whenever possible. The reader is encouraged to verify this result.

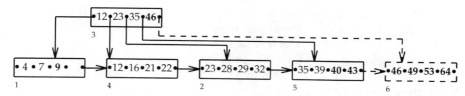

Figure 7.54 Inserting the records with keys 64, 9, 49, 53, and 40, into the B_2^+ structure of Figure 7.53.

Insert 42. This is our final example. The target block (block 5) is an overflow block; redistribution is not applicable; therefore, the block splits. The median, 40, is rewritten (block 7), since the overflow block is a leaf node; it is also promoted to the parent node. The parent node is full; the block splits; but the median, 35, is *only* promoted (*not* rewritten), since the split node is a branch node. The new structure obtained from the insertion of the key in the structure in Figure 7.54 is shown in Figure 7.55.

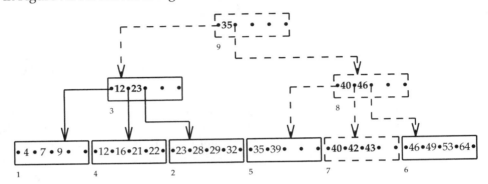

Figure 7.55   Inserting the record with key 42 into the B_2^+ structure of Figure 7.54. Compare with the B_m structure of Figure 7.47.

We close this section with the obvious remark that the search length for this operation depends on each particular case, but the equations derived in the previous section remain valid here.

7.6.1.4   The *Delete_One* Operation.   Following the discussion in the previous section, one would expect that the techniques employed in the case of a B_m structure would be similar to the ones employed here. *Redistribution* and *concatenation* are used here, *but* the fundamental difference is that the key that must be deleted *always* resides in a leaf node. The occurrence of a key with the same value as the key of the target record in a branch node is a duplicate.[30] The deletion process is illustrated via the two examples that follow.

Delete 64, 46.   The target block (block 6) contains more than two keys. Hence, key 64 is deleted as well as is the associated pointer to the data record. When the next record with key 46 is to be deleted, the node is still not an underflow node. Therefore, the record is deleted as before. But this record has an associated key (the leftmost key in the sequence set node) in the parent node, and the question of how it is to be handled arises. There are basically two ways. The first is to promote the new leftmost key of the sequence node in its position; the second method is to flag the occurrence of that key in the parent node.[31] In other words, the tree structure will be the one in Figure 7.56 if the latter method is chosen.

Delete 7, 9.   The deletion of the first record is uneventful, but deletion of the second record leads to an underflow node. Assuming *right redistribution* of the keys, we can see that this operation will handle this particular case. The leftmost

---

[30] Unless the record has already been deleted.

[31] This way the parent node will never be an underflow node.

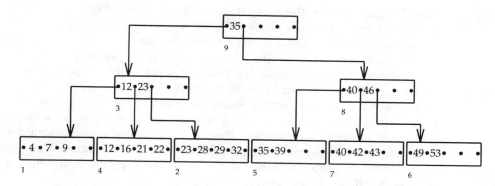

Figure 7.56 Deleting the records with keys 64 and 46 from the B_2^+ structure of Figure 7.54.

key of the right sibling is copied as before into the appropriate position of the underflow node, and the new leftmost node of the right sibling replaces the key occurrence of the borrowed key into the parent node. Figure 7.57 illustrates the resultant structure.

The last case that one may encounter is a deletion that requires concatenation as a request for deletion of the record with key 38. The algorithm for this case is an exercise for the reader.

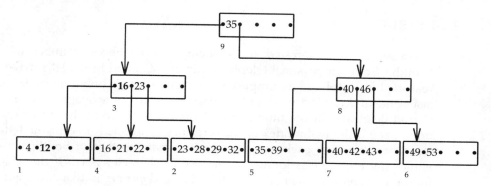

Figure 7.57 Deleting the records with keys 7 and 9 from the B_2^+ structure of Figure 7.56.

7.6.2 The Initial Loading Operation

At the beginning of our discussion we indicated that the cost associated with the initial loading operation for a B_m^+ is considerably less than its B_m counterpart given that the logical records are presented in increasing sequence of their keys.[32] The method that makes this possible is very simple. As soon as a logical

---

[32] This stipulation is not necessary. But if the records are presented in this order, the cost of the operation insert in the sequence set will be higher than in this case.

record is inserted into the data set, the address of the record (along with its key) is inserted in order into a physical-linked sequential file that implements the sequence set.[33] When a block of the sequence set has been written (i.e., when EBF records have been written), the address of that block together with the minimum key of the records in that block (i.e., the key at position k_1) is passed to the "insert into a B_m-tree" procedure. This way only $NBLK_{seq} - 1$ indexes must be inserted, as opposed to NR indexes that would be required for insertion into a B_m structure. Furthermore, it should be clear that this method is far superior to the method of inserting a record into the B^+ structure that was illustrated in an earlier section. As a simple example consider the file in Figure 7.58, which was constructed with this method over the same file in Figure 7.55, which was constructed by the straightforward method of insertion.

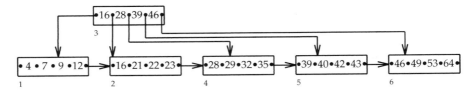

Figure 7.58   The result of the loading algorithm into an initially empty B_2^+ structure.

7.7 TRIE STRUCTURES

Suppose we are interested in retrieving the telephone number of a friend "Smith" from our personal telephone directory. In addition, let's make two unrealistic but simplified assumptions—namely, there is only one friend with that last name and the last names of all friends appear in lexicographic ordering. It should be clear that the time required for the retrieval of that record would be minimized if the main index of the directory is scanned first for the letter S. Instead of examining each name to see if it matches that of Smith, we scan the names until a name is found whose second character is m. If this character is found, we then scan the names from that record *forward* until a name whose third character, i is found. Observe that if a character greater than m is encountered, the search terminates unsuccessfully. The process continues until a match or a nonmatch is encountered.

The above discussion indicates that the search that was performed is fundamentally different from all searches that we have encountered so far because the search for the target record was performed on a character-by-character fashion. It should be clear immediately that when the target record exists, the

---

[33] The effective blocking factor usually is selected so that it is greater than or equal to 0.5 but strictly less than 1. This way the definition of the B^+ is satisfied and future insertions will not necessitate an immediate split.

search length of this operation is approximated very closely by the size of the key (viewed as a string), and it is independent of the number of logical records in the file. At the other extreme (i.e., the target record does not exist), the search length of this operation could be as little as one random access but never greater than the search length of the successful search. Moreover, the comparison test that is performed on a character-by-character basis is independent of the length of the keys of the records, unlike the previous search methods, in which entire key strings were compared. Therefore, this search does not impose any restrictions on the key lengths; it performs equally well on a file of records with variable size keys.

A structure that facilitates this type of fast retrieval is referred to as a trie, a word derived from the word re*trie*val. In such an organization all keys are assumed to be character strings over a certain alphabet A. If the keys are numeric (such as 1022), the key is assumed to be a character string over the alphabet $A = \{0, 1, 2, 3, 4, 5, 6, 7, 8, 9\}$. From now on we will assume that the alphabet A contains n characters ($n \geq 1$).

Logically a trie is viewed as a tree structure, but the type as well as the significance of the branch nodes is different from that of the leaf nodes, since branch nodes contain "indexes", while leaf nodes contain pointers to the stored records. In addition, leaf nodes signify that keys have been completed. As a simple example consider a file of just two records with keys Smith and Smythenson. A trie configuration can be viewed as the tree structure in Figure 7.57.

Examination of Figure 7.59(a) indicates that only five accesses and four comparisons are needed to access an existing target record; note that the fourth comparison is needed because there is the possibility that one of the strings, "Smi" or "Smy," is a prefix of the key of the target record. The above discussion suggests that the number of accesses required to access an existing record never exceeds the length of the key by three. Moreover, the search length in terms of accesses is two more than the length of the path that defines the *longest* common prefix of the target key with the other keys of the records in the file. Recall that given two nonnull[34] strings x and y over the same alphabet, the string x is said to be a prefix of the string y if and only if there exits a third nonnull string z over the same alphabet such that $y = x \cdot z$ where $\cdot$ represents the concatenation operator. For example, the strings S, Sm, Smi, and Smit are all prefixes of the string Smith.

Keys that are prefixes of others could pose a problem. For instance if the record with the key Sm is to be inserted in the *trie* in Figure 7.59(a), how should the application program handle the insertion? The solution to this problem is simple. When a record is to be inserted, its key is padded to the right with a special character that does not belong to the alphabet A. Usually this character is the blank character; this convention will be assumed in future discussions.

---

[34] Recall that a null string is a string of no characters.

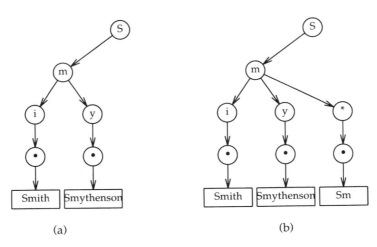

Figure 7.59 The trie before insertion of the record with key Sm (a) and after (b). The character * represents the blank character.

Under these circumstances the insertion of the record with key Sm is not different from the insertion of other records; Figure 7.60(b) illustrates the modifications to the trie structure of Figure 7.59(a) after insertion of the new record has been completed.

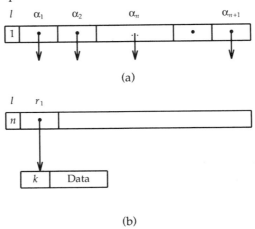

Figure 7.60 The node type of a branch node (a) and a leaf node (b) of a *trie* structure.

Recall that at the beginning of this section we indicated that a scan is performed whenever we wish to locate a record whose ith character matches that of the key of the target record. For example, we stated that after the first record whose key begins with the character *S* has been located, a scan of the subsequent records is performed until a record is found (or not found) and whose key's second character is *m*. We will show that if the structure of Figure 7.59 is modified, the computationally expensive scan operation can be altogether eliminated. In other words, *only* one access will be needed to determine the existence or nonexistence of that key. This modification is based on the observation that whenever the *i*th character of a key is encountered, this character could be any one of $n + 1$ possible characters. Therefore, each branch node of the tree structure should contain $n + 1$ pointer fields; a setting of one of these pointers, say *j*, to *Nil* indicates that there is no record with a prefix equal to one completed so far; otherwise, the search proceeds to the next lower level pointed to by that pointer.

The discussion above suggests that each branch node contains, minimally, $n + 2$ fields, whereas a leaf node should contain only two. Figure 7.60(a) and 7.60(b) illustrates branch and leaf nodes, respectively.

The first field in both types represents the *leaf indicator (l)*; a setting of this field to the bit 0 indicates a leaf node; otherwise, a branch node is indicated. In the former case, the other field, r_1, is a pointer to the block that contains the logical record whose key or prefix of the key was completed in the previous level. In the latter case the node contains $n + 1$ pointer fields, as defined earlier, such that the *i*th pointer corresponds to the α_i character of the alphabet *A*, while the $(n+1)$st pointer corresponds to the blank character.

Using the above conventions a trie organization of a file of 6 records with keys AAB, ABBBC, BAA, BCCAA, BC, and CABB over the alphabet $\{A, B, C\}$ is presented in Figure 7.61. It is worth noting that each path from the root to a node determines uniquely a prefix of a key or keys; and a key is completed only via a path that terminates at a leaf level.

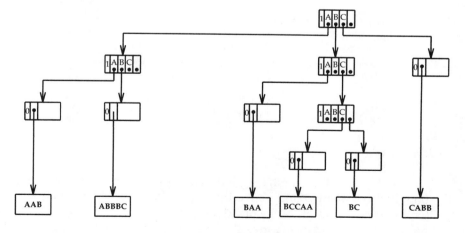

Figure 7.61 A trie organization of a file of six records with keys AAB, ABBBC, BAA, BCCAA, BC, and CABB.

7.7.1 The Operations

In the following sections the algorithms that perform a number of basic operations on a trie structure will be developed. We will assume the model that was presented earlier. Moreover, the notation α[**Key**[i]] will be employed to access that pointer in a node that is indexed by the ith character of the key **Key.**

7.7.1.1 The *Retrieve_One* Operation.   The algorithm that performs the *Retrieve-One* operation is presented in Table 7.17 (page 303). Unless the structure is empty ([1]), a search is initiated at step [2]. The loop variable i is used to point to the ith character of the given key. Observe that an exit from the loop can occur either if the pointer corresponding to the ith character at the $(i - 1)$st level is equal to *Nl* or if a leaf node is reached. In the former case, the target record does not exist, whereas in the latter case further examination is required. In particular, the string formed by the path that was followed could have been a prefix of both the *New_Key* and the key of the record pointed to by the α[1] pointer. As an example, consider the structure of Figure 7.61 and consider a request for the retrieval of the record with key "ABB." A leaf node will be reached, since the string "AB" is a prefix of the *New_Key;* but the stored record's key is different from the *New_Key.*

TABLE 7.17   The algorithm *Retrieve_One* in a trie.

```
Algorithm Retrieve_One(Header,New_Key);

[1]  Next ← Header.lptr;
[2]  If (Next = Nil) then {write ('record not found') and exit};
[3]  Read_Index_Block(Index_Buffer,Next);
[4]  i ← 1;
     while ((Index_Buffer.c = B'1') and (Index_Buffer.α[New_Key[i]] ≠ Nil))
           {Next ← Index_Buffer.α[i];
            Read_Index_Block(Index_Buffer,Next);
            i ← i+1;}
[5]  if (Next = Nil) then write('record not found')
                     else
                         {Read_Block(Data_Buffer,Next);
                          if (Data_Buffer.Key ≠ New_Key)
                            then write('record not found')
                            else write(Data_Buffer);}
[6]  exit;
```

In terms of the search length of this operation, if the record exists the cost is bounded below by 3 and above by $length(New\_Key) + 2$ random block accesses. On the other hand, if the record does not exist, the cost could be as little as one random access and as great as that of the previous case. But it should be intuitively clear that the average search length for this operation is dramatically reduced from that of any other organization of unsuccessful searches.

7.7.1.2 The *Insert_One* Operation.   We begin by illustrating the technique that is employed for the insertion operation via two examples. Our starting point is the *trie* structure of Figure 7.61 and our assumption is that the key of the record to be inserted is not a duplicate.

Insert "A." This is the simplest of the two cases. Note that during the search process the pointer corresponding to the blank character in the leftmost node of the first level is found to be *Nil*. In this case a new leaf node and a new data block is allocated; the appropriate pointers are adjusted, as illustrated in Figure 7.62.

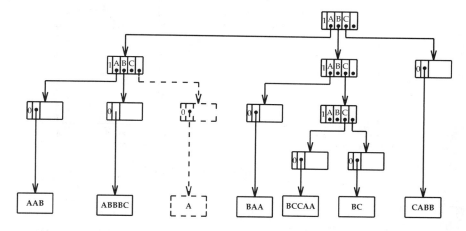

Figure 7.62   Inserting the record with key "A" in the trie structure of Figure 7.61.

With regard to the search length, notice that after the search has been completed, the last accessed index block is rewritten at a cost of one sequential access; two random accesses are required to rewrite the new leaf and data block. In symbols

$$SL[Insert\_One, T] = SL[Search, T] \; rba + 2 \; rba + 1 \; sba$$

Insert ABB. This is the second case that one may encounter. Observe that the search process detects a leaf block, since the string BB is a prefix of both the stored record and of the *New_Key*. In this case, we are required to allocate new branch nodes as well as a new leaf node and a new data block. The question is, How many branch nodes must be generated? Each allocation of an index block increases the size of the common prefix by one; therefore, the number of blocks that must be allocated must be such that the string that is formed by the path from the root to the latest allocated block is the *longest* common prefix of the *New_Key* and the key of the stored record. In our example two branch nodes are allocated. Figure 7.63 illustrates the structure of Figure 7.62 after the insertion of this record.

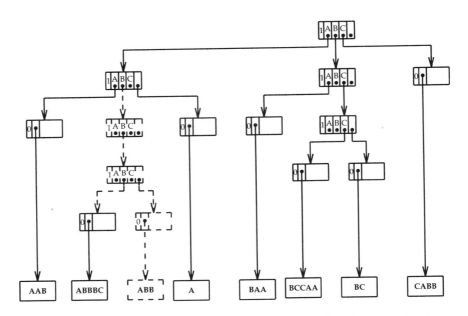

Figure 7.63   Inserting the record with key ABB in the trie structure of
Figure 7.62.

In terms of the search length, in order for the stored record to be accessed a
number of $SL[Search, T] + 2$ random accesses are required; $SL[Search, T]$
denotes the number of accesses required to access the youngest branch node,
while two random accesses are needed to access the leaf and data block.
Moreover, if we let LP represent the length of the longest prefix of the key of the
stored record and the *New_Key*, one can see that a number of
$LP - SL[Search, T] + 1$ random accesses are required to rewrite the youngest
branch node as well as the newly allocated branch nodes. Finally, two more
random accesses are required to write the new leaf and data block. Combining
the above quantities we obtain that the search length is given by

$$SL[Insert\_One, T] = LP + 3 \quad rba$$

The algorithm that performs this task is given in Table 7.18. The reader is
encouraged to study it.

7.7.1.3 The *Delete_One* Operation.   The *Delete_One* operation is similar
to the *Retrieve_One* algorithm and is presented in Table 7.19. A nonexistent
record is detected either when a *Nil* pointer is encountered or whenever a leaf
node is not reached. But even if a leaf node is reached, as in the case of the retrieval operation, the stored record could not be the target record. If it is, the leaf
node as well as the data node are deallocated; the corresponding pointer of the
Parent node is set to *Nil* [5].

TABLE 7.18   The algorithm *Insert_One* in a trie.

```
Algorithm Insert_One(Header,New_Key);

[1]   Next ← Header.lptr;
[2]   If (Next = Nil)
         then
              {Header.lptr ← Get_Free_Index_Block;
              Clear(Index_Buffer);
              New_Leaf ← Get_Free_Index_Block;
              Index_Buffer.l ← B'1';
              Index_Buffer.α[New_Key[1]] ← New_Leaf;
              Write_Block(Index_Buffer,Header.lptr);
              Clear(Index_Buffer);
              Index_Buffer.l ← B'0';
              Index_Buffer.α[1] ← Get_Free_Data_Block;
              Write_Block(Index_Buffer,New_Leaf);
              Write_Block(Data_Buffer,Index_Buffer.α[1]);
              exit;}
[3]   Read_Index_Block(Index_Buffer,Next);
[4]   i ← 1;
      while ((Index_Buffer.c = B'1') and (Index_Buffer.α[New_Key[i]] ≠ Nil))
            {Parent ← Next;
             Next ← Index_Buffer.α[New_Key[i]];
             Read_Index_Block(Index_Buffer,Next);
             i ← i+1;}
[5]   if (Next = Nil)
         then
              {New_Index_Block ← Get_Free_Index_Block;
              Index_Buffer.α[New_Key[i]] ← New_Index_Block;
              Write_Block(Index_Buffer,Next);
              Clear(Index_Buffer);
              Index_Buffer.l ← B'0';
              Index_Buffer.α[New_Key[1]] ← Get_Free_Data_Block;
              Write_Block(Index_Buffer,New_Index_Block);
              Write_Block(Data_Buffer,Index_Buffer.α[New_Key[1]]);
              exit;}
[6]   Read_Block(Data_Buffer,Next);
      if (Data_Buffer.Key = New_Key) then {write('duplicate record');
                                                   exit;}
[7]   save1 ← Parent.α[New_Key[i]];
      save2 ← Get_Free_Index_Block;
      j ← min(length(New_Key),length(Data_Buffer.key));
[8]   while ((i <= j) and (Data_Buffer.key[i] = New_Key[i]))
            { attach ← Get_Free_Index_Block;
             Parent_Buffer.α[New_Key[i]] ← attach;
             Write_Block(Parent_Buffer,Parent);
             Clear(Parent_Buffer);
             Parent_Buffer.l = B'1';
             Parent ← attach;
             i ← i+1;}
[9]   i ← i-1;
[10]  if ((i ≠ j) or ((i = j) and (length(New_Key) = length(Data_Buffer.Key))))
         then
```

```
              {Parent_Key.α[Data_Buffer.Key[i] = save1;
               Parent_Key.α[New_Key[i]] = save2;
          else
              {if (length(Data_Buffer.Key) < j)
                  then
                      {Parent_Buffer.α[n+1] = save1;
                       Parent_Key.α[New_Key[j]] = save2}
                  else
                      {Parent_Buffer.α[n+1] = save2;
                       Parent_Key.α[New_Key[j]] = save1;}}
[11] Write_Block(Parent_Buffer,Parent);
     Clear(Data_Buffer);
     Data_Buffer ← New_Record;
        Clear(Index_Buffer);
     Index_Buffer.l ← B'0';
     Index_Buffer.α[1] ← Get_Free_Data_Block;
     Write_Block(Index_Buffer,save2);
     Write_Block(Data_Buffer,Index_Buffer.α[1]);
[12] exit;
```

TABLE 7.19   The algorithm *Delete_One* in a trie.

```
Algorithm Delete_One(Header,New_Key);

[1]  Next ← Header.lptr;
     Parent ← Next;
[2]  If (Next = Nil) then {write ('record not found') and exit}
                       else Parent ← Next;
[3]  Read_Index_Block(Index_Buffer,Next);
[4]  i ← 1;
     while ((Index_Buffer.c = B'1') and (Index_Buffer.α[New_Key[i]] ≠ Nil))
        {Parent ← Next;
         Next ← Index_Buffer.α[i];
         Read_Index_Block(Index_Buffer,Next);
         i ← i+1;}
[5]  if (Next = Nil) then write('record not found')
                     else
                        {Read_Block(Data_Buffer,Next);
                         if (Data_Buffer.Key ≠ New_Key)
                           then write('record not found')
                           else
                              {Free_Data_Block(Next);
                               Free_Index_Block(Index_Buffer.α[i]);
                               Index_Buffer.α[i] ← Nil;
                               Write_Index_Block(Index_Buffer,Parent);}
[6]  exit;
```

The algorithm presented above performs its task, but does not repair the *trie*. For example, if the deleted record from the *trie* of Figure 7.63 was the one with key "ABB," the structure would have not been the "optimal" structure of Figure 7.62. Coding the "repairing" algorithm is an exercise that the reader should work through.

Finally, it should be clear that the search length for this operation is the same as that of the *Retrieve_One* operation for nonexistent records while an extra overhead of one random access is required to rewrite the branch node last accessed.[35]

7.7.2 Storage Requirements

In the design of our model we opted for a separate data set area or file. The reason is that all the index nodes have the same size, whereas the logical records could have variable lengths, so the total storage requirements could be minimized with the use of two separate files. Moreover, even if the logical records are of a fixed length, the probability that their size is equal to that of the index blocks is very small. In this unlikely possibility, one could have saved storage by storing the logical records in the *leaves*. This modification leads to a savings in terms of the search length of the random operations, but it also precludes the possibility of blocking of the logical records.

At any rate, we will derive the storage requirements for our model. First, let $NBLK_{dat}$ denote the number of data blocks in the data set. Second, with respect to the index notice that the block size, $NBLK_{ind}$, is equal to $(n + 2) \cdot 6$ bytes, assuming 6-byte pointers. But the number of index nodes in a tree structure depends on a number of factors, such as the size of the alphabet, the number of keys, the size of the keys, and the interrelationships between keys (in terms of prefixes). What is absolutely clear here is that the size of each index block is very large. If the alphabet A is the English alphabet, we can see that the size of each index block is equal to 180 bytes. Therefore, with this structure we gain speed for the retrieval operations by sacrificing a considerable amount of storage.

7.8 *C-TRIE* STRUCTURES

Earlier it was shown that the major drawback of trie structures is the excessive amount of storage required for the index blocks. In this section we will present a variation of the trie structure, the *C-Trie*, in which the amount of storage required for each index block is reduced from $(n + 2) \cdot 6$ bytes to $\max\{ \lceil clg(\frac{n + 2}{8}) + 1 \rceil, 7 \}$ bytes. In the case of keys over the English alphabet, the storage requirement falls from 180 to 7 bytes. But, consistent with our theme, the price that we must pay is that the new structure will not permit the operation of insertion; therefore, when such operations are to be performed, they must be done in batch mode, which implies that the structure is reorganized each time.

The storage gains obtained can be seen by simply observing that when we deal with a static tree structure, the structure can be implemented as a physical

---

[35] Not counting the cost of repair of the *Free_Chains*.

sequential file, as opposed to the physical linked sequential organization required for the dynamic *trie* structure of the previous section. Specifically, when a static tree structure is involved, each node (block) can be identified uniquely by its *distance* from the leftmost node in its level. If we consider the *trie* of Figure 7.63, the distance of each block from its leftmost node is reflected in the number that appears in the northwest corner of the blocks of Figure 7.64. The result is that all pointer fields of all branch nodes are replaced by bit fields, whereas the pointers that appear in the structure are only those that point to the stored records and that reside in the leaves.

Consider a request to retrieve the record with key "BC." Examination of the root node (in Figure 7.65) indicates that the node pointed to by the pointer corresponding to character *B* must be examined. In the case of the *trie* in the previous section, the actual block pointer (cylinder, track, block number) was stored at this position. In the case of the C-trie, a *bit* is set to indicate that further looking-up is necessary; but the address of the appropriate child is *computed* in terms of its distance from the leftmost node at its level. This computation is straightforward. The distance (offset) is equal to the number of blocks in the next level that must be "skipped," beginning with the leftmost node, but this number is equal to the number of bits that have been set in the root node in the preceding positions. Here only one preceding bit has been set (the one corresponding to the character *A*); the block that must be accessed is equal to the address of the leftmost node in the next level plus the offset. So the child block (the second block in the next level) is accessed. The position α_3 (corresponding to the character *C*) of the current block is examined; the bit value is 1; therefore, the child block pointed to by that pointer in the next level must be accessed. The addressing scheme presented earlier will not necessarily work because the number of blocks that must be skipped from the leftmost node of that level is equal to the number of preceding set bits (as before) of the current block *plus* the number of children of all the nodes in the current level that lie to the left of the current block. That number which is numerically equal to the number of bits that have been set in all structural pointer fields of all preceding blocks[36] is stored (at the time of creation) in the extra field, which appears to the right of each node. Hence, the addressing scheme is very simple, provided that the addresses of the leftmost nodes of each level are known. Therefore, at the time of creation these addresses must be saved and, consequently, stored.

We close this section with three remarks. First, the deletion of records in a random and not a batch fashion is *always* possible given that no blocks are deallocated and that the deleted logical records are flagged. Second, the insertion of records is possible only if the insertion does not require the creation of new branch nodes. Third, the algorithms applicable to *trie* structures are still valid with minor modifications.

---

[36] The number of set bits in a leaf node is assumed to be zero, since leaf nodes have no children.

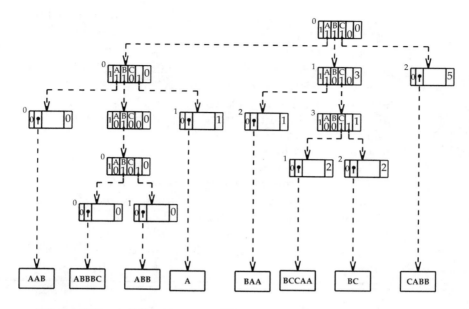

Figure 7.65 A *C*-Trie structure. The counterpart of the trie structure of Figure 7.64.

7.9 EXERCISES

1. Suppose that we insert data records with keys 1, 2, 3,..., 15 (in this order) into an initially empty B-tree, where each node can contain two data records.
   a. Draw the resulting structure after the insertion of these 15 records.
   b. Which record (i.e., key value) would cause the root node of the B-tree to be at level 6 for the first time if the scheme used in part (a) was used to insert records with keys 1, 2, 3,..., *N*? Justify briefly.

2. Suppose that we insert data records with keys 100, 120, 110, 80, 86, 102, 115, 85, 86, 107, 114, 111, 112, 107, 106, 105, and 109 (in this order) into an initially empty binary search tree.
   a. Draw the resulting structure after the insertion of these 17 records.
   b. Draw the resultant structure after the completion of each of the following operations: Delete 86, Delete 100, Delete 110.

3. Suppose that we insert data records with keys 100, 120, 110, 80, 86, 102, 115, 85, 86, 107, 114, 111, 112, 107, 106, 105, and 109 (in this order) into an initially empty *AVL*-tree. Draw the resulting structure after the insertion of these 17 records.

4. Suppose that we insert data records with keys 3, 6, 9, 12, 15, 18, 21, 24, 27, 30, 33, 36, 39, 42 (in this order) into an initially empty B^+-tree, where each data level node can contain three data records. In addition, we assume that

the blocking factor of the index nodes is 5 and the initial loading factor is 100%.

a. Draw the resulting structure after insertion of these 14 records.

b. Draw the resultant B^+ structure after completion of each of the following operations: Insert 16, Insert 8, Delete 42, Delete 36.

5. Suppose that we insert data records with keys 3, 6, 9, 12, 15, 18, 21, 24, 27, 30, 33, 36, 39, 42 (in this order) into an initially empty B-tree where each data level node can contain two data records.

a. Draw the resulting structure after the insertion of these 14 records.

b. Draw the resultant B-tree structure after the completion of each of the following operations: Insert 16, Insert 8, Delete 42, Delete 36.

6. Give the pseudocode of the procedure *Rotate_and_Adjust* of step [7] of the algorithm *Insert_One_AVL* (Table 7.14).

7. Recode the algorithm *Delete_One* in a *trie* (Table 7.19) in such a way that after the deletion is performed, the *trie* structure is "optimal."

7.10 VSAM FILE ORGANIZATIONS

Under the IBM file system a B^+-tree-like structure can be implemented via the *key-sequenced data set (KSDS)* file organization. This file organization is one of the three principal file organizations supported by the *virtual storage access method (VSAM)* file management system; the other two file organizations are the *entry-sequenced data sets (ESDS)* and the *relative record data sets (RRDS)*; they may be employed whenever one wishes to implement a one-level indexed structure.

Before these organizations are discussed, the two principal advantages they have over other file organizations (discussed in earlier chapters) should be stated. First, all these organizations are *device independent*. Second, each such file can be extended automatically beyond its originally declared size[37] whenever additional storage space is required.

7.10.1 The File Structure

The unit of information that the file system transfers between secondary storage and virtual memory as a result of a physical *READ* or *WRITE* request is the *control interval (CI)*. Unlike the *ISAM* file organization, the size of the *CI* is not necessarily a track; instead, its size is fixed either by the user or by the *VSAM* itself. At this point recall that the organizations supported by *VSAM* are *portable* in the sense that a physical file could be ported from one secondary device to another

---

[37] The maximum size is 4.3 million bytes.

regardless of their characteristics. The rationale that makes this work is that the *VSAM* divides the track of each device into a number of *physical* records; the size of each is a multiple of 512 bytes, but it does not exceed 8192 bytes. The value of the multiple selected is the one that utilizes track space best. The control interval size is always a multiple of 512 bytes;[38] therefore, a control interval will always be equivalent to a multiple of physical records. Figure 7.66 illustrates these concepts.

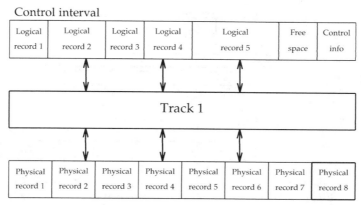

Figure 7.66   The mapping of physical records onto the track and to the control interval.

When this file is ported into a new device whose track capacity is three-fourths of the previous track capacity, the mapping from the control interval to the disk space via the physical record concept will be as illustrated in Figure 7.67.

VSAM keeps track of each control interval via its *relative byte address (RBA)*. An *RBA* is a nonnegative integer that reflects the offset of the beginning of a control interval from the physical beginning of the file; for example, the *RBA* of the first control interval of the file, control interval 0, is equal to zero; the *RBA* of the second control interval is equal to the size of the control interval; and so on. Similarly, the logical records are accessed not by their disk address but via their *RBA* that (as in the case of the control intervals) is equal to the offset in bytes of the beginning of the logical record from the beginning of the file. As Figure 7.66 indicates, *VSAM* organizations support variable-length records; *RRDS* organizations accept fixed-length logical records only. The *Control Info* field overhead[39] is used by the system to keep track of the logical records (location within the control interval and their size) and the free space in the control interval. At this point we should emphasize that the notion of *blocking* is not supported by the

---

[38] Its maximum size is 32,768 bytes and 8192 bytes for data and index control intervals, respectively.

[39] Its size is equal to 4 bytes required for its definition plus 2 more bytes for each record definition.

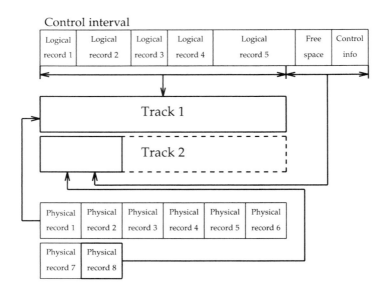

Figure 7.67 The mapping of physical records defined for the device of Figure 7.66 onto the track set of a different device. Notice that the control interval "overflows" to the "next" track.

VSAM organizations;[40] the system will store in each control interval as many logical records as possible. Notice that VSAM allows the user to allocate *free space* within a control interval in order to facilitate future insertions.[41]

VSAM "groups" a fixed number of control intervals into a storage structure which is referred to as a *control area (CA)* (Figure 7.68). As a matter of fact, whenever additional file space is needed, VSAM will allocate as many additional control areas as necessary. The size of this area may be specified by the user, but the VSAM file system may adjust it to utilize storage space best. For example, in order to facilitate fast sequential processing, each control area should occupy a cylinder; if the user specifies an area larger than a cylinder, VSAM overrides the user specification by taking its size equal to that of a cylinder.[42]

7.10.2 Relative Record Files

This organization is a natural extension of the **REGIONAL** file organization discussed in Chapter 5. In particular, this organization expects fixed-length records of the same size, *RECSIZE*, and subdivides each control interval's data area into

[40] Supported indirectly in the case of the *RSDS* file organization.

[41] As a matter of fact, the free space can be distributed *unevenly* among the control intervals according to the user's requirements.

[42] This adjustment will require adjustments of the sizes of the control intervals that again are handled by VSAM.

Control Area

Logical Record 1	Logical Record 2	Logical Record 3	Logical Record 4	Logical Record 5	Free Space	Control info

Logical Record 6	Logical Record 7	Logical Record 8	Logical Record 9	Logical Record 10	Free Space	Control info

Logical Record 11	Free Space	Control info

Logical Record 12	Free Space	Control info

Figure 7.68 A control area consisting of four control intervals.

as many "slots" of size *RECSIZE* as possible. Each such slot is addressed via a positive integer that reflects the position of the slot within the slot set. The first slot bears the address 1; the second, the address 2; and so on.

Records can be inserted either sequentially or randomly. In the former case, the record is inserted in the slot "next" to the current one;[43] in the latter case the application program can request the insertion to take place in the desired slot by providing the slot number to the access method via the **KEYFROM** option of the **WRITE** statement.[44] In the latter case, the application program should be aware of the used slots as well as the unused slots. This is accomplished by requesting that the access method return to the application program the address of the slot number where a record is inserted via the **KEYTO** option of the **READ** statement. Figure 7.69 illustrates such an organization.

Figure 7.69 A relative-sequence file organization consisting of eight control intervals and 32 slots. An asterisk marks the *Control Information* field.

The last remark indicates that the *application program* (and not the *VSAM*) may build a one-level index to the relative record file by utilizing the returned slot numbers. This index may be used whenever the application program must access records *directly* by supplying the slot address to the access method.

Finally, deletions can be accomplished either via the **KEYFROM** option or without it. In the latter case, the logical record last accessed is deleted; otherwise, the record occupying the slot number indicated by the **KEYFROM** option is

---

[43] If this slot is occupied, the **ERROR** condition is raised.
[44] If this slot is occupied, the **KEY** condition is raised.

deleted. After a deletion *VSAM* will *reclaim* the slot vacated. In other words no flags are set and there is no need to check for empty slots.

7.10.3 Entry-Sequence Files

Entry-sequence file organization differs in a number of respects from the one in the previous section. Specifically, it permits the use of variable-length records; insertion of records takes place *only* at the end of the file; and it does not support deletions. Figure 7.70 illustrates such an organization.

| 4 | 7 |22|21|*|35|12|23|39|*|16|32|29|46|*|28|43|64| 9 |*|49|53|40|42|*|24|60| Free |*| Free |*| Free |*|
0   1   2   3   4   5   6   7

Figure 7.70 An entry-sequence file organization consisting of eight *control intervals*. The records, whose keys are shown, are inserted in order of their arrival. Notice the absence of slots.

The only similarity between the two types of organization is that the file can be accessed either sequentially or directly. In the latter case the access of a record is accomplished via its *relative record address (RBA)*, which can be known to the application program at the time that the record is read or written via the **KEYTO** option of the appropriate **READ** or **WRITE** statement. The application program is also capable in this case of building a one-level index that would permit eventual direct access to a record via its *RBA*.

We close this section by noting that although explicit **DELETE** operations are not allowed, a record may replace another via the **REWRITE** operation. *But* in order for this to be possible, the two records must have the same length.

7.10.4 Key-Sequence Files

As we stated earlier, the *KSDS* organization is *based* on the B$^+$-tree structure that was discussed earlier. In the next few paragraphs their similarities as well as their differences will be briefly discussed. We first present a *KSDS* organization in Figure 7.71.

The reader should have already noticed that *VSAM* maintains the *index set* as well as the data set.[45] Each node of the sequence set is associated with a control area. Each key value in this node is associated with a pointer that points to a control interval which contains as many records as can "fit" into it whose keys are *less than or equal* to the key value appearing in the sequence set.

Deletions are accomplished by *VSAM* via reclaiming the freed storage area and "movement" of the records in the target control interval. But unlike the case

---

[45] In IBM terminology a file is referred to as the data set. We use the terminology that we have adopted so far—namely; that the data set is an area separate from the index set where logical records are stored.

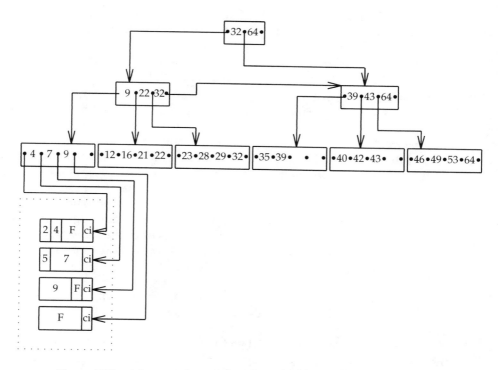

Figure 7.71   A key-sequence file organization.   Only one control area of four control intervals is shown;   in fact, each sequence set index node is associated with a control area.   We denote by an *F* a free space.

of the B$^+$-tree structure, no special treatment (redistribution or concatenation) of underflow nodes takes place.

Insertions are accomplished by inserting the target record in the appropriate control interval.   If the target control interval is an overflow node, the treatment is similar to that of the B$^+$ in that the control interval splits.   But splitting in this case is accomplished in the following fashion.   If an empty control interval in the target control area exists, control interval splitting takes place; otherwise, the control area is split by introducing a new control area at the end of the file and a new sequence set node.   In either case *VSAM* "moves" the contents of some control intervals into new control intervals, while the new record is placed in its appropriate position.

The record movement technique during a split depends on the mode employed and is outlined below.

- **Control interval split.** In the case of *direct* processing, half the records of the target control interval are moved into the empty control interval and the new record is inserted into the appropriate control interval.   In the case of *sequential* processing, if the insertion is to take place at the *end* of the target control interval, the record is inserted in the empty control interval and no other records are moved. On the other hand, if the record is inserted at any other position, all records in the target control interval with keys larger than the new record are moved into the empty control interval and the record is inserted in the target control interval.

- **Control area split.** In the case of *direct* processing, half the control intervals with record keys larger than the key of the new record are moved to the new control area, and the new record is inserted in its target control interval.[46] In the case of *sequential* processing, if the insertion is to take place at the *end* of the last control interval, the record is inserted in the first control interval of the new control area and no other records are moved. On the other hand, if the record is inserted at any other position of the last control interval, then this interval is moved to the new control area and the new record is inserted there with the appropriate control interval split. Finally, in any other case all control intervals after the target control interval are moved to the new control area, followed with the appropriate control interval split of the target control interval.

Figure 7.72 illustrates the result of deleting the record with key 4 and inserting the record with key 6 in the *KSDS* organization of Figure 7.70 assuming direct processing.

The record with key 4 is deleted without adjustment of the sequence node; moreover, *VSAM* reclaims the space in the control interval occupied by that logical record. Insertion of the new record with key 6 forces a control interval split; half the records (in this case, only the record with key 6) are moved to the empty control interval; the new record is inserted in this control interval (since 5 < 6 < 7).

We close by stating that the *VSAM* file system provides the user with a number of features that, if employed, will yield improved performance. As a first example, the user may request that each index record of the sequence set be stored at the beginning of its associated control area. In this case there is no need for any seeks if one desires to access the index record and data records of this control area. As a second example, we note that indexes in higher levels than the sequence set are *compressed*;[47] the net result being that the storage space allocated to these indexes is reduced. The interested reader is referred to the appropriate and extensive IBM manuals.

---

[46]Notice that a control interval split will take place according to the technique discussed earlier.

[47]Consider the following ordered sequence of five-digit, $d_1d_2d_3d_4d_5$, numeric keys 11324, 11345, and 16458. The mapping defined by

$$d_1d_2d_3d_4d_5 \rightarrow d_3d_4$$

maps the three keys to the three new keys, 32, 34, and 45, respectively. Notice that the new keys have a smaller length than the original ones, and they uniquely identify the latter. This simple example illustrates the compression technique.

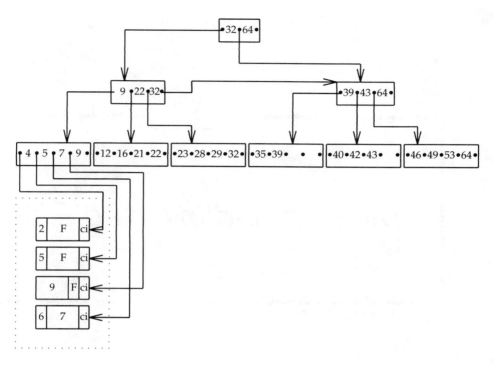

Figure 7.72   Deleting the record with key 4 and inserting the record with key 6 in the *KSDS* of Figure 7.70. We denote a free space by *F*.

8

Multilist and Inverted Files

Up to this point the discussions related to file organizations have been restricted to primary access methods. These file organizations were designed and organized under the assumption that logical records were retrieved subject to their primary key value. Retrieval of a record (or records) subject to some *secondary* key value has not been discussed. The reason is that all organizations that have been discussed so far require $NBLK_{dat}$ accesses, an unacceptably large search length to satisfy any retrieval request that involves secondary key values. This is a direct result of the fact that the mapping from the set of secondary key values to the set of logical records is not a one-to-one mapping, as was the case with the set of the primary key values.

Consider a file of student records, where each record has the following type.

```
STUDENT = RECORD
                  SOCIAL_SECURITY : ARRAY [1..9] OF CHAR;
                  SEX             : (MALE,FEMALE) ;
                  SCHOOL          : (BUS, ENG, LAS);
                  CLASSIFICATION  : (1,2,3,4,5,6,7,8,9);
                  LAST_NAME       : ARRAY [1..20] OF CHAR;
                  MIDDLE_NAME     : ARRAY [1..20] OF CHAR;
                  FIRST_NAME      : ARRAY [1..20] OF CHAR;
                  TELEPHONE       : ARRAY [1..10] OF CHAR;
                  ADDRESS         : RECORD
                        STREET : ARRAY [1..20] OF CHAR;
                        CITY   : ARRAY [1..20] OF CHAR;
                        STATE  : ARRAY [1..4] OF CHAR;
                     END;
        END;
```

The primary key is the SOCIAL_SECURITY number; assume for the sake of simplicity that all requests for retrieval involve at *most* the secondary key values SEX and SCHOOL. Using this assumption each logical record could be viewed (and will be throughout this chapter) as though it had been defined via the declaration of Table 8.1.

TABLE 8.1

```
STUDENT = RECORD
                  SOCIAL_SECURITY : ARRAY [1..9] OF CHAR;
                  SEX             : (MALE,FEMALE) ;
                  SCHOOL          : (BUS, ENG, LAS);
                  DATA            : REST_OF_DATA;
        END;
```

The stored record will be denoted as shown in Figure 8.1.

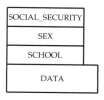

Figure 8.1   The representation of a stored student record.

Now consider a physical linked representation of this file, as in Figure 8.2.

Observe that the request "Retrieve all students such that (SCHOOL = 'ENG')" will yield the first 11 logical records from the linked sequential file in Figure 8.2. The query "Retrieve all students such that ((SEX = 'FEMALE') **or** (SCHOOL = 'LAS'))" will yield a set of 7 records of the file. At the other extreme, the query "Retrieve all students such that ((SEX = 'FEMALE') **and** (SCHOOL = 'LAS'))" will yield no records. Regardless of the number of records

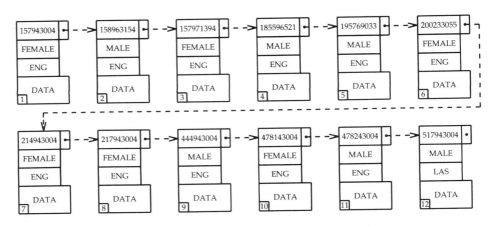

Figure 8.2   The Physical Linked Sequential file.

that will be retrieved, *all* logical records must be retrieved at a cost of 12 random accesses.

One could argue that if the records were blocked, then the number of accesses would fall to 3, as in the case of the cellular linked file organization of Figure 8.3. This is true, but still *all* blocks must be accessed, and *all* logical records must be examined while in main memory to see if the required condition is satisfied. In this chapter we will present a number of file structures suitable for secondary access methods. We will begin by discussing queries.

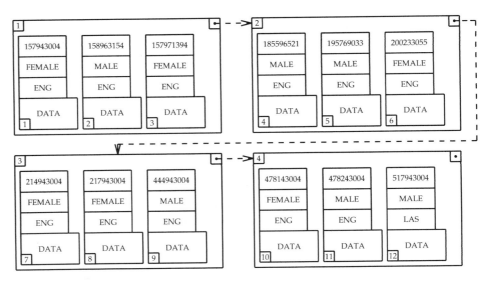

Figure 8.3   The cellular Physical Linked Sequential file.

8.1 QUERIES

Throughout this chapter we will be working with a file of *NR* logical records; we will denote the primary key by k and the set of n secondary keys that could be involved in retrieval requests by $s_1, s_2, s_3, s_4, ..., s_n$. Despite the informal syntax of the example queries given above, it follows that the allowable format of a query has the following form.

"Retrieve all records such that (expression)"

where **expression** is defined in its simplest form as

$$(\text{condition}_1)$$

and in general as

$$(\text{condition}_1) \text{ or } (\text{condition}_2) \text{ or } ... \text{ or } (\text{condition}_m)$$

A **condition** on the other hand has as its simplest form

$$(s_j = \text{'value'})$$

or, in general, the form

$$(s_{j_0} = \text{'value}_0\text{'}) \textbf{ and } (s_{j_1} = \text{'value}_1\text{'}) \textbf{ and } (s_{j_2} = \text{'value}_2\text{'}) \textbf{ and } ... \textbf{ and } (s_{j_m} = \text{'value}_m\text{'})$$

In addition to the relational operator =, one can define the relational operators $\neq$, $<$, $>$, $\geq$, and $\leq$. It is obvious that these new operators are defined in terms of the logical operators and the relational operator = in the natural way. That is,

$$(s_j \neq \text{'value'}) = (\textbf{not } (s_j = \text{'value'}))$$

To define the other relational operators, it is assumed that the variable "value" takes its values on a finite, ordered, and discrete set $D = \{ d_1, d_2, ..., d_n \}$. If it is assumed that $value = \text{'}d_k\text{'}$ for some k, then

$$(s_j < \text{'value'}) = ((s_j = \text{'}d_1\text{'}) \textbf{ or } (s_j = \text{'}d_2\text{'}) \textbf{ or } (s_j = \text{'}d_3\text{'}) \textbf{ or } ... (s_j = \text{'}d_{k-1}\text{'}))$$

The definition of the other relational operations follow.

$$(s_j \neq \text{'value'}) = (\textbf{not}\,(s_j = \text{'value'}))$$
$$(s_j < \text{'value'}) = (\textbf{not}\,(s_j \geq \text{'value'}))$$
$$(s_j > \text{'value'}) = (\textbf{not}\,(s_j \leq \text{'value'}))$$

On the other hand, we have seen that *every* retrieval query that involves secondary key values retrieves a *set*[1] of records that satisfy a given condition (or a set of conditions). Moreover, that condition can be written as an expression that involves the logical operators **and, or,** and **not** and the relational operator =. Hence, with no loss of generality we may assume that such a retrieval query involves only those three operators.

[1] This set could be empty.

In addition, it is simple to see that the logical operators behave as the set operators intersection, $\cap$, union, $\cup$, and complement, $'$. Therefore, to satisfy a query of the form

"Retrieve all records such that $((\mathbf{s_i} = 'value_i')$ **or** $(\mathbf{s_j} = 'value_j'))$"

one should take the *union* of the set of logical records that satisfies the first condition with the set of all logical records that satisfies the second condition.[2] On the other hand, to satisfy a query of the form

"Retrieve all records $((\mathbf{s_i} = 'value_i')$ **and** $(\mathbf{s_j} = 'value_j'))$"

one would take the *intersection* of the set of logical records that satisfies the first condition with the set of all logical records that satisfies the second condition. Finally, to satisfy a query of the form

"Retrieve all records (**not** $(\mathbf{s_j} = 'value_j'))$"

one would take the *complement* (relative to the set of logical records) of the set of logical records that satisfies the condition $(\mathbf{s_j} = 'value_j')$.

The above discussion suggests that file structures facilitating fast retrieval of queries that involve secondary keys will be structures in which the sets discussed above can be identified as such. The basic principle consists of *linking* all records according to their secondary key value. Notice that each secondary key s_i can take up to m_i values $d_{i_1}, d_{i_2}, ..., d_{i_j}$ for $1 \le j \le m_i$ and $1 \le i \le n$. Since one list must be maintained for each pair (s_i, d_{i_j}), we can see that the total number of chains that must be maintained is equal to

$$\sum_{i=1}^{n} \sum_{j=i}^{m_i} j \qquad [8.1]$$

To comprehend the magnitude of this number, consider the moderate case of 10 secondary keys and assume that each can take 100 values. Then the above sum indicates that 1000 chains must be maintained.

The two most common file structures employed in this case are the *Multilist* and *Inverted* file organizations. Their difference lies in the fact that linked lists are maintained in the data blocks under the former organization, while they are maintained separately from the data blocks in the latter organization. We will discuss each one in turn.

8.2 MULTILIST FILES

As we mentioned earlier, logical records are linked according to the pair secondary key and secondary key value. In other words, all records having the same value, $value_{i_1}$, of their s_i key belong in the same list; similarly, all records whose

[2]Notice that records that satisfy both conditions appear only once in the union.

s_i key have the same value, $value_{i_2}$, belong in the same list; but the two lists must be *disjoint*. Figure 8.4 illustrates a *Multilist* structure over the file of Figure 8.2. All records whose SEX value is FEMALE are linked together with a system of dashed pointers. Similarly, all records whose SEX value is MALE are linked together with a system of solid pointers. These two lists are disjoint. Finally, two more lists are shown relative to the value of their secondary key SCHOOL. One list contains only one logical record (record 12); another list (dotted arrows) links together all other records whose SCHOOL key value is ENG.

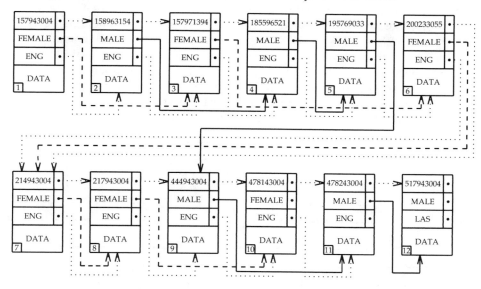

Figure 8.4   A Multilist file structure.

Closer examination of Figure 8.1 indicates that identification of the sets discussed above is done via the multisystem of block pointers; therefore, a savings in the cost of satisfying this type of query vis-à-vis the physical linked sequential file of Figure 8.2 is apparent. But there are also certain queries whose search length remains unacceptably large. For instance, the search length in such a query is equal to the sum of two terms, the *length* of the list and the *distance*[3] of the first record in this chain from the first data block. For example, the retrieval of all records satisfying the three independent conditions ('SEX' = 'FEMALE'), ('SEX' = 'MALE'), and ('SCHOOL' = 'LAS') requires $(0 + 6) = 6$, $(1 + 6) = 7$, and $(1 + 11) = 12$ accesses, respectively. At the other extreme, the retrieval of all records satisfying the condition ('SCHOOL' = 'BUS') requires $(12 + 0) = 12$ accesses; that is because the corresponding list is empty.

To optimize the search length, the Multilist structure can be modified by introducing an index set. The index set contains two levels. In the lower level a set

[3] In terms of physical blocks.

of n index *sets* is allocated. Each index set i contains m_i indexes where m_i denotes, as before, the number of discrete values $d_{i_j}, 1 \le j \le m_i$, that the secondary key s_i can assume. Each index entry contains two components; the first component contains the value d_j and the second field is a pointer to the first record in the list of logical records whose s_i value is equal to d_j. The upper level is used to index the lower level. Specifically, this level contains n indexes. Each index again has two components; the first component contains the secondary key s_i, while the second is a pointer to the index set i in the next level.

Figure 8.5 illustrates a two-level Indexed Multilist structure. Since the number of secondary keys in our example is assumed to be two, we have $s_1 =$ 'SEX' and $s_2 =$ 'SCHOOL.' Hence, the first level contains two indexes. Furthermore, the secondary key s_1 takes its values from a discrete set of two elements; i.e., $d_1 =$ 'FEMALE' and $d_2 =$ 'MALE.' Consequently, the index in the second level corresponding to that key contains two indexes. Finally, the pointer associated with the key value FEMALE points to the first block of the data set, which is the first record in the list corresponding to that key value.

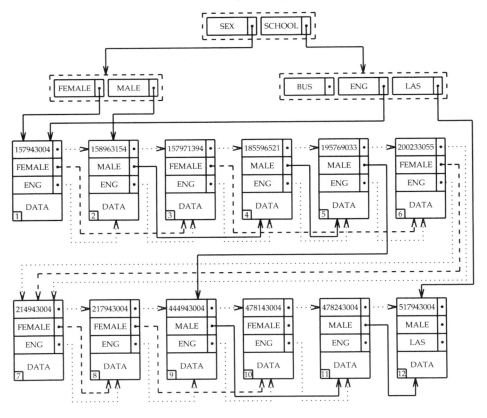

Figure 8.5   A two-level Indexed Multilist file structure.

Before we close this section, it should be emphasized that such a structure could be implemented physically by the employment of up to $n + 2$ files. One file could be dedicated to the index set of the first level, one could be dedicated to each of the n index sets of the second level; and the last file would contain the data set. In addition, the blocking factors, as well as the file organization of these files, could be different. The designer would need to utilize the techniques and discussions of previous chapters in selecting those appropriate file organizations and parameters so that the cost of the required operations would be optimal.

8.2.1 The Operations

In our example we opted for an *ordered* sequential file (relative to the primary key). In addition, we assumed a highly volatile file of records; therefore, we were forced to select a physical linked sequential organization. With this type of organization random insertions and deletions would require large search lengths; therefore, in such a case we should instead sacrifice storage space to obtain smaller search lengths. Consequently, *all* lists in Figure 8.5 would be *doubly* linked, even though this has not been shown. Whenever a record is to be inserted (or deleted), exactly n chains in the data set must be repaired; in some cases up to n indexes must be adjusted in the n index sets of the second level.

8.2.1.1 The *and* Operator.   Earlier it was shown that in order to satisfy the *and* query, the intersection of *all* lists that satisfy each of the conditions must be formed. Brute-force traversal of these lists can be avoided if one observes that the intersection of all these lists will be a sublist of the one among them having the minimal length. Hence, all records must be accessed in that *minimal* length list, and those logical records in the list that do not satisfy any of the other conditions must be "weeded out."

The above discussion suggests that whenever such a query is encountered, the list with the minimal length must be found. This is a simple matter to resolve. The length of each chain is stored in the second index level alongside the index component that points to that list. The application program responsible for maintaining the correct length by adjusting it appropriately during insertions and deletions will be able to determine the minimal length list from examination of these fields.

8.2.1.2 The *or* Operator.   The *or* operation requires *all* lists that satisfy each of the conditions in the query be traversed and all nonduplicate records be output. The process of weeding out the duplicate records as well as the mechanism for retrieval of records subject to the *or* operator is straightforward whenever the underlying data set comprises an *ordered* file, as is the case in our example. In the next paragraph we indicate this mechanism for the case in which the query is of the form

"Retrieve all records such that $((s_i = \text{'}value_i\text{'})$ **or** $(s_j = \text{'}value_j\text{'}))$"

The necessary modifications of this algorithm in the case of the more general query as well as the case of the underlying unordered data set are an exercise for the reader.

The first step consists of accessing the pointers to the logical records associated to the indexes $(s_i, \textbf{value}_i)$ and $(s_j, \textbf{value}_j)$. Let the pointers be p_1 and p_2, respectively. The first step consists of accessing both logical records pointed to by these two pointers (if $p_1 = p_2$, only one access is required). If the key of the logical record pointed to by p_1 is less than that pointed to by p_2 we let $k = 1$; if the keys are equal we set $k = 0$; otherwise, we let $k = 2$. If $k = 0$ or $k = 1$, then the record pointed to by p_1 is output; otherwise, the one pointed to by p_2 is output. If $k = 0$ we then set p_1 and p_2 to the pointer values associated with the s_i and s_j fields; otherwise, only the pointer p_k is set to the pointer value associated with the s_k field of that record and the process is repeated. If at any instant a *Nil* pointer is encountered, then from that point on all records associated with the other list are retrieved. The advantage of this algorithm over simply accessing all elements of both lists and then weeding out the duplicate records is that both lists are traversed in "parallel" in the sense that no logical record is accessed twice; moreover, the retrieval of the records has been accomplished in an *ordered* fashion.

8.2.2 Cellular Multilists

So far we have seen that search lengths can be reduced whenever logical records are blocked. Therefore, our current task is to modify the structure that was presented in an earlier section so that the logical records of the data set can be blocked.

One possible modification is illustrated in Figure 8.6. This modification consists of removing *all* pointer fields associated with each logical record and introducing a number of block pointers equal to the number of distinct values that the secondary keys may assume. In our specific example, the total number of distinct values is equal to five, which actually leads to a pointer saving. This is not always the case because the savings in pointer fields (by blocking the logical records with a blocking factor *BF*) is equal to $BF \cdot n$ per block, since a number of block pointers equal to the one given by equation [8.1] must be introduced in each block.

8.3 INVERTED FILES

Another popular organization is that of an *Inverted* file. This organization differs from the Multilist organization in that the linked lists are implemented by removing the pointers from the stored records and storing them in an *index*like fashion. There is no savings in terms of storage since the number of pointer fields is not reduced, but the management of these pointer fields becomes much

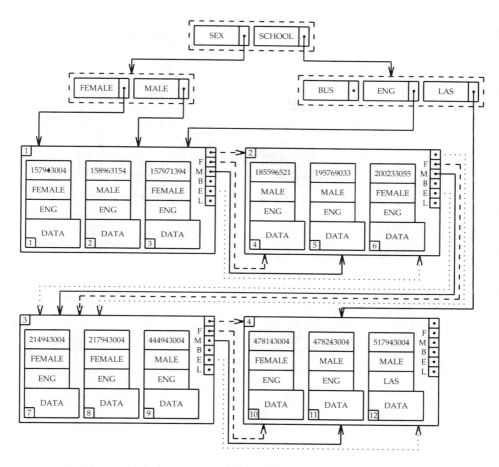

Figure 8.6   The cellular *Indexed Multilist* Linked Sequential file.

easier. Figure 8.7 illustrates such a structure, while Figure 8.8 illustrates its cellular counterpart.

It is apparent that most of the discussions of previous sections can be extended with minor modifications to this file structure. But before we close this section we should note the significant gains in terms of the response time relative to the "or" operator attained with this file organization vis-à-vis the Multilist organization. Assume that the pointers in each list are maintained in sorted order. Then in order to form the union of two such lists, it is enough to access all records pointed to by all these pointers and at the same time to perform a weeding out of duplicate records. As an example, consider the file structure of Figure 8.7 and the query

"Retrieve all students such that ((SEX = 'FEMALE') **or** (SCHOOL = 'ENG'))"

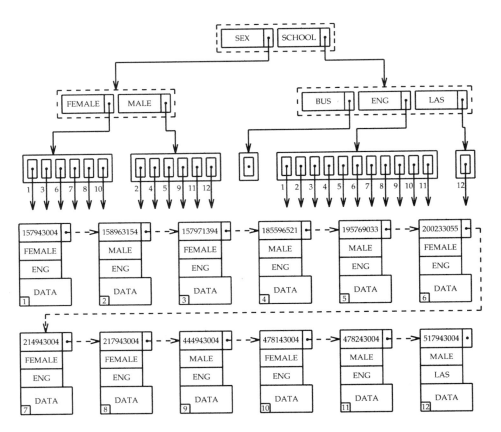

Figure 8.7 An *Inverted* file structure.

The first pointer of each list is compared. If they are equal, the logical record pointed to by one of them is accessed and the next two pointers (one from each list) are compared and the process is repeated. Otherwise, the record pointed to by the smaller pointer is accessed; the next pointer to it is compared with the nonselected pointer and the process is repeated. At any rate, when all the elements of any one list are exhausted, all records pointed to by the remaining pointers of the other list are accessed.

8.4 EXERCISES

1. Assume a sequential file containing a set of logical records of type STUDENT, as defined in Figure 8.1. Implement the two-level Indexed Multilist file organization of Figure 8.5 over the set of these records. In addition, implement the following four operations.

   a. Delete a student (by the primary key).

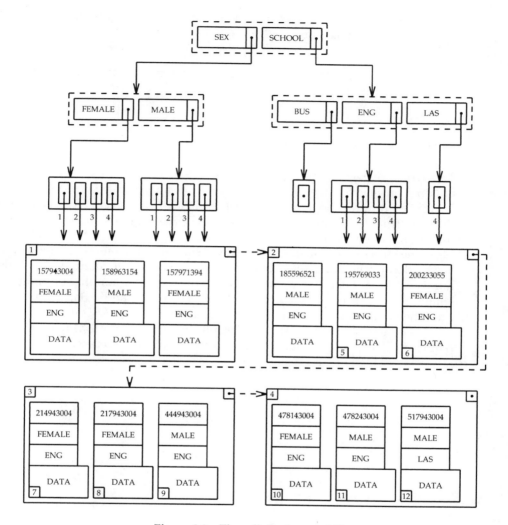

Figure 8.8   The cellular Inverted file.

b. Retrieve all students such that ((SEX = 'gender') and (SCHOOL = 'initials')).

c. Retrieve all students such that ((SEX = 'gender') or (SCHOOL = 'initials')), where 'gender' can take either of the values MALE or FEMALE and 'initials' can take one of the values LAS, ENG, and BUS.

2. Assume a sequential file containing a set of logical records of type STUDENT as defined in Figure 8.1. Implement the cellular Inverted file of Figure 8.8 over the set of these records. In addition implement the following four operations.

a. Delete a student (by the primary key).

b. Retrieve all students such that ((SEX = 'gender') and (SCHOOL = 'initials')).

c. Retrieve all students such that ((SEX = 'gender') or (SCHOOL = 'initials')), where 'gender' can take either of the values MALE or FEMALE and 'initials' can take one of the values LAS, ENG, and BUS.

8.5 *VSAM* FILE ORGANIZATIONS

The *Virtual Storage Access Method* (VSAM) file management system is capable of building an *inverted*-like file organization over an existing *Entry-Sequenced Data Set* (ESDS) or a *Key-Sequenced Data Set* (KSDS) *alternate index*[4] for each key field different from the primary key for the *KSDS* organizations and any key field for the *ESDS* file organizations.

The structure of an alternate index is similar to the one presented in an earlier section on inverted files. Specifically, it contains the alternate key value, a number of pointers to the appropriate data records, the number of pointers, the length of the pointers, the length of the alternate key, and a flag field that indicates the organization of the underlying data set (*ESDS* or *KSDS*).

The interested reader should consult the appropriate IBM manuals for the required JCL and PL/I statements that are available in each case.

---

[4] IBM terminology.

9

External Sorting

Recall that a file is said to be *sorted* if the records of the file are arranged in such a way that the keys of the records form either an *increasing* or a *decreasing* sequence. Unfortunately, seldom at the time of the initial creation of a file is that file sorted; therefore, algorithms are needed to perform the sorting of a file. The reader should already have been exposed to a number of *internal* sorting operations such as *bubble sort, quick sort, binary sort, shell sort,* and so forth. As the term *internal sort* suggests, these sorting techniques can be used only in the cases in which the given file is sufficiently small to permit the loading of the entire file into main memory at once. Files are usually so large that only a small portion—specifically, only a fixed number of blocks—of a file can exist in main memory at any specific instant. Therefore, the internal sorting algorithms become inappropriate; hence, there exists the need for new sorting operations, i.e., *external sortings.*

All external sorting algorithms are based on the same principle. The starting point is the creation of one or more *sorted partition* files from the original unsorted file. The next step consists of a number of passes through these files until the data is sorted. The difference between the various external sorting techniques or algorithms lies primarily in their attempt to minimize the number of passes through the data, and, consequently, to attain the *best* performance possible. As there is a plethora of available sorting algorithms, there is not *a best,* (in the sense of performance), external sorting algorithm. The best algorithm depends on a number of factors, as will be seen.

9.1 SORTED PARTITION FILES

A *sorted partition file* is a physical sequential file in which the first n records can be grouped into an ordered set P_1, the next m records into an ordered set P_2; and, continuing in this fashion, the last r records can be grouped into an ordered set P_k such that the records in each set P_i, for $1 \le i \le k$, are sorted in increasing key sequence (Figure 9.1). The set P_i is called the *ith partition* or the *ith run*, while the number of the records of a partition P_j is called the *partition length* of the jth partition and is denoted by $PL[j]$, where $1 \le i, j \le k$. Finally, the number k is appropriately referred to as the *number of partitions* of the sorted partition file.

$$\boxed{4\ 8\ 24\ \mid\ 23\ 27\ 29\ 31\ \mid\ 2\ 7\ 11\ 16\ 19}$$

Figure 9.1   A sorted partition file with three partitions. Partitions are separated by the symbol "|".

In Figure 9.1 the physical boundary of any two successive partitions has been marked by the symbol |. The obvious question then is how should one mark the boundaries between any two successive partitions in the physical file. The answer is simple. No such marking is required, since it is a simple matter for the application program to detect the boundaries. In particular, a physical boundary is detected whenever a *stepdown* occurs. Observe that within a partition and traversing the file towards its physical end, the next record belongs in the current partition if and only if its key is larger than that of the previous record. The phenomenon in which the key of a record is smaller than that of its predecessor is what is known as a stepdown.

Recall that at the beginning of this chapter it was noted that all external sortings require the creation of a sorted partition file. The reader should have observed by now that *every* file *is* a sorted partition file. For example the physical sequential file consisting of ten records with integer keys 1, 10, 9, 8, 7, 5, 4, 6, 2, and 3 is a sorted partition file with seven partitions in which three of the partitions have a length of 2 and the remaining five have a length of 1. Hence, the question is, Why the need for a new sorted partition file? The answer lies in the fact that the running time of the external sorting algorithms is a decreasing function of the number of partitions in the initial sorted partition file. In other words, the smaller the number of partitions the better the performance of the external sorting algorithm. Hence, the aim is to work towards the development of algorithms that will provide a sorted partition file with a minimum number of partitions. To this end two algorithms are presented to perform this task, the *simple sorted partition generator* and the *replacement sorted partition generator*.

9.1.1 The Simple Sorted Partition Generator

Assume a physical sequential file MASTER with $NREC$ records, loading density LD of 1, $NBLK$ blocks, and blocksize BS bytes. Moreover, assume for the sake of simplicity, that two buffers have been allocated, one for input and one for output, each of size BS;[1] assume also that there is sufficient storage available in the data area to which the contents of the input buffer can be transferred. The simple sorted partition generator algorithm whose pseudoalgorithm appears in Table 9.1 creates from the file MASTER a new sorted partition physical sequential file NMASTER and proceeds as follows. The first block of the file MASTER is transferred into the storage area AREA in main memory via the procedure *Read_a_Block*(MASTER,AREA) (step [1]); the records presently in the program variable AREA are sorted via the procedure Sort(AREA), which is none other than an internal sorting algorithm (step [2]). The contents of the variable AREA are now written into the NMASTER file via the *Write_a_Block*(NMASTER,AREA) procedure (step [3]). Finally, the last step ensures that the entire process is repeated until all blocks and, consequently, all records of the original file MASTER have been processed. An example is given in Figure 9.2.

TABLE 9.1   The pseudocode of the simple sorted partition generator.

```
Simple Sorted Partition Generator;

[1]     Read_a_Block(MASTER,AREA);
[2]     Sort(AREA);
[3]     Write_a_Block(NMASTER,AREA);
[4]     If EOF(MASTER) then exit
[5]                     else go to step [1];
```

24 4 8 19 12 7 2 20 18 6 17 9 16 10 11 21 22 1 23 3 13 15 14 5

(a) The MASTER file.

4 8 24 ǀ 7 12 19 ǀ 2 18 20 ǀ 6 9 17 ǀ 10 11 16 ǀ 1 21 22 ǀ 3 13 23 ǀ 5 14 15

(b) The NMASTER file.

Figure 9.2   The initial file (a) and the new sorted partition file (b), consisting of eight partitions each of length 3, generated by the simple sorted partition generator with $BF = 3$. Note that the marker " ǀ ", used to mark the physical boundaries of the partitions, is absent from the physical file.

---

[1] It will become apparent in the sequence that the blocksize of the output file depends on the sorting algorithm that will eventually be employed.

The above algorithm provides a sorted partition file of at most $clg(NREC/BF)$ partitions, each of which has a length of at least BF with the possible exception of the last partition, whose minimum length is given by $NREC - (NBLK \cdot BF)$. Note that the exact number of generated partitions depends on the buffer size. Hence, it could be stated that the simple partition generator provides partitions of length equal to the buffer size.

The next algorithm provides partitions of *average* length equal to $2BF$; therefore, the number of generated partitions is on the average half of those contributed by the simple partition generator.

9.1.2 The Replacement Sorted Partition Generator

Let's examine the previous algorithm a little more closely. After step [1] has been completed, the contents of the input buffer can be replaced by the contents of the second block of the MASTER file without affecting the next step. Now, if the smallest key among the records in the structure AREA is *less* than or *equal* to the key of the "next" record in the input buffer, this suggests that the latter record *is* a member of the first partition of the NMASTER file. Unfortunately, the simple sorted partition generator will output this record as a member of the *next* partition. The replacement selection partition generator takes into account this observation and outputs this record in the current partition, the result of which is that the length of the current partition increases, which in turn forces a decrease in the number of generated partitions.

Using this algorithm the record with the *smallest* key of those in the structure AREA is output; then, that record is replaced in the structure AREA by the next record in the input buffer. A search is then performed on the structure ARRAY to locate that record with the smallest key that is greater than the key of the record previously output. The result of this search dictates the next action to be taken. Specifically, if the search is successful, then the located record is output; otherwise, the record with the smallest key among those currently in the structure AREA is output. In either case, the record that was just output is replaced in the structure AREA by the next record from the input buffer and the search step is repeated. Notice that after the end of the file has been reached, no replacement takes place. Instead, the records that remain in the structure AREA that have not been output yet are sorted; these are then output and the algorithm terminates. Finally, it is easy to see that the algorithm detects a physical boundary between two successive partitions whenever the search is unsuccessful.

The algorithm utilizes a number of subroutines whose function and significance is outlined below and whose pseudocode is given in Table 9.2.

- **AREA:** A BF element array of records.
- *LAST_KEY:* A program variable that receives a key from a record.
- **I:** An integer program variable.
- **Key(AREA[I]):** A function that returns the key of the Ith record.

TABLE 9.2 The pseudoalgorithm for the replacement sorted partition generator.

```
Replacement Sorted Partition Generator;

[1]    Read_a_Block(MASTER,AREA);
[2]    I ← Smallest_Key(AREA);
[3]    LAST_KEY ← Key(AREA[I]);
       Write_Record(AREA[I],NMASTER);
[4]    If NOT(EOF(MASTER)) then Read_Record(MASTER,AREA[I])
                           else {Clear(AREA) and exit};
[5]    I ← Next_Greater_Key(AREA,LAST_KEY);
       If I = 0 then go to [2] else go to [3];
```

- *Smallest_Key*(**AREA**): A function that returns the position of the record with the smallest key among all the records stored in the array AREA.

- *Read_a_Block*(**MASTER,AREA**): A procedure that transfers (via the input buffer) the first block of file MASTER into the array AREA.

- *Read_Record*(**AREA[I]**): The standard procedure that transfers the next record from the input buffer associated with the MASTER file into the Ith element of the array AREA. Notice that when a logical READ is issued and the input buffer is empty, then the access method will transfer the next block from MASTER unless the end of file has been encountered.

- *Write_Record*(**AREA[I],NMASTER**): The standard write procedure that transfers a record stored at location AREA[I] into the next available slot in the output buffer associated with the NMASTER file. Notice that if the last write caused a full output buffer, then the entire contents are written into the physical file NMASTER.

- **Clear(AREA)**: This procedure outputs in increasing order all records presently in the array AREA that have not been output previously.

- *Next_Greater_Key*(**AREA,LAST_KEY**): A function that returns the position I of a record within the array AREA and whose key is the smallest among those in the array AREA and greater than or equal to the LAST_KEY. If such a key is not found, then the function returns the value 0.

In Table 9.3 a step-by-step trace is provided of the algorithm above under the assumptions that *BF* is equal to 3, that the buffers can hold just one block, and that the MASTER file contains nine records with their keys in the order 3, 8, 12, 9, 6, 7, 1, 4, 22.

It was noted earlier that the average length of the partitions generated via the replacement sorted partition generator is equal to twice the blocking factor. To understand this, assume a buffer capable of holding *BF* records, an array AREA of *BF* elements, and a random distribution of the keys of the records; i.e., given the key of a specific record, the probability that the key of its successor is greater than it *is equal* to the probability that the key of its successor is less than it. In other words, half of the time the key of the "next" record from the input

TABLE 9.3   Trace of the replacement sorted partition
generator over the input file MASTER of Figure 9.2.

STEP	AREA	I	LAST_KEY	INP_BUFFER	OUTPUT
1	3 8 12	-	-	9 6 7	-
2	3 8 12	1	-	9 6 7	-
3	3 8 12	1	3	9 6 7	3
4	9 8 12	1	3	9 6 7	-
5	9 8 12	2	3	9 6 7	-
3	9 8 12	2	8	9 6 7	8
4	9 6 12	2	8	9 6 7	-
5	9 6 12	1	8	9 6 7	-
3	9 6 12	1	9	9 6 7	9
4	7 6 12	1	9	1 4 22	-
5	7 6 12	3	9	1 4 22	-
3	7 6 12	3	12	1 4 22	12
4	7 6 1	3	12	1 4 22	-
5	7 6 1	0	12	1 4 22	-
2	7 6 1	3	12	1 4 22	-
3	7 6 1	3	1	1 4 22	1
4	7 6 4	3	1	1 4 22	-
5	7 6 4	3	1	1 4 22	-
3	7 6 4	3	4	1 4 22	4
4	7 6 22	3	4	1 4 22	-
5	7 6 22	2	4	1 4 22	-
3	7 6 22	2	6	1 4 22	6
4	7 6 22	3	22	1 4 22	7, 22

buffer will be greater than the key LAST_KEY of the last record output. Consider now the mechanism of generating any partition. Recall that the first step is to output the record with the *smallest* key among all records stored in the structure AREA. This suggests that all remaining records in AREA *are* members of the current partition; hence, the length of the partition is at least *BF*. In addition, when a record is output, this record is replaced by the next record in the buffer. Given the fact that half the time the key of the latter record is greater than that of the last output record, then that *new* record must output as a member of the current partition. Hence, one can conclude that, on the average, each output record will force a new record (from the buffer) to be output. But, recall that all the records that initially were stored in the structure AREA will eventually be output as members of the current partition; since each one of those records contributes one more in the current partition, we can see that the length of the current partition is equal to 2*BF*. Figure 9.3 illustrates this fact.

One should notice that the MASTER file is the same as the one in Figure 9.2, which illustrates the amount of savings in the generated number of partitions under this new algorithm.

9.1.2.1 The *Next_Greater_Key*(AREA,LAST_KEY) Function.   As has been discussed the I/O time required for the generation of the sorted partition

24 4 8 19 12 7 2 20 18 6 17 9 16 10 11 21 22 1 23 3 13 15 14 5

(a) The MASTER file.

4 8 12 19 24 I 2 7 18 20 I 6 9 10 11 16 17 21 22 23 I 1 3 13 14 15 I 5

(b) The NMASTER file.

Figure 9.3   The initial file (a) and the new sorted partition file (b), consisting of five partitions generated by the replacement sorted partition generator with $BS = 3$. Note that the marker " I ", used to mark the physical boundaries of the partitions, is absent from the physical file.

file depends heavily on the number of required physical data transfers. This is due to the fact that it has been assumed that the internal processing time is so small compared to that of data transfer that it is negligible. The reader should have noticed that a significant amount of internal processing is required by the *Next_Greater_Key*(AREA,LAST_KEY) function. Specifically, this function must determine the smallest of the keys of the records currently in the data area AREA and also which key is greater than or equal to the previously output key.

There are a number of ways to accomplish this task. We are searching for the specific method that would minimize the internal processing time or, equivalently, for that algorithm of the smallest order.

Notice that the algorithm is required to sort the keys of the records of the data area AREA each and every time a record is written into the output buffer. This is a result of the fact that the record just previously written is replaced by the next record from the input buffer into the AREA. An algorithm is presented below that would accomplish this task in the minimal possible time. The algorithm is based on the idea of the *tournament sort*. Despite the fact that the reader has undoubtedly encountered this algorithm, it will be presented below for the sake of completeness.

The Tournament Sort.   Assume that the following task is assigned. A file, relatively small in size, consisting of a number n of positive integers is given, and these integers must be sorted in increasing order. Also assume that the integer n is some integral power, e.g., m, of two; in other words, $n = 2^m$.

The first step toward our goal is the creation of a *full* and *complete* binary tree with n leaf nodes occupied by n given positive integers in the same order as the given file from left to right. In Figure 9.4, the constructed tree is presented as a result of the given set of $n = 4$ positive integers {13, 2, 1, 8}.

The second step consists of advancing the *winner* (largest) of every pair of siblings to their parent node. This procedure is necessarily repeated until the winner has reached the root node. For example, Figure 9.5 indicates that the winner between the siblings {13, 2} is 13, whereas the winner between the

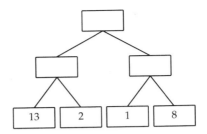

Figure 9.4 The full, complete binary tree constructed from the keys {13, 2, 1, 8} in the first step of tournament sort.

siblings {1, 8} is 8. Furthermore, the winner between the siblings {13, 8} is 13. Hence, as Figure 9.5 indicates, the integer 13 occupies the root position. The so obtained tree is called the *winners tree.*

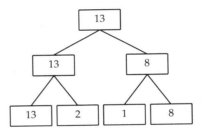

Figure 9.5 The winners tree constructed in the first step from the keys {13, 2, 1, 8} in the first step of tournament sort.

It should be clear that in this way the largest of the integers of the given set have been determined. How does one determine the second largest key? The answer is quite simple; the largest key, that is, the one that has just been output, does not participate any longer in the tournament. Thus, the second largest element will be the winner among the remaining players (elements). In particular, the contents of the leaf node corresponding to the current winner are replaced by a marker, such as $-\infty$, and the process is repeated. For example, the winner between {$-\infty$, 2} is 2, whereas the winner between {1, 8} is 8. Finally, the winner between {2, 8} is 8, which actually is the larger number of the remaining players and, equivalently, the second largest number of the original sequence. Figure 9.6 indicates the second step.

It is clear that the above process is repeated as many times as is necessary; then the sorting process is completed. As a matter of fact the process is repeated until the root node contains $-\infty$ or, equivalently, all but one of the leaf nodes contain $-\infty$; the latter would then contain the smallest integer of the given file.

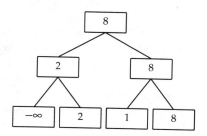

Figure 9.6   The winners tree (the second step) of the tournament sort over the file {13, 2, 1, 8}.

Hence, the tournament sort algorithm is as follows:

```
Construct winners tree;

While ( (contents of the root node) ≠ −∞) do
     {Output contents of the root node;
      Replace contents of the leaf node containing the winner by −∞;
      Readjust;}
exit;
```

Observe, therefore, that the order of the algorithm depends primarily on the number of times that the "while" loop is executed and on the number of comparisons that are required for the "readjust" step.

If instead of propagating the winner, the *loser* of any two siblings was propagated into their parent node, then the integers would be output into an increasing order. Hence, the basic principle upon which the *Next_Greater_Key* function is based is the above algorithm; the losers tree, with some modifications, is the data structure of the AREA, which is discussed below and is called the *selection tree*.

The Selection Tree.   Notice that the losers tree and the above given algorithm cannot be used as they stand in generating the partitions. The first modification that must be made is that when a key is output, the leaf position corresponding to that key must be replaced by the key of the "next" record currently in the input buffer, unless, of course, the logical end of file has been reached. Moreover, after the key has been replaced and the selection tree has been readjusted, the key occupying the root position is the smallest of the keys of the records in the AREA, but it *may not* be greater than or equal to the one that had been output previously. Consequently, it cannot be output in the current partition. In that case a flag is simply set in the corresponding leaf node position, and the selection tree is readjusted by modifying the propagation test. In particular, the determination of the loser between any two siblings will not only depend on the magnitude of the keys occupying the respective node positions but also on whether or not either of the flags of these key values has been set. If neither key has its flag set, then the loser is advanced; if only one key has its associated flag set, then this key does not participate; therefore, the key of its sibling is advanced. Lastly, if both keys have their flags set, then its parent must not participate either; and, in that case, the loser is advanced, but *the flag* of its parent is also set. If after the readjustment the key occupying the root position is greater than or equal to the one previously output, then we output this key; otherwise, we set the flag in the corresponding leaf position and readjust.

The question that naturally arises is what would be done if the root node had its flag set. This occurs if and only if all the keys that occupy the leaf positions are strictly less than the last output key. Hence, this suggests that whenever the setting of the flags is propagated all the way to the root node, then one can conclude that this is a signal that a new partition is to be generated; according to our algorithm, the corresponding tree is a selection tree. In that case, the flags of all nodes of the tree are *reset*; the key occupying the root node is output and the contents of its corresponding leaf node are replaced with the next record from the input file. Figure 9.7 illustrates these events. The first key output is key 4, the second is 5, and the third is 6. The smallest key of those in the AREA is 2, which is less than 6; as a result, the flag of the corresponding node is set (a flagged node is indicated by the appearance of an asterisk before and after the key). The tree is readjusted, and now key 8 is output, since it is greater than 6.

Finally, notice that in Figure 9.7(k) the flag of the root is set; and, therefore, a new partition is generated; key 1 is output and all flags are reset.

9.1.2.2 Implementation.

The idea of using the selection tree has a number of obvious benefits and a definite drawback. Both of these will be analyzed below.

The drawback is that there is some storage overhead relative to the nodes of the tree not at the leaf level. It is an easy matter to calculate that overhead and it will be shown below. Let h be the height of the tree. Since the tree is full and complete binary at level 1, there must be 2^1 nodes; at level 2, there are exactly 2^2 nodes. Continuing in this fashion it can be seen that at the last level, $h-1$, there will be $2^{(h-1)}$ nodes. But it has been assumed that there are exactly $n = 2^m$ nodes at the last level; therefore, there must be

$$2^{(h-1)2} = 2^m = n$$

or,

$$h = (m+1) = \log_2 n + 1 \qquad\qquad [4.1]$$

In addition, since the height of the tree is h, then the number of nodes ND is given by

$$ND = \sum_{k=0}^{h-1} 2^k$$

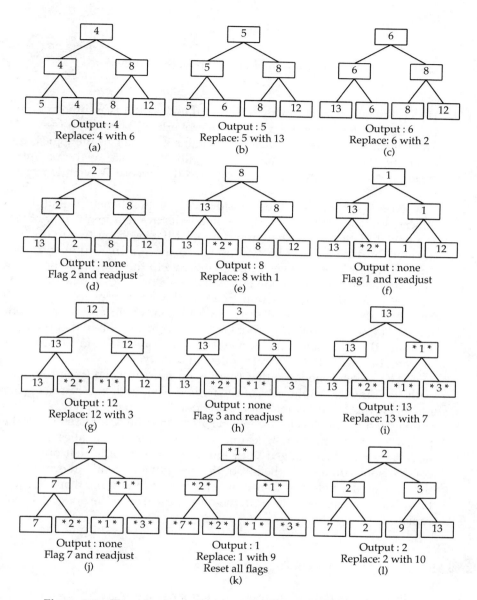

Figure 9.7   The selection tree over the file {5, 4, 8, 12, 6, 13, 2, 1, 3, 7, 9, 10}

But the finite series above is a geometric sum of ratio 2; therefore,

$$ND = \frac{1 - 2^{(h} - 1) + 1}{1 - 2}$$

or, by simplifying,

$$ND = 2^h - 1$$

Taking into account equation [4.1], the above equation yields

$$ND = 2^{\log_2 n} \cdot 2 - 1 = 2 \cdot n - 1$$

Hence, the overhead is exactly $[(2 \cdot n - 1)]$ nodes. If it is assumed that the pointer size requires PS bytes, then the storage overhead is equal to $(n-1) \cdot PS$ bytes.[2] The reason for this is that each *leaf* contains a pointer to the logical record and, similarly, the *loser* record does not actually propagate to the parent node; instead, a pointer to the leaf that points to that record is recorded in the parent node.

Now the benefits will be considered. The first benefit is that the tree is not allocated dynamically; instead, the data structure required is that of an array. It is a trivial matter to see that an ordering of the selection tree in the natural left-to-right (breadth-first) order will assign to the root the number 1, the leftmost node of the first level (level 1), the number 2 to the next node on that level, the number 3 in the leftmost node of the next level (level 2), and so on. In particular, using the fact that the selection tree is full, complete binary ensures that each branch node will have two sons. In addition, given any branch node with a number i assigned to it, it is trivial to see that the left son of that node is the node $2 \cdot i$ and the right son is the node $(2 \cdot i) + 1$. Conversely, given any node i, then its parent is the node $flr(i \ div \ 2)$, unless of course $i = 1$.

The second benefit is that there is no need to keep track separately of the path from the leaf to the root of the node during each readjustment. The reason for this is that in the branch nodes the pointer to that leaf node, which has been propagated to this level, is stored. Hence, after the readjustment has been completed, the root points to the leaf node that contains the smallest key. Hence, this node is replaced or flagged with the direct result being that only a number of comparisons equal to the height of the tree must be made in order to determine the next smallest element, since the only nodes of the tree that were affected are those nodes along the path from the root of the tree to the node that has just been replaced.

9.2 BALANCED MERGE SORTS

Recall from the data structures course that when there are two files, *File_1* and *File_2*, of m and n logical records of the same type, with each file sorted in increasing order by record keys, a new sorted file, *File_3*, can be obtained by applying the two-way merge sort algorithm. For the sake of completeness the pseudoalgorithm is discussed briefly below.

---

[2] It is assumed that the number of leaf nodes n is an integral power of 2 and that enough data transfers occurred so that all the leaf nodes are initially occupied by logical records.

At the outset, assume that the logical records of both files, *File_1* and *File_2*, have been stored in two arrays, α, β, of *m* and *n* elements, respectively; and assume that their primary key value is stored in the field *key* of these records. The algorithm presented in Table 9.4 merges the elements of the two files into a new file, *File_3*, whose logical records are stored in the array γ of (*m* + *n*) elements.

TABLE 9.4   The internal two-way merge algorithm.

```
Algorithm Internal 2-way Merge Sort;
```

$l \leftarrow \text{minimum}(m, n);$
$k \leftarrow i \leftarrow j \leftarrow 1;$
while $((i \le l)$ and $(j \le l))$ do
        {if $\alpha[j].key \le \beta[j].key$ then
                                                                    $\{\gamma[k] \leftarrow \alpha[i];$
                                                                     $i \leftarrow i + 1\}$
                                                                            else
                                                               $\{\gamma[k] \leftarrow \beta[j];$
                                                                 $j \leftarrow j + 1\}$
        $k \leftarrow k + 1\}$
if $i > m$ then
                        {while $(j \le n)$ do
                                 $\{\gamma[k] \leftarrow \beta[j];$
                                  $k \leftarrow k + 1;$
                                  $j \leftarrow j + 1;\}\}$
            else
                        {while $(i \le m)$ do
                                 $\{\gamma[k] \leftarrow \alpha[j];$
                                  $k \leftarrow k + 1;$
                                  $i \leftarrow i + 1;\}\}$
```
exit;
```

Examination of the internal two-way merge algorithm indicates that its order is $O(m + n)$.

9.2.1   The External Two-way Balanced Merge Sort

Consider now an arbitrarily large file *Init_File* that is to be sorted. The idea is that since the file is arbitrarily large and since it cannot be loaded in its entirety in main memory, then "chunks" of that file are loaded into main memory, where they are sorted. In particular, since the internal two-way merge sort requires two "files" in order to perform its task, two partitions (of the same file) at a time are loaded in the place of the two "files." The two partitions are merged via the internal two-way merge sort; therefore, any two partitions will contribute a single, new partition. When all partitions of the file have been read in and have been merged, a new sorted partition file is obtained; but the number of partitions is almost half the number of the partitions of the *Init_File*. If the number of partitions of the new file is equal to 1, then that means that the file has been sorted; otherwise, more *passes* are performed.

Before the pseudoalgorithm is presented, we must remark that the above discussion indicates that at each stage of the sort *two* partitions must be merged. To facilitate this task, it is required that the sorted partition generator that is used output the generated partitions *alternately* to two new sorted partition files, *File_A1* and *File_A2*. In other words, assuming that the first partition is identified as partition number 1, the second as partition number 2, and so on, then the odd numbered generated partitions are written into the file *File_A1*, while the even numbered generated partitions are written into the file *File_A2*. During each pass the ith partition of *File_A1* is merged with the ith partition of *File_A2*. The newly generated partitions from this pass are written *alternately* again into two files in order to facilitate the merging process of the partitions during the next pass.

A tracing of this algorithm over the file, *Init_File*, is presented in Figure 9.8. Notice that initially (Figure 9.8(a)) the file contains eight blocks. The simple selection generator is employed; and the eight generated partitions are written alternately into the two new files (Figure 9.8(b)), *File_A1* and *File_A2*. The result of the first pass is indicated in Figure 9.8(c), where the ith partition of *File_A1* is merged via the internal two-way merge sort with the ith partition of *File_A2* for $i = 1, 2, 3, 4$. Notice that the generated partitions during this pass are again written *alternately* into the two new sorted files *File_C1* and *File_C2*. The next pass, the last required pass for this example, is merging the first and only partition from file *File_C1* with the first and only partition of file *File_C2*; then, the sorted file *Sorted_File* of Figure 9.8(e) is obtained.

The pseudoalgorithm is presented in Table 9.5 and its basic steps are explained below.

In step [1], a sorted partition file is generated; it ensures that the generated partitions are written alternately into the two files, *File_1* and *File_2*, so that their distribution into those two files is *balanced*. The *While* loop in step [3] is executed as many times as is necessary until the output of some *pass* consists of exactly two partitions. In that case, it is clear that there will be just one partition in each of the two files; therefore, the next pass of step [8] will provide the desired sorted file. Notice that the loop of step [4] is executed a number of times equal to the minimum number of partitions in the two files, *File_1* and *File_3*. Notice that step [6] ensures that when the number of partitions generated by the previous pass is odd, then the last partition is always written out in *File_3*. Finally, step [5] ensures that the generated partitions are distributed evenly in the two files.

9.2.1.1 The Blocking Factor and Buffer Requirements.

The pseudoalgorithm of Table 9.5 presents the basic steps of the external two-way balanced merge sorting method, but there are a number of important issues associated with the implementation of the above algorithm that require consideration.

First, notice that since at each stage two partitions are merged, their logical records must be read in main memory sequentially. That suggests that the structure of all files involved in the merging process is physical sequential.

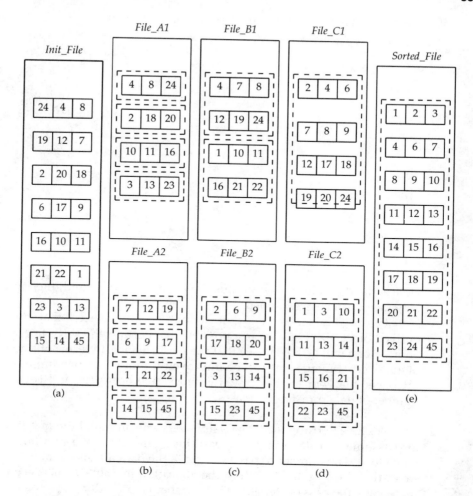

Figure 9.8 The trace of the two-way balanced merge sort over the file in (a). The first step is the generation of the Sorted Partition file shown in (b) where the partitions are enclosed by dashed rectangles. Notice that three passes of the two-way merge sort are required. The input and output file of each pass is shown above.

Secondly, the determination of the blocking factor depends entirely on the available buffer area. To see this, observe that if *BFA* bytes are available as a buffer area, then the *minimum* requirements of this sort is that this area must be divided into three buffer areas; two areas will be used to transfer the blocks from the two files, *File_1* and *File_2*, and the third will be used as an output buffer.[3]

[3] When the host language is a high-level language, then normally two output buffers are allocated, one per output file.

TABLE 9.5 The External Two-way Balanced Merge Algorithm.

```
Algorithm External Two-way Balanced Merge;

[1]   Call Sorted Partition Generator;
      Write partitions alternately to File_1 and File_2;
[2]   Partitions_Number = Partitions (File_1) + Partitions (File_2);
[3]   While Partitions_Number > 2 do
          {for i:=1 to min(partitions(File_1),Partitions(File_2) do
              {merge ith partition of File_1 and File_2;
[4]              if odd(i) then write the partition in File_3
                          else write the partition in File_4;}
[5]          if partitions(File_1)≠min(partitions(File_1),Partitions(File_2)
                 then write ith partition of File_1 to File_3;
[6]          rename(File_3) to File_1;
[7]          rename(File_4) to File_2;
             Partitions_Number = Partitions (File_1) + Partitions (File_2);}
[8]   Merge the only partition of File_1 and File_2
          and write it to Sorted_File;
[9]   exit;
```

Hence, the data block size BS must be equal to $BFA/3$, and, therefore, the blocking factor can be determined.

Before this section ends, it should be emphasized that the previously derived block size is the largest possible that permits the sort to perform its task. Shortly, one will be able to see that the performance, in terms of actual I/O time, of an external merge sort can be improved if more than one input buffer is allocated per file; but in that case, the block size decreases and consequently the number of data transfers increases.

9.2.1.2 Performance Analysis.

Assume an initial file of NR records, and also assume that the number of partitions generated by a partition generator is equal to k. The number of passes through the data, PN, is equal to the number of times that the loop of step [3] of the algorithm in Table 9.5 is executed plus one more pass, the pass of step [8]. That number is easily derived.

To this end, notice that after the first pass the number of partitions is equal to $clg(k/2)$, or, approximately, $k/2$. Clearly then, the approximated number of partitions, as a result of the second pass, will be $(k/2)/2$, or $k/(2^2)$. By generalizing the result after the last pass, pass PN, there must be $k/(2^{PN})$ partitions. But since the sorting is complete, we must have

$$\frac{k}{2^{PN}} = 1$$

or

$$2^{PN} = k$$

and, therefore,

$$PN = \log_2 k$$

Finally, accounting for the approximation we obtain

$$PN = clg\,(\log_2 k) \tag{9.1}$$

Notice now that in each pass all records must be read, which indicates that $NR \cdot PN$ records must be read in order to complete the sort. But all records must be written out during each pass; hence, the total number of records that must be processed during the entire merge, not accounting for the generation of the sorted partition file, is equal to

$$2 \cdot NR \cdot clg\,(\log_2 k)$$

The above equation indicates that the total number of records processed, as well as the number of passes for a given file, is a function of k. Therefore, the best performance of the two-way merge sort will be obtained whenever the number of initially generated partitions k is as small as possible. Hence, given our earlier discussion, the use of the replacement sorted partition generator will reduce the number of partitions generated by the simple partition generator by a factor of two; therefore, the required number of passes will also decrease.

The above-mentioned comments are illustrated in Figure 9.9. In particular, the sort is performed over the same file as the one in Figure 9.8, but the number of initially generated partitions is equal to 4 as opposed to 10 generated by the simple partition generator. The direct result is that now only two passes of the two-way balanced merge sort are needed as opposed to the three previously required. The immediate result is a considerable savings.

9.2.1.3   The Required I/O Time.   Now we will concentrate on obtaining the required I/O time by first deriving the number of required block accesses.

Recall that the number of passes through the data is equal to

$$clg\,(\log_2 k)$$

where k is the number of initially generated partitions. In each pass all the logical records of the file and, consequently, all blocks of the file must be read and also written out. Assuming a number $NBLK$ of blocks, it can be seen in view of the equation above that the total number of data transfers is given by

$$2 \cdot NBLK \cdot clg\,(\log_2 k) \tag{9.2}$$

The actual required I/O time depends on the type of external storage devices used; each of them will be examined in turn.

Sorting with Tapes.   Assume that the available medium is magnetic tapes and that the selection partition generator has already been applied. One can see that the generated partitions are distributed into two files; therefore, two tape drives will be needed. Moreover, during each pass of the two-way merge the merged partitions must be output alternately into two new files; consequently, two more tape drives will be needed. Hence, one can see that in order to

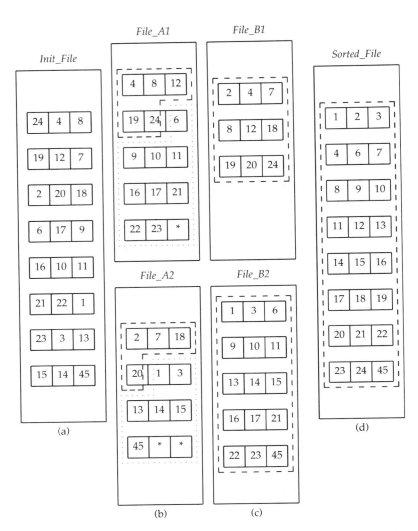

Figure 9.9 The trace of the two-way balanced merge sort over the same file as in Figure 9.8. Notice the improved performance of the sort as a result of the fewer number of initially generated partitions due to the use of the replacement selection partition generator. Asterisks indicate dummy records.

perform a two-way merge with tapes the basic requirement[4] is the availability of four tapes and four tape drives.

---

[4] The minimal requirement is only three tape drives, but in such a case the merged partitions generated during one pass must be written in one file, and then the partitions must be redistributed before the next pass begins. The result is considerable delays.

Furthermore, when a merge pass is completed and before the next pass starts, all four tapes must be rewound. Specifically, if gt is the time spent in the interblock gap in ms, r is the time in ms required to read a block of user data, r_w is the time in ms required to rewind a tape that contains the entire file, and $NBLK$ is the number of blocks in the file, then the total time required, assuming overlap of I/O and internal processing,[5] can be approximated via the following equation.

$$\left\{2 \cdot NBLK \cdot clg\,(\log_2 k) \cdot (gt + r)\right\} + \left\{\frac{clg\,(\log_2 k) + 2m - 1}{m}\right\} \cdot r_w \text{ ms} \qquad [9.3]$$

The first term represents the time required for all data transfers, while the second term represents the time required for rewinding the tapes.

Equation [9.3] was derived under the following three important assumptions:

1. No overlap of I/O is assumed.[6]
2. Rewinding of the tapes is required.
3. No interference with other user's jobs occurs.

Observe that the delay encountered due to the second assumption above can be eliminated or at least reduced if two extra tape drives and two extra tapes are dedicated and also if the tape drives can read backward. To understand how this may be accomplished, assume that the tape drives and tapes are identified via an integer value from 1 to 6. One may also assume that the initially generated partitions have been written out onto tapes 1 and 2, respectively. Since the tape drives can read backward by modifying the two-way merging algorithm, the partitions are merged onto fresh reels mounted on tape drives 3 and 4, respectively. While the next pass of the merging process takes place and while the merged partitions are written out onto fresh reels mounted on tape drives 5 and 6, the tapes on drives 1 and 2 are rewound so that when the pass is completed the merged partitions from tapes 5 and 6 will be written out on the "fresh" reels on drives 1 and 2; the process is repeated until the merge is complete. Be aware of the fact that if the number of required passes is odd, then the file must be written out one more time, since the output of the final pass will be a sorted, decreasing-order file; on the other hand, if the number of required passes is even, then no extra write is needed.

---

[5] The term "overlap of I/O internal processing and I/O" means that the application program is never interrupted due to lack of data. In other words, when a logical *READ* is issued, an empty buffer is never encountered; similarly, when a logical *WRITE* is issued, a full output buffer is never encountered. In order for this to be possible, double buffers must be allocated per file.

[6] A 100% I/O overlap occurs whenever input and output can be done in parallel. In other words, at the same time one can read the next block from a partition and also write out the contents of the output buffer. Notice that theoretically this is possible if there are enough channels and devices available and the partitions have almost the same length.

Returning to the first assumption, it was hypothesized than no I/O overlap occurs. If I/O overlap is assumed then one can easily see that the time required to transfer two blocks is equivalent to the time required to transfer one block with no I/O overlap. The net effect is that the required time has been cut by a factor of 2.

Sorting with Disks. Assuming that all four files involved in the merging process reside on the same disk and that I/O overlaps with internal processing time, then the total I/O time required is given by

$$\left\{ \left\lceil 2 \cdot NBLK \cdot clg\,(\log_2 k) \right\rceil \cdot (s + l + r) \right\}$$ [9.4]

where s denotes the average seek time, l the average latency, and r the time required to read or write the block. Notice that two important assumptions are made here:

1. There is only one R/W head.
2. No overlap of I/O time is assumed.

It is clear that the above time can be reduced considerably if a fixed-head disk is available—i.e., a disk in which there are as many R/W heads as there are cylinders. In that case, all seeks are eliminated and equation [9.4] yields

$$\left\{ \left\lceil 2 \cdot NBLK \cdot clg\,(\log_2 k) \right\rceil \cdot (l + r) \right\}$$ [9.5]

Finally, in the case of I/O overlap, the same remark that was made in the case of magnetic tapes is valid here; therefore, the required time would be cut by a factor of 2.

9.2.2 The External *m*-way Balanced Merge

Recall that the number of passes of the two-way merge sort is equal to $clg\,(\log_2 k)$, where k is the total number of initially generated partitions. It is easy to see that the number of passes can be reduced to

$$clg\left\lceil \frac{\log_2 k}{\log_2 m} \right\rceil$$ [9.6]

for arbitrary values greater than 2 of the integer m. To accomplish this, the initially generated k partitions are written into m, with $k \geq m$, distinct sorted partition files in such a way that the partitions are, as before, evenly distributed. Then by using the internal m-way merge, the ith partition of each file is merged for all possible values of $i \geq 1$.

9.2.2.1   The Algorithm.   Assume an m-way balanced merge over a given unsorted file *Init_file* and let $\{File\_k\}_{k=1}^{2m}$ be the required $2m$ working files. To simplify the notation it will be assumed that at the beginning of each pass the files $\{File\_k\}_{k=1}^{m}$ will be the input files, while the files $\{File\_k\}_{k=m+1}^{2m}$ will be the output files.[7] The pseudoalgorithm that performs an m-way balanced merge is given in Table 9.6.

TABLE 9.6   The m-way balanced merge sort algorithm.

```
Algorithm External m-way Balanced sort;
```

[1]   Call Sorted Partition Generator;

[2]   Write Partitions alternately to $\left\{File\_k\right\}_{k=1}^{m}$;

[3]   Partitions_Number $\leftarrow \sum\limits_{k=1}^{m} Partitions(File\_k)$;

[4]   While Partitions_Number $\neq 1$ do

$\qquad$ {for i=1 to $\max_{(1 \le k \le m)} \left\{Partitions(File\_k)\right\}$ do

[5]   {merge ith partition of $\left\{File\_k\right\}_{k=1}^{m}$;

$\qquad$ write the partition in $File\_[(m+i+1)mod\,(m+1)]$;}

[6]   rename $File\_(m+i)$ to $File\_(i)$ and conversely $1 \le i \le m$;}

[7]   exit;

Observe that the internal m-way merge (step [5]) has the task of determining the smallest of the m keys that occupy the current first position in each of the m partitions. Notice that this determination must be made in the minimum possible time in order to accomplish the overlap between internal processing time and I/O. A straightforward comparison between these m keys will yield an algorithm of order $O(m)$; the reader should have noticed that the same task can be accomplished in $O(\log_2 m)$ if the selection tree were used that was presented earlier. Specifically, each leaf node of the selection tree contains a pointer to each current logical record from each of the m current partitions; the loser among the keys to the pointed records is output; the corresponding leaf pointer is set to the next logical record of the same partition and the process is repeated. There is one point that must be addressed here—namely, there is the possibility that the number of logical records in the ith partition of *File_k* is greater than the number of logical records in the ith partition of $File\_(k+j)$ for some k, j such that $1 \le k, k+j \le m$. In this case the elements of the ith partition of $File\_(k+j)$ will be exhausted before those of *File_k*; therefore, in order to avoid incorrectly merging partitions any two partitions are separated by a marker such as (∞) so that when the marker is encountered for some partition, it signals its logical end, the corresponding leaf position in the selection tree is flagged, and logical as well as

---

[7]Notice that the file *Init_file* can be used as *File_k* for some k such that $(m+1) \le k \le 2m$ after the initial distribution run.

physical transfers from the file *File_(k + j)* are suspended until the moment that all leaf nodes contain that special marker ∞, which indicates that the merging of the (*i* + 1) partitions is ready to begin.

Figure 9.10 illustrates the effect of the external four-way merge sort over the same file as in Figure 9.8. In particular, the replacement selection partition generator generates four partitions which are distributed evenly among the four files *File_Ai* for i = 1, 2, 3, 4; and then, only one pass of the four-way merge sort is required.

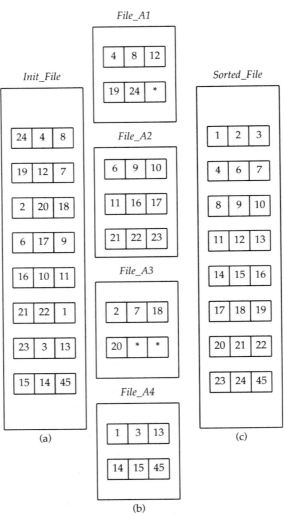

Figure 9.10 The trace of the four-way balanced merge sort over the same file as in Figure 9.8. Notice that only one pass is required. Asterisks indicate dummy records.

Comparing equations [9.1] and [9.6], one could *erroneously* infer that the larger the order of the merge m, the better the performance that is to be expected. In order to see this at the outset, it must be noted that if tape files are used, then one needs at least $2m$ tape drives and obviously at least $2m$ tapes. Moreover, in order to perform the internal m-way merge, there must be resident in main memory at least one block from each of the m input files. This implies that the available size of the buffer area BFA must be divided into at least $2m$ buffer areas, the first m areas employed as input buffers for each of the m input files and the m remaining areas employed as output buffers. The latter observation indicates that the block size is considerably affected; therefore, a larger value of m implies a smaller block size, which in turn implies a considerably larger number of blocks, which ultimately indicates a considerable increase in the number of required data transfers during one pass.

9.2.2.2 The Required I/O Time of an External m-way Merge.   In the previous section it was remarked that when the value of the order of the merge m increases, the number of required passes of the merge decrease. *But* the required I/O time for the sorting process does not necessarily decrease. The analysis that follows will indicate that in a number of instances the I/O time actually *increases* dramatically. Since the required I/O time also depends on the type of available external memory devices, the performance will be analyzed in the case where files reside on magnetic disks and also in the case where files reside on magnetic tapes.

Disk Files.   Assume that all files involved in the external m-way sorting process reside on an arbitrary but specific disk. In addition, assume that the disk is furnished with a single R/W head and the following characteristic parameters. The average seek time is s ms, the average latency is l, the $MDTR$ is v bytes/millisecond, and the block system overhead is negligible.

If the input buffer area available to our application program has a size of BFA bytes and if the sort that is to be performed is an m-way, the buffer area must be subdivided into $2m$ equal areas assuming double input buffer allocation per file. Moreover, if it is assumed that the number of logical records in the initial file is equal to NR, the size of each logical record is RS bytes, and the output of the employed partition generator consists of k partitions, then the total I/O time required for the sorting process is a function of m, denoted by $\delta_t(m)$, and in view of equations [9.4] and [9.6] it is given by

$$\delta_t(m) = 2 \cdot \left[s + l + \left\lceil \frac{BFA}{2mv} \right\rceil \right] \cdot \left\lceil \frac{NR \cdot RS}{\frac{BFA}{2m}} \right\rceil \cdot clg\left\lceil \frac{\log_2 k}{\log_2 m} \right\rceil \qquad [9.7]$$

Assuming a continuous environment and letting

$$\alpha = \frac{BFA}{v}, \quad \beta = \frac{NR \cdot RS}{BFA}, \quad \gamma = s + l \qquad [9.8]$$

equation [9.7] becomes

$$\delta_t(m) = 2 \cdot \left[\gamma + \left(\frac{\alpha}{2m}\right)\right] \cdot \left[\beta \cdot (2m)\right] \cdot \left(\frac{\ln k}{\ln m}\right) \quad \text{[9.9]}$$

Simplifying the above equation, we obtain the desired equation

$$\delta_t(m) = 2 \cdot \beta \cdot \ln k \cdot \left[\frac{\gamma \cdot (2m) + \alpha}{\ln m}\right] \quad \text{[9.10]}$$

Differentiating the above equation with respect to m, we obtain

$$\frac{d\,\delta_t(m)}{dm} = 2 \cdot \beta \cdot \ln k \cdot \left[\frac{2\gamma \ln m - \dfrac{\gamma(2m) + \alpha}{m}}{(\ln m)^2}\right]$$

and by simplifying,

$$\frac{d\,\delta_t(m)}{dm} = 2 \cdot \beta \cdot \ln k \cdot \left[\frac{2\gamma m\,(\ln m - 1) - \alpha}{m\,(\ln m)^2}\right] \quad \text{[9.11]}$$

Clearly the constants α, β, γ, m, and $\ln k$ are positive; therefore, in view of equation [9.11], the sign of $d\,\delta_t(m)/dm$ is the same as that of the expression

$$\left[2\gamma m\,(\ln m - 1) - \alpha\right] \quad \text{[9.12]}$$

It is obvious that the sign of the above expression depends on the relative values of the constants α and γ for each fixed value of the constant m. Their values may be approximated by considering the typical case in which $s = 25\ ms$, $l = 8\ ms$, and $v = 1204\ bytes/millisecond$. Then the constants α and γ will be approximately equal for the value of the constant BFA equal to 33,792 bytes, a value larger than the usually allocated buffer area. Despite the fact that in a normal case the size of BAF will be less than the one assumed, which, in turn, will cause the magnitude of the term α to be less than the one under the above-assumed quantities, the following expression for [9.12] is obtained:

$$\left[2\gamma m\,(\ln m - 1) - \gamma\right]$$

or, equivalently,

$$\gamma \cdot \left[2m\,(\ln m - 1) - 1\right] \quad \text{[9.13]}$$

Table 9.7 indicates the values of the expression $m\,(\ln m - 1)$ for some selected values of m.

Taking into account the values shown in Table 9.7, it is clear that the expression in [9.13] is negative for $2 \leq m \leq 3$; given the fact that the expression $m\,(\ln m - 1)$ is a strictly increasing function of m, the expression remains positive for any value of the integer m greater than or equal to 4.

The remarks made above imply the following:

TABLE 9.7 Computed values
of the expression $m(\ln m - 1)$ for
different values of the variable m.

m	$m(\ln m - 1)$
2	−0.6138
3	0.2958
4	1.5452
5	3.4520
6	4.7508
7	6.6213

1. The function $\delta_t(m)$ increases when the order of the merge increases for all values of m greater than or equal to 4; therefore, the required I/O time also increases.

2. The function $\delta_t(m)$ decreases when the order of the merge increases for all values of m greater than or equal to 2 and less than or equal to 3; therefore, the required I/O time decreases respectively.

Hence, taking into account the apparent continuity of the function $\delta_t(m)$ and the above remarks, one can see that the absolute minimum required I/O time will be obtained at either $m = 3$ or $m = 4$, depending on the relative values of $\delta_t(3)$ and $\delta_t(4)$.

At this point, the reader should wonder what the result would have been when the available disk was a fixed-head disk. The I/O time would definitely have been less for an m-way merge as opposed to the same merge under the previously used disk device, but the fact of the matter is that the I/O time increases with an increase in the order of the merge. The analysis below parallels the technique used above and thereby proves this assertion.

Observe that in the present situation the function expressing the I/O time in terms of the order of the merge will be identical to the one derived above with only one exception—namely, the value of s will be zero. Hence, the same computations lead to the I/O function $\delta_t(m)$ that is given by equation [9.10] in which the values of the constants α, β are the same as in [9.8], while the value of the constant γ is equal to l. Again, as before, one can show that the first derivative of $\delta_t(m)$ satisfies equation [9.11], and similarly, that the sign of the first derivative is the same as the sign of the expression

$$\left[2\gamma m (\ln m - 1) - \alpha \right] \tag{9.14}$$

Using the same average values (i.e., $l = 8$ ms, $v = 1024$ bytes/ms, BFA = 33,792 bytes), we obtain that $\alpha \approx 4.2\gamma$; therefore, [9.14] yields

$$2 \cdot \gamma \cdot \left[m (\ln m - 1) - 2.1 \right] \tag{9.15}$$

Again using the derived values of the expression $m(\ln m - 1)$ from Table 9.7, it can be seen that the derivative of $\delta_t(m)$ is negative for $2 \le m \le 4$, whereas it remains positive for all values of m greater than or equal to 5. Hence, the same conclusion can be made; namely, the absolute minimum I/O time is obtained for either $m = 4$ or $m = 5$; and the I/O time increases for all larger values of m.

One more remark can be made with respect to this issue. Notice that in both of the above cases the function $\delta_t(m)$ is given by an expression of the form

$$\delta_t(m) = 2 \cdot \beta \cdot \ln k \cdot \left[\frac{\gamma \cdot (2m) + \alpha}{\ln m} \right]$$

where the constants α, β, γ are independent of m. By taking the limit of the above function when m becomes arbitrarily large, one can get an idea of the magnitude of the I/O time. To this end,

$$\lim_{m \to \infty} \delta_t(m) = \lim_{m \to \infty} \left\{ 2 \cdot \beta \cdot \ln k \cdot \left[\frac{\gamma \cdot (2m) + \alpha}{\ln m} \right] \right\}$$

By applying L'Hôpital's rule we obtain

$$\lim_{m \to \infty} \delta_t(m) = 2 \cdot \beta \cdot \ln k \cdot \left[\lim_{m \to \infty} \left[\gamma \cdot 2m \right] \right] = \infty$$

Hence, one can conclude that the required I/O time becomes arbitrarily large for large values of m.

The only possibility that has not been considered is the possibility of I/O overlap. Notice that I/O overlap can be accomplished theoretically on the order of 100% given that fixed-head disks are used, that $2m$ channels are available, and that we operate in a single-user environment. In that extreme case the I/O time function is the one obtained from equation [9.10] provided that it is divided by the term $2m$, which represents the number of blocks that can be read and written at the same instant given the assumption of 100% overlap. Hence, we obtain

$$\delta_t(m) = 2 \cdot \beta \cdot \ln k \cdot \left[\frac{\gamma \cdot (2m) + \alpha}{2m \ln m} \right]$$

By taking the limit as m approaches infinity, the equation below can be obtained.

$$\lim_{m \to \infty} \delta_t(m) = \lim_{m \to \infty} \left\{ \beta \cdot \ln k \cdot \left[\frac{\gamma \cdot (2m) + \alpha}{m \ln m} \right] \right\} = \lim_{m \to \infty} \frac{2 \cdot \gamma \cdot \beta \cdot \ln k}{\ln m + 1} = 0 \qquad [9.16]$$

On the other hand, by differentiating the equation $\delta_t(m)$ with respect to m, we obtain

$$\frac{d \, \delta_t(m)}{dm} = -2 \cdot \beta \cdot \ln k \cdot \left[\frac{\alpha(\ln m + 1) + 2\gamma m}{(m \ln m)^2} \right] \qquad [9.17]$$

Closer examination of this derivative indicates that its sign remains negative for all values of m greater than or equal to 2, since all quantities appearing on the right-hand side of the equation are positive. Therefore, one can infer that the I/O time improves as the order increases. Hence, the performance of the m-way balanced merge sort increases constantly for larger values of m. We leave it as an exercise to show that the rate of increase in performance caused by the rate of increase in the order of the sort is relatively small. Hence, dedication of an inordinate amount of resources in order to improve performance is not justified.

It can be concluded, therefore, that the order of the merge depends on the situation at hand; nevertheless, the order selected almost *always* remains between 2 and 8.

Sorting with Tapes.   Assume for the sake of simplicity that the m-way merge sort algorithm does not require any rewinding of the tapes. Thus, if by GS we denote the interblock gap size, then the equation $\tau_t(m)$ of the I/O time required to perform an m-way merge sort, in view of [9.6], is given by

$$\tau_t(m) = 2 \cdot \left[\left[\frac{GS}{v_1} \right] + \left[\frac{BFA}{(2m)v_1} \right] \right] \cdot \left[\frac{NR \cdot RS}{\frac{BFA}{(2m)}} \right] \cdot clg \left[\frac{\log_2 k}{\log_2 m} \right] \qquad [9.18]$$

Assuming a continuous environment and by letting

$$\alpha_1 = \frac{BFA}{v_1,} \qquad \beta = \frac{NR \cdot RS}{BFA,} \qquad \gamma_1 = \frac{GS}{v_1} \qquad [9.19]$$

equation [9.18] becomes

$$\tau_t(m) = 2 \cdot \left[\gamma_1 + \left[\frac{\alpha_1}{(2m)} \right] \right] \cdot \left[\beta(2m) \right] \cdot \left[\frac{\ln k}{\ln m} \right] \qquad [9.20]$$

Simplifying,

$$\tau_t(m) = 2 \cdot \beta \cdot \ln k \cdot \left[\frac{\gamma_1 \cdot (2m) + \alpha_1}{\ln m} \right] \qquad [9.21]$$

Differentiating the above equation with respect to m, we obtain

$$\frac{d\tau_t(m)}{dm} = 2 \cdot \beta \cdot \ln k \cdot \left[\frac{2\gamma_1 \ln m - \dfrac{\gamma_1(2m) + \alpha_1}{m}}{(\ln m)^2} \right]$$

and, by simplifying

$$\frac{d\tau_t(m)}{dm} = 2 \cdot \beta \cdot \ln k \cdot \left[\frac{2\gamma_1 m (\ln m - 1) - \alpha_1}{m (\ln m)^2} \right] \qquad [9.22]$$

Clearly the constants α_1, β, γ_1, $\ln k$, and m are positive; therefore, the sign of $d\tau_t(m)/dm$ is the same as that of the expression

$$\left[2\gamma_1 m (\ln m - 1) - \alpha_1 \right] \qquad [9.23]$$

Assume now a typical tape of density 1600 bytes/inch, $GS = 0.6$ in., $v_1 = 192$ bytes/milliseconds, and $BFA = 33{,}792$ bytes. Then $\gamma_1 = 5$ ms, while $\alpha_1 = 211.2$ms. Therefore, $42.24\gamma_1 \approx a_1$.

Hence, we arrive at the same conclusion as before—namely, the I/O time increases for $m \geq 10$, while it decreases for $2 \leq m \leq 9$.

Finally, one can show that the I/O time constantly decreases if 100% overlap occurs. But the m-way sort requires $2m$ tape drives, an unrealistically large requirement even for a value of $m = 5$.

9.2.2.3 m-way Merge on Disks versus m-way Merge on Tapes.

The derived equations for the I/O time required for an m-way sort may be used in order to decide on what order the merge must be and also in order to determine what storage medium should be selected. As an example consider the case in which both magnetic tapes/drives and magnetic disks are available. Then the difference in performance can be measured by the difference

$$\delta_t(m) - \tau_t(m)$$

for each value of m. Notice that the value of the difference depends on the computer system's environment, on the available resources, and on the characteristics of the available secondary devices.

As an example, consider the case of the typical disks and tapes discussed in the above sections. If no I/O overlap is assumed and there is no interference from other jobs, then the above difference is equal to

$$2 \cdot \beta \cdot \ln k \cdot \left[\frac{(2m)(\gamma - \gamma_1) + (\alpha - \alpha_1)}{\ln m} \right]$$

or

$$2 \cdot \beta \cdot \ln k \cdot \left[\frac{28(2m) - 181.2}{\ln m} \right]$$

Hence, the performance of an m-way sort is better on a disk device if and only if $m \leq 3$. Notice that if the required time for rewinding the tapes is considered, then the value of m will be larger.

9.3 THE m-WAY POLYPHASE MERGE

In the previous section it was shown that the external m-way balanced merge sort requires, for purposes of efficiency, the use of $2m$ files; in the case of the tape medium, $2m$ drives are required. The external merge sort that will be presented here is based on the idea of the m-way balanced merge sort. But instead of outputting the merged partitions into m files, the partitions are output into a single file. In other words, the file requirement of this m-way sort is only $(m + 1)$ files, which leads to a considerable savings. There is one more fundamental difference between these two sorts: The initial distribution scheme of the generated partitions by the partition generator is significantly different from the balanced distribution scheme followed by the m-way merge sort. Before the general distribution scheme that is followed in this case is represented, an example of a three-way polyphase merge sort will be given.

Consider an unsorted physical sequential file *Init_file*, and assume that the employed partition generator generates a total of seventeen partitions. Since a three-way polyphase merge is to be performed, four files, *File_1*, *File_2*, *File_3*, and *File_4*, are available. The 17 generated partitions are distributed in such a way that the first file receives 7 partitions; the second, 6 partitions; the third, the remaining 4 partitions; and the fourth file remains empty (Figure 9.11).

	File_1	File_2	File_3	File_4
Number of partitions	7	6	4	0

Figure 9.11   The initial distribution of the 17 partitions.

Now, the three-way merge is applied. But instead of processing all the partitions, *only* that number of partitions equal to the number contained in the file with the *fewest* partitions are processed and merged. The merged partitions are then written out in the empty file. In our case the smallest file (in terms of the number of partitions that it contains) is *File_3*; therefore, the first four partitions of each of the three nonempty files are three-way merged, and the four generated partitions are written out into the empty file, *File_4*. The result is that *File_1* contains three partitions, *File_2* contains two partitions, *File_4* contains four partitions, and *File_3* is now empty (Figure 9.12).

	File_1	File_2	File_3	File_4
Number of partitions	3	2	0	4

Figure 9.12   Merging the first four partitions of the nonempty files.

The second step follows the approach of the previous step. In other words, the smallest file presently is *File_2*; therefore, the first two partitions of each of the non-empty files are three-way merged; and the merged partitions are written out into the presently empty *File_3*. Figure 9.13 illustrates the result of this step.

	File_1	File_2	File_3	File_4
Number of partitions	1	0	2	2

Figure 9.13   The distribution of the merged partitions after the completion of the second step.

The third step consists of merging the first partitions of each of the nonempty files and writing the generated partition to *File_2*, as Figure 9.14 illustrates.

	File_1	File_2	File_3	File_4
Number of partitions	0	1	1	1

Figure 9.14 The distribution of the merged partitions after the completion of the third step.

The fourth and final step completes the merging process. In particular, the three-way merge applied to the nonempty files with their present structure as in Figure 9.14 provides us with a single partition that is written out to *File_1* (Figure 9.15); the merge is complete, since all other *m* files are empty and the only nonempty file contains a single partition.

	File_1	File_2	File_3	File_4
Number of partitions	1	0	0	0

Figure 9.15 The sorted file *File_1* after the completion of the last step.

The reader who followed the basic steps of the three-way polyphase merge should have noticed that only four files are needed as opposed to six for the comparable order balanced merge; there is also another welcomed side effect—namely, the number of blocks, or, equivalently, the number of initial partitions that were read and written out during this merge is significantly less than the corresponding number of partitions processed via the three-way merge. To see this observe that the number of passes required for a three-way balanced merge is equal to

$$clg \left\lceil \frac{\ln k}{\ln 3} \right\rceil = clg \left\lceil \frac{\ln 17}{\ln 3} \right\rceil = clg \left\lceil \frac{2.8332}{1.0986} \right\rceil = clg \left\lceil 2.57 \right\rceil = 3$$

Therefore, 51 partitions must be processed.

On the other hand, the number of partitions processed during the three-way polyphase merge, as we will see, is equal to 48. In other words, the savings is equal to the input and output of three partitions. Of course, the magnitude of the savings does not appear to be considerable, but this is due to the extremely small number of assumed initial partitions.

9.3.1 The Initial Partition Distribution

Notice that the merge process of the example above worked perfectly; it worked perfectly in the sense that no unnecessary processing of partitions took place. The reason for that lies in two basic facts—the facts being that there was an *awareness*, before the merging process started, of

1. The number of required initial partitions, and

2. The required distribution of the initial partitions into three files.

This mechanism will be explained by first studying a specific example of a three-way polyphase merge; then, the result will be generalized for an *m*-way polyphase merge of arbitrary *m*. To this end, assume that it is *known* that the partition generator provides *exactly* 57 initial partitions. It turns out that the distribution of the initial partitions must be as shown in Figure 9.16.

	File_1	File_2	File_3	File_4
Number of Partitions	24	20	13	0

Figure 9.16 The required distribution of the 57 initially generated partitions.

In Table 9.8 the contents of the involved files are shown at the end of each step until the sorting process is completed.

TABLE 9.8 The trace of the three-way polyphase merge.

Step	File_1	File_2	File_3	File_4
S_0	24	20	13	0
S_1	11	7	0	13
S_2	4	0	7	6
S_3	0	4	3	2
S_4	2	2	1	0
S_5	1	1	0	1
S_6	0	0	1	0

This table will be modified in the following way:

1. Each row of the new table will contain the elements of the corresponding row of the above table, but the elements will be listed left to right in decreasing order. The zero elements corresponding to the empty file of each row will be omitted.

2. At the end of the new table two rows will be appended, which will consist of only zero elements.

3. Each row will be provided with an index such that one can refer to each element of the first column as α_i, and each element of the second column as β_i, each element of the third column as γ_i, where *i* is the index associated with each row with $i = 0, 1, 2, ...$; and the last (bottom) row will have an index of zero.

The table so obtained is shown as Table 9.9.

Assume now that the number of initial partitions was 58, that is, larger than 57. In this case, the values of α_9, β_9, and γ_9 must be determined so that the question marks appearing in Table 9.9 can be replaced by the required values.

TABLE 9.9 The trace of the three-way
polyphase merge.

Index	α	β	γ
9	?	?	?
8	24	20	13
7	13	11	7
6	7	6	4
5	4	3	2
4	2	1	1
3	1	1	1
2	1	0	0
1	0	0	0
0	0	0	0

How will γ_9 be determined? Closer examination of Table 9.9 indicates that the value of γ_i is equal to the value of the element $\alpha_{(i-1)}$ for every possible value of i. Hence, $\gamma_9 = \alpha_8 = 24$; more importantly, however, it has been derived that

$$\gamma_i = \alpha_{(i-1)} \qquad \text{for } all \ i \geq 0 \qquad\qquad [9.24]$$

Similarly, from Table 9.9, one can infer that

$$\beta_i = \alpha_{(i-1)} + \gamma_{(i-1)} \qquad \text{for } all \ i \geq 0 \qquad\qquad [9.25]$$

which indicates that $\beta_9 = \alpha_8 + \gamma_8 = 37$, and, finally, that

$$\alpha_i = \alpha_{(i-1)} + \beta_{(i-1)} \qquad \text{for } all \ i \geq 0 \qquad\qquad [9.26]$$

Therefore, $\alpha_9 = \alpha_8 + \beta_8 = 44$. Notice that the sum of α_9, β_9, and γ_9 is equal to 105. In other words, the polyphase merge required 105 initial partitions while only 58 had been assumed, in which case $105 - 58$, or 47, *dummy* partitions must be generated in order for the initial requirements to be met. This issue will be addressed again later.

The equations derived above indicate that the determination of α_i, β_i, and γ_i is a trivial matter if the values of $\alpha_{(i-1)}$, $\beta_{(i-1)}$, and $\gamma_{(i-1)}$ are known. The question then is how those latter values can be determined. This is a simple matter; the only requirement is that the values of α_i for each value of index i be known. To understand this, observe that equation [9.24], in view of equation [9.25], yields:

$$\beta_i = \alpha_{(i-1)} + \alpha_{(i-2)} \qquad \text{for } all \ i \geq 0. \qquad\qquad [9.27]$$

Then, equation [9.26], in view of [9.27], implies that

$$\alpha_i = \alpha_{(i-1)} + \alpha_{(i-2)} + \alpha_{(i-3)} \qquad \text{for } all \ i \geq 0. \qquad\qquad [9.28]$$

Summarizing the above derived equations [9.24], [9.27], and [9.28], we obtain that for all $i \geq 0$

$$\alpha_i = \alpha_{(i-1)} + \alpha_{(i-2)} + \alpha_{(i-3)} \qquad\qquad [9.29a]$$

$$\beta_i = \alpha_{(i-1)} + \alpha_{(i-2)} \qquad\qquad [9.29b]$$

$$\gamma_i = \alpha_{(i-1)} \qquad\qquad [9.29c]$$

and it can be concluded, as mentioned earlier, that the determination of the terms α_i, β_i, and γ_i, for all $i = 1, 2, \ldots$, depends on the values of the sequence α_i.

Notice equation [9.28] indicates that the value of α_i is equal to the sum $\alpha_{(i-1)} + \alpha_{(i-2)} + \alpha_{(i-2)}$ for each i. In other words, this indicates that the value of each term a_i is equal to the sum of its *three* predecessors. In particular, examining Table 9.9 again, one can verify that the remark made above is true; and, it also explains why the two extra rows of zero elements at the end of the table were appended.

Recall now that a Fibonacci sequence of order m, denoted by $\left\{\chi_i^m\right\}_{i=0}^{\infty}$, is a sequence of nonnegative integers where the following hold:

1. The value of each of its first $m - 1$ terms is equal to zero.
2. The value of its mth term is equal to 1.
3. The value of all of the other terms is equal to the sum of the values of its m predecessors.

In symbols,

$$\chi_i^m = \begin{cases} \displaystyle\sum_{k=1}^{m}\chi_{(i-k)}^m & \text{if } i > (m-1) \\ 1 & \text{if } i = (m-1) \\ 0 & \text{if } 0 \le i < m-1 \end{cases} \qquad [9.30]$$

The above discussion indicates that the sequence at hand, α_i, is none other than a Fibonacci sequence of order $m = 3$; in symbols, for each $i \ge 0$ we have $\chi_i^{(3)} = \alpha_i$.

The results derived above for the case of the three-way polyphase merge can be generalized for the case of the m-way polyphase merge for arbitrary values of m; they are summarized below:

1. Exactly $m + 1$ files, $\left\{File\_k\right\}_{k=1}^{m+1}$, must be allocated.

2. The n partitions initially generated must be distributed in such a way that each file, $File\_k$, for $k = 1, 2, \ldots, m$, receives exactly $v_j^{(k)}$ partitions where $k = 1, 2, \ldots, m$; and the index j_0 is the *smallest* nonnegative integer j such that the total number of partitions π_{j_0} satisfies

$$\pi_{j_0} = \sum_{k=1}^{m} v_{j_0}^{(k)} \ge n \qquad [9.31]$$

3. If the above inequality is strict, that is, if $\pi_{j_0} > n$, then exactly $\pi_{j_0} - n$ dummy partitions must be generated and added to the n initially generated partitions.

4. The sequence $\left\{ v_j^{(1)} \right\}_{j=0}^{\infty}$ is a Fibonacci sequence of order m.

5. Finally, the determination of the values of the sequences $\left\{ \left\{ v_j^{(k)} \right\}_{k=1}^{m} \right\}_{j=0}^{\infty}$ is accomplished via the $m - 1$ equations below.

$$v_j^{(k)} = \sum_{p=1}^{m+1-k} v_{j-p}^{(1)} \quad \text{for } each\ j \geq 0 \text{ and } 1 \leq k \leq m. \qquad [9.32]$$

6. The number of total partitions π_j for each fixed value of the index j is equal to

$$\pi_j = \sum_{k=1}^{m} v_j^{(k)} \qquad [9.33]$$

or, in view of equation [9.33],

$$\pi_j = \sum_{k=1}^{m} \left[\sum_{p=1}^{m+1-k} v_{(j-p)}^{(1)} \right] \qquad [9.34]$$

$$= \sum_{k=1}^{m} \left[(m+1-k) \cdot v_{j-k}^{(1)} \right] \qquad [9.35]$$

As an example consider a six-way polyphase merge, where the partition generator produces 636 partitions. We know that the sequence $\left\{ v_j^{(1)} \right\}_{j=0}^{\infty}$ forms a Fibonacci sequence of order 6. Taking into account equation [9.30], we obtain:

$$v_j^{(1)} = \chi_j^6 = \begin{cases} \sum_{k=1}^{6} \chi_{(j-k)}^6 & \text{if } j > 5 \\ 1 & \text{if } j = 5 \\ 0 & \text{if } 0 \leq j < 5. \end{cases} \qquad [9.36]$$

Hence, we obtain the sequence $\left\{ v_j^{(1)} \right\}_{j=0}^{\infty}$ some of the terms of which are listed below.

$$v_0^{(1)} = 0,\ v_1^{(1)} = 0,\ v_2^{(1)} = 0,\ v_3^{(1)} = 0,\ \ v_4^{(1)} = 0,\ \ v_5^{(1)} = 1,\ \ v_6^{(1)} = 1,$$

$$v_7^{(1)} = 2,\ v_8^{(1)} = 4,\ v_9^{(1)} = 8,\ v_{10}^{(1)} = 16,\ v_{11}^{(1)} = 32,\ \ v_{12}^{(1)} = 63,\ \ v_{13}^{(1)} = 125$$

The next step is to determine that particular smallest index j_0 that satisfies the inequality of [9.31]. In view of [9.35], it is easy to see that $\pi_j = 0$ for all j such that $j \leq 4$. More involved calculations indicate that

$$\pi_5 = 1, \qquad \pi_6 = 4, \qquad \pi_7 = 11, \qquad \pi_8 = 21, \qquad \pi_9 = 41$$

For the sake of completeness π_{12} is calculated. Equation [9.35] in this case becomes

$$\pi_{12} = \sum_{i=1}^{6} \left[(7-i) \cdot v_{12-i}^{(1)} \right]$$

or

$$\pi_{12} = 6 \cdot v_{11}^{(1)} + 5 \cdot v_{10}^{(1)} + 4 \cdot v_9^{(1)} + 3 \cdot v_8^{(1)} + 2 \cdot v_7^{(1)} + 1 \cdot v_6^{(1)}$$

Substituting the values for $v_j^{(1)}$ found above,

$$\pi_{12} = 6 \cdot 32 + 5 \cdot 16 + 4 \cdot 8 + 3 \cdot 4 + 2 \cdot 2 + 1 \cdot 1 = 321$$

Observe that 321 is less than 636; hence, it is clear that the smallest integer j satisfying [9.31] is 13. Hence, the values of $v_{13}^{(k)}$ for $k = 2, ..., 6$ must be determined. Equations [9.32] yield

$$v_{13}^{(2)} = v_{12}^{(1)} + v_{11}^{(1)} + v_{10}^{(1)} + v_9^{(1)} + v_8^{(1)}$$

$$v_{13}^{(3)} = v_{12}^{(1)} + v_{11}^{(1)} + v_{10}^{(1)} + v_9^{(1)}$$

$$v_{13}^{(4)} = v_{12}^{(1)} + v_{11}^{(1)} + v_{10}^{(1)}$$

$$v_{13}^{(5)} = v_{12}^{(1)} + v_{11}^{(1)}$$

$$v_{13}^{(6)} = v_{12}^{(1)}$$

The initial distribution and the trace of the six-way polyphase merge are shown in Table 9.10.

TABLE 9.10   The trace of the six-way polyphase merge.

Index j	$v^{(1)}$	$v^{(2)}$	$v^{(3)}$	$v^{(4)}$	$v^{(5)}$	$v^{(6)}$	$v^{(7)}$
13	125	123	119	111	95	63	0
12	62	60	56	48	32	0	63
11	30	28	24	16	0	32	31
10	14	12	8	0	16	16	15
9	6	4	0	8	8	8	7
8	2	0	4	4	4	4	3
7	0	2	2	2	2	2	1
6	1	1	1	1	1	1	0
5	0	0	0	0	0	0	1

This section closes with one more observation. Closer examination of equation [9.33] indicates that π_j is defined in terms of $v_j^{(k)}$, but the latter terms are also defined in terms of $v_i^{(1)}$. Therefore, it is possible to define each π_{j+1} in terms of $v_i^{(1)}$. That relation is defined below.

First note that equation [9.33] implies

$$\pi_{j+1} = \sum_{k=1}^{m} v_{j+1}^{(k)} \qquad [9.37]$$

or, in view of equation [9.32], equation [9.33] becomes

$$\pi_{j+1} = \sum_{k=1}^{m} \left[\sum_{p=1}^{m+1-k} v_{(j+1-p)}^{(1)} \right] = \sum_{k=1}^{m} \left[\sum_{p=1}^{m+1-k} v_{(j-(p-1))}^{(1)} \right]$$

By letting $q = (p-1)$ in the above equation, we obtain

$$\pi_{j+1} = \sum_{k=1}^{m} \left[\sum_{q=0}^{m-k} v_{(j-q)}^{(1)} \right] = \left\{ \sum_{k=1}^{m} v_{j}^{(1)} \right\} + \left\{ \sum_{k=1}^{m} \left[\sum_{q=1}^{m+1-k} v_{(j-q))}^{(1)} \right] \right\} - \left\{ \sum_{k=1}^{m} v_{(j-(m-k+1))}^{(1)} \right\}$$

or, equivalently,

$$\pi_{j+1} = \left\{ m \cdot v_{j}^{(1)} \right\} + \pi_{j} - \left\{ \sum_{k=1}^{m} v_{(j-(m-k+1))}^{(1)} \right\}$$

But, the last sum in the above equation is equal to the sum $\sum_{i=1}^{m} v_{(j-i)}^{(1)}$, which according to [9.38] is equal to $v_{j}^{(1)}$; therefore, the last equation implies the desired
result; namely,

$$\pi_{j+1} = \pi_{j} + (m-1) \cdot v_{j}^{(1)} \qquad\qquad [9.38]$$

9.3.2 Estimating the Number of Passes Through the Data

Recall from the analysis of the m-way merge sort that the performance of a sort
can be measured from the number of blocks that were read and written out during the merging process. To find that number one must multiply the number of
blocks $NBLK$ by the number of *passes*. A pass is defined as the processing of the
entire file. In this case

$$NBLK \approx \left\{ \frac{RS \cdot \sum_{i=1}^{NP} PL(i)}{BS} \right\} \qquad\qquad [9.39]$$

where $PL(i)$ is the partition length of the ith partition of the NP initial partitions,
RS is the record size, and BS is the block size. If, in addition, it is assumed for
simplicity that all initial partitions have the same length l, then the above equation can be written as

$$NBLK \approx \left\{ \frac{RS \cdot l}{BS} \right\} \cdot NP = \xi \cdot NP$$

The above equation implies that the $NBLK$ is proportional to the number of the
initial partitions NP. Hence, a pass can be defined alternatively as the processing
of the *entire set* of *initial* partitions. So, in order to calculate the number of passes,
$PN(m)$, the number of *initial* partitions that were processed during the sorting
process must be found; that number must be divided by the number of initial

partitions NP. Assuming the notation of the previous section, it is already known that the total number of initial partitions NP that is required is given by π_{j_0}. Notice that the sum of all π_i terms *does not* provide one with the number of initial partitions that were processed! To see this refer to Table 9.10. It can be seen that 63 partitions from *each* of the six files were processed during the first step for a total of $63 \cdot 6$ partitions. During the next step, s_1, 32 partitions were processed from *each* of the six files. One could then erroneously conclude that the number of initial partitions processed is $32 \cdot 6$ by direct analogy with the previous calculations; this is not so. The reason is that each partition of the file, *File_7*, before this merge had a length equal to six initial partitions since at the first step six initial partitions were merged into one partition of that file; therefore, the actual number of initial partitions processed during this step is equal to $32 \cdot (1 + 1 + 1 + 1 + 1 + 6)$. The five 1s indicate the lengths of the partitions of files *File_1* through *File_5*. Similarly, one can see that in the next step the number of initial partitions processed is equal to $16 \cdot (1 + 1 + 1 + 1 + 11 + 6)$ where the four 1s represent the length of the partitions of *File_1* through *File_4* and 11 and 5 are the lengths (in terms of initial partitions) of the files, *File_6* and *File_7*, respectively.

Table 9.10 is transformed into Table 9.11, where a notation such as 63_6 indicates that the respective file contains 63 partitions each of length equal to the length of six initial partitions. Moreover, the notation σ_j is used to indicate the number of initial partitions processed in this step.

TABLE 9.11   The trace of the six-way polyphase merge.

j	File1	File2	File3	File4	File5	File6	File7	π	σ
13	125_1	123_1	119_1	111_1	95_1	63_1	0	636	0
12	62_1	60_1	56_1	48_1	32_1	0	63_6	321	378
11	30_1	28_1	24_1	16_1	0	32_{11}	31_6	161	352
10	14_1	12_1	8_1	0	16_{21}	16_{11}	15_6	81	336
9	6_1	4_1	0	8_{41}	8_{21}	8_{11}	7_6	41	328
8	2_1	0	4_{81}	4_{41}	4_{21}	4_{11}	3_6	21	324
7	0	2_{161}	2_{81}	2_{41}	2_{21}	2_{11}	1_6	11	322
6	1_{321}	1_{161}	1_{81}	1_{41}	1_{21}	1_{11}	0	6	321
5	0	0	0	0	0	0	1_{636}	1	636

A general formula will be derived shortly for determining the number of initial partitions processed during an *m*-way polyphase merge. To this end, Table 9.12 is constructed, in which the entries *Index j*, π_j, and σ_j have been extracted from the corresponding entries of Table 9.11 and the values of $v_j^{(1)}$ have been calculated.

Closer examination of the table reveals that

$$\sigma_{12} = v_{12}^{(1)} \cdot \pi_6, \quad \sigma_{11} = v_{11}^{(1)} \cdot \pi_7, \quad \sigma_{10} = v_{10}^{(1)} \cdot \pi_8, \quad \sigma_9 = v_9^{(1)} \cdot \pi_9$$

$$\sigma_8 = v_8^{(1)} \cdot \pi_{10}, \quad \sigma_7 = v_7^{(1)} \cdot \pi_{11}, \quad \sigma_6 = v_6^{(1)} \cdot \pi_{12}, \quad \sigma_5 = v_5^{(1)} \cdot \pi_{13}$$

Hence, the pattern has become apparent:

TABLE 9.12 The Modified Table 9.11.

Index j	$v^{(1)}$	π	σ
13	125	636	0
12	63	321	378
11	32	161	352
10	16	81	336
9	8	41	328
8	4	21	324
7	2	11	322
6	1	6	321
5	1	1	636

$$\sigma_k = v_k^{(1)} \cdot \pi_{(j_0+m-1)-k} \quad \text{for all } k \text{ such that } (m-1) \le k \le (j_0-1)$$

Therefore, for a polyphase merge of order m, the total number of initial partitions processed is given by

$$\sum_{k=m-1}^{j_0-1} \sigma_k = \sum_{k=m-1}^{j_0-1} v_k^{(1)} \cdot \pi_{(j_0+m-1)-k} \qquad [9.40]$$

It follows that the number of passes through the data, $PN(m)$, of an m-way polyphase merge is given by

$$PN(m) = \frac{\sum_{k=m-1}^{j_0-1} v_k^{(1)} \cdot \pi_{(j_0+m-1)-k}}{\pi_{j_0}} \qquad [9.41]$$

9.3.3 The Required I/O Time

As in the analysis of the m-way balanced merge sort, the I/O time depends on the available resources. Both cases are considered below.

9.3.3.1 Disk Files. Assume that all files involved in the m-way polyphase merge sorting process reside on an arbitrary but a specific disk. In addition, assume that the disk is furnished with a single R/W head and the following characteristic parameters. The average seek time is s milliseconds; the average latency is l milliseconds; the $MDTR$ is v bytes/millisecond; and the block system overhead is negligible.

If the buffer area available to our application program has a size of BFA bytes and if the sort that is to be performed is m-way, we must subdivide the buffer area into $m+1$ equal areas assuming single buffer allocation per file (m input buffers and 1 output buffer). Moreover, if it is assumed that the number of records in the initial file is equal to NR, the size of each logical record is RS bytes, and the output of the employed partition generator consists of k partitions, then the total I/O time required for the sorting process is a function of m denoted by $\delta_t(m)$ and in view of equation [9.41] is given by

$$\delta_t(m) = 2 \cdot \left\{ s + l + \left[\frac{BFA}{((m+1)v} \right] \right\} \cdot \left[\frac{NR \cdot RS}{\frac{BFA}{(m+1)}} \right] \cdot \left[PN(m) \right] \qquad [9.42]$$

Letting

$$\alpha = \frac{BFA}{v}, \quad \beta = \frac{NR \cdot RS}{BFA}, \quad \gamma = s + l \qquad [9.43]$$

equation [9.42] becomes

$$\delta_t(m) = 2 \cdot \left\{ \gamma + \left[\frac{\alpha}{((m+1)} \right] \right\} \cdot \left[\beta \cdot (m+1) \right] \cdot \left[PN(m) \right] \qquad [9.44]$$

Simplifying the above equation, we obtain the desired equation.

$$\delta_t(m) = 2 \cdot \beta \cdot \ln k \cdot \left[\gamma \cdot (m+1) + \alpha \right] \cdot \left[PN(m) \right] \qquad [9.45]$$

It remains as an exercise for the reader to verify that the I/O time in this case approaches infinity for large values of *m*. In addition, the reader can check that the I/0 time approaches zero for large values of *m* in the case of a fixed-head disk.

9.3.3.2 Tape Files.   Since the analysis of this case parallels that of the analysis of the *m*-way balanced merge sort, the desired equation will be stated under the assumption that the sorting algorithm does not require any rewinding of the tapes. Thus, if by *GS* we denote the interblock gap size, then the equation $\tau_t(m)$ of the I/O time required to perform an *m*-way polyphase merge sort, is given by

$$\tau_t(m) = 2 \cdot \left\{ \left[\frac{GS}{v_1} \right] + \left[\frac{BFA}{(m+1)v_1} \right] \right\} \cdot \left[\frac{NR \cdot RS}{\frac{BFA}{(m+1)}} \right] \cdot \left[PN(m) \right] \qquad [9.46]$$

9.4 THE *m*-WAY CASCADE MERGE

The external *m*-way cascade merge sort resembles the *m*-way polyphase merge sort in that it requires $m+1$ files, $\{File\_k\}_{k=1}^m$, and in that it requires perfect initial distribution of the initially generated partitions. The fundamental difference between this merge and the polyphase merge lies in the fact that each *step* of this merge consists of exactly[8] $(m-1)$ *phases*. If the phases of each step are indexed by the index i, phase(1) is just an *m*-way polyphase merge. If it is assumed that as a result of this merge the file, $File\_(m-1)$, is empty, then phase(2) consists of an $(m-1)$-way polyphase merge performed on the set of files $\{File\_k\}_{k=1}^{m-2}$. If it is assumed for simplicity again that the empty file which resulted from this phase

---

[8] Except the very last step.

is file, $File\_(m-2)$, then phase(3) consists of an $(m-2)$-polyphase merge performed on the set of files $\{File\_k\}_{k=1}^{m-3}$. Continuing in this fashion and under the assumption that as a result of each phase(i) the empty file is $File\_(m-i)$, then the last phase of each step, phase($m-1$), will be a two-way polyphase merge performed on the set of files $\{File\_k\}_{k=1}^{2}$.

Before the general distribution scheme that is followed in this case is presented, an example of a three-way cascade merge sort will be given.

Consider an unsorted physical sequential file $Init\_file$ and assume that the partition generator generates a total of 31 partitions. Since a three-way cascade merge is performed, four files, $File\_1$, $File\_2$, $File\_3$, and $File\_4$ are available. The 31 generated partitions are first distributed in such a way that the first file receives 14 partitions; the second, 11 partitions; and the third, the remaining 6 partitions, while the fourth file remains empty (Figure 9.17).

File_1	File_2	File_3	File_4
14	11	6	0

Figure 9.17   The initial distribution of the 31 partitions.

Phase(1) of the first step consists of a three-way polyphase merge. The result is that $File\_1$ contains 8 partitions, $File\_2$ contains 5 partitions, and $File\_4$ contains 6 partitions, while $File\_3$ is empty (Figure 9.18).

	File_1	File_2	File_3	File_4
Phase(1)	8	5	0	6

Figure 9.18   The result of phase(1) of the first step.

The second and last phase of the first step consists of a two-way polyphase merge on files $File\_1$, $File\_2$, and $File\_3$. Figure 9.19 illustrates the result of this phase, which actually is the result of the *first step*.

	File_1	File_2	File_3	File_4
Phase(2)	3	0	5	6

Figure 9.19   The distribution of the merged partitions at the completion of the first step.

The second step again consists of two phases, a three-way polyphase followed by a two-way polyphase, the results of which are summarized in Figure 9.20. The sequence of the phases defined above is repeated until a sorted file is obtained.

Table 9.13 summarizes the tracing of this merge. Notice that we employ the same notation as in the case of the polyphase merge; i.e., an entry in the table

	File_1	File_2	File_3	File_4
Phase(1)	0	3	2	3
Phase(2)	2	3	0	1

Figure 9.20   The distribution of the partitions during the two phases of the second step.

such as 6_3 indicates that the respective file contains six partitions each of length equal to the length of three initial partitions. Moreover, the value of π indicates the total number of partitions, while σ denotes the number of initial partitions processed in this phase.

TABLE 9.13   The trace of the three-way cascade merge.

Step	Phase	File1	File2	File3	File4	π	σ
0	—	14_1	11_1	6_1	0	31	0
1	1	8_1	5_1	0	6_3	19	18
1	2	3_1	0	5_2	6_3	14	10
2	1	0	3_6	2_2	3_3	8	18
2	2	2_5	3_6	0	1_3	6	10
3	1	1_5	2_6	1_4	0	4	4
3	2	0	1_6	1_4	1_{11}	3	11
4	1	1_{41}	0	0	0	1	41

It is clear from Table 9.13 that a perfect distribution of the initial partitions ensures that the last step consists of only *one* phase, namely, an m-way polyphase merge.

9.4.1 The Initial Partition Distribution

Assume an m-way cascade merge. Let $\{File\_k\}_{k=1}^{m+1}$ denote the set of working files involved in this merge; and let $v_{i_j}^{(k)}$ denote the number of partitions contained in the file, *File_k*, at the beginning of phase j, step i. One must calculate $v_{i_1}^{(k)}$ for each $k = 1, 2, ..., m$ and for each step i. If it is assumed that the total number of steps is n, then it is known that only one phase is needed for this step. The output of this phase consists of just one nonempty file, which contains exactly one partition; clearly, then, $v_{n_2}^{(1)} = 1$, while $v_{n_2}^{(k)} = 0$ for each $k = 2, 3, ..., m$. But, in order for this to be possible, at the end of the last phase, $m - 1$, of the previous step, $n - 1$ (i.e., the beginning of the nth step), one should have obtained that $v_{n_1}^{(k)} = 1$ for each $k = 1, 2, ..., m$.

Look more closely at the $(n-1)$th step. In its first phase, an m-way polyphase merge is performed. Therefore, at its beginning exactly one file must contain one partition, while all other files must contain at least two partitions; therefore, $v_{n-1_1}^{(m)} = 1$. In the second phase an $(m-1)$-way-polyphase merge is performed on the remaining files; therefore, exactly one of these files must contain *exactly* one partition, while the remaining files must contain at least three partitions. Hence, at the beginning of this step that file must have had exactly two partitions, since in the previous phase one of its partitions was merged with the only partition of file *File_m*. Hence, $v_{n-1_1}^{(m-1)} = 2$. Continuing in this manner we obtain that $v_{n-1_1}^{(m-2)} = 3,, ...,$ and $v_{n-1_1}^{(1)} = \sum_{p=1}^{m} p$.

Inductively, we obtain the general formula for each $k = 1, 2, ..., m$.

$$v_{i_1}^{(k)} = \begin{cases} 1 & i = 1 \text{ and } k = 0 \\ 0 & i = 1 \text{ and } k \neq 0 \\ \sum_{p=1}^{m-k+1}\left\{v_{i-1_1}^{(p)}\right\} & \text{otherwise} \end{cases} \qquad [9.47]$$

It is easy to see now that the total number of partitions, π_i, obtained at step i is given by

$$\pi_i = \sum_{k=1}^{m} v_{i_1}^{(k)} = \begin{cases} 1 & i = 1 \text{ and } k = 0 \\ 0 & i = 1 \text{ and } k \neq 0 \\ \sum_{k=1}^{m}\sum_{p=1}^{m-k+1}\left\{v_{i-1_1}^{(p)}\right\} & \text{otherwise} \end{cases} \qquad [9.48]$$

As an example, consider a six-way cascade merge performed on a sorted partition file of 321 initial partitions. Then equation [9.47] becomes

$$v_{i_1}^{(k)} = \begin{cases} 1 & i = 1 \text{ and } k = 0 \\ 0 & i = 1 \text{ and } k \neq 0 \\ \sum_{p=1}^{7-k}\left\{v_{i-1_1}^{(p)}\right\} & \text{otherwise} \end{cases}$$

Hence, for $i = 1$ the above equation yields that $v_{1_1}^{(1)} = 1$, while $v_{1_1}^{(k)} = 0$ for all k = 2, 3, 4, 5, 6. Therefore, given the values derived above as well as equation [9.47], we obtain $v_{1_1}^{(k)} = 1$ for all k = 1, 2, 3, 4, 5, 6.

Equation [9.47] for $i = 2$ yields that

$$v_{2_1}^{(k)} = \sum_{p=1}^{7-k}\left\{v_{1_1}^{(p)}\right\}$$

for each k = 1, 2, ..., 6. Calculation indicates that

$$v_{2_1}^{(1)} = 6, \; v_{2_1}^{(2)} = 5, \; v_{2_1}^{(3)} = 4, \; v_{2_1}^{(4)} = 3, \; v_{2_1}^{(5)} = 2, \; v_{2_1}^{(6)} = 1$$

Continuing in this fashion the results appearing in Table 9.14 are obtained and where the notation introduced earlier is used. Notice that the values in boldface indicate values computed via equation [9.47].

TABLE 9.14   The trace of the six-way cascade merge.

Step	Phase	File1	File2	File3	File4	File5	File6	File7
0	—	91_1	85_1	74_1	59_1	41_1	21_1	0
1	1	70_1	64_1	53_1	38_1	20_1	0	21_6
1	2	40_1	44_1	33_1	18_1	0	20_5	21_6
1	3	32_1	26_1	15_1	0	18_4	20_5	21_6
1	4	17_1	11_1	0	15_3	18_4	20_5	21_6
1	5	6_1	0	11_2	15_3	18_4	20_5	21_6
2	1	0	6_{21}	5_2	9_3	12_4	14_5	15_6
2	2	5_{20}	6_{21}	0	4_3	7_4	9_5	10_6
2	3	5_{20}	6_{21}	4_{18}	0	3_4	5_5	6_6
2	4	5_{20}	6_{21}	4_{18}	3_{15}	0	2_5	3_6
2	5	5_{20}	6_{21}	4_{18}	3_{15}	2_{11}	0	1_6
3	1	4_{20}	5_{21}	3_{18}	2_{15}	1_{11}	1_{91}	0
3	2	3_{20}	4_{21}	2_{18}	1_{15}	0	1_{91}	1_{85}
3	3	2_{20}	3_{21}	1_{18}	0	1_{74}	1_{91}	1_{85}
3	4	1_{20}	2_{21}	0	1_{59}	1_{74}	1_{91}	1_{85}
3	5	0	1_{21}	1_{41}	1_{59}	1_{74}	1_{91}	1_{85}
4	1	1_{371}	0	0	0	0	0	0

9.5 COMPARISON OF SORTING METHODS

Assume that the partition generator applied to a physical sequential file S generates 321 partitions. Table 9.15 illustrates the tracing of a six-way polyphase merge over the generated sorted partition file.

TABLE 9.15   The trace of the six-way polyphase merge.

Step	File1	File2	File3	File4	File5	File6	File7	σ
1	63_1	62_1	60_1	56_1	48_1	32_1	0	—
2	31_1	30_1	28_1	24_1	16_1	0	32_6	192
3	15_1	14_1	12_1	8_1	0	16_{11}	16_6	176
4	7_1	6_1	4_1	0	8_{21}	8_{11}	8_6	168
5	3_1	2_1	0	4_{41}	4_{21}	4_{11}	4_6	164
6	1_1	0	2_{81}	2_{41}	2_{21}	2_{11}	2_6	162
7	0	1_{161}	1_{81}	1_{41}	1_{21}	1_{11}	1_6	161
8	1_{321}	0	0	0	0	0	0	321

From Table 9.15 one may easily determine that a total of 1304 initial partitions must be processed during this merge. On the other hand, examination of Table 9.14 shows that the number of initial partitions that must be processed during a six-way cascade merge performed over the same sorted partition file is equal to 1031. Hence, one can see that there is an improvement on the order of 21%. Moreover, it should be pointed out that this improvement is attained despite the fact that 51 additional dummy partitions are required to be introduced in order to guarantee that the six-way cascade merge proceeds smoothly.

Combining the above results, it can be seen that despite the fact that the six-way cascade merge starts with 14.5% more partitions than the comparable order polyphase merge, it processes 21% fewer partitions. In general, one can show that the m-way cascade merge is faster than the comparable polyphase merge if and only if $m \geq 6$.

Examination of Table 9.15 again indicates that the number of passes required for the six-way polyphase merge is equal to $(1304/321) \approx 4.06$, while the number of passes for a three-way balanced merge is equal to 6. The direct result is a considerable savings. In general, it can be shown that the m-way polyphase merge is faster than a comparable order balanced merge if and only if $m \leq 8$.

9.6 EXERCISES

1. Consider a physical sequential sorted partition file S consisting of 2028 partitions; each partition has a length of 4000 bytes, while each logical record is equal to 200 bytes. Assume that the total available buffer area is equal to 16,000 bytes. Calculate the required I/O time in seconds in order to perform an m-way balanced merge for m = 4, 8, 12, 16, 20, 24 under the following assumptions.
   a. The sort is done by using tapes. The number of available tape drives and tapes is equal to $4m$ for each value of m. The characteristics of each available tape are as follows: Length = 2400 ft, Density = 1600 bytes/inch, GS = 0.6 in. and $v = 10$ ft/s.
   b. Internal processing overlaps with I/O.
   c. There is no interference from other users' jobs.

2. Repeat Exercise 1 assuming 100% I/O overlap.

3. Consider a physical sequential sorted partition file S consisting of 2028 partitions; each partition has a length of 4000 bytes, while each logical record is equal to 200 bytes. Assume that the total available buffer area is equal to 16,000 bytes. Calculate the required I/O time in seconds in order to perform an m-way balanced merge for $m = 4, 8, 12, 16, 20, 24$ under the following assumptions.
   a. The sort is done by using tapes. The number of available tape drives and tapes is equal to $m + 1$ for each value of m. The characteristics of each available tape are as follows: Length = 2400 ft, Density = 1600 bytes/inch, GS = 0.6 in. and v = 10 ft/s.
   b. Internal processing overlaps with I/O.
   c. There is no interference from other users' jobs.

4. Consider a physical sequential sorted partition file S consisting of 2028 partitions; each partition has a length of 4000 bytes, while each logical record is equal to 200 bytes. Assume that the total available buffer area is equal to 16,000 bytes. Calculate the required I/O time in seconds in order to perform an m-way balanced merge for $m = 4, 8, 12, 16, 20, 24$ under the following assumptions.
   a. The sort is done on the same disk device and employs $2m$ files. The characteristics of the device are as follows: Cylinders = 555, tracks/cylinder = 39, density = 19200 bytes/track, average seek time = 25 ms, time required for one revolution = 18.6 ms, IBG size negligible, format used: count-data.

    b. Internal processing overlaps with I/O.

    c. There is no interference from other users' jobs.

5. Repeat exercise 4 assuming a fixed-head disk.

6. Consider a physical sequential sorted partition file S consisting of 2028 partitions; each partition has a length of 4000 bytes, while each logical record is equal to 200 bytes. Assume that the total available buffer area is equal to 16,000 bytes. Calculate the required I/O time in seconds in order to perform an m-way balanced merge for $m = 4, 8, 12, 16, 20, 24$ under the following assumptions:

    a. The sort is done on the same disk device and employs $m+1$ files. The characteristics of the device are as follows. Cylinders = 555, tracks/cylinder = 39, density = 19,200 bytes/track, average seek time = 25 ms, time required for one revolution = 18.6 ms, IBG size negligible, format used: count-data.

    b. Internal processing overlaps with I/O.

    c. There is no interference from other users' jobs.

7. Repeat Exercise 6 assuming a fixed-head disk.

8. Consider a physical sequential sorted partition file S consisting of 2028 partitions; each partition has a length of 4000 bytes, while each logical record is equal to 200 bytes. Assuming that we are to perform a four-way polyphase merge, find each of the following.

    a. The initial partition distribution.

    b. The number of dummy partitions that must be generated.

    c. The trace of the merge via a table similar to Table 9.11.

    d. The number of passes through the data.

9. Consider a physical sequential sorted partition file S consisting of 2028 partitions; each partition has a length of 4000 bytes, while each logical record is equal to 200 bytes. Assuming that we are to perform a four-way cascade merge, find each of the following.

    a. The initial partition distribution.

    b. The number of dummy partitions that must be generated.

    c. The trace of the merge via a table similar to Table 9.11.

    d. The number of passes through the data.

10. Consider a physical sequential sorted partition file S consisting of 2028 partitions; each partition has a length of 4000 bytes, while each logical record is equal to 200 bytes. Assume that the total available buffer area is equal to 16,000 bytes. Calculate the required I/O time in seconds in order to perform an m-way polyphase merge for $m = 4, 8, 12, 16, 20, 24$ under the following assumptions.

    a. The sort is done by using tapes. The number of available tape drives and tapes is equal to $m+1$ for each value of m. The characteristics of each available tape are as follows. Length = 2400 ft, Density = 1600 bytes/inch, GS = 0.6 in. and v = 10 ft/s.

    b. Internal processing overlaps with I/O.

    c. There is no interference from other users' jobs.

11. Consider a physical sequential sorted partition file S consisting of 2028 partitions; each partition has a length of 4000, bytes while each logical record is equal to 200 bytes. Assume that the total available buffer area is equal to 16,000 bytes.

Calculate the required I/O time in seconds in order to perform an m-way polyphase merge for $m = 4, 8, 12, 16, 20, 24$ under the following assumptions.

   a. The sort is done on the same disk device. The characteristics of the device are as
      follows. Cylinders = 555, tracks/cylinder = 39, density = 19200 bytes/track,
      average seek time = 25 ms, time required for one revolution = 18.6 ms, IBG size
      negligible, format used: count-data.

   b. Internal processing overlaps with I/O.

   c. There is no interference from other users' jobs.

12. Repeat Exercise 11 assuming a fixed-head disk.

13. Consider a physical sequential sorted partition file S consisting of 2028 partitions;
    each partition has a length of 4000 bytes, while each logical record is equal to 200
    bytes. Assume that the total available buffer area is equal to 16,000 bytes. Calcu-
    late the required I/O time in seconds in order to perform an m-way cascade merge
    for $m = 4, 8, 12, 16, 20, 24$ under the following assumptions.

   a. The sort is done by using tapes. The number of available tape drives and tapes
      is equal to $m + 1$ for each value of m. The characteristics of each available tape
      are as follows. Length = 2400 ft, Density = 1600 bytes/inch, GS = 0.6 in. and v =
      10 ft/s.

   b. Internal processing overlaps with I/O.

   c. There is no interference from other users' jobs.

14. Consider a physical sequential sorted partition file S consisting of 2028 partitions;
    each partition has a length of 4000 bytes, while each logical record is equal to 200
    bytes. Assume that the total available buffer area is equal to 16,000 bytes. Calcu-
    late the required I/O time in seconds in order to perform an m-way cascade merge
    for $m = 4, 8, 12, 16, 20, 24$ under the following assumptions.

   a. The sort is done on the same disk device. The characteristics of the device are as
      follows. Cylinders = 555, tracks/cylinder = 39, density = 19200 bytes/track,
      average seek time = 25 ms, time required for one revolution = 18.6 ms, IBG size
      negligible, format used: count-data.

   b. Internal processing overlaps with I/O.

   c. There is no interference from other users' jobs.

15. Repeat Exercise 13 assuming a fixed-head disk.

16. Consider a physical sequential unsorted file *Init_File*. Assume that the replace-
    ment selection generator is invoked. We have seen that all generated initial parti-
    tions are first distributed into m files and then merged according to the external m-
    way merge sort employed. We will describe one more scheme that will permit us to
    sort the file. The fundamental difference between the type of sort that is to be
    described and the type of sorts that have been studied in this chapter lies in the fact
    that instead of distributing *all* partitions, a number of partitions are distributed and
    merged and the process is repeated. Notice that under this scheme we oscillate
    between distributing and merging; therefore, the name of this sort is the m-way os-
    cillate merge.

   In order for this sort to perform, $m + 1$ files are needed in addition to the *Init_File*.
Initially, *exactly* m partitions are generated, which are written alternately into files
$\{File\_k\}_{k=1}^{m}$; hence, each of these files has received exactly one partition. Now an m-way

balanced merge is performed with input files $\{File\_k\}_{k=1}^{m}$; the result of this merge is just one partition that is written out to $File\_(m + 1)$.

At this point *exactly m* new partitions are generated, which are written out alternately into files $\{File\_k\}_{k=2}^{(m+1)}$. Observe that at this instant one file, $File\_1$, is empty; $(m - 1)$ files contain exactly one partition, files $\{File\_k\}_{k=2}^{m}$; and, one file, $File\_(m + 1)$, contains two partitions (the one merged in the preceding step plus the new one that was just written into it). Now the m-way balanced merge is applied and the generated merged partition is written out into $File\_1$. The m input partitions of this step are only the m *new* partitions. In other words, the old partition that was written into the file, $File\_(m + 1)$, at the conclusion of the previous merge step remains as is in the same file $File\_(m + 1)$. In order for this to be possible, this partition must be "*hidden*" by the new partition that was distributed to this file; this can be accomplished by using only tapes. Even more crucial to the issue is the use of tape drives that can read backward.

The procedure above is repeated a number of times. Take note of the fact that after a total of m-distribute/merge passes, there will be exactly m files, each one containing a partition of length equal to that of the m initial partitions, except $File\_m$, which is presently empty. At this instant (before we distribute from the $Init\_File$) an m-way balanced merge is performed on this set of files. The generated merged partition of length equal to m^2 initial partitions is written out to $File\_m$. The above sequence of steps is repeated until all partitions generated from the $Init\_File$ are exhausted.

a. Assume now that a three-way oscillate merge must be performed. Show in pictorial fashion the trace of that sort, assuming for simplicity that the initial partitions are one logical record in length and the partitions are (in the order that will be generated)

$$12, 8, 72, 31, 46, 62, 33, 38, 24$$

b. Assuming that a four-way oscillate merge is to be performed on a file that contains 16 partitions, show in the form of a table the trace of this merge.

c. If an m-way oscillate merge is to be performed and if the merge is to process smoothly, what must be the number of initially generated partitions, as a function of m?

9.7 HOST LANGUAGE: PL/1

9.7.1 Data Manipulation Sublanguage

An algorithm will be presented here that performs an four-way balanced merge over an $Init\_File$, which will be assumed to be the unordered file CHECKS that was discussed in Chapter 4. Specifically, we will assume a set of data cards, each of which has the information recorded relative to a $Checking\_Account$. Eventually the sorted file CHECKS will be produced.

In order to be able to perform the above-mentioned sort, four sorted partition files must be generated first via the replacement selection generator. Notice that according to our earlier discussions, a subset of these files will be input files at the beginning of a pass, while the rest will be output files at the beginning of the next pass. Since all involved files here will be `CONSECUTIVE` files and each file must be opened for only one operation, some mechanism is needed that permits us not only to rename (at run time) files but also to be able to oscillate between `INPUT` and `OUTPUT` files.

The PL/1 data manipulation sublanguage provides us with this capability, and, in particular, provides us with two distinct ways, which will be presented below.

9.7.1.1 File Variables.
PL/1 permits the definition of file variables. The only thing that is needed is the following declaration.

```
DCL MYFILE(6) FILE VARIABLE
```

The above declaration informs the compiler that six files have been declared, `MYFILE(1)` through `MYFILE(6)`. From that point on, one can associate any file variable to any file structure whose *logical_filename* has been declared via the usual `DCL` statement by a simple assignment. For example, consider the following sequence of declarations.

```
DCL (AFILE) FILE ENV(CONSECUTIVE);
DCL (BFILE) FILE ENV(CONSECUTIVE);
DCL FILES(2) FILE VARIABLE;
FILES(1) = AFILE;
. . . . . . . . . . . . . . . . . . . . . . . . . . . . . . . . . . . . . . .
FILES(2) = AFILE;
FILES(1) = BFILE;
```

The first assignment statement permits us to manipulate file `AFILE` via its alias `FILES(1)`, while the third assignment establishes `FILES(1)` to be an alias for `BFILE`. From that point on, every file can be referred to via its alias and the latter can be opened for any purpose.

9.7.1.2 The TITLE Option.
There is another way to establish an alias for a logical filename: via the `TITLE` option of the open statement. Consider the following piece of PL/1 code:

```
DCL (AFILE) FILE ENV(CONSECUTIVE);
DCL (BFILE) FILE ENV(CONSECUTIVE);
OPEN FILE (AFILE) TITLE('FILE1') INPUT;
OPEN FILE (BFILE) TITLE('FILE2') OUTPUT;
```

```
. . . . . . . . . . . . . . . . . . . . . . . . . . . . . . . . . . . . .
     OPEN FILE (BFILE) TITLE('FILE1') INPUT;
     OPEN FILE (AFILE) TITLE('FILE2') OUTPUT;
```

The first **OPEN** statement establishes that **FILE1** is the alias for **AFILE** and the file has been opened for **INPUT**. On the other hand, the fourth **OPEN** statement establishes that **FILE2** is the alias for **AFILE**; but now the file has been opened for **OUTPUT**. This permits us to oscillate[9] the purpose of a file between **INPUT** and **OUTPUT** by referring to it by its alias name.

9.7.2 Examples

9.7.2.1 The Replacement Selection Generator.   Recall from Chapter 4 that the PL/1 declaration of the logical records of the **CHECKS** file is

```
DCL 1 CHECKS_TYPE
      2   ACCOUNT CHAR(11),
      2   NAME    CHAR(20),
      2   ADDRESS CHAR(15),
      2   BALANCE FLOAT DECIMAL(8);
```

Assume now that each customer's record has been written to a **CONSECUTIVE** file, **UNSORT**; we will produce the sorted partition file **MASTER** via the PL/1 code that follows.

```
     PARTGEN:PROC OPTIONS(MAIN);
     DCL (BEOF) BIT(1) INIT('1'B);
/*
**   Integer division will be performed via the builtin function TRUNC.
*/
     DCL TRUNC  BUILTIN;
*
**   Declaration of the file that contains the original unsorted data.
*/
     DCL UNSORT FILE RECORD ENV(CONSECUTIVE F RECSIZE(54));
/*
**   Declaration of the file that will contain sorted partitions after
**   processing.
*/
     DCL MASTER FILE RECORD ENV(CONSECUTIVE FB RECSIZE(54) BLKSIZE(540));
/*
**   Declare variable to hold key of last record output.
*/
     DCL LASTOUT CHAR(11);
```

---

[9] Recall that a file must be closed between any two openings.

```
      DCL (COUNTER,POINTER,LEAVES,I,J,N) FIXED BIN(31);
      OPEN FILE(UNSORT) INPUT, FILE(MASTER) OUTPUT,
      ON ENDFILE(UNSORT) BEOF = '0'B;
/*
**    Read in number of leaf nodes (LEAVES) and assign it to N.
**    Notice that N must be an integral power of 2.
*/
      GET LIST(N);
      LEAVES = N;
/*
**    Dynamic allocation of the array AREA and the tree structure TREE follows:
*/
      BEGIN
/*
**    Declaration of the array AREA that will hold the records read in.  Size
**    of AREA should be at least equal to the number of leaf nodes
**    (LEAVES) in the tree to be used.
*/
      DCL 1 AREA(N),
            2 ACCOUNT  CHAR(11),
            2 NAME     CHAR(20),
            2 ADDRESS  CHAR(15),
            2 BALANCE  FLOAT DECIMAL(16);
/*
**    Declaration of the tree structure to be used. Size of TREE should
**    be at least equal to 2*LEAVES - 1. Positions LEAVES through
**    2*LEAVES - 1 will index the array AREA.
*/
      DCL 1 TREE(2*N-1),
            2 KEYFIXED BIN(31),
            2 FLAG     BIT(1) INIT('1'B);
/*
**    Read in the first N records into the allocated array AREA.
*/
      DO I=1 TO N;
            READ FILE(UNSORT) INTO(AREA(I));
      END;
/*
**    Call procedure to construct the tree structure by filling in the
**    correct indices.
*/
      CALL BLDTREE;
/*
**    Assign key of the record indexed by the root of the tree to LASTOUT and
**    write it to the file MASTER.
*/
      LASTOUT = AREA(TREE(TREE(1).KEY).KEY).ACCOUNT;
      WRITE FILE(MASTER) FROM(AREA(TREE(1).KEY-LEAVES+1));
```

```
/*
**    Read in the next record into the proper position of the array AREA.
*/
      READ FILE(UNSORT) INTO(AREA(TREE(1).KEY-LEAVES+1));
      DO WHILE(BEOF);
/*
**    Call procedure to readjust the nodes of the tree, propagating the
**    lowest key that is larger than the key of the last record written out
**    (LASTOUT).
*/
            CALL RADJUST(TREE(1).KEY);
/*
**    If the following condition is true, then all nodes in the tree are
**    flagged and it is time to begin a new partition.  The record indexed
**    by the root is written out and the flags for all nodes are reset.
*/
            IF (TREE(1).FLAG = '0')
            THEN DO;
                  LASTOUT = AREA(TREE(TREE(1).KEY).KEY).ACCOUNT;
                  WRITE FILE(MASTER) FROM(AREA(TREE(1).KEY-LEAVES+1));
                  DO I=1 TO 2*LEAVES-1;
                        TREE(I).FLAG = '1'B;
                  END;
            END;
/*
**    Else write the record indexed by the root, assign LASTOUT to the
**    key of that record.
*/
            ELSE DO;
                  LASTOUT = AREA(TREE(TREE(1).KEY).KEY).ACCOUNT;
                  WRITE FILE(MASTER) FROM(AREA(TREE(1).KEY-LEAVES+1));
            END;
/*
**    Read in the next record into the array AREA.  If the key is less than the key
**    of the last record written out or if at the end of file UNSORT,
**    flag that node.
*/
            READ FILE(UNSORT) INTO(AREA(TREE(1).KEY-LEAVES+1));
            IF (AREA(TREE(TREE(1).KEY).KEY).ACCOUNT < LASTOUT) |
                              (BEOF = '0'B)
                  THEN TREE(TREE(1).KEY).FLAG = '0'B;
      END;
/*
**    Call readjust procedure and write out any records left in the tree
**    when end of file UNSORT is reached. This loop will only write
**    out records that belong to the current partition.  A counter  will
**    denote how many there are.  Each time a record is written out that
**    node is flagged and the tree readjusted.
```

```
*/
      CALL RADJUST(TREE(1).KEY);
      COUNTER = 1;
      DO WHILE(TREE(1).FLAG = '1'B);
           COUNTER = COUNTER + 1;
           WRITE FILE(MASTER) FROM(AREA(TREE(1).KEY-LEAVES+1));
           TREE(TREE(1).KEY).FLAG = '0'B;
           CALL RADJUST(TREE(1).KEY);
      END;
/*
**    When the end of file UNSORT is reached there may have been some
**    records in the tree that were flagged denoting that they belong in a
**    new partition. There are LEAVES-COUNTER of these.  The following
**    will reset the flags of all nodes,readjust the tree, and write out
**    these last records.  */
      DO I = 1 TO 2*LEAVES-1;
           TREE(I).FLAG = '1'B;
      END;
      CALL RADJUST(TREE(1).KEY);
      DO I = 1 TO LEAVES-COUNTER;
           WRITE FILE(MASTER) FROM(AREA(TREE(1).KEY-LEAVES+1));
           TREE(TREE(1).KEY).FLAG = '0'B;
           CALL RADJUST(TREE(1).KEY);
      END;
      CLOSE FILE(MASTER);
/*
**    End of main procedure.
*/
      RETURN;
/*
**    The following function will take two indices and return the index of the
**    node with the lesser key.
*/
      LOSER:PROC (I2,J2);
           DCL (I2,J2) FIXED BIN(31);
           IF AREA(TREE(I2).KEY).ACCOUNT <= AREA(TREE(J2).KEY).ACCOUNT;
                THEN RETURN(I2);
                ELSE RETURN(J2);
      END;
/*
**    The following procedure will build the structure TREE.
*/
      BLDTREE:PROC;
/*
**    Assign the indices of the records in AREA to the proper nodes.
**    TREE(LEAVES) will hold the first record in AREA,
**    TREE(LEAVES+1) will hold the second and so on.
*/
```

```
      DO I=1 TO N;
           TREE(LEAVES+I-1).KEY = I;
      END;
/*
**    Set all the flags of all nodes to '1'.
*/
      DO I=1 TO 2*LEAVES-1;
           TREE(I).FLAG = '1'B;
      END;
/*
**    The following will assign the correct indices of the remaining nodes
**    to establish the parent and sibling relationships. The children of
**    node I are in positions 2*I and 2*I+1.
*/
      POINTER = LEAVES;
      DO WHILE(POINTER <= 2*LEAVES-1);
           TREE(TRUNC(POINTER / 2)).KEY = LOSER(POINTER,POINTER+1);
           POINTER = POINTER + 2;
      END;
      POINTER = TRUNC(LEAVES / 2);
      DO WHILE(POINTER > 1);
           I = POINTER;
           DO WHILE(I <= 2*POINTER-1);
                TREE(TRUNC(I / 2)).KEY = LOSER(TREE(I).KEY,TREE(I+1).KEY);
                I = I + 2;
           END;
           POINTER = TRUNC(POINTER /2);
      END;
      END;
/*
**    The following procedure is used by procedure RADJUST to assign the
**    proper index of the root node. If the flags of the children are the same
**    then the loser is propagated else the index of the node that is not
**    flagged is propagated.
*/
      CNDMIN1:PROC (I3);
      DCL I3 FIXED BIN(31);
      IF (TREE(2*I3).FLAG = TREE(2*I3+1).FLAG)
      THEN DO;
           TREE(I3).KEY  = LOSER(2*I3,2*I3+1);
           TREE(I3).FLAG = TREE(2*I3).FLAG;
      END;
      ELSE DO;
           IF TREE(2*I3).FLAG
           THEN TREE(I3).KEY = 2*I3;
           ELSE TREE(I3).KEY = 2*I3+1;
      END;
      RETURN;
```

```
    END;
/*
**    The following procedure is used by procedure RADJUST to assign the
**    proper index to all nodes between the root and the leaves. The decision
**    of which index to propagate is the same as in procedure CNDMIN1.
*/
    CNDMIN2:PROC (I3);
    DCL I3 FIXED BIN(31);
    IF (TREE(2*I3).FLAG = TREE(2*I3+1).FLAG)
    THEN DO;
        TREE(I3).KEY  = LOSER(TREE(2*I3).KEY,TREE(2*I3+1).KEY);
        TREE(I3).FLAG = TREE(2*I3).FLAG;
    END;
    ELSE DO;
        IF TREE(2*I3).FLAG
            THEN TREE(I3).KEY = TREE(2*I3).KEY;
            ELSE TREE(I3).KEY = TREE(2*I3+1).KEY;
    END;
    RETURN;
    END;
/*
**    The following procedure will readjust the indices of the tree after a
**    record is written out. It calls both CNDMIN1 and CNDMIN2.
*/
    RADJUST:PROC (I);
    DCL (I,TEMP) FIXED BIN(31);
    TEMP = I;
    CALL CNDMIN1(TRUNC(TEMP / 2));
    TEMP = TRUNC(TEMP / 2);
    DO WHILE(TEMP > 1);
        CALL CNDMIN2(TRUNC(TEMP/2));
        TEMP = TRUNC(TEMP / 2);
    END;
    RETURN;
    END;
    END;
    END;
/**
** JCL follows.
/*
//SYSPRINT DD SYSOUT=A
//GO.UNSORT DD DSNAME=UF.B0069143.S1.UNSORT,DISP=(OLD,KEEP),
//    UNIT=SYSDA
//GO.MASTER DD DSNAME=UF.B0069143.S1.MASTER,DISP=(NEW,CATLG),
//    UNIT=SYSDA,SPACE=(TRK,(1,1))
/*
```

9.7.2.2 The Four-way Balanced Merge Sort. It is assumed that the PARTGEN has been employed in such a way that the generated partitions of the UNSORT file have been distributed evenly in the four CONSECUTIVE files F1, F2, F3, and F4. The following algorithm produces a sorted CONSECUTIVE file SORTF1 in the case in which the number of initially generated partitions was even or TF5 otherwise.

```
        FOURWAY:PROC OPTIONS(MAIN);
        DCL (NOTDONE,READIT) BIT(1) INIT('1'B);
        DCL (TRUNC,MOD)   BUILTIN;
/*
**      An array of BEOF flags will be used for convenience.
*/
        DCL BEOF(4) BIT(1) INIT('1'B);
/*
**      Declaration of the 8 files to be used in the merge. Files F1-F4
**      initially hold the sorted partitions.
*/
        DCL
        F1 FILE RECORD ENV(CONSECUTIVE FB RECSIZE(54) BLKSIZE(540)),
        F2 FILE RECORD ENV(CONSECUTIVE FB RECSIZE(54) BLKSIZE(540)),
        F3 FILE RECORD ENV(CONSECUTIVE FB RECSIZE(54) BLKSIZE(540)),
        F4 FILE RECORD ENV(CONSECUTIVE FB RECSIZE(54) BLKSIZE(540)),
        F5 FILE RECORD ENV(CONSECUTIVE FB RECSIZE(54) BLKSIZE(540)),
        F6 FILE RECORD ENV(CONSECUTIVE FB RECSIZE(54) BLKSIZE(540)),
        F7 FILE RECORD ENV(CONSECUTIVE FB RECSIZE(54) BLKSIZE(540)),
        F8 FILE RECORD ENV(CONSECUTIVE FB RECSIZE(54) BLKSIZE(540));
/*
**      Declaration of FILE variable to facilitate switching of files for
**      input and *output. FILES(1-4) will represent the input files,
**      positions (5-8) will represent output files.
*/
        DCL FILES(8) FILE VARIABLE;
/*
**      Size of AREA now equals 4 because there will be one leaf node
**      per input file.
*/
        DCL   1 AREA(4),
                2 ACCOUNT  CHAR(11),
                2 NAME     CHAR(20),
                2 ADDRESS  CHAR(15),
                2 BALANCE  FLOAT DECIMAL(16);
/*
**      TREE size equals 2*LEAVES-1
```

```
*/
      DCL   1 TREE(7),
              2 KEY   FIXED BIN(31),
              2 FLAG BIT(1) INIT('1'B);
      DCL (COUNTER,FILCNT,LEAVES,PASS,ACTIVEFILS) FIXED BIN(31),
      LASTOUT CHAR(11),  (I,J,N,PARTITIONS) FIXED BIN(31);
/*
**    Initialize N and LEAVES to 4, number of passes and PARTITIONS to 0.
**    ACTIVEFILS will represent the number of input files active in
**    each pass.
*/
      N = 4;
      LEAVES= N;
      PASS = 0;
      PARTITIONS = 0;
      ACTIVEFILS = 4;
/*
**    Continue making passes until the number of partitions generated is equal
**    to one.  At the beginning of each pass increment passes and set
**    PARTITIONS = 1 since you are ready to write the first partition.
*/
      DO WHILE(PARTITIONS ^= 1);
            PARTITIONS = 1;
            PASS = PASS + 1;
/*
**    If number of passes is even, files F5-F8 are input while F1-F4 are
**    output.
*/
            IF (MOD(PASS,2) = 0)
            THEN DO;
                  FILES(1) = F5;   FILES(5) = F1;
                  FILES(2) = F6;   FILES(6) = F2;
                  FILES(3) = F7;   FILES(7) = F3;
                  FILES(4) = F8;   FILES(8) = F4;
            END;
/*
**    else F1-F4 are input and F5-F8 are output.
*/
            ELSE DO;
                  FILES(1) = F1;   FILES(5) = F5;
                  FILES(2) = F2;   FILES(6) = F6;
                  FILES(3) = F3;   FILES(7) = F7;
                  FILES(4) = F4;   FILES(8) = F8;
            END;
```

```
/*
**   Open required files; both input and output files are opened in
**   ascending order as needed.
*/
          DO I = 1 TO ACTIVEFILS;
               OPEN FILE(FILES(I)) INPUT, FILE(FILES(I+4)) OUTPUT;
               BEOF(I) = '1'B;
          END;
          ON ENDFILE(FILES(1)) BEOF(1) = '0'B;
          ON ENDFILE(FILES(2)) BEOF(2) = '0'B;
          ON ENDFILE(FILES(3)) BEOF(3) = '0'B;
          ON ENDFILE(FILES(4)) BEOF(4) = '0'B;
/*
**   Read first record from each active file into designated position of
**   AREA ARRAY.
*/
          DO I=1 TO ACTIVEFILS;
               READ FILE(FILES(I)) INTO(AREA(I));
          END;
/*
**   FILCNT will index which output file is currently being written to
**   and is initialized to the first output file.
*/
          FILCNT = 5;
          CALL BLDTREE;
/*
**   If all input files are not participating, flag the appropriate nodes of
**   tree that will not participate in merge. Index nodes are handled first,
**   then leaf nodes.
*/
          IF ACTIVEFILS < LEAVES
          THEN DO;
               DO I=ACTIVEFILS+1 TO 3;
                    TREE(I).FLAG = '0'B;
               END;
               DO I=ACTIVEFILS+4 TO LEAVES+3;
                    TREE(I).FLAG = '0'B;
               END;
          END;
/*
**   Write first record to set LASTOUT and read the next record from the
**   appropriate input file.
*/
          LASTOUT = AREA(TREE(TREE(1).KEY).KEY).ACCOUNT;
```

```
             WRITE FILE(FILES(FILCNT)) FROM(AREA(TREE(1).KEY-LEAVES+1));
             READ FILE(FILES(TREE(1).KEY-3)) INTO
                         (AREA(TREE(1).KEY-LEAVES+1));
```

```
/*
**   NOTDONE will later be based on the end-of-file flags for the active
**   input files, but now it can be set to true.
*/
```

```
             NOTDONE = '1'B;
             DO WHILE(NOTDONE);
                   CALL RADJUST(TREE(1).KEY);
```

```
/*
**   If root is flagged then begin new partition to be written to next
**   output file.  If fourth output file is current one then begin writing
**   to first output file again.
*/
```

```
                 IF (TREE(1).FLAG = '0')
                 THEN DO;
                       PARTITIONS = PARTITIONS + 1;
                       IF FILCNT = 8
                             THEN FILCNT = 5;
                             ELSE FILCNT = FILCNT + 1;
```

```
/*
**   Update LASTOUT and reset flags of index and leaf nodes.
**   Determination of participation of leaf nodes and READIT
**   is based on BEOF of the file corresponding to that node.
*/
```

```
                       LASTOUT = AREA(TREE(TREE(1).KEY).KEY).ACCOUNT;
                       WRITE FILE(FILES(FILCNT)) FROM
                                   (AREA(TREE(1).KEY-LEAVES+1));
                       DO I=1 TO TRUNC((2*ACTIVEFILS+1)/2);
                             TREE(I).FLAG = '1'B;
                       END;
                       DO I=1 TO ACTIVEFILS;
                             TREE(I+3).FLAG = BEOF(I);
                       END;
                       IF BEOF(TREE(1).KEY-3)
                             THEN READIT = '1'B;
                             ELSE READIT = '0'B;
                 END;
```

```
/*
**   else if record key indexed by root is less than LASTOUT, flag that
**   node, readjust, and set READIT to false.
*/
```

```
                 ELSE DO;
```

```
                          IF AREA(TREE(TREE(1).KEY).KEY).ACCOUNT < LASTOUT
                          THEN DO;
                                  TREE(TREE(1).KEY).FLAG = '0';
                                  CALL RADJUST(TREE(1).KEY);
                                  READIT = '0'B;
                          END;
/*
**    else write record indexed by root and update LASTOUT. READIT is set based
**    on BEOF for that particular leaf node. If end of file, then flag
**    that leaf node.
*/
                          ELSE DO;
                                  LASTOUT = AREA(TREE(TREE(1).KEY).KEY).ACCOUNT;
                                  WRITE FILE(FILES(FILCNT)) FROM
                                               (AREA(TREE(1).KEY-LEAVES+1));
                                  IF BEOF(TREE(1).KEY-3)
                                  THEN READIT = '1'B;
                                  ELSE DO;
                                      READIT = '0'B;
                                      TREE(TREE(1).KEY).FLAG = '0'B;
                                  END;
                          END;
                      END;
/*
**    If READIT was set, then read next record from appropriate file and
**    update tree node. If end of file or key of new record is less than
**    LASTOUT, flag the node.
*/
                      IF READIT
                      THEN DO;
                              READ FILE(FILES(TREE(1).KEY-3)) INTO
                                       (AREA(TREE(1).KEY-LEAVES+1));
                              IF (BEOF(TREE(1).KEY-3)='0') |
                                  (AREA(TREE(TREE(1).KEY).KEY).KEY < LASTOUT)
                              THEN TREE(TREE(1).KEY).FLAG = '0'B;
                      END;
/*
**    Check if end of all active files and set NOTDONE accordingly.
*/
                      IF ((ACTIVEFILS=4)&(BEOF(1) | BEOF(2)|BEOF(3)|BEOF(4)))
                          | ((ACTIVEFILS=3)&(BEOF(1) | BEOF(2) | BEOF(3)))
                          | ((ACTIVEFILS=2)&(BEOF(1) | BEOF(2)))
                          | ((ACTIVEFILS=1)&(BEOF(1)))
                      THEN NOTDONE = '1'B;
```

```
                    ELSE NOTDONE = '0'B;
              END; /*  end of NOTDONE loop - 1 complete pass done  */
/*
**    Readjust tree and dump out any records belonging to current partition.
*/
              CALL RADJUST(TREE(1).KEY);
              COUNTER = 0;
              DO WHILE(TREE(1).FLAG = '1'B);
                    COUNTER = COUNTER + 1;
                    WRITE FILE(FILES(FILCNT)) FROM
                          (AREA(TREE(1).KEY-LEAVES+1));
                    TREE(TREE(1).KEY).FLAG = '0'B;
                    CALL RADJUST(TREE(1).KEY);
              END;
/*
**    If there were any records that belong in a new partition then update
**    FILCNT, increment PARTITIONS, and write them out.
*/
              IF (COUNTER < LEAVES)&(COUNTER > 0)
              THEN DO;
                    PARTITIONS = PARTITIONS + 1;
                    DO I = 1 TO 2*ACTIVEFILS-1;
                          TREE(I).FLAG = '1'B;
                    END;
                    IF FILCNT = 8
                          THEN FILCNT = 5;
                          ELSE FILCNT = FILCNT + 1;
                    CALL RADJUST(TREE(1).KEY);
                    DO I = 1 TO LEAVES-COUNTER-1;
                          WRITE FILE(FILES(FILCNT)) FROM
                                (AREA(TREE(1).KEY-LEAVES+1));
                          TREE(TREE(1).KEY).FLAG = '0'B;
                          CALL RADJUST(TREE(1).KEY);
                    END;
              END;
/*
**    Calculate the number of active input files for next pass and close all
**    files so they can be reopened in the proper mode on the next pass.
*/
              IF PARTITIONS < 4
                    THEN ACTIVEFILS = PARTITIONS;
                    ELSE ACTIVEFILS = 4;
              DO I = 1 TO 8;
                    CLOSE FILE(FILES(I));
```

```
            END;
        END;
/*
**    If the total number of passes was even, then final sorted file is in
**    the physical file associated with logical filename F1, else it
**    is in the file associated with logical file F5.
*/
        IF (MOD(PASS,2) = 0)
            THEN PUT SKIP LIST(' FINAL RESULTS IN FILE SORTF1 DATA');
            ELSE PUT SKIP LIST(' FINAL RESULTS IN FILE SORTF5 DATA');
        RETURN;
END;
10
10 JCL follows
10
  /*
//SYSPRINT DD SYSOUT=A
//GO.F1 DD DSNAME=UF.B0069143.S1.SORTF1,DISP=(OLD,KEEP),
//    UNIT=SYSDA
//GO.F2 DD DSNAME=UF.B0069143.S1.SORTF2,DISP=(OLD,KEEP),
//    UNIT=SYSDA
//GO.F3 DD DSNAME=UF.B0069143.S1.SORTF3,DISP=(OLD,KEEP),
//    UNIT=SYSDA
//GO.F4 DD DSNAME=UF.B0069143.S1.SORTF4,DISP=(OLD,KEEP),
//    UNIT=SYSDA
//GO.F5 DD DSNAME=UF.B0069143.S1.SORTF5,DISP=(NEW,CATLG),
//    UNIT=SYSDA,SPACE=(TRK,(1,1))
//GO.F6 DD DSNAME=UF.B0069143.S1.SORTF6,DISP=(NEW,CATLG),
//    UNIT=SYSDA,SPACE=(TRK,(1,1))
//GO.F7 DD DSNAME=UF.B0069143.S1.SORTF7,DISP=(NEW,CATLG),
//    UNIT=SYSDA,SPACE=(TRK,(1,1))
//GO.F8 DD DSNAME=UF.B0069143.S1.SORTF8,DISP=(NEW,CATLG),
//    UNIT=SYSDA,SPACE=(TRK,(1,1))
  /*
```

9.8 EXERCISES

1. Write the code required to perform a six-way polyphase merge on the file UNSORT.

2. Write the code required to perform a five-way polyphase merge on the file UNSORT.

3. Write the code required to perform a six-way cascade merge on the file UN-SORT.

4. Write the code required to perform a five-way cascade merge on the file UN-SORT.

5. Write the code required to produce the number of passes required for an m-way balanced, polyphase, and cascade merge over a sorted partition file consisting of k partitions.

A

The UNIX File System

A.1 THE FILE SYSTEM

The primary responsibility of the file system is the management of computer files. Specifically, it keeps track of the location of a physical file, its use, its status, the opening and the closing of the file, allocating external storage according to the needs of the application program, the status of the I/O buffers, the secondary devices, and their characteristics. In the following sections some of the tasks of this system will be discussed.

A.1.1 The Directory

The directory maintained by the file system is a hierarchical structure similar to the one presented in Section 3.2.1.4.2. Recall from these discussions that a directory is a file. The algorithm that is employed for the determination of the location of a specific file parallels the algorithm given in Table 3.2. Unix assigns a unique number to each filename, which is referred to as an *inode* number. In particular, the inode number is stored in the circular nodes appearing in Figure 3.11. This number indicates the location in the secondary device of a structure (which will be discussed shortly) that is referred to as *inode.*

A.1.1.1 Secondary Storage Space, File Storage Space. In this section two important issues will be addressed: First, the mechanism by which the file system allocates storage in response to a user's request, and second, the mechanism through which the access method can access a particular block within a given file that contains the target record.

Device Storage Allocation First and foremost, the file system must be aware of what blocks are in use and which ones are free. The Unix file system keeps track of which blocks are allocated to specific files by recording their location in the corresponding file inode. On the other hand, all free blocks form a linked list[1] which is referred to as a *free list*. In this case, only the address of the first block of the chain must be known; this address is stored in the *super block* of the file system. Specifically, the super block records primarily the size of the file system (*size*), the number of blocks in the file system (*nblk*), the maximal number of files (*maximal nfiles*) that can be accommodated by the file system, the size of the inode list (*inode size*) as well as the number of free inodes (*free inodes*) together with a pointer to the first free inode (*to free inodes*). Finally, the pointer to the free list (*to free list*) is stored there. These fields are illustrated in Figure A.1.

Super block

Size	nblk	Maximal nfiles	Inode size	Free inodes	To free inodes	To free list

Figure A.1 The primary fields of the super block.

The first inode in the inode list is referred to as the *root inode*, which reflects the directory structure of the file system. The inode list follows the super block and the latter follows the very first block, which is referred to as the *boot block* and which contains the *bootstrap* code that initializes the operating system. Finally, as Figure A.2 illustrates, the data blocks follow the inode list.

Boot block	Super block	Inode list	Data blocks

Figure A.2 The structure of the file system.

File Storage Allocation Each file under Unix is a *relative stream* file, i.e., a sequence of characters (bytes), each of which is individually addressable. The bytes of the file are numbered consecutively, with the first byte bearing the number 0, the second 1, the third the number 2, and so on. The file system does

---

[1] This structure has been replaced by a bit map in the Berkley 4.2 implementation.

not block or deblock logical records but instead it blocks and deblocks strings of bytes. Each physical block consists of a collection of 512 bytes;[2] therefore, it is a simple matter to determine the number of the block where a specific byte resides. It is important to notice that the block size is the same for all files in the system at the time of initial creation of the file system. The address of each data block of a file is determined from the contents of its associated *inode*. The inode structure is illustrated in Figure A.3 and contains three principal fields; the first two, *owner* and *time stamps,* identify the owner of the file, the type of file (i.e., whether the file is a directory or a file),[3] its protection, and the times of its initial creation, its last modification, and its last access. The third field serves as the *file allocation map* and consists of an array of 13 block pointers,[4] each 4 bytes wide. The first pointer points to the first data block; if another block is needed, a block is allocated and the second pointer is set to point to it. The process continues until the number of data blocks reaches 10.

When more storage is required, a new block is allocated, the eleventh pointer is set to point to it, and the new block is employed as an index block to subsequently allocated data blocks. Notice that up to 128 data blocks can be allocated, and each is accessible via *double indirection.* Finally, if more space is required, two more blocks are allocated. The first (which is pointed to by the twelfth pointer of the inode) serves as an index to the second one; and, the latter indexes subsequently allocated data blocks. With this scheme the first index block can index up to 128 index blocks; each of the latter can index up to 128 data blocks; however, each one of the data blocks[5] is accessible via *triple indirection.* If more space is required, the thirteenth pointer is used by accessing the data blocks via the triple indirection mechanism just described.

Finally, when the file shrinks in size, unused blocks are unlinked and inserted into the free list. The end result is that for a highly volatile file the blocks are dispersed in the disk device, due to the frequent insertion and deletion of records.

A.1.2 I/O Buffers

When a file is opened, the inode that corresponds to the opened file is read into main memory. Given the discussion in the previous section, the transfer of a physical block requires between one and three random accesses. The operating system attempts to minimize the disk accesses by storing a number of data blocks into main memory. These blocks are stored in an internal buffer pool referred to as *disk buffers* or *buffer cache.* Therefore, whenever an application program wants to access data from the disk, the file system examines its disk buffers

---

[2] 1024 under the system V and any power of 2 greater than or equal to 4096 bytes under Berkley 4.2.

[3] There are two more types of files that are supported: *special files* and *pipes.*

[4] The number of block pointers is implementation dependent but is usually between 5 and 13.

[5] This mode is not supported under Berkley 4.2

File descriptor (inode)

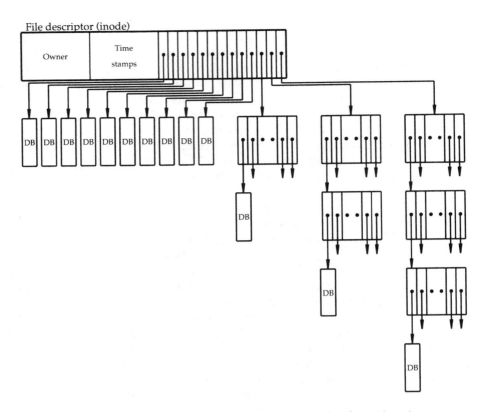

Figure A.3 The inode structure. Notice that the first 10 pointers directly access the first 10 data blocks of the file. The eleventh block pointer points to a block which contains 128 block pointers; each pointer of the latter block points directly to a data block. The last two block pointers of the inode require triple indirection to access the data blocks.

to see if the target data are there; if not, a physical transfer takes place. Figure A.4 illustrates these concepts.

A.1.3 Access Modes and Access Techniques

The earlier discussions can be summarized as follows. The *access mode* supported by the Unix file system (for files that reside on disks) is the *random access* mode.[6] Moreover, the only access technique employed is the *basic access technique*. In other words, the file system performs only physical block transfers; therefore, blocking/deblocking of logical records is the responsibility of the application program.

---

[6] Despite the fact that logical sequential processing is possible.

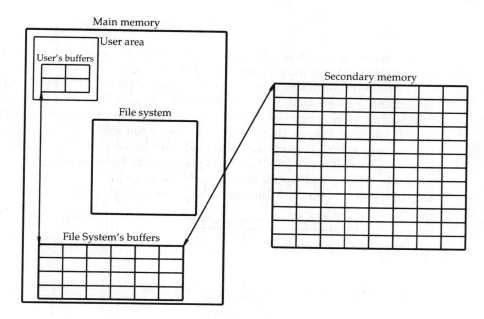

Figure A.4   The disk buffers.

A.2 HOST LANGUAGE: C

A.2.1 Data Manipulation Sublanguage

A.2.1.1 Opening a File.   When it becomes necessary to perform an operation on a file, that file must first be opened. Subsequently the file can be accessed via a pointer to FILE. For example, the following piece of code opens a file under the logical filename my_file and thereafter is accessed via the pointer **fileptr** returned by the **fopen** function.[7]

```
main()
{
    FILE *fileptr,*fopen();

    fileptr = fopen("my_file","r");
    ..........
    ..........
}
```

Consistent with the preceeding piece of code, the format of the C statement that accomplishes this task follows

---

[7] If the file cannot be accessed either because the file does not exist or there are too many files open at that instant, the value of the pointer returned is NULL.

```
fileptr = fopen("filename","options");
```

where `filename` represents the logical name of the file and `options` indicates the *type* of operation that must be performed on the file.

Before the allowable options are discussed, we would like to remark that logically the `fileptr` that is returned via the `fopen` call can be thought of as a pointer to a specific byte of the physical file.[8] For example, assume a 730-byte file *my_file* and also assume that the file has been opened for reading. The value of the `fileptr` returned from the `fopen` call will be zero, indicating that the first read request will commence from this position. In addition, if we read 14 bytes, then the `fileptr` will be updated in such a way so that it points to the fifteenth byte of the file. Figure A.5 illustrates these concepts.

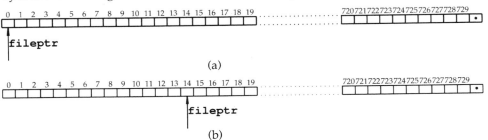

Figure A.5 The position of the `fileptr` (a) immediately after the open call (with the read option) and (b) immediately after the reading of 14 bytes.

There are six possible options, as summarized in Table A.1. Examination of Table A.1 indicates that a file is opened for a *specific* operation.

TABLE A.1 The allowable `options` and operations.

OPTION	READ	WRITE
r	Yes	No
w	No	Yes
a	No	Yes
r+	Yes	Yes
w+	Yes	Yes
a+	Yes	Yes

- A file opened with the option `r` can only be read. No writes are permitted. Moreover, the `fileptr` is set to point to the physical beginning of the file.

---

[8] This is the logical interpretation. As a matter of fact, the `fileptr` points to a data structure which records the information pertaining to the file as well as the current position within the file.

- A file opened with the option **w** can only be written to. Moreover, the **fileptr** is set to point to the physical beginning of the file.

- A file opened with the option **a** can be written to. But the only writing permitted under this option is at the end of the existing file. Of course if the file does not exist, this option may be used to create it. Moreover, the **fileptr** is set to point to the physical end of the file.

- A file opened with either of the options **r+**, **a+**, or **w+**, can be either read or written to.[9] The **fileptr** is positioned at the beginning of the file for the **r+** and **w+** option but at the end of the file for the **a+** option. However, if the file is opened via the **w+** option, and if the file exists, all its contents are deleted. Finally, both reads and writes may be used, with the limitation that an **fseek**, **rewind**, or reading an **end-of-file** must be used between a read and a write or vice versa.

A.2.2 The Logical READ Request

C provides a number of functions that permit one to read from a file. Some of these are discussed below.

The fread function. Whenever "reads" are permitted from an opened physical file, a number of bytes can be read via the following C statement:

```
fread(ptr, size, #items, fileptr)
```

ptr is a pointer to a user defined block structure; **size** is the size in bytes of an item; and, **fileptr** is the pointer to the file. Each time the above statement is executed, the access method will transfer **size · #items** bytes into the block structure pointed to by **ptr** (starting from the current location within the physical file that the **fileptr** points to). For example, assuming the following declarations

```
#define recordsize sizeof (struct recordtype)
struct recordtype
    {
    char    deleted, blockflag;
    long    address, overflow;
    short   key;
    char    name[31];
    };
```

If one assumes that **record** is of the type **recordtype**, the statement

```
fread (&record, recordsize, 1, fileptr);
```

[9]These types do not exist in all systems. Those systems treat the type as if the **+** was present.

will cause `recordsize` bytes (starting at the location pointed to by the `fileptr`) to be transferred to the structure `record` (with the necessary conversions indicated by the type of variables to be made). Notice that after the transfer is completed, the "value" of the `fileptr` is adjusted accordingly (`fileptr +recordsize` in this case). `fread` returns the number of items actually read; if the returned value is zero, this indicates an error in the reading process.

The fgets function.   The function `fgets` reads $n - 1$ characters or up to a newline character, whichever comes first, from the file pointed to by `fileptr` into the string `s`; a null character is appended to the latter. `fgets` returns the first argument of the string `s` unless an error occurs, in which case it returns the null pointer. The syntax follows.

```
char *fgets(s,n,filerptr)
char *s;
FILE *fileptr;
int  n;

fgets(s,n,fileptr);
```

The gets function.   The function `gets` reads a string (that is terminated by a newline character) from the standard input stream, *stdin*, into the string `s` by replacing the newline character by the null character. Also, `gets` returns the first argument of the string `s` unless an error occurs, in which case it returns the null pointer. The syntax follows.

```
char *gets(s)
char *s;

gets(s);
```

The getchar and fgetc functions.   Both the getchar and fgetc functions return the next character of the named input stream unless an error has occured,[10] in which case they return the constant value EOF. Their difference lies in the fact that the `getchar()` reads and returns by default the next character from the standard input stream *stdin*, while the `fgetc` reads and returns the next character from the indicated file. The syntax follows.

```
int   fgetc(fileptr)
FILE  *fileptr;

int getchar()
```

---

[10] If the end of file has been reached, subsequent calls to these functions will continue to return EOF.

```
                    fgetc(fileptr);
                    getchar();
```

A.2.3 The logical WRITE request

C provides a number of functions that permit one to write to a file. Some of these are discussed below.

The fwrite function.   Whenever "writes" are permitted from an opened physical file, a number of bytes can be written via the following C statement:

```
            fwrite(ptr, size, #items, fileptr)
```

`ptr` is a pointer to a user defined block structure, `size` is the size in bytes of an item, and `fileptr` is the pointer to the file. Each time the above statement is executed, the access method will transfer `size` ·`#items` bytes from the block structure pointed to by `ptr` (starting from the current location within the physical file that the `fileptr` points to) into the file. For example, assuming the following declarations:

```
        #define recordsize sizeof (struct recordtype)
        struct recordtype
           {
               char   deleted, blockflag;
               long   address, overflow;
               short  key;
               char   name[31];
           };
```

If one assumes that `record` is of the type `recordtype`, the statement

```
        fwrite (&record, recordsize, 1, fileptr);
```

will cause the `recordsize` bytes contents of the structure `record` to be written into the file (starting at the location pointed to by the `fileptr`). Notice that after the transfer is completed, the "value" of the `fileptr` is adjusted accordingly (`fileptr` + `recordsize`, in this case). The function `fwrite` returns the number of items actually written; if the returned value is zero, this indicates an error in the writing process.

The fputs function.   The function `fputs` writes the null-terminated string `s` into the file pointed to by `fileptr` by first truncating the terminal null character. Also, `fputs` returns the last character written unless an error occurs, in which case it returns the constant `EOF`. The syntax follows.

```
int   fputs(s,fileptr)
char *s;
FILE *fileptr;

fputs(s,fileptr);
```

The puts function. The **puts** function writes the null-terminated string **s** into the standard output stream, *stdout*, by first replacing the terminal null character with the newline character. Also, **fputs** returns the next-to-last character written unless an error occurs, in which case it returns the constant **EOF**. The syntax follows.

```
int   puts(s)
char *s;

puts(s);
```

The putchar and fputc functions. Both the putchar and fputc functions[11] append the next character of the named input stream unless an error has occured, in which case they return the constant value **EOF**. Their difference lies in the fact that the **putchar(c)** writes and returns by default the character **c** into the standard output stream *stdout*, whereas the **fputc** writes the character into the file pointed to by **fileptr**. The syntax follows.

```
int   fputc(c,fileptr)
FILE  *fileptr;
char  c;
int   putchar(c)

fputc(c,fileptr);
putchar(c);
```

A.2.4 Positioning into the File

The previous discussions suggest that one could process a file either sequentially or randomly. The former mode is accomplished via successive read or write requests, whereas the latter is accomplished via repositioning of the **fileptr** between two reads or writes. C permits one to position the **fileptr** at any point in the file at hand. Moreover, the application program may request and receive the current location within the file. The C functions that are used for this purpose are briefly discussed next.

The fseek function. The **fseek** function is used to reposition the **fileptr** within the file. The format of the C statement that performs this task follows.

---

[11] **putchar** has been implemented as a macro.

```
int    fseek(fileptr,offset,code)
long   offset;
short  code;

fseek(fileptr, offset, code)
```

Execution of this statement causes the `fileptr` to be set to a position given by *position* + `offset` , where the value of the position depends on the value of the `code`. Specifically, if the value of the `code` is 0, then the position is assumed to be the physical beginning of the file. If the value of the `code` is 1, then the position is assumed to be the current position; if the value of the `code` is 2, however, the position is assumed to be the physical end of the file. If an improper seek is requested, then the `fseek` function will return the value −1.

The rewind function.   Notice that repositioning of the `fileptr` at the physical beginning of the file can be accomplished via the following statement.

```
rewind(fileptr)
```

The ftell function.   Finally, the current position can always be found via the call

```
ftell(fileptr)
```

which returns the current (long) offset in bytes from the beginning of the named file.

A.3.5 Closing a File

A file can be closed via the statement

```
fclose(fileptr)
```

A.3 AN EXAMPLE

The C program that follows implements and demonstrates a hashed file with separate overflow area. Each block in the main and overflow files has the following structure:

- A flag indicating if the record has been deleted.
- A flag indicating if the record has synonyms in the overflow file.
- The address of the block.
- The address of the first block in the overflow file that contains synonyms for this record, if any.

- A data field for the key.
- A data field for the name.

The overflow file is a separate file with the filetype of .ovf. It begins with a header that gives the address (offset) of the first free block in the file.

The code that follows is not very elegant. It should be broken into separate source files, and the functions should be decomposed a little more. But, it serves as a starting point to illustrate the capabilities as well as the usage of C functions to manipulate files.

```c
#include <stdio.h>
#define EOF -1
#define HASH_DIVISOR 47
#define ADDRESS_SPACE HASH_DIVISOR-1
#define RECORDSIZE  sizeof (struct recordtype)
#define clearscreen  printf ("%c[1;1H%c[2J",27,27)
                                            /* Escape sequence for VT-100 */


struct recordtype                   /* Structure of a block */
    {
        char   deleted, blockflag;  /* 'y' if record deleted, 'n' if not */
        long   address, overflow;   /* Address of current and next record */
        short  key;                 /* Key and name data  */
        char name[31];
    };

struct headertype                   /* Structure of overflow file header */
    {
        long firstblock;
    };



/*********************************************************************************

The main program displays a menu to allow the user to add, delete, or list
records.
**********************************************************************************/
  main () {
    char menuchoice;
    char line[80];

    while (1)                            /* Loop until user breaks out */
      {
      menuchoice='0';
      while ((menuchoice<'1') || (menuchoice>'4'))
      {
      printf("%c[1;1H%c[2J%c[1;4m",27,27,27);
```

```
     printf("%c[16C Hashed Direct File with Separate Overflow Area%c[0m0,
            27,27);
     printf("%c[25C 1  Add a record0,27);
     printf("%c[25C 2  Delete a record0,27);
     printf("%c[25C 3  Display a record0,27);
     printf("%c[25C 4  Exit the program0,27);
     printf("%c[25C Please make one of the above choices: ",27);
     gets(line);
     menuchoice = line[0];
     }
   clearscreen;
   switch (menuchoice)
      {
      case '1': add();
               break;
      case '2': delete();
               break;
      case '3': list();
               break;
      }

    if (menuchoice == '4')
       {
       clearscreen;
       break;
       }
   }
 }




/***********************************************************************
    This function gets the file pointer and filename for addrecord below.
 ***********************************************************************/

add()

   {
   char filename[80];                             /* File to be added to */
   struct recordtype record;

   clearscreen;
   printf ("Enter the name of the file: ");
   gets(filename);
   loadrecord(&record);                           /* User loads name & key */
   addrecord(&record, filename);
   }
```

```
/********************************************************************

This function passes a pointer to an empty block, loads the block with the key
and name specified by the user, and sets the "deleted" flag to 'n'.

********************************************************************/

loadrecord (recptr)
struct recordtype *recptr;

    {
      printf ("Enter the key of the record to be added: ");
      scanf ("%hd%*c", &(recptr->key));
      printf ("Enter the name in the record to be added: ");
      gets (recptr->name);
      recptr->deleted = 'n';
      recptr->blockflag = 'n';
      recptr->overflow = 0L;
    }

/********************************************************************
    This function gets the file pointer and filename for delete record below.
********************************************************************/

delete()

    {
    char filename[80];
    int key;

    clearscreen;
    printf ("Enter the name of the file: ");
    gets(filename);
    printf ("Enter the key to be deleted: ");
    scanf ("%d%*c",&key);
    delrecord (filename, key);
    }



/********************************************************************
    This function gets the file pointer and filename for list record below.
********************************************************************/

list()
    {
    char filename[80];
    int key;
```

```
        clearscreen;
        printf ("Enter the name of the file: ");
        gets   (filename);
        printf ("Enter the key of the record to be displayed: ");
        scanf ("%d%*c",&key);
        listrec(filename, key);
        }


/*************************************************************************
    This function pauses until the user presses a key.
*************************************************************************/

pause()

{
 printf("%c%c[23;40H%c[7m Please press RETURN to continue... %c[0m",
        7,27,27,27);
 scanf ("%*c");
 clearscreen;
 }


/*************************************************************************

This function, when called, adds a record to the overflow file.

1) If it is the first overflow record, the address of the record in the
   overflow file is returned.
2) If there are already overflow records present, they are searched to see if
   the record that is to be added is already there.
   a) If it is present, -1 is returned as an error indicator.
   b) Otherwise, the record is added:
      i) If the slot in the main file is empty (the overflow file is being
         searched because the blockflag has been set), the new record is placed
         in that slot.
     ii) Otherwise, the record is placed in the first available slot of the
         overflow chain (either in the first empty slot where a record had
         been deleted or at the start of the free chain.)

*************************************************************************/

long add2overflow(recptr, filename, deleted, overfaddr)
    struct recordtype *recptr;          /* Pointer to the record to be added */
    char deleted, filename[];           /* Set to 'y' if main record deleted */
    long overfaddr;                     /* Pointer to next block with synonyms */

{
 struct recordtype overec;          /* Buffer for record from overflow file */
 long ftell(), firstblank;          /* Address of 1st deleted record found */
```

```
struct headertype header;            /* Buffer for overflow header */
FILE *fopen(), *fileptr;
int fread(), fwrite(), hash;         /* Variable which holds hashed address */

strcat (filename,".ovf");
fileptr = fopen(filename,"r+b");
if (fileptr == NULL)         /* File doesn't exist-write header and record */
   {                         /* then return address of the record */
   fileptr = fopen(filename,"wb");
   fseek(fileptr, (long) (sizeof(header)), 0);
   recptr->address = ftell(fileptr);
   fwrite(recptr, RECORDSIZE, 1, fileptr);
   header.firstblock = ftell(fileptr);
   rewind (fileptr);
   fwrite (&header, sizeof(header), 1, fileptr);
   fclose (fileptr);
   return (recptr->address);
   }
else         /* Search overflow records to see if key is already present */
   {
   if (overaddr == 0L)         /* If pointer is null, skip search and add */
      {                        /* since this is the 1st overflow block  */
      rewind (fileptr);
      fread (&header, sizeof(header), 1, fileptr);
      fseek (fileptr, header.firstblock, 0);   /* Find start of free chain */
      recptr->address = ftell (fileptr);
      fwrite (recptr, RECORDSIZE, 1, fileptr);
      header.firstblock = ftell (fileptr);
      rewind (fileptr);
      fwrite (&header, sizeof(header), 1, fileptr);
      fclose (fileptr);
      return (recptr->address);
      }
   else                              /* Find the overflow block the main */
   {                                 /* record points to and keep reading  */
    fseek (fileptr, overaddr, 0);  /* until the key is found or the end  */
    firstblank = -1L;              /* of the chain is reached.  */

    do {
        fread (&overec, RECORDSIZE, 1, fileptr);
        if (overec.deleted == 'y' && firstblank == -1L)
           firstblank == overec.address;       /* Note the 1st empty block  */
        fseek (fileptr, overec.overflow, 0);
        }
    while ((overec.key != recptr->key) && (overec.overflow > 0L));

    if (overec.key == recptr->key && overec.deleted == 'n')
       {                                /* Key exists - return error flag */
```

```
        fclose (fileptr);
        return (-1L);
        }
else if (deleted == 'y')    /* Key isn't here, will be added in main file */
        {                    /* since the record there had been deleted  */
        fclose (fileptr);
        return (0L);
        }
    else if (firstblank != -1L)     /* A deleted record was found */
            {                       /* Write the record here     */
            fseek (fileptr, firstblank, 0);
            fread (&overec, RECORDSIZE, 1, fileptr);
            overec.key = recptr->key;
            strcpy(overec.name, recptr->name);
            overec.deleted = 'n';
            fseek (fileptr, firstblank, 0);
            fwrite (&overec, RECORDSIZE, 1, fileptr);
            fclose (fileptr);
            return (0L);
            }
        else    /* The record is added at the head of the free chain -
                   get the address from the header,  update the overflow
                   pointer  on the last old overflow block,  and rewrite
                   the old and  new  overflow  blocks  and  the  updated
                   header.  */
            {
            rewind (fileptr);
            fread (&header, sizeof(header), 1, fileptr);
            overec.overflow = header.firstblock;
            fseek (fileptr, overec.address, 0);
            fwrite (&overec, RECORDSIZE, 1, fileptr);
            fseek (fileptr, header.firstblock, 0);
            recptr->address = ftell (fileptr);
            fwrite (recptr, RECORDSIZE, 1, fileptr);
            header.firstblock = ftell (fileptr);
            rewind (fileptr);
            fwrite (&header, sizeof(header), 1, fileptr);
            fclose (fileptr);
            return (0L);
            }
        }
    }
}
```

/**

This function performs a key-to-address transformation by dividing the key by
a prime number and returning the remainder.

```
**********************************************************************/

hash (key)
    int key;
    {
     return (key % HASH_DIVISOR);
    }
/*********************************************************************
```

This function passes a pointer to a filename and a key, then adds that record to
the file.

1) If the file does not exist, it is created and the record is added to the
   address found by the KTA transformation.
2) If the file exists, the address returned by the transformation is checked.
   a) If it is empty and there are no overflow records, the record is added
      at that address.
   b) If it is not empty or if there are overflow records, the Add2Overflow
      function is called. This function searches the overflow file for the key,
      returning an error flag if it is found. If the address in the main file
      is vacant, the record is added in the main file; otherwise, the record
      is added in the overflow file.

```
**********************************************************************/


addrecord (recptr, filename)
    struct recordtype *recptr;
    char filename[];


    {
    struct recordtype mainrec;                    /* Buffer read into  */
    FILE *fopen(), *fileptr;                      /* Pointer to the file */
    int i, fread(), fwrite (), hash();
    char initchar;
    long overflow, add2overflow();

    fileptr = fopen(filename, "r+b");             /* Open for R/W */
    if (fileptr == NULL)                          /* If file nonexistent */
        {
        fileptr = fopen(filename, "wb");          /* Create file */
        printf ("The file %s is being initialized...0, filename);
        initchar = '_';                           /* Initialize the file */

        for (i=1; i<= RECORDSIZE * ADDRESS_SPACE; i++)
          fwrite(&initchar, 1, 1, fileptr);

        recptr->address = (long)((hash(recptr->key))*RECORDSIZE);
```

```
        fseek (fileptr, recptr->address, 0);
        fwrite(recptr,RECORDSIZE, 1, fileptr);
      }
else                                        /* file exists; find hashed address */
   {
   fseek (fileptr, (long)((hash(recptr->key)) * RECORDSIZE), 0);
   fread (&mainrec, RECORDSIZE, 1, fileptr);
   if (mainrec.deleted == 'n' && mainrec.key == recptr->key )
      {
      printf ("The key %d already exists in the file %s.0,
              recptr->key,filename);
      pause();
      }
   else if (mainrec.deleted != 'n' && mainrec.blockflag != 'y')
          {                              /* No record here, & no overflow */
           recptr->address = (long)((hash(recptr->key))*RECORDSIZE);
           fseek (fileptr, recptr->address, 0);
           fwrite(recptr,RECORDSIZE, 1, fileptr);
          }
      else { /* Add the record to the overflow  file.  If  the  add-to-
               overflow  function returns -1,  the record was already
               present in the overflow file.  Otherwise,  the address
               of  the  first block in the overflow file is returned.
               If record.deleted != 'n' (there is no  record  present
               in  the  current position of the main file), the over-
               flow function does not actually add the record to  the
               overflow file, but just searches for its presence.  It
               will be added into the main file. */

               overflow = add2overflow (recptr, filename,
                  mainrec.deleted, mainrec.overflow);
               if (overflow == -1L)
                  {
                  printf ("The key %d already exists in the file %s.0,
                  recptr->key,filename);
                  pause();
                  }
               else {  /* Copy the record info to the main record if the
                          slot is empty. Regardless, rewrite it with the
                          new overflow pointer returned by the overflow
                          function.                                    */
                    if (mainrec.deleted != 'n')
                       {
                       mainrec.key = recptr->key;
                       strcpy(mainrec.name, recptr->name);
                       mainrec.deleted = 'n';
                       }
                    else {
```

```
                                    if (overflow > 0L)
                                        mainrec.overflow = overflow;
                                    }
                            mainrec.blockflag = 'y';
                            fseek (fileptr, mainrec.address, 0);
                            fwrite(&mainrec,RECORDSIZE, 1, fileptr);
                            }
                    }

        }
    fclose (fileptr);
  }



/*************************************************************************

This function passed a pointer to a filename and a key, and retrieves that
record, if it exists, from the file.

*************************************************************************/


listrec(filename, key)
    char filename[];
    int key;

  {
    struct recordtype  record;
    FILE *fopen(), *fileptr;
    int fread(), hash();

    fileptr = fopen(filename, "rb");         /* Open for reading */
    clearscreen;

    if (fileptr == NULL)
        {
         printf ("The file %s does not exist.0, filename);
         pause();
         }
    else
        {                                     /* See if it's in the main file */
        fseek (fileptr, (long)((hash(key))*RECORDSIZE), 0);
        fread (&record, RECORDSIZE, 1, fileptr);
        if (record.key == key && record.deleted == 'n')
            printf ("%d%s0,record.key, record.name);
        else if (record.blockflag != 'y')
                {
```

```
                printf ("The key %d does not exist in the file %s.0,
                    key, filename);
                }
         else    {                           /* Open the overflow file */
                fclose (fileptr);
                strcat(filename, ".ovf");
                fileptr = fopen(filename,"rb");
                if (fileptr == NULL)
                    printf("***** OVERFLOW OPEN ERROR ****0);

                while ((record.overflow != 0L)&&(record.key != key))
                    {
                    fseek(fileptr,record.overflow,0);
                    fread (&record,RECORDSIZE, 1, fileptr);
                    }

                if (record.key == key && record.deleted == 'n')
                    printf ("%d%s0,record.key, record.name);
                else {
                     printf("The key %d does not exist.0, key);
                     }
                }
    fclose (fileptr);
    pause();
    }

}
```

```
/******************************************************************************
```

This function passed a pointer to a filename and a key, deletes that record
if it exists in the file by setting the "deleted" flag to 'y.' The deleted
record is not added to the free list, but remains as an empty "slot" with
pointers to the next overflow record, if any. When any records are added that
hash to the same value as the deleted record, they are added in the vacant
slot.

```
******************************************************************************/
```

```
delrecord(filename, key)

    char filename[];
    int key;

{
    struct recordtype  record;
```

```
FILE *fopen(), *fileptr;
int fread(), hash();

fileptr = fopen(filename, "r+b");        /* Open for read/write */
clearscreen;

if (fileptr == NULL)
    {
     printf ("The file %s does not exist.0, filename);
     pause();
     }
else
    {                                    /* See if it's in the main file */
    fseek (fileptr, (long)((hash(key))*RECORDSIZE), 0);
    fread (&record, RECORDSIZE, 1, fileptr);

    if (record.key == key && record.deleted == 'n')
        {                               /* Record found - delete it */
        printf ("Record %d has been deleted from %s0,record.key,filename);
        record.deleted = 'y';
        fseek (fileptr, record.address, 0);
        fwrite (&record, RECORDSIZE, 1, fileptr);
        }
    else if (record.blockflag != 'y')
           printf ("The key %d does not exist in the file %s.0,
                    key, filename);
         else    {                       /* Open the overflow file */
                 fclose (fileptr);
                 strcat(filename, ".ovf");
                 fileptr = fopen(filename,"r+b");
                 if (fileptr == NULL)
                     printf("***** OVERFLOW OPEN ERROR *****0);

                 while ((record.overflow != 0L)&&(record.key != key))
                     {
                     fseek(fileptr,record.overflow,0);
                     fread (&record,RECORDSIZE, 1, fileptr);
                     }

                 if (record.key == key && record.deleted == 'n')
                     {                   /* Record found - delete it */
                     printf ("Record %d has been deleted from %s0,
                       record.key,filename);
                     record.deleted = 'y';
                     fseek (fileptr, record.address, 0);
                     fwrite (&record, RECORDSIZE, 1, fileptr);
                     }
                 else printf("The key %d does not exist in the file %s.0,
```

```
                              key, filename);
                       }
fclose (fileptr);
pause();
}


}
```

Index

Note: Boldface, uppercase entries are PL/1 keywords. Boldface, lowercase entries are C functions.

ACCESS, 201, 243-44
Access length, I/O and, 107-10
Access method area, 80
Access methods, 14-18, 88. *See also* ISAM file(s)
Access mode(s), 65-66, 195-96, 197
  binary, 15-16
  direct, 196, 199, 246
  random, 15-16, 65
  sequential, 15-16, 22, 65, 196, 197, 198-99, 244, 245, 246
    245, 246
  UNIX, 404
Access path, 15
Access techniques, 65-66, 404
Actuator, 38
Address(es)
  home, 44, 146
  relative byte (RBA), 319
  virtual, 92
Address size (B), 146, 155-57
Address space (R), 146, 155-57
Algorithm(s)
  least recently used (LRU), 93

for *m*-way balanced merge sort, 359-61
  scheduling, 61-65
Alternate keys, 4
and operator, 333
Anticipatory buffering, 57
Application program area, 80
Application programmers, 5-6, 7
Architecture, disk, 42-47
Asynchronous I/O, 66

Balanced merge sorts, 350-66
  external *m*-way, 358-66
  external two-way, 351-58
  four-way, 385-400
Base (track descriptor) block, 44-45
Basic access technique, 66
Basic Direct Access Method (BDAM), 88
Basic Indexed Sequential Access Method (BISAM), 88
  (BISAM), 88
Basic Partitioned Access Method (BPAM), 88

Basic Sequential Access Method (BSAM), 88
Batch operations, 19, 22
    on **CONSECUTIVE** files, 128
    on fixed-length records, 128
    on hash files, 206-9
    on ISAM file, 250-52
    on tape files, 98-99
    on variable-length records, 139-42
Binary access, 15-16
Binary search, 101
Binary search trees, 253-70. *See also* Height-
    balanced (AVL)-trees
    operations on, 256-68
    threaded, 268-70, 271
Bit map, 70-71
Block addressable devices, 42, 44-48
Block descriptor word (BDW), 35
Blocked logical records, 209-14
Blocking factor (BF), 11-13, 18, 29, 352-54
Block movement, 78
Block multiplexor channel, 57
Block overhead, 14, 39, 46-47
Block(s) (physical block), 11, 14, 57, 92
    boot, 402
    contiguous, 48
    count data, 44, 45
    count-key data, 44, 46-47
    file control, 77
    index, dummy, 237
    logical, 11
    number, 43
    organization of, 18
    overflow, 104, 222, 291, 294
    primary (control intervals), 222, 235-36
    relative, 193
    super, 402
    underflow, 105
Block pointers, 14
Block size (BS), 28-29, 31-32
Boot block, 402
Bootstrap code, 402
Boundary folding, 160
B+-trees, 297-306
    height of, 300-301
    initial loading operation, 305-6
    operations on, 300-305
B-trees, 284-97
    height of, 288-89
    operations on, 287-97
Bucket, 146
Buffer(s), I/O, 12, 13, 57-59, 72-74
    allocation of, 18
    disk, 403-4, 405
    multiple, 74
    for two-way balanced merge sort, 352-54
    UNIX, 403-4
Buffer area, 80
Buffer cache, 403-4
Buffer control block list, 77

Buffering, anticipatory, 57
Buffer pool block (BPB), 74
Buffer pool block pointer (BPBP), 74
Buffer pool control block, 74-75
Byte multiplexor channel, 56
Bytes per inch (bytes/inch), 27

Cache, buffer, 403-4
Cache memory, 55-56
Candidate key, 4
Capacity, storage, 27-29, 38
Capstan, 28
Cascade merge, *m*-way, 377-81
Cellular multilists, 334, 335
Central processing unit (CPU), 55, 61-63, 89
Chained block method, 71
Chaining, 71, 168-76, 227
Channel, 55-57, 89-90
Channel address word (CAW), 89
Channel command, 89
Channel program, 55, 80
Channel status word (CSW), 89-90
C language, 405-23. *See also specific C functions*
    closing files in, 411
    data manipulation sublanguage, 405-7
    opening files in, 405-7
    sample code, 412-23
Clustering, 166, 167
Clusters, 48
Coalesced chaining, 169-74
Collision, 147
Command, channel, 89
Composite key, 4
Computer systems, 4-5
Concatenation, 304
Condition code (CC), 89
CONSECUTIVE files, 112-42
    creation of, 124-26, 136-37
    declaring, 112-13
    with fixed-length records, 124-35
    opening, 113-15
    operations on, 123-42
    update of, 137-39
    with variable-length records, 135-42
Control area (CA), 320
Control area split, 324
Control interval (CI), 43-44, 235-36, 318, 323-24
Controller, 47, 57
Count area, 44
Count data format, 44, 45
Count-key data format, 44, 46-47
CPU, 55, 61-63, 89
Critical node (CN), 277
C-SCAN policy, 64
C-Trie structures, 315-17
Current input buffer pointer (CIBP), 72, 73
Current output buffer pointer (COBP), 72, 74
Cyclic check redundancy bytes, 47

Cylinder overflow area, 237
CYLOFL parameter, 243

Data, 9
　　access path to, 15
　　defined, 1
Data area, 45, 80
Data control block (DCB), 76-77, 80, 112
Data Definition (DD) statement, 112
Data definition language, 6, 115
　　for ISAM files, 242-43
　　for **REGIONAL(1)** files, 195
　　for **REGIONAL(2)** files, 200-201
Data event control block (DECB), 75-76
Data management. *See* Operating systems
Data manipulation sublanguage, 6, 113-23
　　C, 405-7
　　closing file, 123
　　fixed-length records, 115-19
　　for four-way balanced merge, 385-86
　　for ISAM files, 243-52
　　opening **CONSECUTIVE** file, 113-15
　　for **REGIONAL(1)** files, 195-99
　　for **REGIONAL(2)** files, 201-2
　　variable-length records, 119-23
Data-program dependence, 9
Data set, 215, 216, 268, 285
　　entry-sequenced, 318, 322, 338
　　key-sequenced, 318, 322-25, 338
　　relative record, 318, 320-22
Data set control block (DSCB), 81
Data Set Name (DSNAME), 112
Data subblock, 39
Data sublanguage, 5-6
Data transfer, 11, 23. *See also* Hardware;
　　Operating systems; Software
　　rate of, 29-32, 39-41
DCB parameter, 242
DCL statement, 195, 200-201, 242
DD keyword, 86
Deblocking, 11-12
DECLARE statement, 85-88
Delete_One operation, 20
　　on binary search trees, 259-65
　　on B⁺-trees, 304-5
　　on B-trees, 295-97
　　on disk files, 100, 101
　　on extendible hashing, 185
　　on full index files, 218
　　on hash file, 165-66
　　on indexed sequential files, 231-32
　　on ISAM files, 241
　　on physical linked sequential files, 103, 105
　　on tape files, 97-98
　　on trie structures, 312-15
DELETE request, 199, 201-2, 247
Deletion of records, 3, 321-22
Density of magnetic tape, 27-29

Descriptor, VTOC, 81-83
Design, file. *See* File design
Designer, 7
Deterministic transformations, 147-50
Device(s). *See also* Disk(s); Tape(s)
　　block addressable, 42, 44-48
　　I/O, 59
　　scheduling algorithm, 63-64
　　sector addressable, 42-44
　　storage allocation, 70-71, 402
Device allocation table, 81, 83-85
Device controller. *See* Controller
Device management, 63-64
Device unit block list, 77
Digit analysis, 157-58
Direct access mode, 196, 199, 246
Direct access storage devices (DASD). *See*
　　Disk(s)
Direct files, 146-47. *See also* Deterministic
　　transformations; Hashing transformations
Direct loading, 160-61
Directory, 48, 66-70, 401-3
Disk(s), 5, 36-50
　　architecture of, 42-47
　　average seek time of, 38-39, 40-42
　　buffer, 403-4, 405
　　capacity of, 38
　　clusters and extents, 48
　　fixed vs. fixed-head, 39, 40
　　general characteristics of, 36-38
　　latency time, 38-39
　　loading density and storage requirements,
　　　　49-50
　　maximal and effective data transfer rate, 39-
　　　　40
　　sorting with, 358, 361-65, 366, 376-77
　　volume table of contents (VTOC) and file
　　　　labels, 48-49
Disk buffers, 403-4, 405
Disk controller, 47
Disk directory, 48, 66-70
Disk drives, 38, 39, 43-44
Disk files, 99-103
Disk pointers, 95
Dispatcher, 62
DISP keyword, 86
Division method of hashing, 158-59
Double hashing, 167-68
Double indirection, 403
Doubly linked sequential file, 107
Drives, disk, 38
Drums, magnetic, 5
Duplication, data, 9
Dynamic address translation (DAT), 92
Dynamic files, 19

EBCDIC format, 26
Effective blocking factor (EBF), 49-50

Effective data transfer rate (EDTR), 30-32, 40-41
Electro-mechanical devices. *See* Disk(s); Tape(s)
Embedded keys, 46-47
end-of-file, 407
End of file, physical and logical, 49
End of reel mark, 25
End-user, 5, 7
Entry-sequenced data sets (ESDS), 318, 322, 338
Entry-sequence files, 318, 322
Error correction code, 47
Extended Binary Coded Decimal Interchange
    Code (EBCDIC) format, 26
Extendible hashing, 177-85, 190
Extents, 48
Extent Sequence Number, 49
Extent Type Indicator, 49

fgetc (C function), 408
fgets (C function), 408
Field(s), 2
    in count-data data block, 45
    in count-key data block, 46
    in data control block, 76-77
    in data event control block, 75-76
    device allocation table, 83
    in file labels, 48-49
    inode, 403
    on tape volume label, 33-34
    on variable-length records, 35
    VTOC descriptor, 81-83
File(s)
    activity of, 20
    closing, 123, 411
    defined, 1-2
    growth of, 19
    headers, 48-49
    labels, 48-49
    logical end of, 49
    maintenance of, 3
    maps, 71-72
    physical end of, 49
    record vs. stream, 9
    size of, 18, 20
    static vs. dynamic, 19
    target, 3
File allocation table, 71
File control block, 77
File design, 18-24
    constraints on, 20
    issues in, 18-19
    logical and physical, 18
    operations, 19-20
    organizations, 21-22
    performance, 22-24
Filenames, user vs. physical, 66
File processing systems, 7-18
File protection ring, 28
fileptr (C function), 405-7

File space, 83-85
File storage allocation, 71-72
File storage space, 70, 402-3
File structure, 14, 235-38, 318-20
File systems, 6-7, 59, 64, 401-23
File variables, 386
First come, first serve (FCFS) policy, 61, 63-64,
    65
Fixed-block architecture (FBA), 43
Fixed disk, 40
Fixed-head disks, 39, 40
Fixed-length records, 34-36, 115-19
    batch mode processing of, 128
    CONSECUTIVE files with, 124-35
    input buffer processing of, 131-33
    locate mode processing of, 115, 117-19, 131-
        35
    move mode processing of, 115-16, 128-31
    output buffer processing of, 133-35
FLAG field, 196, 244
Floor function (*flr*), 47
fopen (C function), 405-7
Four-way balanced merge sort, 385-400
fputc (C function), 410
fputs (C function), 409
Fragmentation of secondary storage, 71
fread (C function), 407-8
Free chain, 71
Free inodes, 402
Free list, 402
fseek (C function), 407, 410-11
ftell (C function), 411
Full index organization, 216-19
fwrite (C function), 409

gest (C function), 408
getchar (C function), 408

Hard sectoring, 43
Hardware, 4-5, 54-59
    central processing system, 55, 61-63, 89
    channel, 55-57, 89-90
    controller, 47, 57
    I/O buffers, 12, 13, 18, 57-59, 72-74, 352-54,
        403-4, 405
    primary storage, 54
    secondary storage, 5, 15, 20, 54-55, 70, 71,
        402-3
Hash files, 147, 160-61, 165-66, 206-9
Hashing transformations, 147, 150-90
    boundary folding, 160
    choice of, 151-57
    digit analysis, 157-58
    division method, 158-59
    double hashing, 167-68
    load and average search length control, 190
    loading hash files, 160-61

midsquare method of, 159-60
overflow management techniques, 161-90
  chaining, 168-76
    extendible hashing, 177-85
    linear hashing, 185-90
    open addressing, 161-68
  radix transformation, 159
  shift folding, 160
  truncation method of, 159
Header label, 33
Headers, file, 48-49
Head flying distance, 38
Head-switching time, 39
Height-balanced (AVL)-trees, 270-82
  insert algorithm for, 277-78
  performance of, 278-82
  rebalancing operation on, 274-77
  rotations, 272-74
Home address, 44, 146
Home records, 169
Host language, 5-6. *See also* C language; PL/1

IBM 3310 disk, 43-44
IBM 3350 disk, 38, 39
Identifier, label, 33
Independent overflow area, 237
Index, 145, 215
  KSDS alternate, 338
  master, 238
  track, 235, 236
Index area, 237-38
Index block, dummy, 237
INDEXED files, 241-52
  declaration of, 242-43
  opening, 243-45
Indexed sequential access method (ISAM). *See* ISAM file(s)
Indexed sequential files, 66, 219-35
  height of, 223-26
  initial loading operation, 227-28
  model of, 226-33
  multilevel, 220-23
  operations on, 228-32
  performance analysis, 223-26
  reorganization points of, 232-33
Index marker, 44
Index records, 235
Index set, 177-78, 179, 215, 216, 268, 285
Indirection, double and triple, 403
Information, defined, 1
Inodes, 401, 402-4
INPUT, 196, 244
Input buffer pointer (IBP), 72, 73
Input buffer processing, 78, 117-18, 122-23, 131-33
Input/output (I/O). *See also* Buffer(s), I/O
  access length and, 107-10
  asynchronous, 66

device handler, 63
devices, 59
  under MVT system, 85-90
  in *m*-way balanced merge sort, 361-66
  in *m*-way polyphase merge, 376-77
  record and stream, 12
  scheduler, 63
  search length and, 23-24
  synchronous, 66
  traffic controller, 60, 63
  in two-way balanced merge sort, 355-58
Insert algorithm for height-balanced (AVL)-trees, 277-78
Insertion of records, 3, 49, 163-64, 321, 323-25
Insert_One operation, 20
  on binary search trees, 258-59
  on B+-trees, 302-4
  on B-trees, 289-95
  on disk files, 100, 101
  on extendible hashing, 179-85
  on full index files, 218
  on indexed sequential files, 230-31
  on ISAM files, 238-41
  on physical linked sequential files, 103, 105
  on tape files, 97-98
  on trie structures, 311-12
Integrity of data, 9
Interblock gap (IBG), 28-29, 45, 47
Interrupts, 89-90
Interval, control (CI), 43-44, 235-36, 318, 323-24
INTO clause, 117-18
Inverted files, 334-36
I/O. *See* Input/output (I/O)
ISAM file(s), 235-52
  batch mode direct update of, 250-52
  BISAM, 88
  creation of, 247-50
  file structure, 235-38
  operations on, 238-41
  PL/1 implementation of, 241-52

Job control language (JCL), 85-86, 112-13, 242
Job file control block (JFCB), 88
Job scheduler, 60, 80

KEY condition, 195-96, 244
KEYED attribute, 197, 243-44, 245
KEYLENGTH parameter, 242, 245, 247
Key redistribution, 292-93
Keys, 3-4, 18-19, 46-47, 235-36, 298
Key-sequenced data sets (KSDS), 318, 322-25, 338
Key-to-address (KTA) transformation, 145-46, 150

Label format, 81

Label identifier, 33
Labels, 32-34, 48-49, 83-85
Language(s), 53. *See also* C language; PL/1
    data definition, 6, 115, 195, 200-201, 242-43
    host, 5-6
    job control, 85-86, 112-13, 242
    query, 5
Latency time of magnetic disks, 38-39
Least recently used (LRU) algorithm, 93
Linear hashing, 185-90
Linear search, 161-66
List(s)
    buffer control block, 77
    data control block, 76-77
    data event control block, 75-76
    device unit block, 77
    free, 402
    request, 90
    service request (SR), 64
Loader, 79
Load factor (LF), 146, 155-57, 190
Loading density, 49-50
Load point mark, 25
LOCATE, 246
Locate mode processing, 77-78, 115, 117-19,
    121-23, 131-35
Logical block, 11
Logical file structure, 14
Logical record, 11, 236, 298

Magnetic storage. *See* Storage, secondary
Maintenance of files, 3
Marker, index, 44
Master directory, 67-68
Master index, 238
Maximal data transfer rate (MDTR), 30, 39-40
Memory, 55-56, 59, 90-93
Memory, secondary. *See* Storage, secondary
Memory management, 60
Merge sorts, balanced. *See* Balanced merge
    sorts
Midsquare method of hashing, 159-60
Movable-head disks, 39
MOVEAREA declaration, 117
Move mode processing, 77, 115-16, 121, 128-31
Multifile-processing system, 7-9
Multilevel indexed sequential files, 220-23
Multilist files, 330-34, 335
Multiple buffer allocation, 74
Multiprogramming systems, 59, 60. *See also*
    Operating systems
MVS (Multiple Virtual Storage) system, 90-94
MVT (Multiprogramming with Variable
    Number of Tasks) system, 79-90
    device allocation table, 83-85
    first logical I/O, 85-90
    gaining control, 80-81
    primary storage allocation, 54, 79-80

region partitions, 80
VTOC, 81-83
m-way balanced merge sort, external, 358-66
    algorithm, 359-61
    on disks, 361-65
    required I/O time, 361-66
    on tapes, 365-66
m-way cascade merge, 377-81
m-way polyphase merge, 366-77
    estimating number of passes through data,
        374-76
    initial partition distribution, 368-74
    required I/O time, 376-77

Next_Greater_Key (**AREA, LAST_KEY**)
    function, 344-48
Node(s). *See also specific types of tree-based files*
    critical (CN), 277
    underflow, 295-96
Node splitting, 292-93, 302
Nonembedded keys, 46-47
Nonlinear search, 166
N-SCAN policy, 64
NTM parameter, 243

Open addressing, 161-68
OPEN statements, 88, 195
Operating systems, 54, 59-78
    data management component of, 64-78
        access modes and techniques, 65-66
        buffer pool control block, 74-75
        data control block list, 76-77
        data event control block list, 75-76
        device storage allocation, 70-71
        directory, 66-70
        file storage allocation, 71-72
        I/O buffers, 72-74
        locate mode processing, 77-78
    device management component of, 63-64
    memory management components of, 60
    multiple virtual storage (MVS), 90-94
    multiprogramming with variable number of
        tasks (MVT), 79-90
    processor management component of, 60-63
    UNIX, 401-23
OPTCD parameter, 243
OPTION modes, 113-14, 195-96, 201, 243-44
Ordered sequential fashion, 4
or operator, 333-34
OUTPUT, 196, 198, 244
Output. *See* Input/output (I/O)
Output buffer. *See* Buffer(s), I/O
Output buffer pointer (OBP), 72, 74
Output buffer processing, 78, 119, 123, 133-35
Overflow, track, 47
Overflow area, 169, 174-76, 222, 237
Overflow block, 104, 222, 291, 294

Overflow chain, 227
Overflow entry, 236
Overflow records, 147, 150, 155-57
  chaining of, 168-76
  linear hashing and, 185-90
  in multilevel indexed sequential files, 221-23
  number of accesses required to retrieve, 174
  performance and, 232
Overhead, block, 14, 39, 46-47

Paged trees, 282-83
Page fault, 93
Page map table, 92
Pages, 91-92
Paging supervisor, 92
Parity checking, 26-27, 47
Partition files, sorted. *See* Sorted partition files
Partitions, 79-80
Passes, sorting, 374-76
Pathnames, 67
Performance. *See also* Search length, average
    (ASL)
  of AVL-tree, 278-82
  of deterministic transformations, 148-50
  file design and, 22-24
  of indexed sequential files, 223-26
  overflow records and, 232
  of two-way balanced merge sort, 354-55
Physical block. *See* Block(s) (physical block)
Physical file structure, 14
Physical linked sequential files, 14, 95-96, 103-7
Physical sequential file, 14, 95-103
PL/1. *See also* **CONSECUTIVE** files;
    INDEXED files; **REGIONAL** files; *specific
    keywords*
  direct files manipulation in, 193-214
  four-way balanced merge using, 385-400
  ISAM file implementation in, 241-52
  sequential file operations in, 112-42
Pointer(s), 117-18
  block, 14
  buffer pool block, 74
  disk, 95
  in I/O buffers, 72-73
  split block (sb), 186
Pointer variables, 117-18, 121-22
Poisson distribution, 153-55
Polyphase merge, *m*-way, 366-77
Primary blocks (control intervals), 222, 235-36
Primary clustering, 166
Primary key, 3, 18-19
Primary (prime) area, 169, 222, 235
Probing, 162, 166
Processor management, 60-63
Processors, 59
Processor scheduler, 60
Processor sharing policy, 62
Program, channel, 55, 80

Program-data dependence, 9
Programmers, 5-6, 7
Program status word, 90
Pseudokey, 178-79
putchar (C function), 410
puts (C function), 410

Quantum, 62
Queries, 329-30
Query language, 5
Queue, 62-63, 90
Queued access technique, 66
Queued Indexed Sequential Access Method
    (QISAM), 88
Queued Sequential Access Method (QSAM), 88

Radix transformation, 159
Random accesses in full index files, 216-17
Random access methods, 15-16, 22
Random access mode, 15-16, 65
Random distribution, 151-55
Random probing, 166
Random processing, 145
READ request, 11-12, 201-2
  logical, 11-12, 115-16, 197-98, 245, 407-8
  physical, 11-12
Read/write head, 38, 55
Real memory, 90-93
Record(s), 2. *See also* Block(s) (physical block);
    Fixed-length records; Overflow records;
    Variable-length records; *specific operations
    on records*
  accessing through keys, 3-4
  blocked, 209-14
  home, 169
  index, 235
  internal view of, 14
  I/O, 12
  logical, 11, 202-9, 236, 298
  spanned, 35-36
  target, 3
  unblocked, 202-9
Record descriptor word (RDW), 35
Recorded key, 235-36
Record file, 9, 318, 320-22
Record movement, 78
Record terminator, 43
RECSIZE parameter, 247
Redistribution, 292-93, 294, 302, 304-5
REGIONAL files, 193-214
  properties of, 193-94
  REGIONAL(1) files, 195-99, 202-14
  REGIONAL(2) files, 199-202
Region numbers, 193
Regions (partitions), 79-80
Rehashing, 166-67, 185
Relative block (region), 193

Relative byte address (RBA), 319
Relative record data sets (RRDS), 318, 320-22
Relative stream file, 402-3
Replacement selection generator, 387-92
Replacement sorted partition generator, 243-50, 342-50
Request element, 90
Request queue, 90
Response time, 20, 22-23
Retrieve_All operation, 19
    on binary search trees, 265-68
    on B+-trees, 301-2
    on B-trees, 289
    on full index files, 218
    on indexed sequential files, 228-29
    on physical linked sequential files, 103
    on tape files, 97
Retrieve_Few operation, 20
Retrieve_Next operation, 19
Retrieve_One operation, 19
    average search length for, 170
    on binary search trees, 256-58
    on B+-trees, 300-301
    on B-trees, 287-89
    on disk files, 99, 100, 101
    on extendible hashing, 178-79
    on full index files, 218
    on indexed sequential files, 229
    on multilevel index sequential structure, 225
    on tape files, 96, 97
    on trie structures, 310
Retrieve_Previous operation, 19
rewind (C function), 411
REWRITE statement, 246
RKP parameter, 242-43
Root inode, 402
Rotations, 272-74

SCAN policy, 64, 65
Scheduling algorithms, 61-65
Search length, average (ASL), 24
    for binary search tree operations, 256-58, 259, 265
    for B-tree operations, 287-88
    for disk files, 99-100, 101-3
    for full index files, 218
    for hashing transformations, 190
    I/O time and, 23-24
    for linear and extendible hashing, 190
    for physical linked sequential files, 104-5
    for pumped vs. nonpumped insertion, 163-64
    for *Retrieve_One* operation, 170
    of separate file overflow technique, 175-76
    for tape files, 96, 99
Search mechanism, access path and, 15
Search techniques, 101, 161-66
Secondary clustering, 167
Secondary key, 3

Sector addressable devices, 42-44
Sectors, 43
Seek time of magnetic disks, 38-39, 40-42
Segment descriptor word (SDW), 35-36
Segments, 91
Selection tree, 347-50
Selector channel, 56
Separate file overflow area technique, 174-76
Sequence-preserving transformation, 147
Sequence set, 221, 298
Sequential access mode, 15-16, 65, 196, 197, 198-99, 244, 245, 246
Sequential files, 95-111
    doubly linked, 107
    ordered and unordered, 95
    physical, 14, 95-103
    physical linked, 14, 95-96, 103-7
    PL/1 implementation of, 112-42
    required I/O time, 107-10
Sequential loading, 161
Sequential organization, 14
Serial number, volume, 33
Service queue (SQ), 62-63
Service request (SR) list, 64
SET clause, 118, 246
Shift folding, 160
Shortest cylinder next (SCN) policy, 64, 65
Shortest job next (SJN) policy, 61-62
Simple sorted partition generator, 341-42
Slice (quantum), 62
Soft sectoring, 43
Software, 4-5. *See also* Operating systems
Sorted partition files, 340-50
    replacement sorted partition generator, 243-50, 342-50
    simple sorted partition generator, 341-42
SPACE parameter, 243
Spanning, 35-36
Spindle, 38
Split block (sb) pointer, 186
Split functions, 186, 189-90
START instruction, 89
Static files, 19
Stepdown, 340
Step search, 101
STOP instruction, 89
Storage, primary, 54, 79-80
Storage, secondary, 5, 15, 20, 54-55, 70, 71, 402-3. *See also* Disk(s); Tape(s)
Storage allocation, 70-72, 79-80, 402
Stream file, 9, 402-3
Stream I/O, 12
Subdirectories, 67
Sublanguage, 53. *See also* Data manipulation sublanguage; Data sublanguage
Super block, 402
Synchronous I/O, 66
Synonyms, 147
Systems programmer, 6, 7

Table of contents, volume (VTOC), 48-49, 68
Tables, 92
  device allocation, 81, 83-85
  file allocation, 71
  page map, 92
Tape(s), 5, 25-36
  advantages and disadvantages of, 36
  density, capacity, utilization, 27-29, 30
  fixed- and variable-length records and, 34-36
  general characteristics, 25-26
  maximal and effective data transfer rate, 29-32
  sorting with, 355-58, 365-66, 377
  vertical and longitudinal parity check, 26-27, 47
  volume, header, and trailer labels, 32-34
Tape files, 96-99
Target file, 3
Target record, 3
TEST instruction, 89
Threaded binary search trees, 268-70, 271
TITLE option, 386-87
Tournament sort, 345-47
Track descriptor (base) block, 44-45
Track index, 235, 236
Track overflow, 47
Tracks, 25
Track utilization, 47
Traffic controller, 60, 63
Trailer label on magnetic tapes, 33
Transfer of data, 11, 23. *See also* Hardware;
  Operating systems; Software
Transfer rate. *See* Data transfer rate
Transformation. *See* Deterministic
  transformations; Hashing transformations
Tree-based files. *See* Binary search trees; B⁺-
  trees; B-trees; Height-balanced (AVL)-
  trees; Paged trees; Trie structures; VSAM
  file organizations
Trees, 67, 346, 347-50
Trie structures, 306-17
Triple indirection, 403
Truncation method of hashing, 159
Two-way balanced merge sort, external, 351-58
  blocking factor and buffer requirements,
  352-54

  performance analysis, 354-55
  required I/O time, 355-58

Unblocked logical records, 202-9
Underflow block, 105
Underflow node, 295-96
Unit control block (UCB), 76-77
UNIX file system, 401-23
UPDATE, 197, 198, 244
Update_One operation, 20
  on disk files, 99, 101
  on tape files, 97-98
Updating of records, 3, 49, 137-39
Users, 5-7

Variable-length records, 34-36, 43, 57, 119-23
  batch mode update of, 139-42
  in **CONSECUTIVE** files, 135-42
  locate mode processing of, 121-23
  move mode processing of, 121
Verification, write, 27
Virtual addresses, 92
Virtual (file) page table, 92
Virtual memory, 90-93
Virtual sequential access method (VSAM). *See*
  VSAM file organizations
Volume labels, 32-33, 48-49
Volume serial number, 33
Volume table of contents (VTOC), 48-49, 68,
  81-83
VSAM file organizations, 88, 318-25
  entry-sequence files, 318, 322
  file structure, 318-20
  inverted-like file organization from, 338
  key-sequence files, 318, 322-25
  relative record files, 318, 320-22

Wait time, 22-23
Winner tree, 346
WRITE operation, 12, 198-99, 201-2, 246
  in C, 409
  for sequential files, 116
Write verification, 27